BARRON'S

HOW TO PREPARE FOR THE COLLEGE BOARD ACHIEVEMENT TESTS

ENGLISH

ENGLISH COMPOSITION TEST WITH ALL
MULTIPLE-CHOICE QUESTIONS
ENGLISH COMPOSITION TEST WITH ESSAY
LITERATURE TEST

SIXTH EDITION

BY
JEROME SHOSTAK
Former Supervisor of Guidance
District 27, New York City

BARRON'S

BARRON'S EDUCATIONAL SERIES, INC.
New York/London/Toronto/Sydney

English Composition and Literature test questions
selected from *The College Board Achievement Tests,
14 Tests in 13 Subjects,* College Entrance
Examination Board, 1986. Essay Topic selected
from *Taking the Achievement Tests,* College
Entrance Examination Board, 1985. Reprinted by
permission of Educational Testing Service, the
copyright owner of the sample questions.

Permission to reprint the above material does
not constitute review or endorsement by
Educational Testing Service or the College
Board of this publication as a whole or of
any other testing information it may contain.

Questions appear on pp. 3–8, 11, 13–15, 57, 59, 266–67, 289–292.

All inquiries should be addressed to:
Barron's Educational Series, Inc.
250 Wireless Boulevard
Hauppauge, NY 11788

Library of Congress Catalog Card No. 87-17916

International Standard Book No. 0-8120-2993-3

Library of Congress Cataloging-in-Publication Data

Shostak, Jerome.
  Barron's how to prepare for the College Board achievement tests,
English : English composition test without essay, English
composition test with essay, literature test / by Jerome Shostak. —
6th ed.
    p. cm.
  Rev. ed. of: How to prepare for College Board achievement tests,
English. 1984.
  ISBN 0-8120-2993-3
  1. English composition test—Study guides. 2. English language—
Composition and exercises—Examinations, questions, etc.
3. English literature—Examinations, questions, etc. 4. American
literature—Examinations, questions, etc. I. Shostak, Jerome. How
to prepare for College Board achievement tests, English. II. Title.
III. Title: How to prepare for the College Board achievement tests.
English.
PE1411.S5 1987
808',042'076—dc19   87-17916
                                          CIP
                                          AC

PRINTED IN THE UNITED STATES OF AMERICA

9 100 98765

CONTENTS

BARRON'S

Test-Taker's Checklist
for the English Achievement Tests

On the Day of the Test

1. Check and recheck date, time, place of exam. Avoid last minute rush and anxieties.

2. Before you leave home, check for
   - admission notice
   - identification
   - pen
   - pencils
   - watch

3. Clear your head. Don't clutter your mind with extraneous thoughts. You can cross only one bridge at a time!

4. <u>Budget your time.</u> Do not linger on questions you cannot answer but return to them when you have completed the rest. Check off the questions in the test book that you plan to return to.

5. Guess if you know that one or more of the choices for a question is definitely wrong. The way the tests are scored, it is generally to your advantage to guess from the remaining choices after eliminating at least one of the choices. Random guessing, however, is unlikely to increase your score.

6. Before marking your answer, consider all the choices given, to make sure you have not overlooked the best choice.

7. Mark your answer sheet clearly. Use a soft-lead (No. 2) pencil and blacken the choice completely, keeping within the space. Be sure erasures are done cleanly with a good eraser.

8. If you are taking the examination with essay writing, spend only the 20 minutes allotted for the question, and then promptly begin the multiple-choice questions. If you finish these and have time to spare, then you can return to the essay.

Introduction

COLLEGE ENTRANCE EXAMINATIONS

The College Entrance Examination Board provides standardized tests for admission to many colleges in the United States. A number of colleges require applicants to take the College Board's Scholastic Aptitude Test (SAT). About one-third of the colleges requiring the SAT also require two or three of the Board's Achievement Tests.

SCHOLASTIC APTITUDE TEST (SAT)

The SAT is a three-hour test of all multiple-choice questions designed to measure ability to do general college work. It measures potential rather than achievement. It consists of two sections evaluating verbal skills and two sections evaluating general number concepts. The verbal skills involve the extent of candidates' vocabulary and their ability to extract data, inferences, and conclusions from what they read.

TEST OF STANDARD WRITTEN ENGLISH (TSWE)

The TSWE is a half-hour examination administered with the SAT. The multiple-choice questions evaluate basic grammar and usage skills. It is scored separately and is not included in the SAT score.

ACHIEVEMENT TESTS

The College Board Achievement Tests (CBAT) are one-hour examinations designed to measure achievement in a particular subject. These tests are offered in thirteen subject areas. The results are used to help colleges not only to reach admission decisions, but also to decide which applicants can be exempted from courses covering material they already know, especially in English, mathematics, and foreign languages.

ACHIEVEMENT TESTS IN ENGLISH

The College Board provides three achievement tests for measuring student ability in the general field of English.

- English Composition Achievement Test multiple-choice questions only

- English Composition Achievement Test essay writing plus multiple-choice questions

- Literature Achievement Test

WHICH TEST SHOULD YOU TAKE?

Usually the colleges make the decision whether a candidate should take the Scholastic Aptitude Test (SAT). However, the situation with the Achievement Tests is more complex. Some colleges stipulate the specific test or tests that must be taken.

Some, for example, may require the English Composition Test with Essay; some may require the English Composition Test without the essay, or the Literature Test only or in combination with one form of the English Composition Test. Still others leave to the applicant which Achievement Tests to take and only require that the student take a definite number of achievement examinations.

If the college leaves the choice to you, then the material that follows will prove invaluable in helping you decide whether to take the English Composition Test with Essay or without the essay, or the Literature Test. By taking the practice examinations in the book, you will be able to determine what the areas include and assess your strengths in each.

REGISTRATION AND FEES

To register for either the English Composition Test with all multiple-choice questions, the English Composition Test with Essay, or the Literature Test, pick up a registration form and *Student Bulletin* in the guidance office of your school or write or call the College Board ATP (Admissions Testing Program) at

College Board ATP CN6200   Box 1025
Princeton, NJ 08541-6200   Berkeley, CA 94701
(609) 771-7600   *or*   (415) 849-0950

Monday through Friday between 8:30 A.M. and 4:30 P.M.

Currently, the fee allows you to take one to three Achievement Tests on one date. It also entitles you to have test scores sent (1) to you, (2) to your school, and (3) to three colleges of your choice. These reports will be mailed within six weeks after the test, together with a booklet explaining your score. For an additional fee, reports can be sent to other colleges.

IF YOU ARE TAKING THE ENGLISH COMPOSITION ACHIEVEMENT TEST

The English Composition Test has two distinctly different versions: English Composition Test (all multiple-choice) and English Composition Test (multiple-choice with essay).

ENGLISH COMPOSITION TEST (ALL MULTIPLE-CHOICE)

The Composition Test without essay is given in November, January, May, and June. This is a one-hour examination with an additional 15 minutes for initial instruction. There are approximately 90 multiple-choice questions.

Scope of the Test

Through a series of multiple-choice questions, the Achievement Test in Composition evaluates your ability to handle the common writing problems that handicap college students. The following are the areas on which the questions are based.

- Being consistent
- Expressing ideas logically
- Being clear and precise
- Following conventions

See Section One, Digest of Grammar and Usage, for a complete outline of these writing problems.

Questions Used in the Test

Three types of multiple-choice questions are currently used in the English Composition Achievement Test. The directions that follow are those used on the test. The sample questions are from the May 1983 administration.

TYPE ONE (IDENTIFYING THE ERROR)

This form tests your ability to detect an error in underlined portions of a sentence. No corrections are required.

DIRECTIONS: The following sentences contain problems in grammar, usage, diction (choice of words), and idiom.

Some sentences are correct.

No sentence contains more than one error.

You will find that the error, if there is one, is underlined and lettered. Assume that all other elements of the sentence are correct and cannot be changed. In choosing answers, follow the requirements of standard written English.

If there is an error, select the one underlined part that must be changed in order to make the sentence correct, and blacken the corresponding space on the answer sheet.

If there is no error, mark answer space E.

EXAMPLE:

It is far easier to ride a bicycle
      A

than explaining in words exactly how a bicy-
  B   **C**

cle is ridden. No error
   D   **E**

ANSWER   Ⓐ ● Ⓒ Ⓓ Ⓔ

The error is a lack of parallelism. In the comparison, to ride should be matched by to explain. (B) is the answer.

Sample Questions and Analysis of Answers

DIRECTIONS: Block out your choice before reading the *Analysis* for each of the following.

1. The report Alexander is discussing, a report
                A

   prepared jointly by he and the committee, does
             B

   not take into account the socioeconomic status
      C

   of those interviewed. No error
     D   **E**

               Ⓐ Ⓑ Ⓒ Ⓓ Ⓔ

Analysis: (B) Case of Pronoun   The report was prepared by him and the committee. The object form him rather than the subject form he is required as object of the preposition by.

2. Austria did not fare well in Third World markets
        (A)   **B**

   because they exported too few of the goods
         C   **D**

   needed for the development of Third World

   nations. No error
       E

               Ⓐ Ⓑ Ⓒ Ⓓ Ⓔ

Analysis: (C) Pronoun Reference   There is no plural noun for they to refer to. Austria requires it.

3. Driving less frequently is one way to save en-
        A

   ergy; to turn off all appliances when they are
       B   **C**

   not being used is another. No error
         D   **E**

               Ⓐ Ⓑ Ⓒ Ⓓ Ⓔ

Analysis: (B) Lack of Parallelism   Driving should be followed by another *-ing* form of the verb, turning, and not by the infinitive to turn.

4. When rumors of a merger began to spread, nei-
     A   **B**

   ther of the company presidents were available
                   C

   for comment. No error
      D   **E**

               Ⓐ Ⓑ Ⓒ Ⓓ Ⓔ

Analysis: (C) Lack of Subject-Verb Agreement   The singular neither requires the singular was available.

5. The accidental meeting of the distant cousins
            A

   came about through an incredulous series of
      B   **C**   **D**

   coincidences. No error
       E

               Ⓐ Ⓑ Ⓒ Ⓓ Ⓔ

Analysis: (C) Diction   Incredible (hard to believe) rather than incredulous (naive) is required.

6. Each of Beethoven's many acts of ungracious-
              A

   ness seems to have been balanced by an act of
      B   **C**   **D**

   kindness. No error
       E   Ⓐ Ⓑ Ⓒ Ⓓ Ⓔ

Analysis: (E) No error   Each is singular and requires the singular seems.

7. In the opinion of the lecturer, a belief in Chris-
       A   **B**

   tianity is not a condition necessary in
                        C

   the enjoyment of medieval literature. No error
      D   **E**

               Ⓐ Ⓑ Ⓒ Ⓓ Ⓔ

Analysis: (C) Idiom   Necessary should be followed by for, not by in.

8. The living conditions of some migrant workers
    <u>having been improved</u>   <u>primarily</u>
           A   B
    <u>through the efforts</u> of <u>people like</u> Cesar
          C   D
    Chavez. <u>No error</u>
           E

    Ⓐ Ⓑ Ⓒ Ⓓ Ⓔ

Analysis: (A) Sentence Fragment   The use of
the participle <u>having</u> instead of a finite form of the
verb (such as <u>has</u>) creates an incomplete sentence.

9. <u>Being absent</u> the time his enemies <u>voted down</u>
        A   B
    his proposal, Selby <u>is worried</u> about
                             C
    <u>missing further</u> meetings of the Board of Direc-
          D
    tors. <u>No error</u>
         E

    Ⓐ Ⓑ Ⓒ Ⓓ Ⓔ

Analysis: (A) Sequence of Tense   The absence
preceded the being worried; therefore, <u>Having been
absent</u> rather than <u>Being absent</u> is required.

10. <u>Also supported</u> by the commission <u>was</u> the pro-
         A   B
    posed health clinics and the proposed <u>center</u> to
                                  C
    distribute information <u>on job-training</u> opportu-
                        D
    nities. <u>No error</u>
          E

    Ⓐ Ⓑ Ⓒ Ⓓ Ⓔ

Analysis: (B) Subject-Verb Agreement   The
subject is not <u>commission</u>, but rather <u>clinics</u> and
<u>center</u>; therefore, the verb <u>were</u> rather than <u>was</u> is
required.

TYPE TWO (CORRECTING ERRORS)

This multiple-choice question tests your ability to
identify an error in a sentence and to select the best
revision of the unacceptable form.

DIRECTIONS: In each of the following sentences,
some part of the sentence or the entire sentence is
underlined. Beneath each sentence you will find five
ways of phrasing the underlined part. The first of
these repeats the original; the other four are different. If you think the original is better than any of

the alternatives, choose answer A; otherwise
choose one of the others. Select the best version
and blacken the corresponding space on your answer sheet.

This is a test of correctness and effectiveness of
expression. In choosing answers, follow the requirements of standard written English; that is, pay attention to grammar, choice of words, sentence construction, and punctuation. Choose the answer that
best expresses the meaning of the original sentence.
Your choice should produce the most effective sentence—clear and precise, without awkwardness or
ambiguity.

EXAMPLE:

During the labor dispute, barrels of potatoes
were emptied across the <u>highway, and they
thereby blocked it to all traffic</u>.

(A) highway, and they thereby blocked it to
    all traffic
(B) highway and therefore blocking it to all
    traffic
(C) highway, by which all traffic was there-
    fore blocked
(D) highway, and therefore this had all traffic
    blocked
(E) highway, thereby blocking all traffic

ANSWER   Ⓐ Ⓑ Ⓒ Ⓓ ●

The error is in pronoun reference. In (A) the
pronoun <u>they</u>, in (C) the pronoun <u>which</u>, and
in (D) the pronoun <u>this</u> have no <u>one</u> noun to
refer to. In (B), <u>therefore</u> changes the meaning. In (E), the correct answer, the vague pron-
omial reference has been eliminated, and the
sense of the sentence is clear.

Sample Questions and Analysis of Answers

DIRECTIONS: Block out your choice before reading
the *Analysis* in each of the following.

1. The representatives of the parking-lot operators
    asserted <u>as to the defensibility of their practices
    as legal and ethical</u>.

    (A) as to the defensibility of their practices as
        legal and ethical
    (B) as to their practices and their defensibility
        on legal and ethical grounds

(C) that their practices, that is the operators, are defensible in legal terms as well as ethics

(D) that in regards to defensibility their practices are legally and ethically defensible

(E) that the practices of the operators are legally and ethically defensible

Ⓐ Ⓑ Ⓒ Ⓓ Ⓔ

Analysis: (E)   The idiom is <u>assert that</u>, not <u>assert as to</u>, thus eliminating (A) and (B). (C) is wordy and changes the meaning by substituting <u>ethics</u> and <u>legal terms</u> for the parallel <u>legal</u> and <u>ethical</u>. (D) contains a <u>their</u> that could refer either to the representatives or to the operators.

2. <u>The age of ninety having been reached</u>, the photographer Imogen Cunningham became interested in photographing others who had achieved that age.

(A) The age of ninety having been reached

(B) At ninety, when she reached that age

(C) The age of ninety being reached

(D) When she reached the age of ninety

(E) When having reached the age of ninety

Ⓐ Ⓑ Ⓒ Ⓓ Ⓔ

Analysis: (D) Unclear Modification or Reference   In (A), (C), and (E), who or what reached the age of ninety is not clearly defined. (B) has an awkward involution not present in (D).

3. The major reasons students give for failing to participate in the political process <u>is that they have demanding assignments and work at</u> part-time jobs.

(A) is that they have demanding assignments and work at

(B) are demanding assignments and they work at

(C) are that they have demanding assignments and that they have

(D) is having demanding assignments and having

(E) are demanding assignments, in addition to work at

Ⓐ Ⓑ Ⓒ Ⓓ Ⓔ

Analysis: (C)   <u>Part-time jobs and demanding assignments</u> should be in parallel construction, thus eliminating (A), (B), and (E); (D) changes the meaning.

4. Although Jonathan is very much interested in Mexican culture, <u>he does not speak Spanish and has never visited Mexico.</u>

(A) he does not speak Spanish and has never visited Mexico

(B) it is without being able to speak Spanish or having visited there

(C) he does not speak Spanish nor has he ever visited there

(D) he does not speak Spanish and has never visited there

(E) it is without speaking Spanish nor having visited there

Ⓐ Ⓑ Ⓒ Ⓓ Ⓔ

Analysis: (A) Pronoun Reference   (B) contains vague <u>it</u>. (B), (C), (D), and (E) contain a vague <u>there</u> without a word (Mexico) as antecedent.

5. <u>Returning to Dayville after ten years, the small town seemed much livelier to Margo</u> than it had been when she was growing up there.

(A) Returning to Dayville after ten years, the small town seemed much livelier to Margo

(B) Having returned to Dayville aften ten years, it seemed a much livelier town to Margo

(C) After Margo returned to Dayville in ten years, the small town seemed much livelier

(D) Margo returned to Dayville after ten years, and then she thought the small town much livelier

(E) When Margo returned to Dayville aften ten years, she thought the small town much livelier

Ⓐ Ⓑ Ⓒ Ⓓ Ⓔ

Analysis: (E) Unclear Modification   (A) has <u>Returning</u> and (B) has <u>Having returned</u> modifying <u>the small town</u> instead of <u>Margo</u>. (D) lacks the <u>subordination</u> found in (E). (C) changes the meaning.

6. Allowed to remain in any warm place, a covered flour mixture will grow the yeast for a sourdough <u>starter, the problem being that the bread</u> may not have the desired taste.

(A) starter, the problem being that the bread

(B) starter, but the problem is the using the starter to make the bread

(C) starter; in using it to make the bread, you

(D) starter, but bread made from that starter

(E) starter; the problem is that in making bread from it, it

ⓐ ⓑ ⓒ ⓓ ⓔ

Analysis: (D) Coordination and Subordination   The flour mixture and the problem of bread made from it are coordinate ideas. (A) subordinates the problem of the bread and clouds the meaning. (B) changes the meaning. (C) and (E) omit the important meaning carried by but.

7. Whether the ancient Egyptians actually sailed or did not to South America remains uncertain, but that they could have was demonstrated by Heyerdahl's Ra II expedition.

(A) Whether the ancient Egyptians actually sailed or did not
(B) Whether in actuality the ancient Egyptians sailed or did not
(C) The actuality of whether the ancient Egyptians sailed
(D) That the ancient Egyptians actually did sail
(E) That the ancient Egyptians may actually have sailed

ⓐ ⓑ ⓒ ⓓ ⓔ

Analysis: (D) Verb Form   (A) and (B) require "sailed or did not sail." (C) and (E) change the meaning. (D) is correct even though it avoids the sailed-sail problem.

8. Journalists should present a balanced view of the news but with their goal to stir discussion, to unsettle complacent thinkers.

(A) with their goal to stir
(B) ought also to stir
(C) aiming at the same time to stir
(D) also trying to stir
(E) its goal should also be in stirring

ⓐ ⓑ ⓒ ⓓ ⓔ

Analysis: (B) Parallelism   (B) keeps should and ought parallel. (E) changes the subject unnecessarily from journalists to news. (C) and (D) introduce an -ing form to parallel should. (A) omits necessary action word.

9. Many people are alarmed by the recent Supreme Court ruling that gives judges discretionary power to determine about closing trials to the public.

(A) about closing trials

(B) whether he or she ought to close trials
(C) if he or she should close trials
(D) whether or not trials should be closed
(E) the closing of trials, if they wish,

ⓐ ⓑ ⓒ ⓓ ⓔ

Analysis: (D) Idiom   The idiom is not (A) determine about but (D) determine whether or not. (B), (C), and (E) change the emphasis of the given sentence.

10. Separated by the sea from any major population center, the aborigines of Australia have developed a unique culture.

(A) have developed a unique culture
(B) have developed into a very unique culture
(C) have a unique development, their culture
(D) had developed a very unique culture
(E) had developed their culture uniquely

ⓐ ⓑ ⓒ ⓓ ⓔ

Analysis: (A)   (B) and (D) unnecessarily qualify unique with very. (C) and (E) change the meaning of the sentence. (A) is the correct response.

TYPE THREE (EDITING)

The third type of question involves the sort of editing you usually do in your own writing to change emphasis in a sentence or to achieve variety in sentence structure. You are not asked to find errors or to correct errors; you are given an acceptable sentence and asked to rephrase it in a specified way.

DIRECTIONS: Each of the following sentences is to be rephrased according to the directions that follow it. You should make only those changes that the directions require. Keep the meaning of the revised sentence as close to the meaning of the original sentence as the directions for that sentence permit.
  If you think that more than one good sentence can be made according to the directions, select the sentence that

  retains, insofar as possible, the meaning of the original sentence;
  is most natural in phrasing and construction;
  meets the requirements of standard written English; and is the best sentence in terms of conciseness, idiom, logic, and other qualities found in well-written sentences.

When you have thought out a good rephrasing of the original sentence, find in choices (A) through (E) the word or entire phrase that you have included in your revised sentence and blacken the corresponding space on your answer sheet. Be sure that the choice you select is the fullest expression of your revision available in the choices; that is, for example, if your revised sentence contains was playing and both was playing and playing are offered as choices, playing would not be an acceptable answer.

> EXAMPLE:
>
> The creation of Black Studies programs was based on the belief that existing academic offerings did not take the contribution of Black people into account.
>
> Begin with Those who favored.
>
> (A) based on believing
> (B) based their belief about
> (C) had a belief
> (D) were believing
> (E) believed
>
> ANSWER   Ⓐ Ⓑ Ⓒ Ⓓ ●
>
> (E) Your rephrased sentence will probably read:
>
>   Those who favored the creation of Black Studies programs believed that existing academic offerings did not take the contributions of Black people into account. (A) changes the meaning of the sentence. (B) contains an error in the use of the idiom based on. (C) is wordy. (D) changes tense unnecessarily.

Sample Questions and Analysis of Answers

DIRECTIONS: Block out your choice before reading the Analysis in each of the following.

1. The supervisor was able, or so he thought, to make the decision himself.
    Change able to capable.

    (A) to be making
    (B) of having made
    (C) of making
    (D) to have made
    (E) to make

    Ⓐ Ⓑ Ⓒ Ⓓ Ⓔ

    Analysis: (C)   The rephrase will probably read: The supervisor was capable, or so he

thought, of making the decision himself. The new sentence contains choice (C), the only choice possible with the idiom capable of, which must be followed by the -ing form of the verb.

2. Probably nothing threatens our economy more than our dependence on foreign oil.
    Begin with There is probably.

    (A) no more a threat than
    (B) no greater threat to
    (C) not as much of a threat as
    (D) nothing to threaten
    (E) nothing threatening so much

    Analysis: (B)   The rephrase will probably read: There is probably no greater threat to our economy than our dependence on foreign oil. (A) is too wordy. (C) and (D) change the meaning. (E) makes inclusion of "our economy" awkward. (B) is the correct choice.

3. A great many reforms resulting from the French Revolution were of benefit to the bourgeoisie.
    Begin with The French Revolution.

    (A) resulting benefits
    (B) that benefited
    (C) with a benefit
    (D) a result was the benefit
    (E) and the benefit

    Ⓐ Ⓑ Ⓒ Ⓓ Ⓔ

    Analysis: (B)   The rephrase will probably read: The French Revolution resulted in a great many reforms that benefited the bourgeoisie. (D) and (C) change the meaning. (A) and (E) do not lead to acceptable sentences.

4. Gandhi started out with the normal ambitions of a young Indian student and adopted his nationalist opinions only by degrees.
    Begin with Starting.

    (A) he only adopted
    (B) Gandhi adopted
    (C) only adopting
    (D) Gandhi had only adopted
    (E) and only adopting

    Ⓐ Ⓑ Ⓒ Ⓓ Ⓔ

    Analysis: (B)   The rephrase will probably read: Starting with the normal ambitions of a young Indian student, Gandhi adopted his nationalist opinions only by degrees. (A), (C), and

(D) change the meaning. (E) results in a sentence fragment.

5. The discoveries made by Freud have undermined rationalistic conceptions of mind as effectively as Copernicus' theory undermined classical accounts of the heavens.
Begin with Just as Copernicus'.

(A) thus
(B) so
(C) also
(D) similarly
(E) as well

Ⓐ Ⓑ Ⓒ Ⓓ Ⓔ

Analysis: (B)   The rephrase will probably read: Just as Copernicus' theory undermined classical accounts of the heavens, so the discoveries made by Freud have undermined rationalistic conceptions of mind. (A) introduces an unjustified causal relationship. (C), (D), and (E) change the meaning.

6. The appreciation of painting, as well as of other forms of art, demands the interplay of judgment and imagination.
Begin with The interplay.

(A) demands
(B) is demanded by
(C) is essential to
(D) are essential to
(E) demand

Ⓐ Ⓑ Ⓒ Ⓓ Ⓔ

Analysis: (C)   The replacement will probably read: The interplay of judgment and imagination is essential to the appreciation of painting as well as other forms of art. (A) and (B) reverse the roles of the demander and what is being demanded. (D) and (E) present a plural verb form for a singular subject (interplay).

7. The administrators of the federal agencies that assist education have held long discussions about giving increased support to county colleges.
Change discussion to discussed.

(A) at length about giving
(B) about giving at length
(C) the idea of giving
(D) the idea of giving, at length,
(E) at length giving

Ⓐ Ⓑ Ⓒ Ⓓ Ⓔ

Analysis: (E)   The replacement will probably read: The administrators of the federal agencies that assist education have discussed at length giving increased support to county agencies. (A) has redundant about. In (B) and (D), the placement of at length makes the phrase ambiguous. (C) makes no sense.

8. Given the choice of living in the past, the present, or the future, many adventurous individuals doubtless would choose the least certain, most unpredictable future.
Omit the past.

(A) less certain, most unpredictable
(B) less certain and unpredictable
(C) least certain, unpredictable
(D) less certain, more unpredictable
(E) least certain and unpredictable

Ⓐ Ⓑ Ⓒ Ⓓ Ⓔ

Analysis: (D)   The replacement will probably read: Given the choice of living in the present or the future, many adventurous individuals would choose the less certain, more unpredictable future. Since two items are being compared, the comparative less and more are required; therefore, (D) is the correct choice. (A), (C), and (E) contain the superlative least or most. (B) changes the meaning.

9. Although the composer Ethel Smyth was famous in England in the early years of this century for her operas and symphonies, she is almost unknown in this country.
Begin with Almost unknown.

(A) country, despite being famous for
(B) country, the composer
(C) country, the English
(D) country, although she was famous
(E) country and famous

Ⓐ Ⓑ Ⓒ Ⓓ Ⓔ

Analysis: (B)   The replacement will probably read: Almost unknown in this country, the composer Ethel Smith was famous in England in the early years of this century for her operas and symphonies. (A), (D), and (E) lead to a sentence fragment. (C) changes the meaning.

10. In 1978 Mary Clarke became the first woman to achieve the rank of Major General in the United States Army. She was the commander

of Fort McClellan, Alabama.
Combine these two sentences into one.

(A) Clarke, the commander
(B) Clarke, the first woman whose
(C) Clarke, and she was
(D) Clarke, and so she became
(E) Clarke, being the commander

Ⓐ Ⓑ Ⓒ Ⓓ Ⓔ

Analysis: (A)   The replacement will probably read: In 1978 <u>Mary Clarke, the commander</u>
of Fort McClellan, Alabama, became the first
women to achieve the rank of Major General in
the United States Army. (B), (D), and (E)
change the meaning of the sentence. (C) creates
a weak sentence lacking effective subordination
of the second independent clause.

Tips on Handling Multiple-Choice Questions

1. Look first for the most common errors. In
order to achieve a range in scores, the items must
vary in difficulty with most of them in the grasp of
the average candidate. If the mistake doesn't jump
out of the page at you, check for the more common
errors: dangling modifiers, lack of parallelism, pro-
noun-antecedent problems, sequence of tenses,
error in use of idiom or verb form.

> EXAMPLE:
>
> The tutor entered <u>the room</u> and <u>began</u> to shout
>   A   B
> at us <u>which</u> annoyed me <u>very much</u>. <u>No error</u>
>   C   D   E
>
> Ⓐ Ⓑ ● Ⓓ Ⓔ

Analysis: If the <u>which</u> doesn't plead for analysis
the moment you see the sentence, you will have to
go through your list of favorite common errors (similar to the one given above). When you reach pro-
noun-antecedent, you will realize that *which* cannot
refer to *us*, but does refer to the entire sentence and
not to a specific word. Case resolved!

2. Even if you are positive that you have caught
the error, check all other choices. Put a line through
the letter of each one that you check—to save yourself from over-confidence.

3. Before guessing on a difficult one, put a big
check or large star in the margin and go on to the
next. After you have done two or three more, *return*
to the stubborn one. The chances are that your mind

has had time to clear up the confusion. In most instances, the difficulty that seemed so impossible becomes so simple on the rerun! If it continues to elude
you, let it go! If time permits, you can return at the
end of the test.

4. When working with Type One questions (identifying the error), concentrate only on the underlined elements. Look for errors involving the underlined parts only. Rewording the sentence to
eliminate the problem is not involved in your
choices. For example, if you have a sentence in
which the subject is singular and the verb is plural,
you could consider either one wrong. However, if
only the noun is underlined, the error for that item
is the noun.

> EXAMPLE:
>
> Jack <u>is</u> one of <u>those</u> stalwarts who <u>takes</u> a daily
>   A   B   C
> swim <u>regardless</u> of the weather. <u>No error</u>
>   D   E
>
> Ⓐ Ⓑ ● Ⓓ Ⓔ

Analysis: Since <u>who</u> refers to <u>stalwarts</u>, a plural
noun, <u>who</u> requires the plural <u>take</u>. You could rewrite the sentence to avoid the error. You could say,
for instance, "Jack, a typical stalwart, *takes* . . ."
or "Jack, who is a typical stalwart, *takes* . . ."
However, as the sentence stands, you are not offered these possibilities. You have to choose from
the underlined choices on the printed page. Don't
confuse yourself!

5. In Type Two questions (correcting errors), if
something in the underlined section strikes you as
an obvious error, you can eliminate any answer
choices that repeat the same error. A dangling participle is wrong in as many choices as it appears.

> EXAMPLE:
>
> Separated by the sea from any major popu-
> lation center the aborigines of Australia <u>have</u>
> <u>developed a unique culture.</u>
>
> (A) have developed a unique culture
> (B) have developed a very unique culture
> (C) had developed a very unique culture
> (D) have developed their culture uniquely
> (E) had developed their culture uniquely
>
> ● Ⓑ Ⓒ Ⓓ Ⓔ

Analysis: Because *very* is not permitted as a modifier for *unique*, (B) is wrong. If (B) is wrong, then (C) must be wrong.

6. The correct choice *must not* change the meaning of the given sentence. In the previous example in Hint 5, (D) is wrong because it states incorrectly that the development and not the culture is unique. So, if (D) is wrong, so is (E), which also has *develop* and *unique* linked. (A) becomes the only possible choice!

7. With Type Three questions (editing), there is one approach that works best: Follow the directions and mentally create the sentence prescribed. If necessary, *begin* to write it. Try to imagine the reason, the grammatical principle, behind the suggested revision. Your final check-up should be to test all five choices with the directions for revision.

For additional preparation for the English Achievement Test (All Multiple-Choice) turn to Section One.

ENGLISH COMPOSITION TEST (MULTIPLE CHOICE WITH ESSAY)

The English Achievement Test with Essay is given only in December when the all-multiple-choice version is not given. It is a one-hour test with an additional 15 minutes for initial instruction. The test consists of

- an essay to be written in the first 20 minutes
- 70 multiple questions to be completed in 40 minutes.

Multiple-Choice Questions

The essay version of the composition test contains only Type One and Type Two of the multiple-choice questions currently used in the English Composition Achievement tests.

The Essay

Each administration of the test offers only one topic. The topic is planned so that the candidates can react quickly and begin to write almost immediately. The topic allows for a wide variety of responses and the expression of diverse points of view.

This is not a test meant to analyze particular strengths and weaknesses in a student's writing ability. It is meant to provide an indication of the candidate's ability to do the kind of writing required in most college classes. Therefore, no subscore for the essay alone is reported.

SCORING THE ESSAY

The essay is read by two members of a panel of about 150 high-school and college English teachers. The readers have been trained in the standards of expectation for an essay written in 20 minutes by a high-school senior.

The essays are scored on a scale from 1 to 6, with 6 as the highest and 1 the lowest. Those receiving widely divergent scores are read a third time to reconcile the discrepancies. The total score, the sum of the two reader's scores, is weighted to equal one-third of the score for the examination.

CRITERIA IN SCORING

The reader's judgment is based on a totality of impression. Rather than deduct for weaknesses, the reader scores for what the student has done well and not for what he has failed to do. The score is based on every aspect of the essay. Both content and writing technique are evaluated, including

- spelling
- punctuation
- organization
- choice of words
- usage control
- development of ideas
- paragraphing
- clarity of message or purpose.

SAMPLE ESSAYS

DIRECTIONS: You have twenty minutes to plan and write an essay on the topic assigned below. DO NOT WRITE ON ANOTHER TOPIC. AN ESSAY ON ANOTHER TOPIC IS NOT ACCEPTABLE.

The essay is assigned to give you an opportunity to show how well you can write. You should, therefore, take care to express your thoughts on the topic clearly and effectively. How well you write is much more important than how much you write, but to cover the topic adequately you may want to write more than one paragraph. Be specific.

Your essay must be written on the lines provided on your answer sheet. You will receive no other paper on which to write. You will find that you have enough space if you write on every line, avoid wide margins, and keep your handwriting to a reasonable size. It is important to remember that what you write will be read by someone who is not familiar with your handwriting. Try to write or print so that what you are writing is legible.

DO NOT WRITE IN YOUR TEST BOOK. You will receive credit only for what you write on your answer sheet.

The Essay Topic for December 4, 1982

Consider carefully the following quotation and the assignment following it. Then, plan and write your essay as directed.

"People seldom stand up for what they truly believe; instead they merely go along with the popular view."

Assignment: Do you agree or disagree with this statement? Write an essay in which you support your opinion with specific examples from history, contemporary affairs, literature, or personal observation.

Essays with a Total Score of 12 (Each Reader Gave the Essay a Score of 6.)

Although essays in this category differ in approach and style and have slight differences in quality, they all have the same characteristics: good organization, good command of the language, and an interesting style. These essays are not perfect, nor are they expected to be, for each is only a first draft written in the 20 minutes allotted. The essay that follows, which is representative of this category, received the highest possible score.

ESSAY I

I agree that most of us merely go along with the popular views; we seldom stand up for what we believe if it goes counter to the stand taken by the majority.

Take any teenage group. In order for the group to function, there has to be consensus.

Whether the decision is to go to a party, to hold a picnic, or even to help a local political candidate running for office, there can be only one view if the group is to go into action. To remain a group, therefore, most go along even when some do disagree.

However, when the stakes are high enough or the risk demanding enough, then we do stand up for what we believe. Going to a party just to "please the guys" is one thing, but going on a rumble or taking part in a robbery is completely different. There is a point where we draw the line. This is the point at which we have to stand up for what we believe. Fortunately, we seldom meet such occasions.

Yes, conformity is an essential component for living in a social group. Most frequently we compromise our individual beliefs for the benefit of the group. However, at the rare moments when our conscience demands that we go counter to group demands, many of us do stand up for what we believe.

Analysis: Essay I has traditional structure; the first paragraph states the topic; the second and third present examples from personal observation and experience. The fourth concludes the essay, affirming what was said in the first paragraph. The sentence structure varies; the vocabulary is controlled and effective.

The point of view taken is an unusual one. The essay has some bits of repetition, but given the 20-minute time limit imposed upon the writer, the essay must be considered well done.

Essays with a Total Score of 8 (Each Reader Gave the Essay a Score of 4.)

Essays in this category, as in every category, vary in quality. In this group, the essays might be described as ranging from good to merely competent. Although the papers show that the writers have a basic command of the skills needed for good writing, they have the kinds of flaws that keep them out of the highest range. They may lack such qualities as a forceful presentation or adequate development of the basic argument.

ESSAY II

I believe that not many people stand up for what they believe; for the most part, they merely go along with the popular view. This can be seen in the everyday world around us.

One of the best examples of people standing up for what they believe has to be the protesters against the development of nuclear weaponry and power plants. Numerically, this group is relatively small, but they demand notice because of the way in which they stand up to be counted throughout the nations of the world. They have been gassed; they have been beaten; they have been jailed; they have even been maimed and killed; but they keep coming and protesting. Their courage and determination set standards for all who have conviction of the right of their stand.

On the other hand, most people do go along with the popular view. The world of today's teenagers gives us the proof. How else can we explain the uniformity in dress of most high-school students! When crack became the in-thing, how quickly the addiction epidemic started! When some of the kids in the crowd took to the drug, the others quickly followed to be part of the crowd. Some of the teenagers did this merely to go along with the popular views.

In summary, it is true that while few people stand up for what they believe, most of us merely go along with the popular view—even if it hurts!

Analysis: Essay II is competently written. The writer presents the thesis in the first paragraph and then proceeds to offer supporting examples in the second and third paragraphs. The fourth paragraph contains a summarizing conclusion. However, the essay is weakened by the lack of connection or transition in the handling of teenage dress and crack. The sentence structure has variation but there is some repetition. The writer went off on a tangent in overdeveloping the anti-nuke group.

Essays with a Total Score of 6 (Each Reader Gave the Essay a Score of 3.)

Essays in this category, in comparison with the other essays being scored, have faults that override whatever merits they may have. Although the essays show that the writers have a fairly good grasp of English sentence structure, they usually have such problems as limited development of the argument, few explicit connections between ideas, and inexactness and ineffectiveness of expression.

ESSAY III

On the whole, I agree almost completely with the given statement because as the result of what I have seen and heard, I have often concluded that people would rather go along with the popular view rather than tell others exactly what they believe.

As I sit here a perfect example comes to my mind. It's personal, but I am certain that something like this has happened to all of us. The group of teenagers who are my best friends wanted to drop one of the guys from the group. I saw nothing really too much wrong with him. All of us are not perfect. He does not have too many very good qualities and one or two faults. He just talks too much.

Anyway, I voted along with the others. I truly felt sorry for him, but I thought that I would lose the group if I did not go along. As you can readily see, I believe that most of us would rather go along with the majority view than tell others how we really feel.

Analysis: The writer of Essay III has constructed an argument and provided an example to support that argument, but he is too verbose. The essay rambles rather than makes a point and then going on to the next. Words and ideas are repeated in a self-conscious style.

Essays with a Total Score of 2 (Each Reader Gave the Essay a Score of 1.)

Essays in this category are the poorest of those being scored. They are seriously flawed. No important feature of an essay in this category is well done enough to lift the essay out of the bottom category. Usually, the problems in these essays so interfere with communication that it is difficult to understand exactly what the writer is trying to say.

ESSAY IV

People find it difficult to handle their own beliefs when under pressure. It is always easier to give in and accept what the others want you to believe. Don't you agree?

It is easy to prove that this is true. All you have to do is think of what peer pressure can force you to do. It really can twist you around into doing the exact opposite of what you had intended. Sometimes it is better to stop thinking so you can have your own peace of mind. You don't like to be different because it makes you stand out, and this would make you unhappy about the people you are with.

Analysis: The first paragraph is primarily the given topic rewritten—without being focused on the primary obligation of the writer: to show the extent of agreement with the topic. The second paragraph promises proof without telling what is to be proved. The last sentence changes the complete direction of the essay. Although almost every sentence is syntactically correct, the ideas contained are not related.

For more specific preparation for the English Achievement Test With Essay turn to Section Three, page 116.

IF YOU ARE TAKING THE LITERATURE TEST

The Literature Test is given in November, December, January, May, and June on the same test dates as both of the English Composition Tests.

The Literature Test is a one-hour examination with an additional 15 minutes for initial instruction. It attempts to measure how well you can read and interpret literary material. The test consists of multiple-choice questions based on six to eight reading selections, about half of which are poetry and half prose. The selections are complete short poems or excerpts from various forms of literature, including longer poems, novels, nonfiction writing, or drama, selected from British or American literature of the past 300 years. The questions may be on content, vocabulary, or elements of form and style.

This is a test designed to measure how well you have learned to interpret literary prose and poetry. It does *not* test your knowledge of literary periods, lives of authors, or evaluation of a work by critics. You do not need an extensive knowledge of literary terminology although control of the more basic terms is expected. Basic terms include the following:

allegory	moral
alliteration	personification
blank verse	speaker
context	stanza
image	theme
irony	tone

Areas Measured

- Meaning: basic ideas, effect, argument, theme
- Form: structure, method of organization
- Narrative Voice: characterization of speaker, listeners
- Language: imagery, figures of speech, allusions

- Diction: meaning of specific words or phrases in the context of the passage, denotation, syntax denotation, implication

Types of Questions

Three types of questions are used in the test. However, all of the questions are of the five-choice completion, the fundamental form for most College Board examinations.

TYPE ONE (BEST CHOICE)

You are required to select the most precise or the most suitable of the responses from the five offered. All five responses may be at least partly true.

Samples

1. Lines 8–9 refer to the dream as though it were a

    (A) dangerous vagrant
    (B) valuable possession
    (C) distant relative
    (D) young creature requiring care
    (E) mysterious but beneficent force

2. The primary effect of the change of tempo in line 11 is to suggest that the speaker

    (A) is putting aside the temptation to dream and returning to the reality at hand
    (B) is excited by the possibilities she has just imagined
    (C) is unaccustomed to sustaining a pessimistic mood for any length of time
    (D) is angry because she has missed the opportunity to get hot water

(E) recognizes the need for haste in finishing the chores so that important decisions can be made

Ⓐ Ⓑ Ⓒ Ⓓ Ⓔ

TYPE TWO (NOT OR EXCEPT)

This type is a reversal of the usual. You are given four appropriate choices and one inappropriate choice that you must identify.

Samples

3. Which of the following pairs of words does NOT correctly illustrate the contrast in content between the two parts of the poem (lines 1–6 and lines 7–10)?

(A) "man" (line 2) and "Old Age" (line 9)
(B) "Nimrod" (line 2) and "Old Age" (line 9)
(C) "speedy" (line 3) and "stealing" (line 9)
(D) "greyhounds" (line 3) and "nets" (line 10)
(E) "we breathe" (line 6) and "we panting die" (line 10)

Ⓐ Ⓑ Ⓒ Ⓓ Ⓔ

4. As it is used in the poem, "giddy" (line 2) can be understood in all of the following senses EXCEPT

(A) dizzy
(B) flighty
(C) ephemeral
(D) impractical
(E) raucous

Ⓐ Ⓑ Ⓒ Ⓓ Ⓔ

TYPE THREE (ROMAN NUMERALS)

Several statements labeled by Roman numerals follow the question. The statements are followed by five lettered choices, each of which consists of some combination of the Roman numerals that label the statements. You are asked to select the choice that best answers the question.

Samples

5. Which of the following statements about the author's intent are true?
    I. Statement One
    II. Statement Two

III. Statement Three
IV. Statement Four
V. Statement Five

(A) I and II only
(B) II only
(C) II and IV only
(D) III and V only
(E) none of them

Ⓐ Ⓑ Ⓒ Ⓓ Ⓔ

6. In this poem, the woman functions as which of the following?
    I. A symbol of the emptiness of modern life
    II. The representative of a social class
    III. The personification of the power of love

(A) I only
(B) II only
(C) I and III only
(D) II and III only
(E) I, II, and III

Ⓐ Ⓑ Ⓒ Ⓓ Ⓔ

Most of the questions, more than 85%, are Type One, Best Choice. Type Three, Roman Numeral questions, are the fewest.

Sample Questions and Analysis of Answers

DIRECTIONS: This sample consists of a selection from a literary work and questions on its content, form, and style. After reading the passage, choose the best answer to each question and blacken the corresponding space.

Note: Pay particular attention to the requirement of questions that contain the words NOT, LEAST, or EXCEPT.

Questions 1–8. Read the following passage carefully before you choose your answers.

But Leander got the last word. Opening Aaron's copy of Shakespeare, after it had begun to rain, Coverly found the place marked with a note in his father's hand. "Advice to my sons," it read.
(5) "Never put whisky into hot water bottle crossing borders of dry states or countries. Rubber will spoil taste. Never make love with pants on. Beer on whisky, very risky. Whisky on beer, never fear. Never eat apples, peaches, pears,
(10) etc., while drinking whisky except long French-style dinners, terminating with fruit. Other

viands have mollifying effect. Never sleep in
moonlight. Known by scientists to induce madness. Should bed stand beside window on clear
(15) night draw shades before retiring. Never hold
cigar at right angles to fingers. Hayseed. Hold
cigar at diagonal. Remove band or not as you
prefer. Never wear red necktie. Provide light
snorts for ladies if entertaining. Effects of
(20) harder stuff on frail sex sometimes disastrous.
Bathe in cold water every morning. Painful but
exhilarating. Also reduces horniness. Have
haircut once a week. Wear dark clothes after 6
p.m. Eat fresh fish for breakfast when available.
(25) Avoid kneeling in unheated stone churches. Ec-
clesiastical dampness causes prematurely gray
hair. Fear tastes like a rusty knife and do not
let her into your house. Courage tastes of blood.
Stand up straight. Admire the world. Relish the
(30) love of a gentle woman. Trust in the Lord.''

1. With which of the following is Leander's advice
   most concerned?

   (A) practical knowledge and sensible living
   (B) fortitude and salvation
   (C) accomplishment and material success
   (D) determination and moral rectitude
   (E) wit and serenity

   Ⓐ Ⓑ Ⓒ Ⓓ Ⓔ

2. The first sentence suggests that the

   (A) sons tried to be unlike their father in every
       way they could
   (B) father was never able to communicate with
       his sons
   (C) father was never more profound than in his
       note
   (D) sons exercised great control over their own
       lives
   (E) sons and father debated about the conduct
       of the sons' lives

   Ⓐ Ⓑ Ⓒ Ⓓ Ⓔ

3. The humor of the advice given in lines 5-7
   (''Never . . . taste'') depends primarily on the
   fact that Leander

   (A) is aware that his sons enjoy whisky
   (B) thinks it likely that his sons have hot water
       bottles
   (C) assumes that his sons will be traveling
   (D) assumes that his sons' cars will be
       searched

   (E) is unconcerned about his sons' breaking the
       law.

   Ⓐ Ⓑ Ⓒ Ⓓ Ⓔ

4. Which of the following pieces of advice is most
   probably based on superstition?

   (A) ''Never make love with pants on.'' (lines
       7-8)
   (B) ''Never eat [fruit] while drinking whisky.''
       (lines 9-10)
   (C) ''Never sleep in moonlight.'' (lines 12-13)
   (D) ''Never hold cigar at right angles to fin-
       gers.'' (lines 15-16)
   (E) ''Bathe in cold water every morning.'' (line
       21)

   Ⓐ Ⓑ Ⓒ Ⓓ Ⓔ

5. Which of the following pairs best points up the
   contrast in levels of diction in the passage?

   (A) ''viands'' (line 12) . . . ''snorts'' (line 19)
   (B) ''mollifying'' (line 12) . . . ''entertaining''
       (line 19)
   (C) ''sleep'' (line 12) . . . ''retiring'' (line 15)
   (D) ''Painful'' (line 21) . . . ''exhilarating'' (line
       22)
   (E) ''Fear'' (line 27) . . . ''Courage'' (line 29)

   Ⓐ Ⓑ Ⓒ Ⓓ Ⓔ

Analysis:
1. (A)   Of the choices, the only ones stressed in
this selection are practical knowledge and sensible
living.
2. (E)   In that the father, Leander, had the last
word by being placed in the son's notebook, there
had to be a prior discussion with the sons.
3. (E)   Leander is worried about spoiling the
taste of the whisky and not about illegal transportation of whisky.
4. (C)   The only justification for the admonition
not to sleep in moonlight is the unsubstantiated generalization, ''scientists know that it induces madness''—an obvious superstition. The other statements all have empirical proofs.
5. (A)   The term viands is formal or elegant
while snorts is slang or colloquial. The other choices
contain pairs of formal words.
For more specific preparation for the English
Achievement Test in Literature turn to Section
Five, page 208.

The English Composition Test

(All Multiple-Choice Questions)

Section **O N E** : **Correctness and Effectiveness of Expression**

1. *Diagnostic Test*

2. *Digest of Grammar and Usage*

3. *Proper Punctuation and Capitalization*

The English Composition Test (all multiple-choice questions) does not measure writing ability directly. The most valid test in this area would require the actual writing of themes, essays, reports, narratives, and so forth. For this reason, the second form of the English Composition Test has been developed, the English Composition Test with Essay (see pages 116–207).

To obtain objective results using only multiple-choice questions, the College Entrance Examination Board had the Educational Testing Service develop the items in the English Composition Test as indirect methods of measurement. Studies have shown that the scores achieved on this test correlate very closely with the ability to write clearly and forcefully—as shown in subsequent college work.

The multiple-choice questions on the English Composition Test stress the mechanics of writing, ranging from the simpler to the more subtle. The recognition of errors and the ability to eradicate them are emphasized much more than control of literary forms or creative and imaginative approaches.

The English Composition Test evaluates ability in one of the dialects of the language—Standard Written English. This is the language system of oral and written communication used on the college level. The test is a measurement of potential college success. College success depends heavily upon the student's ability to function in an atmosphere almost wholly dominated by Standard Written English; however, there is no underlying assumption of superiority of one dialect over another.

In the College Board publications, the terms *correct* and *incorrect* are used interchangeably with *acceptable* and *not acceptable,* respectively, when referring to specific forms in usage, diction, and spelling. Thus, items labeled here as acceptable in current Standard Written English may be labeled as either *acceptable* or *correct* in directions and in test items on the exam.

1. *Diagnostic Test*

The preparation for each of the reviews and drills for the three tests in English begins with a Diagnostic Test. This test has several purposes. First, it is a tool that will help you to discover strengths and weaknesses. It will aid you in setting up a realistic, practical study program to meet your particular needs. You will be able to check the efficiency of your studying by taking the Practice Tests in Section Two on page 62 and comparing the results with those of the Diagnostic Test.

Another purpose of the Diagnostic Tests is to give you familiarity with the format and level of difficulty of the English Composition multiple-choice questions. You will gain confidence and know-how by experiencing the "traps" set by the test-makers. You will learn to recognize your mistakes, especially if you study the reviews and explanations for the principles you did not know.

Finally, for those of you who still have a choice of which examination to take—all multiple-choice, with essay, or literature—taking the three Diagnostic Tests and comparing results may help you reach your decision.

DIAGNOSTIC TEST
ANSWER SHEET

1 Ⓐ Ⓑ Ⓒ Ⓓ Ⓔ	31 Ⓐ Ⓑ Ⓒ Ⓓ Ⓔ	61 Ⓐ Ⓑ Ⓒ Ⓓ Ⓔ
2 Ⓐ Ⓑ Ⓒ Ⓓ Ⓔ	32 Ⓐ Ⓑ Ⓒ Ⓓ Ⓔ	62 Ⓐ Ⓑ Ⓒ Ⓓ Ⓔ
3 Ⓐ Ⓑ Ⓒ Ⓓ Ⓔ	33 Ⓐ Ⓑ Ⓒ Ⓓ Ⓔ	63 Ⓐ Ⓑ Ⓒ Ⓓ Ⓔ
4 Ⓐ Ⓑ Ⓒ Ⓓ Ⓔ	34 Ⓐ Ⓑ Ⓒ Ⓓ Ⓔ	64 Ⓐ Ⓑ Ⓒ Ⓓ Ⓔ
5 Ⓐ Ⓑ Ⓒ Ⓓ Ⓔ	35 Ⓐ Ⓑ Ⓒ Ⓓ Ⓔ	65 Ⓐ Ⓑ Ⓒ Ⓓ Ⓔ
6 Ⓐ Ⓑ Ⓒ Ⓓ Ⓔ	36 Ⓐ Ⓑ Ⓒ Ⓓ Ⓔ	66 Ⓐ Ⓑ Ⓒ Ⓓ Ⓔ
7 Ⓐ Ⓑ Ⓒ Ⓓ Ⓔ	37 Ⓐ Ⓑ Ⓒ Ⓓ Ⓔ	67 Ⓐ Ⓑ Ⓒ Ⓓ Ⓔ
8 Ⓐ Ⓑ Ⓒ Ⓓ Ⓔ	38 Ⓐ Ⓑ Ⓒ Ⓓ Ⓔ	68 Ⓐ Ⓑ Ⓒ Ⓓ Ⓔ
9 Ⓐ Ⓑ Ⓒ Ⓓ Ⓔ	39 Ⓐ Ⓑ Ⓒ Ⓓ Ⓔ	69 Ⓐ Ⓑ Ⓒ Ⓓ Ⓔ
10 Ⓐ Ⓑ Ⓒ Ⓓ Ⓔ	40 Ⓐ Ⓑ Ⓒ Ⓓ Ⓔ	70 Ⓐ Ⓑ Ⓒ Ⓓ Ⓔ
11 Ⓐ Ⓑ Ⓒ Ⓓ Ⓔ	41 Ⓐ Ⓑ Ⓒ Ⓓ Ⓔ	71 Ⓐ Ⓑ Ⓒ Ⓓ Ⓔ
12 Ⓐ Ⓑ Ⓒ Ⓓ Ⓔ	42 Ⓐ Ⓑ Ⓒ Ⓓ Ⓔ	72 Ⓐ Ⓑ Ⓒ Ⓓ Ⓔ
13 Ⓐ Ⓑ Ⓒ Ⓓ Ⓔ	43 Ⓐ Ⓑ Ⓒ Ⓓ Ⓔ	73 Ⓐ Ⓑ Ⓒ Ⓓ Ⓔ
14 Ⓐ Ⓑ Ⓒ Ⓓ Ⓔ	44 Ⓐ Ⓑ Ⓒ Ⓓ Ⓔ	74 Ⓐ Ⓑ Ⓒ Ⓓ Ⓔ
15 Ⓐ Ⓑ Ⓒ Ⓓ Ⓔ	45 Ⓐ Ⓑ Ⓒ Ⓓ Ⓔ	75 Ⓐ Ⓑ Ⓒ Ⓓ Ⓔ
16 Ⓐ Ⓑ Ⓒ Ⓓ Ⓔ	46 Ⓐ Ⓑ Ⓒ Ⓓ Ⓔ	76 Ⓐ Ⓑ Ⓒ Ⓓ Ⓔ
17 Ⓐ Ⓑ Ⓒ Ⓓ Ⓔ	47 Ⓐ Ⓑ Ⓒ Ⓓ Ⓔ	77 Ⓐ Ⓑ Ⓒ Ⓓ Ⓔ
18 Ⓐ Ⓑ Ⓒ Ⓓ Ⓔ	48 Ⓐ Ⓑ Ⓒ Ⓓ Ⓔ	78 Ⓐ Ⓑ Ⓒ Ⓓ Ⓔ
19 Ⓐ Ⓑ Ⓒ Ⓓ Ⓔ	49 Ⓐ Ⓑ Ⓒ Ⓓ Ⓔ	79 Ⓐ Ⓑ Ⓒ Ⓓ Ⓔ
20 Ⓐ Ⓑ Ⓒ Ⓓ Ⓔ	50 Ⓐ Ⓑ Ⓒ Ⓓ Ⓔ	80 Ⓐ Ⓑ Ⓒ Ⓓ Ⓔ
21 Ⓐ Ⓑ Ⓒ Ⓓ Ⓔ	51 Ⓐ Ⓑ Ⓒ Ⓓ Ⓔ	81 Ⓐ Ⓑ Ⓒ Ⓓ Ⓔ
22 Ⓐ Ⓑ Ⓒ Ⓓ Ⓔ	52 Ⓐ Ⓑ Ⓒ Ⓓ Ⓔ	82 Ⓐ Ⓑ Ⓒ Ⓓ Ⓔ
23 Ⓐ Ⓑ Ⓒ Ⓓ Ⓔ	53 Ⓐ Ⓑ Ⓒ Ⓓ Ⓔ	83 Ⓐ Ⓑ Ⓒ Ⓓ Ⓔ
24 Ⓐ Ⓑ Ⓒ Ⓓ Ⓔ	54 Ⓐ Ⓑ Ⓒ Ⓓ Ⓔ	84 Ⓐ Ⓑ Ⓒ Ⓓ Ⓔ
25 Ⓐ Ⓑ Ⓒ Ⓓ Ⓔ	55 Ⓐ Ⓑ Ⓒ Ⓓ Ⓔ	85 Ⓐ Ⓑ Ⓒ Ⓓ Ⓔ
26 Ⓐ Ⓑ Ⓒ Ⓓ Ⓔ	56 Ⓐ Ⓑ Ⓒ Ⓓ Ⓔ	86 Ⓐ Ⓑ Ⓒ Ⓓ Ⓔ
27 Ⓐ Ⓑ Ⓒ Ⓓ Ⓔ	57 Ⓐ Ⓑ Ⓒ Ⓓ Ⓔ	87 Ⓐ Ⓑ Ⓒ Ⓓ Ⓔ
28 Ⓐ Ⓑ Ⓒ Ⓓ Ⓔ	58 Ⓐ Ⓑ Ⓒ Ⓓ Ⓔ	88 Ⓐ Ⓑ Ⓒ Ⓓ Ⓔ
29 Ⓐ Ⓑ Ⓒ Ⓓ Ⓔ	59 Ⓐ Ⓑ Ⓒ Ⓓ Ⓔ	89 Ⓐ Ⓑ Ⓒ Ⓓ Ⓔ
30 Ⓐ Ⓑ Ⓒ Ⓓ Ⓔ	60 Ⓐ Ⓑ Ⓒ Ⓓ Ⓔ	90 Ⓐ Ⓑ Ⓒ Ⓓ Ⓔ

DIAGNOSTIC TEST

Total Time: One Hour
PART 1 *Suggested Time: 20 Minutes*
Time begun .... Time ended .... Time used ....
Did you complete the section within the time limit? ..

DIRECTIONS: The following sentences contain problems in grammar, usage, diction (choice of words), and idiom.

Some sentences are correct.

No sentence contains more than one error.

You will find that the error, if there is one, is underlined and lettered. Assume that all other elements of the sentence are correct and cannot be changed. In choosing answers, follow the requirements of standard written English.

If there is an error, select the <u>one underlined part</u> that must be changed in order to make the sentence correct, and blacken the corresponding space on the answer sheet.

If there is no error, mark answer space E.

1. Everyone in the class <u>looks</u> <u>well</u> in the gradu-
(A) (B)
ation picture <u>except</u> Margie and <u>me</u>.
(C)   (D)
<u>No error</u>
(E)

2. There <u>are</u> <u>fewer</u> items in this test <u>than</u> in the
(A) (B)   (C)
ones he had given <u>previously</u>. <u>No error</u>
(D)   (E)

3. Her cough so <u>aggravated</u> her condition that the
(A)
doctor had to <u>bring</u> her to the hospital, where
(B)
she <u>lay</u> in the ward awaiting <u>further</u> treatment.
(C)   (D)
<u>No error</u>
(E)

4. There is <u>really</u> no reason for <u>you</u> becoming so
(A)   (B)
<u>annoyed</u> with Bea and <u>me</u> that you can scarcely
(C)   (D)
talk with us. <u>No error</u>
(E)

5. We <u>lived</u> in this house for three years <u>before</u> my
(A)   (B)
father <u>decided</u> to have us move to a <u>newer</u>
(C)   (D)
neighborhood. <u>No error</u>
(E)

6. Sift two <u>cupsful</u> of flour, break the eggs very
(A)
<u>carefully</u>, and <u>then</u> fill the <u>emptied</u> shells with
(B)   (C)   (D)
the flour. <u>No error</u>
(E)

7. <u>Although</u> Milton and I <u>are</u> deeply involved in
(A)   (B)
this matter, the <u>amount</u> of hours we have de-
(C)
voted to it <u>is</u> negligible. <u>No error</u>
(D)   (E)

8. Hardly <u>no one</u> that I <u>have</u> seen in the
(A)   (B)
<u>past</u> two hours <u>had</u> witnessed the performance.
(C)   (D)
<u>No error</u>
(E)

9. Some of the famous opera stars <u>of the past</u>
(A)
<u>who</u> <u>was</u> present <u>approved of</u> our pro-
(B) (C)   (D)
posal, a plan to popularize good music.
<u>No error</u>
(E)

10. The main difficulty <u>was</u> the barriers <u>which</u>
(A)   (B)
<u>were</u> standing in the <u>center</u> of the crosswalk.
(C)   (D)
<u>No error</u>
(E)

11. The most exciting scene occurred <u>when</u> every-
(A)
one <u>in the cast</u> <u>was</u> told to disguise
(B)   (C)
<u>themselves</u> as gypsies. <u>No error</u>
(D)   (E)

12. In the newspaper <u>they</u> say that <u>much more</u>
            (A)   (B)
money must be <u>spent on</u> research; hence,
            (C)
we may confidently expect an <u>increase in</u> our
                       (D)
present grant. <u>No error</u>
          (E)

13. <u>They're</u> the ones who <u>assert</u> that a better bridge
    (A)   (B)
<u>could</u> have been built <u>had</u> we had their assist-
   (C)   (D)
ance. <u>No error</u>
     (E)

14. She said, <u>moreover</u>, that I <u>had</u> not even tried,
       (A)   (B)
<u>which</u> <u>annoyed me</u> very much. <u>No error</u>
 (C)   (D)   (E)

15. Frances <u>has long had</u> the desire <u>to become a</u>
     (A)   (B)
famous writer even though the study of <u>it</u>
                    (C)
would require years of sacrifice on <u>her</u> part.
                  (D)
<u>No error</u>
 (E)

16. When I <u>realized</u> how little I <u>had been</u> able to
    (A)   (B)
accomplish, my <u>fears of failure</u> grew rapidly,
       (C)
<u>robbing</u> me of what little confidence I had had.
 (D)
<u>No error</u>
 (E)

17. <u>Even though</u> it <u>may</u> be the <u>most</u> harmless of
  (A)   (B)   (C)
snakes, I am not <u>enthused</u> about having it in a
        (D)
cage in my room. <u>No error</u>
       (E)

18. <u>Every one</u> who <u>is</u> anyone <u>was</u> invited to attend
  (A)   (B)   (C)
the party for you and <u>me</u>. <u>No error</u>
          (D)   (E)

19. The old tape recorder <u>seems</u> to be much better
           (A)

<u>then</u> any of the <u>newer</u> ones that <u>are</u> on display
 (B)   (C)   (D)
now. <u>No error</u>
    (E)

20. He treats his pets <u>as though</u> they <u>were</u>
           (A)   (B)
humans, <u>showing</u> them every possible consid-
 (C)   (D)
eration. <u>No error</u>
    (E)

21. <u>In regards to</u> your recent request for assistance,
   (A)
I <u>have to</u> report that Allan has stated
  (B)
<u>emphatically</u> that he has no more money to give
 (C)
you or <u>me</u>. <u>No error</u>
   (D)   (E)

22. <u>It</u> was <u>kind of a</u> shock to look <u>into</u> these mat-
 (A)   (B)   (C)
ters and <u>discover</u> that the fault was solely mine.
    (D)
<u>No error</u>
 (E)

23. If taxes <u>raise</u> any <u>higher</u> we <u>would have to</u> move
   (A)   (B)   (C)
elsewhere. <u>No error</u>
 (D)   (E)

24. She will <u>definitely</u> <u>lose out</u> if she studies <u>less</u>
    (A)   (B)   (C)
than any <u>other</u> girl in her class. <u>No error</u>
  (D)   (E)

25. <u>Let</u> it <u>lay</u> where it <u>has</u> fallen until the
 (A) (B)   (C)
<u>demolition</u> squad arrives. <u>No error</u>
 (D)   (E)

26. You <u>will</u> have to make the curves <u>rounder</u>;
   (A)   (B)
otherwise, everyone <u>will be</u> copying your
        (C)
<u>mistakes</u>. <u>No error</u>
 D   (E)

27. Grandmother and I enjoyed your letter
    (A)
    muchly; we are eagerly looking forward to your
    (B)   (C)   (D)
    next communication. No error
                        (E)

28. As he neared the end of the evening, his
        (A)
    voice echoed the hopes that filled everyone's
            (B)   (C)
    heart; he had become the symbol of our hopes.
              (D)
    No error
    (E)

29. Let's play a old record on the machine so that
    (A)   (B)
    we can discover the true worth of this
        (C)
    latest gadget. No error
        (D)   (E)

30. Due to carelessness, the couple will lose their
    (A)   (B) (C)
    savings in this uncalled-for mess. No error
                                 D   (E)

31. Give it to whomever it belongs to; it little mat-
                (A)   (B)   (C)
    ters to me now whose it is. No error
                   (D)   (E)

32. I may not except you from these
      (A)   (B)   (C)
    regulations, regardless of how much pressure
                 (D)
    you put on me to do so. No error
                           (E)

33. When you are among friends and the problem
                   (A)
    is all ready to be solved, it is better that you do
       (B)
    as you are told and not aggravate others.
    (C)   (D)
    No error
    (E)

PART 2 *Suggested Time:* 15 *Minutes*
Time begun .... Time ended .... Time used ....
Did you complete the section within the time limit? ..

DIRECTIONS: In each of the following sentences, some part of the sentence or the entire sentence is underlined. Beneath each sentence you will find five ways of phrasing the underlined part. The first of these repeats the original; the other four are different. If you think the original is better than any of the alternatives, choose answer A; otherwise choose one of the others. Select the best version and blacken the corresponding space on your answer sheet.

34. Mrs. Fitzpatrick is one of those people who is always willing to help others.

    (A) who is always willing
    (B) which are always willing
    (C) whom are always willing
    (D) who are always willing
    (E) which is always willing

35. Having spoken to the principal our anger subsided.

    (A) principal, our anger subsided
    (B) principal, we felt our anger subside
    (C) principal, our anger had subsided
    (D) principal, the discussion caused our anger to subside
    (E) principal, our anger could have subsided

36. A package finally arrived however it is not the one I expected.

    (A) however it is not the one I expected
    (B) which was not the one I had expected
    (C) , however it is not the one I expect
    (D) ; however it was not the one I expect
    (E) . However, it was not the one I had expected

37. It was a awesome sight, much too much for my weakened condition.

    (A) a awesome sight, much too much
    (B) an awesome sight. Much too much
    (C) a awesome sight, much to much
    (D) an awesome sight, much too much
    (E) an awesome sight; much to much

38. If I <u>would have gone</u> there, we could have prevented all of this!

  (A) would have gone
  (B) would of gone
  (C) had gone
  (D) could have gone
  (E) could've gone

39. I can see hardly <u>any reason for their</u> listening to us.

  (A) any reason for their
  (B) no reason for them
  (C) no reason for their
  (D) any reason for them
  (E) any of the reasons for them

40. I hate to <u>loose the ring it really was quit valuable.</u>

  (A) loose the ring it really was quit valuable
  (B) loose the ring; it really was quit valuable
  (C) lose the ring. It really was quit valuable
  (D) lose the ring; it really was quite valuable
  (E) loose the ring. It really had been quit valuable

41. <u>Leave it lay there</u> until we are ready.

  (A) Leave it lay there
  (B) Let it lay their
  (C) Leave it lie their
  (D) Leave it lay there
  (E) Let it lie there

42. Alberta is <u>more sensitive than any girl</u> in her class.

  (A) more sensitive than any girl
  (B) most sensitive
  (C) more sensitive than any other girl
  (D) most sensitive than any girl
  (E) more sensitive than any girls

43. <u>Being Harold had invited me</u>, I had not anticipated such a curt reception.

  (A) Being Harold had invited me
  (B) Being that Harold had invited me
  (C) Being that Harold invited me
  (D) Since Harold had invited me
  (E) Since Harold invited me

44. Everyone <u>except he and I</u> had the necessary visas.

  (A) except he and I
  (B) except him and I
  (C) except I and he
  (D) except me and him
  (E) except him and me

45. The results were better <u>then I should of expected.</u>

  (A) then I should of expected
  (B) than I should of expected
  (C) Then I should have expected
  (D) Than I should of expected
  (E) than I should have expected

46. <u>Is it him who</u> I have to see this morning?

  (A) Is it him who
  (B) Was it he whom
  (C) Is it he whom
  (D) Is it he who
  (E) Was it him who

47. All I can say is <u>that it is a womans' world after all.</u>

  (A) that it is a womans' world after all.
  (B) "That it is a woman's world after all."
  (C) "That it is a woman's world after all"
  (D) that it is a women's world after all.
  (E) that it is a woman's world after all.

48. <u>When the damage is assessed</u>, you pay the costs.

  (A) When the damage is assessed
  (B) After the damage has been assessed
  (C) After the damage is assessed
  (D) When the damage had been assessed
  (E) By the time the damage is assessed

49. Is he one of those doctors <u>who have been experimenting on humans</u>?

  (A) who have been experimenting on humans
  (B) who has been experimenting on humans
  (C) who have been experimenting on human beings
  (D) who has been experimenting on human beings
  (E) which has been experimenting on humans

50. He told us that <u>its a kind of a fools' paradise.</u>

  (A) its a kind of a fools' paradise
  (B) it's a kind of fools' paradise
  (C) its a kind of a fool's paradise
  (D) it's kind of a fool's paradise
  (E) its a kind of fools' paradise

51. <u>Being as everyone of my friends were there</u>, I felt confident.

   (A) Being as everyone of my friends were there
   (B) Being that everyone of my friends was there
   (C) Being that everyone of my friends were there
   (D) Since every one of my friends was there
   (E) Since everyone of my friends were there

52. The case has been decided in our favor; <u>however, it can still be appealed</u>.

   (A) ; however, it can still be appealed
   (B) however it can still be appealed
   (C) ; However, it can still be appealed
   (D) , and however, it can still be appealed
   (E) , however, it could have been still appealed

53. We must make our peace <u>with Mr. Shaw the leader of the opposition</u>.

   (A) with Mr. Shaw the leader of the opposition
   (B) with Mr. Shaw who had been leader of the opposition
   (C) with Mr. Shaw. The leader of the opposition
   (D) with Mr. Shaw. Who has been leader of the opposition
   (E) with Mr. Shaw, the leader of the opposition

54. His favorite complimentary close is that old <u>favorite, *sincerely yours*</u>'.

   (A) favorite, *sincerely yours*'.
   (B) favorite *sincerely yours*.
   (C) favorite *sincerely your's*.
   (D) favorite *Sincerely yours*'.
   (E) favorite, *Sincerely yours*.

55. <u>If I was he</u>, I would drop the discussion at this point.

   (A) If I was he
   (B) If I were he
   (C) If I was him
   (D) If I had been him
   (E) If I were him

56. You will find <u>these here somewhere near the new school</u>.

   (A) these here somewhere near the new school
   (B) these somewhere near the new school
   (C) these here somewheres near the new school
   (D) these here someplace near the new school
   (E) these someplace near the new school

57. He always finds the negative values in whatever I suggest, <u>which annoys me no end</u>.

   (A) , which annoys me no end
   (B) . Which annoys me no end
   (C) , an action which annoys me no end
   (D) ; which annoys me no end
   (E) ; an action which annoys me no end

58. The most exciting scene <u>is when the hero's horse stumbles</u>.

   (A) is when the hero's horse stumbles
   (B) occurs when the heroes' horse stumbles
   (C) is when the heroes' horse stumbles
   (D) occurs when the hero's horse stumbles
   (E) was when the hero's horse stumbles

PART 3 *Suggested Time:* **15 Minutes**
Time begun .... Time ended .... Time used ....
Did you complete the section within the time limit? ..

DIRECTIONS: Each of the following sentences is to be rephrased according to the directions that follow it. <u>You should make only those changes that the directions require</u>. Keep the meaning of the revised sentence as close to the meaning of the original sentence as the directions for that sentence permit.

59. Everyone of the soldiers was given his full set of equipment.
Begin with <u>All of the soldiers</u>.

   (A) were given his
   (B) will be given their
   (C) was given their
   (D) were given their
   (E) will have been given their

60. Ben is the most egotistical man I know.
Substitute <u>more egotistical</u> for <u>the most egotistical</u>.

   (A) than any man I know
   (B) than any man I have ever known
   (C) than any other man I have known
   (D) than any other man I know
   (E) than any man I had ever known

61. Running up the steps, he soon found himself out of breath.
Begin with He ran.

   (A) and then he was found
   (B) and soon found
   (C) and could have found
   (D) which found him
   (E) and then had found

62. Miss Muller, our college adviser and guidance counselor, addressed the assembly.
Begin with Because.

   (A) counselor addressed
   (B) counselor, she could have
   (C) counselor she
   (D) counselor was addressed
   (E) counselor, she

63. Dave along with several other members of the class was seen loitering in the vicinity of the lockers.
Begin with Dave and.

   (A) has been
   (B) are
   (C) is
   (D) were
   (E) was often

64. To be used effectively, the solution must be kept at full strength.
Substitute you must for the solution must.

   (A) When used effectively
   (B) the solution effectively,
   (C) strength of full solution
   (D) To have been used
   (E) When used as a solution,

65. I saw the accident, and therefore I expected to be called as a witness.
Begin the sentence with Because.

   (A) . and therefore
   (B) . Therefore
   (C) accident, I
   (D) and expected
   (E) I saw

66. The body which had been found lying face down in the stagnant pool at the edge of town was finally identified as that of an itinerant day laborer.
Begin the sentence with Found.

   (A) town, the body
   (B) which had been identified
   (C) town, itinerant day laborer
   (D) An itinerant day laborer
   (E) town. Body

67. Was there anyone in the group ready to describe the project at that time?
Substitute any for anyone.

   (A) Had there been
   (B) Were there
   (C) of the group
   (D) Have there been
   (E) Ready to describe

68. I was unprepared for the report, and this soon became very obvious to the members of the committee.
Begin with That I was unprepared.

   (A) report, and this
   (B) report; and this
   (C) report soon
   (D) report and soon
   (E) report, soon

69. I agreed to purchase the new equipment from them, but I really thought that the price was too high.
Substitute however for but.

   (A) , however, I
   (B) ; however, the price
   (C) . However, the new equipment
   (D) . However, I
   (E) ; however, I

70. Frances felt that she was ready, and she asked her instructor to give her the makeup test. Omit the second she.

   (A) , and asked
   (B) and had asked
   (C) but asked
   (D) and asked
   (E) , and asked

71. Being my best friend, Marvin helped me plan my strategy.
Substitute who is for Being.

   (A) Marvin who is
   (B) friend, helped
   (C) Helped
   (D) strategy, who is
   (E) strategy who is

72. I was so angry that I wrote a letter to the company and mailed it immediately.
Substitute which I for and.

(A) company which I
(B) company, which I
(C) which I had
(D) immediately to
(E) Which I

73. How can we measure the worth of the hours which have been frittered away in useless worry!
Substitute time for hours.

(A) time. Which
(B) time, which
(C) which has
(D) which would have been
(E) frittering away

PART 4 *Suggested Time: 10 Minutes*

DIRECTIONS: The following sentences contain problems in grammar, usage, diction (choice of words), and idiom.

Some sentences are correct.

No sentence contains more than one error.

You will find that the error, if there is one, is underlined and lettered. Assume that all other elements of the sentence are correct and cannot be changed. In choosing answers, follow the requirements of standard written English.

If there is an error, select the one underlined part that must be changed in order to make the sentence correct, and on the answer sheet.

If there is no error, mark answer E.

74. I cannot argue with what he said, but I object
(A)   (B)   (C)
to how he said it . No error
(D)   (E)

75. Neither he nor I am unwilling to accept these
(A)   (B)   (C)   (D)
reasonable suggestions. No error
(E)

76. When the pipes burst, the sound was so loud
(A)   (B)
that I could not hardly bear the pain in my ears.
(C)   (D)
No error
(E)

77. My grandparents had lived in Brooklyn
(A)
long before any bridge connected up Manhattan
(B)   (C)
with Long Island. No error
(D)   (E)

78. May we say that we do not want to hear
(A)   (B)
any more about how she blames everything that
(C)
goes wrong on him. No error
(D)   (E)

79. Alice, accompanied by her classmates, are here
(A)
concerning your objections to the guests they
(B)   (C)
chose to invite to the school dance. No error
(D)   (E)

80. Without telling Rose or us , Frances had sent
(A)   (B)
a note to everyone except me, demanding im-
(C)
mediate payment of their pledge. No error
(D)   (E)

81. In this modern world of today, there are so
(A)   (B)
many more gadgets than our grandparents
(C)
had ever dreamed possible. No error
(D)   (E)

82. Being a sensible person does not mean that you
(A)   (B)
intend to allow others to push you around.
(C)   (D)
No error
(E)

83. He could have chosen another equally as good
(A)   (B)   (C)
without having to take ours. No error
(D)   (E)

84. It would be wise to decide that everyone
except her is to be permitted to have access
(A)   (B) (C)   (D)
to the records. No error
(E)

85. There <u>are</u> <u>nowheres</u> <u>nearly</u> enough food sup-
     (A)   (B)   (C)
    plies for the long, cold months <u>ahead</u>.
                                      (D)

    <u>No error</u>
    (E)

86. Who other than Jack and <u>I</u> <u>can</u> enjoy being
                            (A) (B)
    isolated <u>by themselves</u> for hours <u>on end</u>?
             (C)   (D)

    <u>No error</u>
    (E)

87. The problem <u>was when</u> a series of films <u>was</u>
                 (A)   (B)
    transferred <u>into</u> the permanent <u>files</u>. <u>No error</u>
                (C)   (D)   (E)

88. The song he <u>wrote</u> was <u>sung</u> <u>continually</u> <u>over</u>
                (A)   (B)   (C)   (D)
    this station until it caught the public's favor.

    <u>No error</u>
    (E)

89. When I <u>was graduated</u> <u>from</u> high school, there
           (A)   (B)
    <u>were</u> scarcely <u>no</u> jobs that I could qualify for.
    (C)   (D)

    <u>No error</u>
    (E)

90. <u>Bring</u> this recording to the dean so that he can
    (A)
    <u>hear</u> <u>for himself</u> what <u>had really been said</u>.
    (B)   (C)   (D)

    <u>No error</u>
    (E)

ANSWER KEY: DIAGNOSTIC TEST

Part 1	*Part 2*	*Part 3*	*Part 4*
1. (B)	34. (D)	59. (D)	74. (B)
2. (E)	35. (B)	60. (D)	75. (E)
3. (B)	36. (E)	61. (B)	76. (C)
4. (B)	37. (D)	62. (E)	77. (C)
5. (A)	38. (C)	63. (D)	78. (D)
6. (A)	39. (A)	64. (B)	79. (A)
7. (C)	40. (D)	65. (C)	80. (D)
8. (A)	41. (E)	66. (A)	81. (A)
9. (C)	42. (C)	67. (B)	82. (D)
10. (E)	43. (D)	68. (C)	83. (C)
11. (D)	44. (E)	69. (D)	84. (E)
12. (A)	45. (E)	70. (D)	85. (B)
13. (E)	46. (C)	71. (B)	86. (C)
14. (C)	47. (E)	72. (D)	87. (A)
15. (C)	48. (B)	73. (C)	88. (A)
16. (E)	49. (C)		89. (D)
17. (D)	50. (B)		90. (A)
18. (A)	51. (D)		
19. (B)	52. (A)		
20. (C)	53. (E)		
21. (A)	54. (E)		
22. (B)	55. (B)		
23. (A)	56. (B)		
24. (B)	57. (C)		
25. (B)	58. (D)		
26. (B)			
27. (B)			
28. (E)			
29. (B)			
30. (A)			
31. (B)			
32. (E)			
33. (D)			

DETERMINING YOUR RAW SCORE

1. Tabulate Totals
   Number Right _____
   Number Wrong _____
   Number Omitted _____

2. Enter Number Right   A _____
   Divide Number
   Wrong by 4 and
   put result here   B _____

3. Subtract B from A. This
   results in your RAW SCORE _____

   The subtraction of ¼ point for each incorrect answer adjusts for the effect of
   random guessing.

EVALUATING YOUR PERFORMANCE

Excellent	84–90
Very Good	61–83
Good	44–60
Average	33–43
Below Average	16–32
Unsatisfactory	15 or below

ANALYSIS OF ANSWERS: DIAGNOSTIC TEST

Part 1

1. (B) The adjective *good* describes *everyone*.
2. (E) No error
3. (B) The verb *take* rather than *bring* is correct since the action is not toward the speaker.
4. (B) The possessive pronoun *your* is required to modify the gerund *becoming*.
5. (A) The past perfect *had lived* is required since the action preceded past action.
6. (A) Since *cupful* is a unit word, the sign of the plural is added at the end—*cupfuls*.
7. (C) The noun *number* rather than *amount* is used since units (*hours*) are involved.
8. (A) *Hardly* is followed by the positive *anyone*, not the negative *no one*.
9. (C) *Some* is plural and requires *were*.
10. (E) No error
11. (D) The pronoun *everyone* requires the singular *himself* or *herself*, not the plural *themselves*.
12. (A) The pronoun *they* lacks an antecedent.
13. (E) No error
14. (C) The pronoun *which* must relate back to a specific word and not to the general idea of the sentence.
15. (C) The pronoun *it* lacks an antecedent.
16. (E) No error
17. (D) The term *enthused* is nonstandard.
18. (A) The pronoun *everyone* should be spelled as one word.
19. (B) In comparison *than* rather than *then* is used.
20. (C) The standard term is *human beings*, not *humans*.
21. (A) The standard phrase is *in regard to*.
22. (B) The idiom *kind of a* is nonstandard.
23. (A) *Raise* requires an object; *rise* does not take an object.
24. (B) The word *out* is unnecessary.
25. (B) The verb *lie* (rest) and not *lay* (put) is required.
26. (B) Something is either round or not round; it cannot be *rounder* in Standard Written English.
27. (B) The term *muchly* is nonstandard.
28. (E) No error
29. (B) The article *an* and not *a* is needed because the first letter in *old* is a vowel.
30. (A) The phrase *due to* is nonstandard as a synonym for *since* or *because*.
31. (B) The preposition *to* is repeated unnecessarily.
32. (E) No error
33. (D) Nonstandard as a synonym for *irritate* is *aggravate*.

Part 2

34. (D) The pronoun *who* refers to the plural *people,* and therefore it should be followed by a plural verb form.

35. (B) A pronoun is needed for the participle to modify. The words *principle* (rule) and *principal* (chief) are confused.

36. (E) The conjunctive adverb *however* can separate, not unite completely; therefore it cannot be used as a coordinating conjunction.

37. (D) The article *an* is needed because of the initial vowel in *awesome.*

38. (C) The past subjunctive *had* is required since the sentence describes action contrary to what had really happened.

39. (A) No error

40. (D) The word *loose* (lax) is used incorrectly; the two ideas must be punctuated as semi-dependent. The words *quit* (leave) and *quite* (almost completely) are confused.

41. (E) The verbs *let* (allow), not *leave* (depart), and *lie* (rest), not *lay* (put), are required.

42. (C) She could not be more sensitive than herself.

43. (D) The word *being* cannot be used as a substitute for *since* or *because* in standard usage.

44. (E) The preposition *except* should be followed by the objective form.

45. (E) Required are *than* (comparison) and *have.*

46. (C) The subject form is needed for the verb *is.*

47. (E) The noun *women* ends in a consonant; the possessive form, therefore, is *woman's.*

48. (B) The present perfect tense is required to describe action that preceded the present action in the main verb.

49. (C) The plural verb form (*have*) is required; *humans* is not an acceptable standard synonym for *human beings.*

50. (B) The standard term is *kind of.* There is confusion of *its* (possessive) and *it's* (it is), *fool's* (singular possessive) and *fools'* (plural possessive).

51. (D) The term *being as* is a nonstandard synonym for *since.* The singular *every one* should be followed by the singular *was.*

52. (A) No error

53. (E) Appositives are set off by commas.

54. (E) The possessive pronoun *yours* does not require an apostrophe; the complimentary close has an introductory capital letter.

55. (B) The present subjunctive form is required in untrue conditional clauses in the present tense.

56. (B) The word *these* means *the ones here;* therefore, *here* is unnecessary.

57. (C) The pronoun *which* must refer to a specific word.

58. (D) The idiom *is when* is a nonstandard synonym for *occurs when.*

Part 3

59. (D) The pronoun *all* is plural and requires *were* and *their.*

60. (D) The term *more* requires the addition of *other.*

61. (B) The compound verb *ran and found* is the result.

62. (E) Because Miss Muller is our college adviser and guidance counselor, she addressed the assembly.

63. (D) The sentence contains a plural subject *Dave and several other members.*

64. (B) The infinitive phrase *to be used effectively* must not be converted into a dangling infinitive phrase.

65. (C) Because I saw the accident, I . . .

66. (A) Found lying face down in the stagnant pool at the edge of town, the body was finally identified . . .

67. (B) The plural *any* requires the plural verb *were.*

68. (C) That I was unprepared for the report soon became very obvious . . .

69. (D) The conjunctive adverb cannot be punctuated as a coordinating conjunction.

70. (D) The compound verb *felt and asked* requires no comma before *and.*

71. (B) Marvin, who is my best friend, helped me plan my strategy.

72. (D) I was so angry that I wrote a letter which I mailed immediately to the company.

73. (C) The singular *time* requires the singular *has.*

Part 4

74. (B) We argue *with* a person and *against* an idea.

75. (E) No error

76. (C) The adverb *hardly* does not need *not* to carry negative values.

77. (C) The idiom *connect up* is nonstandard.

78. (D) The idiom *blame on* is nonstandard.

79. (A) The singular *Alice* requires the singular *is.*

80. (D) The pronoun *everyone* as subject requires *his or her.*

81. (A) *Modern* world *of today* is verbose.

82. (D) The idiom *push around* is nonstandard.
83. (C) The phrase *equally as* is not standard as a synonym for *equally*.
84. (E) No error
85. (B) The term *nowheres* is a nonstandard equivalent for *nowhere*.
86. (C) The phrase *by themselves* should be omitted since it repeats the idea in *isolated*.

87. (A) *Was when* is a nonstandard equivalent for *occurred when*.
88. (A) The past perfect *had written* is required since it involves action precedent to past action.
89. (D) The adverb *scarcely* is followed by *any*, not *no* or *not*.
90. (A) The verb *take*, not *bring*, is required since the action is not toward the speaker.

STEPS TO A HIGH SCORE

1. Use the results of the Diagnostic Test to assess your strengths and weaknesses.

2. Scan through each group in the units that follow and check the items to review or learn. Do *not* spend time in going over items you have already mastered.

3. Space your learning. Frequent short sessions are more productive than long cram periods. The more frequent the periods of learning, the greater the mastery.

4. After your study sessions, take one of the Practice Tests. Simulate the actual examination in time and privacy; evaluate your progress and discover the areas requiring additional review. These Practice Tests will help you gain confidence by familiarizing you with the style and types of questions to be found on the exam. Your speed and control will increase as the result of the continued practice. Use the scoring results to judge your progress.

2. *Digest of Grammar and Usage*

AN OVERVIEW

In Standard Written English, the range of what is considered unacceptable runs the gamut from errors that would be inexcusable when committed by a high school freshman to errors that involve subtleties of style and tone. You must know how to recognize unacceptable forms and how to correct them.

Study carefully the chart on the next page. It lists all of the common writing problems that are included in the English Composition Achievement Test. (The digests that follow will show you how to correct them.)

SCOPE OF THE TEST

Through a series of multiple-choice questions, the Achievement Test in Composition evaluates your ability to handle the common writing problems that handicap college students. Here are the areas on which the questions are based. A more thorough discussion of each follows this chart.

Writing Problems	Illustrative Sentences
Sequence of tenses	After she entered the room, she tells me the sad news.
Shift of pronoun	If one follows the directions, you will have no difficulties.
Parallelism	She likes scripts that contain exciting action and which keeps you guessing.
Noun agreement	Jack and Phyllis plan to become a lawyer.
Pronoun reference	Helen told Edna that she was wrong.
Subject-verb agreement	The number of inquiries have been slight.

Expressing Ideas Logically	Illustrative Sentences
Coordination and subordination	She enjoyed the book, and she bought three copies to give to her friends.
Logical comparison	He is the best singer of any in the chorus.
Modification and word order	When playing loudly, the piano develops a rattle.

Being Clear and Precise	Illustrative Sentences
Ambiguous and vague pronouns	In our textbook, they quote the relevant statistics.
Diction	He gained great renown as a swindler.
Wordiness	It was the consensus of opinions among the students that the coach should be reprimanded.
Unclear modification	Even students who work hard occasionally fail a test.

Following Conventions	Illustrative Sentences
Pronoun case	He told the story to everyone but Sarah and I.
Verb forms	You should have tooken it.
Idioms	I have great respect of his work.
Comparison of modifiers	Of the three candidates, Lucy is the more capable.
Sentence fragment	When it was finally completed.
Double negative	I have hardly no time for myself.
Recognizing correct sentences	The telephone rang, I rushed to answer it.

HOW MUCH GRAMMAR

Grammar is the systematic description of how a language works. Usage is concerned with alternative choices—the difference between standard and non-standard expressions. On this test you are not being evaluated for your knowledge of grammar; you are not required to know why a form is grammatically acceptable or unacceptable.

Of course, if you can explain a usage in grammatical terms, you will be able to generalize the error and be able to spot it much quicker. Therefore, if you can understand the grammatical reasons, take the few extra minutes to study and gain this advantageous mastery.

However, if you and grammar are separated by misunderstanding and uneasiness, then you would be wasting your valuable time trying to master this approach. Instead, you can easily learn to identify an error by associating it with one of the examples that follow. *Memorize the name of the error, the example, and the correct form.* This method will give you complete examination control of the items being tested.

SEQUENCE OF TENSES

DEFINITION: *Tense is used to define the built-in time factor found in verbs. The verb bears the main responsibility of establishing time relationships. Sometimes this relationship is fairly simple and definite. When the sentence contains a single action, then the verb may be in the present, future, or past. However, when the sentence contains two clauses, then the complications arise when the action in one clause relates to a time different from that found in the other clause.*

The examples that follow cover the areas usually stressed in examinations.

1. Past and Present

Example: When I finally entered the building, he (walks, walked) up to me.

EXPLANATION: When the action is in the past and occurs at the same or nearly the same time in both clauses, the both verbs should be in the past tense. In this example, there is no need for shifting to the present in the main verb.

ACCEPTED FORM: When I finally *entered* the building, he *walked* up to me.

Example: The main thing that Columbus proved is that the world (is, was) round.

EXPLANATION: When an action occurred in the past, the verb should be in the past tense. That rule would explain why the form *proved* is correct. The verb after *world* is governed by a completely different principle since it does not describe a past action but a general truth. A general truth must be in the present tense.

ACCEPTED FORM: The main thing that Columbus proved is that the world *is* round.

Example: The minister preached a sermon last week on the thesis that without hope and faith man was unable to function as a social being.

ACCEPTED FORM: The minister preached a sermon last week on the thesis that without hope and faith man *is* unable to function as a social being.

2. Present perfect and the past

Example: We (lived, have lived) in our present apartment for ten years.

EXPLANATION: The past (*lived*) is used to represent action completed. The present perfect (*have* or *has* plus a past participle—*have lived*) represents an action which took place in the past but has consequences extending right into the present. The present perfect is also used to represent action which began in the past and continues through the present. Since, in this example, the people lived in the apartment in the past and are still living in it, the present perfect should be used.

ACCEPTED FORM: We *have lived* in our present apartment for ten years.

ACCEPTED FORM: I *saw* it! (Action completed at a definite time in the past.)

ACCEPTED FORM: I *have seen* it! (The action is *now* completed.)

3. Past perfect and the past

Example: When he saw us, he (already notified, had already notified) the authorities.

EXPLANATION: The subject had done two things in the past. One of these actions (the notification) had occurred before the other (the seeing). The action completed before another in the past must be expressed in the past perfect.

ACCEPTED FORM: When he saw us, he *had already notified* the authorities.

SHIFT OF PRONOUN

DEFINITION: *A pronoun is a word that refers to a noun or another pronoun. The pronoun must agree with that noun or pronoun (its antecedent) in both person and number. A singular noun demands a singular pronoun. A plural noun requires a plural pronoun (number). A masculine noun is the antecedent of a masculine pronoun, and a feminine noun must be followed by a feminine pronoun (person).*

The problems usually arise with having to choose *them* or *him-her*; *their* or *his-hers-its*; *they* or *he-she*.

1. With indefinite pronouns: The error most frequently involves the indefinite pronouns—*each, everyone, everybody, someone, nobody, anyone, anybody, either, neither.*

TRADITIONAL APPROACH:

Example: Each of the contestants made (his, their) entrance on time.

EXPLANATION: Since *each* is singular, and since the pronoun (*his-their*) must refer to *each* and not to *contestants,* which is not the subject, the singular possessive pronoun *his* must be used.

ACCEPTED FORM: *Each* of the contestants made *his* entrance on time.

Example: Everyone in the group should be given an opportunity to state (his, their) views in this matter.

EXPLANATION: Since the subject is *everyone* and *everyone* is singular, the pronoun referring to it should be singular.

ACCEPTED FORM: *Everyone* in the group should be given an oportunity to state *his* views on this matter.

Example: I thought anyone could have taken it for (himself, themselves).

EXPLANATION: Since *anyone* is singular, the pronoun referring to it must be singular.

ACCEPTED FORM: I thought *anyone* could have taken it for *himself.*

CURRENT USAGE:

However, although these principles still hold in formal written English, the obvious male predominance has been tempered in most modern usage. Most writers attempt to handle this usage in one of three ways:

a. Avoid the use of singular indefinite pronouns when they are to be followed by another pronoun that must be in agreement. The easiest solution is to use plural forms to be followed by *they, them,* or *their.*

AVOID: *Each* of the actors made *his* appearance on time.

PREFER: The *actors* all made *their* appearances on time.

b. Use *he-she, him-her, his-her, his-hers* in tandem and connect each item in the pair with *and* or *or.*

AVOID: *Everyone* in the group should be given an opportunity to state *his* views.

PREFER: *Everyone* in the group should be given an opportunity to state *his* or *her views.*

c. Alternate singular masculine and feminine pronouns.

Example: No one will lose *his* turn. *Each student* must, however, prepare *her* own material.

For examination purposes, it is most likely that questions in this area will no longer be as frequent as in the past. If the candidate must choose between a singular indefinite pronoun followed by *he-him-his* or a plural indefinite pronoun followed by *their,* then the latter is to be selected.

AVOID: *Anyone* who disobeys will lose *his* privileges.

PREFER: *All* who disobey will lose *their* privileges.

If, however, the indefinite pronoun is singular and the choice remains *his-their, him-them, he-they,* then for examination purposes the singular pronoun forms are still the acceptable forms in formal written English.

2. Pronouns used impersonally: When *you* and *one* are used impersonally, they must be followed by their corresponding pronouns.

Example: One must never jump to conclusions hastily. (One, You) must train (oneself, yourself) to see the complete problem before reaching a decision.

EXPLANATION: Since the speaker had begun with *one,* he should not have changed to the *you* form. You must be consistent. If you begin with *you,* then the forms of *you* must be continued. If you begin with *one,* then the forms of *one* must be continued. Usage allows *his, him* to follow *one,* but not *you.*

ACCEPTED FORM: *One* must never jump to conclusions hastily. *One* must train *one's self* to see the complete problem before reaching a decision.

or

You must never jump to conclusions hastily. *You* must train *yourself* to see the complete problem before reaching a decision.

PARALLELISM

DEFINITION: *Elements in a sentence that are equal in importance should be expressed by parallel grammatical constructions.*

Example: He spoke forcefully and with clarity.

EXPLANATION: *Forcefully* and *with clarity* explain how he spoke; therefore, they should be in the same grammatical construction. They should both be adverbs or prepositional phrases, not a mixture.

ACCEPTED FORM: He spoke *with force* and *with clarity*.

or

He spoke *forcefully* and *clearly*.

Example: The men were ordered to see the film, to write a report on its effectiveness, and that they should discuss it afterwards.

EXPLANATION: Two of the commands are infinitive form (*to see, to write*). The third command is a clause, *that they should discuss it afterwards*. Since all three are commands, they should be in the same construction.

ACCEPTED FORM: The men were ordered *to see* the film, *to write* a report, and *to discuss* it afterwards.

Example: The children told us that they enjoy going to the beach, watching the surfboard riders perform, and to eat lunch near the water's edge.

EXPLANATION: Two of the activities enjoyed are gerunds (*going, watching*). The third, *to eat,* is an infinitive. Since all three are equal in importance, they should be in the same construction.

ACCEPTED FORM: The children told us that they enjoy *going* to the beach, *watching* the surfboard riders perform, and *eating* lunch near the water's edge.

Example: During the afternoon lesson, he learned the importance of hand signals, the main purpose of the rearview mirror and how to set the hand brake in an emergency.

EXPLANATION: Two of the items learned are nouns (*importance, purpose*). The third is in an infinitive form and should be converted to agree in form with the other two.

ACCEPTED FORM: During the afternoon lesson, he learned the *importance* of hand signals, the main *purpose* of the rearview mirror, and the *function* of the hand brake in an emergency.

Example: Jack was flighty, extravagant, and liked to let his emotions lead him.

ACCEPTED FORM: Jack was *flighty, extravagant,* and *emotional.*

NOUN AGREEMENT

DEFINITIONS: *Nouns and verbs agree in number. Singular: The package is in the corner. Plural: The members are all present. Nouns agree with pronouns in person and number. Singular: Arthur lost his coat. Plural: Arthur and Peter lost their coats. Nouns agree in number with their antecedents. Singular: George is my confidant. Plural: Jack and Lucille are my only confidants.*

The typical problem in this area involves nouns and antecedents.

Example: Only three of the seniors were accepted as a member of the Reorganization Committee.

EXPLANATION: Since the subject (*three*) is plural, the referring noun (*member*) should be plural.

ACCEPTED FORM: Only three of the seniors were accepted as members of the Reorganization Committee.

PRONOUN REFERENCE

The specific noun or pronoun that a pronoun has as its antecedent must be clear to the reader. Two common types of errors in usage arise in this area.

1. Vague reference

Example: He said that I had not even read the book, which angered me very much.

EXPLANATION: The relative pronoun *which* in the above sentence should refer to a specific noun or pronoun. Instead it refers to the entire idea in the preceding clause. The sentence must be recast so that the error is eliminated.

ACCEPTED FORM: He said that I had not even read the book, a statement which angered me very much.

or

His statement that I had not even read the book angered me very much.

2. Ambiguous reference

Example: Bess told Blanche that she did not understand the assignment.

EXPLANATION: The culprit in this case is the pronoun *she*. Does *she* refer to Bess or to Blanche? In this sentence as it stands the reader cannot tell. The sentence must be recast to eliminate this ambiguity.

ACCEPTED FORM: Bess told Blanche, ''You do not understand the assignment.''

or

Bess told Blanche, ''I do not understand the assignment.''

SUBJECT-VERB AGREEMENT

DEFINITION: *If the subject is singular, the verb that follows must be singular. If the subject is plural, then the verb that follows must be plural.*

The difficulty that the students face lies not in the statement of the rule, but in familiarizing themselves with the following constructions that offer problems.

1. Intervening elements: When a singular subject is separated from its verb by an intervening clause or phrase, the student often tends to make the verb agree with the nearest noun even though it is not the subject of the sentence.

Example: Margery, as well as her three friends, (was, were) invited to try out for the part of Helen in the varsity play.

EXPLANATION: The subject of the sentence is Margery. When the subject is followed by a group of words introduced by *with, together with,* or *as well as,* these words are not part of the subject. Therefore, *friends* is not part of the subject.

ACCEPTED FORM: *Margery,* as well as her three friends, *was* invited to try out for the part of Helen in the varsity play.

Example: A basket of apples (is, are) in the car for you.

EXPLANATION: The subject of the sentence is *basket*. When the subject is followed by a group of words introduced by a preposition, this group is called a prepositional phrase and it modifies the subject. Therefore *apples* cannot be the subject.

ACCEPTED FORM: A *basket* of apples *is* in the car for you.

Example: A group of soldiers (has have) been detailed to guard the munitions dump.

EXPLANATION: The subject is *group*. Since it is *one* group (*a* group), *group* is singular.

ACCEPTED FORM: A *group* of soldiers *has* been detailed to guard the. . . .

Example: A set of four thousand books (lies, lie) on the shelves, waiting for you to catalogue them.

EXPLANATION: It is not *books* that are waiting but *a set*. Since *set* is singular, the verb form must be singular.

ACCEPTED FORM: A *set* of four thousand books *lies* on the shelves. . . .

2. Indefinite pronouns: Although the sentence may seem to carry a plural sense when certain indefinite pronouns are used, the reader must know which of these pronouns are singular and have them followed by singular verbs.

Example: Every one of the four thousand pens (doesn't, don't) work. Everybody (know, knows) that.

EXPLANATION: When *body* and *one* are compounded (*somebody, anybody, nobody, everybody, someone, anyone,* and *everyone*) they are still singular and should be followed by a singular verb. *Either, neither,* and *each* are also singular.

ACCEPTED FORM: *Every one* of the four thousand pens *doesn't* work. *Everybody knows* that.

Example: Some of the men (was, were) ready to leave before noon.

EXPLANATION: Since *some, few, several* are plural in form, they should be followed by plural verbs.

ACCEPTED FORM: *Some* of the men *were* ready to leave before noon.

3. Compound subjects: When *and* is used, the rule is simple.

Example: Edna and Bea (is, are) waiting in the anteroom for the doctor.

EXPLANATION: When *and* joins the elements of the subject, the subject is plural, and the verb must be plural.

ACCEPTED FORM: *Edna and Bea are* waiting in the anteroom for the doctor.

Example: Neither Henry nor his brothers (was, were) present at the meeting.

EXPLANATION: When a compound subject is connected by the correlative conjunctions (*neither . . . nor, either . . . or, not only . . . but also*), the verb is determined by the subject word closest to it. If that word is plural, then the verb must be plural; if that word is singular, then the verb must be singular.

ACCEPTED FORM: *Neither Henry nor his brothers were* present at the meeting.

Example: Either Paula or I (is, am, are) scheduled to lead the discussion.

EXPLANATION: Since the last subject word is *I*, the verb must agree with *I*.

ACCEPTED FORM: *Either Paula or I am scheduled* to lead the discussion.

4. After a relative pronoun: In ordinary cases, there is very little difficulty in discovering which is the correct form to follow a relative pronoun.

Example: Tom is the one who (was, were) to judge the contest.

EXPLANATION: The antecedent of *who* is *one*. Since *one* is singular, the verb form must be singular.

ACCEPTED FORM: Tom is the *one who was* to judge the contest.

Example: It is I who (is, are, am) to make the final decision.

EXPLANATION: Since *I* is the antecedent of *who*, the form that follows *who* must be the form that would follow *I*.

ACCEPTED FORM: It is *I who am* to make the final decision.

Example: I saw him pass the note to one of the men who (has, have) been standing outside the windows.

EXPLANATION: The antecedent of *who* is *men* (the noun closest to it). Therefore the verb must agree with *men*, a plural noun.

ACCEPTED FORM: I saw him pass the note to one of the *men who have* been standing outside the windows.

5. After *there* and *here*: When *there* and, much less frequently, *here* are used to introduce sentences, the subject word *follows* the verb rather than *precedes* it.

Example: There (is, are) several plausible explanations for this phenomenon.

EXPLANATION: The subject is *explanations,* a plural noun, and therefore the verb must be plural.

ACCEPTED FORM: There *are* several plausible *explanations* for this phenomenon.

Example: Here (lie, lies) the heroes fallen in the defense of their country.

EXPLANATION: The subject is *heroes,* plural in form; the verb must be plural.

ACCEPTED FORM: Here *lie* the *heroes* fallen in the defense of their country.

6. Compound subjects as a unit: The elements of a compound subject lose their individuality when they become a single entity in the mind of the speaker.

Example: Ham and eggs (is, are) my favorite cold-weather breakfast.

EXPLANATION: Since *ham and eggs* is treated as a unit, the verb should be singular.

ACCEPTED FORM: *Ham and eggs is* my favorite cold-weather breakfast.

Example: Ham and eggs (is, are) the ingredients of an American meal.

EXPLANATION: Here each of the parts of the compound subject is being treated separately, and therefore the compound subject requires a plural verb.

ACCEPTED FORM: *Ham and eggs are* the ingredients of an American meal.

Example: Twenty dollars (was, were) too much to pay for that article.

EXPLANATION: The sum of money is a unit; therefore, the verb should be singular.

ACCEPTED FORM: *Twenty dollars was* too much to pay for that article.

NOTE: Even collective nouns like *group, army, set, jury,* etc., are affected by the meaning in the mind of the user. Normally these words govern a singular verb, but when the speaker or writer is considering the individuals of the group as separate entities, the verb should be plural.

Example: The jury (is, are) unable to agree on the amount of the settlement.

EXPLANATION: The members of the jury cannot agree. More than one person must be involved in such an action; the speaker actually means the individual members. Therefore, the verb should be plural.

ACCEPTED FORM: The *jury are* unable to agree on the amount of the settlement.

7. Nouns plural in form, singular in meaning

Example: Measles (is, are) dangerous when contracted by adults.

EXPLANATION: Nouns like *billiards, mumps, news, economics, mathematics, civics, molasses, tactics, statistics, physics, comics, aeronautics,* although they end in *s,* are singular in meaning.

ACCEPTED FORM: *Measles is* dangerous when contracted by adults.

8. With fractions and percentages

Example: Seven percent of the dollar bills (is, are) badly frayed.

EXPLANATION: Since individual items (*dollar bills*) are being represented, the verb should be plural. If the noun following *of* is plural, the verb is plural.

ACCEPTED FORM: Seven *percent* of the dollar bills *are* badly *frayed.*

Example: Three-fourths of the dam (is, are) gone!

EXPLANATION: Since only *one* dam is involved, the verb should be singular. If the noun following *of* is singular (*dam*), the verb is singular.

ACCEPTED FORM: *Three-fourths* of the dam *is* gone!

9. Commonly mistaken plurals

Example: No thanks (is, are) due to you for this!

EXPLANATION: The following group of nouns while plural in form and requiring a plural form of the verb are often mistaken as singular.

ashes   clothes   goods   links   nuptials   oats pliers   proceeds   remains   riches   spectacles suds   thanks   thongs   victuals   vitals   wages

Therefore, in the example above, the plural form of the verb should be used:

ACCEPTED FORM: No *thanks are* due to you for this!

NOT ACCEPTED: The wages of sin is death!

ACCEPTED FORM: The *wages* of sin *are* death!

10. Double subject

Example: (Paul and I, we) (Paul and I) will attend the lecture.

EXPLANATION: *Paul and I* form the subject. The word *we* is completely unnecessary and the addition of a second subject is an error.

ACCEPTED FORM: *Paul and I will attend* the lecture.

NOT ACCEPTED: The Puerto Ricans, they are citizens of the United States.

ACCEPTED FORM: The *Puerto Ricans are* citizens of the United States.

NOT ACCEPTED: The radio, it is not playing well tonight.

ACCEPTED FORM: The *radio is* not *playing* well tonight.

11. Subjects joined by *or*

Example: Paul or you (has, have) the right to choose the route.

EXPLANATION: When the conjunction joining a compound subject is *or,* the noun or pronoun *after* the *or* determines the form of the verb. Since *you* is after the *or,* the *form* of the verb must be second person.

ACCEPTED FORM: Paul or *you have* the right to choose the route.

NOT ACCEPTED: Henry or I are mentioned in the dispatch.

ACCEPTED FORM: Henry or *I am* mentioned in the dispatch.

12. *All, none, any, some* as pronouns

Example: (Is, Are) any of the money still in the desk drawer?

EXPLANATION: The pronouns *all, any, none, some* may be singular or plural depending upon their meaning in the sentence. In the example, *any* refers to a single quantity (*money*) and is therefore singular.

ACCEPTED FORM: *Is any of the money* still in the desk drawer?

Example: (Is, Are) any of the teachers still in the building?

EXPLANATION: In this example, *any* refers to individual units and is therefore plural in nature.

ACCEPTED FORM: *Are any of the teachers* still in the building?

NOT ACCEPTED: All that is left are one piece of crumb cake.

ACCEPTED FORM: *All* that is left *is* one piece of crumb cake.

NOT ACCEPTED: All of the books has now been returned.

ACCEPTED FORM: *All of the books have* now been returned.

13. Subjects and predicate nominatives

Example: The major obstacle (is, are) pedestrians crossing at other than intersections.

EXPLANATION: The verb agrees with the subject (*obstacle*) and not with the noun (*pedestrians*) used as a predicate nominative.

ACCEPTED FORM: The major *obstacle is* pedestrians crossing at other than intersections.

ACCEPTED FORM: *Pedestrians are* the major obstacle. . . .

14. Title

Example: My Most Interesting Cases (is, are) compulsory reading for all would-be surgeons.

EXPLANATION: The title of a book is treated as a singular subject even when the title contains a plural idea.

ACCEPTED FORM: *My Most Interesting Cases is* compulsory reading for all would-be surgeons.

COORDINATION AND SUBORDINATION

DEFINITIONS: *Coordination is the joining of equal sentence elements by <u>and</u>, <u>but</u>, <u>or</u>.* Adam and Sarah will be here in an hour. Susanna <u>saw</u> the play <u>and</u> <u>enjoyed</u> it immensely. *Subordination occurs when two unequal ideas are joined by connectives that establish the relationship between them. Some of the common connectives are: <u>if</u>, <u>since</u>, <u>because</u>, <u>that</u>, <u>who</u>.* We left <u>because</u> the room was too crowded. Milton identified the man <u>who</u> had left the scene of the accident.

Faulty subordination occurs when two unequal ideas are joined by <u>and</u>, <u>or</u>, <u>but</u> as though they were of equal importance.

Example: I did not follow the instructions, *and* I messed up the assignment.

EXPLANATION: The two ideas are not equal; one is completely dependent on the other.

ACCEPTED FORM: *Because* I did not follow instructions, I messed up the assignment.

Example: I am going to the bus depot to meet my cousin, and he is coming from San José.

EXPLANATION: The use of *and* does not help to reveal the relationship between the two ideas.

ACCEPTED FORM: I am going to the bus depot to meet my cousin *who* is coming from San José.

LOGICAL COMPARISON

Care must be taken in using some comparative forms, to ensure that the comparison is valid and logical.

Example: Alice is faster than (any typist, any other typist) in her class.

EXPLANATION: Since Alice is herself one of the members of the class, she cannot be faster than all of the girls in her class which includes herself. Therefore the word *other* must be included.

ACCEPTED FORM: Alice is faster than any *other* typist in her class.

Example: She is definitely as (capable, capable as) or more capable than her sister.

EXPLANATION: The two forms for comparison are *as . . . as* and *more . . . than.* Each of these compounds must be completed correctly. If the second *as* is not included in the example given, then the word *than* would go with both *as* and *more,* an incorrect assumption.

ACCEPTED FORM: She is definitely *as* capable *as* or *more* capable *than* her sister.

Example: It was the most unique experience I ever had.

EXPLANATION: Certain adjectives and adverbs cannot have comparative or superlative forms. The adjective *unique,* for example, means *one of a kind.* The noun therefore is either *unique* or *not unique.*

ACCEPTED FORM: The experience I just had was *unique.*

NOTE: Other adjectives that should be used in the positive degree only are *dead, everlasting, final, last, round.*

Example: He not only enjoys playing Mozart but also listening to that master's symphonies.

EXPLANATION: The pairs of correlatives, *not only . . . but also, neither . . . nor, either . . . or,* must be placed immediately before the parallel terms.

ACCEPTED FORM: He enjoys *not only playing* Mozart *but also listening* to that master's symphonies.

MODIFICATION AND WORD ORDER

Adjectives and adverbs, whether they are single words or phrases, must have a word in the sentence that they logically modify. Very often, especially with adjective phrases, the writer or speaker in a hurry to make a point implies this specific word, but omits it from the sentence. The result can be humorous or misleading, but it is always wrong.

1. Dangling participial phrases

Example: Realizing how richly he deserved to win, my feelings of jealousy turned into feelings of admiration.

EXPLANATION: Obviously, *Realizing how richly he deserved to win* is a participial phrase modifying the pronoun *I*, but the speaker omitted *I*. As the sentence stands, (*my*) *feelings* is the only word that the phrase can modify, and *feelings* just *cannot* realize anything. Therefore the phrase dangles without a true noun for it to modify.

ACCEPTED FORM: *Realizing how richly he deserved to win, I* discovered that my feelings of jealousy were turning into feelings of admiration.

2. Dangling gerund phrases

Example: Upon entering the room, the missing ring was soon found on the floor.

EXPLANATION: The gerund phrase, *Upon entering the room,* has no word in the sentence for it to modify. The missing *ring* could not enter the room! A noun or pronoun must be added to the sentence for the phrase to modify.

ACCEPTED FORM: *When I entered the room, I* soon found the missing ring on the floor.

or

Upon entering the room, I soon found the missing ring on the floor.

3. Dangling infinitive phrases

Example: To plan carefully in case of fire, doors must not be kept locked when the auditorium is in use.

EXPLANATION: As the sentence stands, the only known word that *To plan carefully* can modify is *doors*. However, *doors* cannot *plan*. Therefore *To plan* dangles. A satisfying noun or pronoun must be added and the sentence recast if necessary.

ACCEPTED FORM: *To plan carefully in case of fire, you* must make certain that the doors of the auditorium are not locked when it is in use.

4. Dangling elliptical clauses and phrases

Example: When four years old, Paul's father died.

EXPLANATION: As the sentence stands, the father died at the age of four! The sentence must be expanded or recast to make clear just who is being referred to.

ACCEPTED FORM: *When Paul was four,* his father died.

Example: On reaching his fifth birthday, his uncle bought him a tricycle.

EXPLANATION: As the sentence stands, the uncle was five years old.

ACCEPTED FORM: *When Allan reached his fifth birthday,* his uncle . . .

AMBIGUOUS AND VAGUE PRONOUNS

Example: In New York City they are very considerate of visitors who ask questions.

EXPLANATION: The pronoun *they* is used without a definite antecedent. The sentence can be recast so that this indefinite reference can be eliminated.

ACCEPTED FORM: New Yorkers are very considerate of visitors who ask questions.

Example: In this book it states that the price of food is a prime concern of all good governments.

ACCEPTED FORM: The author of this book states that the price of food. . . .

Implied Reference

Example: Although Harold has read much poetry, he has never attempted to write one himself.

EXPLANATION: Obviously, the writer meant by *one* a single poem, but there is no *poem* in this sentence for the word to refer to.

ACCEPTED FORM: Although Harold has read much poetry, he has never attempted to write a poem of his own.

Example: He hopes to become a famous surgeon some day even though the study of *it* will require long years of apprenticeship.

ACCEPTED FORM: He hopes to become a famous surgeon some day even though the study of *surgery* will require long years of apprenticeship.

DICTION

The English language is a composite of many systems of communication both in usage and in diction (choice of words). When different systems of communications (dialects) are being used by the writer and reader, or by the speakers and listeners, only confusion and misunderstanding result.

STANDARD: Words that are used to convey the thoughts of one person to another on the widest communication band. This is the system of our best speakers and writers.

NONSTANDARD: Words that are used by social, geographical, occupational, ethnic, and religious groups to convey thoughts to a restricted number of people.

WORD	STANDARD DEFINITION	NONSTANDARD DEFINITION
scream	loud sound revealing fright: hear a *scream*	funny, amusing: It's a *scream*!
smashed	broken to pieces; destroyed: *smashed* the vase.	drunk: He's *smashed*.
hip	part of body: carry the child on her *hip*.	aware: He's *hip*.
square	even: a geometrical figure: draw a *square*.	old-fashioned, conservative: be a *square*.

Both Standard and Nonstandard words are subdivided into five overlapping groups.

Formal: Words that are used when dignity is the primary requirement. This is the level of sermons, the language of ceremony, the wording of treaties and binding agreements.

Written: Words that are used in written communications for precision and clarity to tell an entire story, to convey a complete idea, or to give a full description.

Informal: Spoken words that are in everyday use when formality and presentation of a complete unit of thought are not being stressed.

Technical: Words that have very specific meaning for those in certain occupations, calling for a precision of identification not needed by the public.

> *macron* (pronunciation)
> *octave* (prosody)
> *anhydrous* (chemistry)

Foreign: Words and phrases that are taken along with their pronunciation, directly from another language. Very often they parallel good, acceptable English words.

> *en passant* (in passing)
> *entre nous* (between us)
> *gaucheries* (awkwardness)

Into this group fall Briticisms—words that are acceptable in England but for which we have American substitutes that are preferred here.

> *braces* (suspenders)
> *lift* (elevator)

Examples of standard words:

FORMAL	WRITTEN	INFORMAL
acquire	obtain	get
inter	bury	bury
scrutinize	examine	look over
irate, enraged	angry	mad
secrete	hide	put away
possess	own	have got
inquired	questioned	asked
relate	describe	tell
complete	finish	end

Nonstandard words are also included in the following classifications:

Archaic: Words that were once in standard usage but are no longer current. Words so labeled may be retained for special purposes—poetical, liturgical.

> *thou forsooth belike eftsoons*

Obsolete: Words that were in standard usage but have fallen completely out of use.

> *swink* (toil) *egal* (equal)
> *hardiment* (a bold deed)

Poetic: Words that are or were once in standard use in poetry but which are no longer acceptable in standard speech, prose, or poetry.

> *o'er ope oft e'en*

Jargon: Words that are occupational in nature, the occupational slang of those working in specific fields; a mixture of two or more existing languages. Pidgin English and Chinook are jargons.

Contractions and Clipped Words: Words that have been abbreviated for everyday oral and written communication.

> *phone* (telephone) *can't* (cannot)
> *chem* (chemistry)

Slang: A loose term for words that are not accepted as part of the Standard English vocabulary. It includes newly coined words and phrases and terms that have been arbitrarily termed unacceptable.

> *flip a lid   cool it, man   in a fix*

Localism: Words that are used with specific meanings only in certain areas of the country and that do not have countrywide acceptance.

> *tote* (carry)   *poke* (paper bag)   *reckon* (think)

WORDINESS

DEFINITION: *Wordiness (verbosity) is the use of repetitive elements that add nothing to the meaning of the sentence and are not justified by any need for special emphasis.*

There are several other terms associated with wordiness:

Circumlocution (deadwood) involves using two or more words for the one exact word.

> *loud and annoying* for *noisy*
> *quiet and peaceful* for *subdued*

Redundancy (tautology) describes the use of words that needlessly repeat the meaning of other words.

> *stoop with lowered shoulders*
> at 3 P.M. *in the afternoon*

The pitfalls of verbosity include the following:

1. **Definition used instead of word itself**
   WORDY: cause to go faster
   CONCISE: accelerate

2. **Relative clause in place of adjective**
   WORDY: a child *who is idle*
   CONCISE: an *idle* child

3. **Redundant phrase in place of briefer term or word**
   WORDY: smaller in size
   CONCISE: smaller

4. **Longer words used for shorter ones**
   carefulness for *care*

5. **Unnecessary preposition added to verb**
   write *up*   descend *down*
   write *down*   ascend *up*
   repeat *again*   redo *again*
   lose *out*   win *out*

Become familiar with the following list of frequently used verbose phrases; they may find their way into examination items.

WORDY PHRASES	CONCISE PHRASES
cooperate together	cooperate
expert in the field of	expert in
seen by the eyes	seen
means to imply	implies
because of the fact	because
green in color	green
few in number	few
same identical	identical
advance notice	notice
of an indefinite nature	indefinite
in order to	to
by means of	by
isolated by himself	isolated
close to the point of	close to
the modern world of today	the world of today
different in a number of ways	different
novelist writes in his novels	novelist writes
New Year's party celebration	New Year's celebration
connected up with	connected with
fundamental principles	principles
attractive in appearance	attractive
at about	about
both alike	alike
consensus of opinion	consensus
endorse on the back	endorse
have need for	need
give instruction to	teach
give encouragement to	encourage
for the purpose of	for
with respect to	about
despite that fact that	though
with a view to	to
come into conflict	conflict
in view of the fact that	because, since
make an adjustment in	adjust
give consideration to	consider
of a confidential nature	confidential
is of the opinion	believes
along the lines of	like
in the amount of	for
in accordance with	by
make inquiry regarding	inquire
on the occasion of	when

WORDY PHRASES	CONCISE PHRASES
for the reason that	since
in the case that	if
have under consideration	is considering

UNCLEAR MODIFICATION

Modifiers may be single words, phrases, or clauses. A modifying word, phrase, or clause must be placed close to the word being modified and not near another word that it could mistakenly seem to modify.

1. Misplaced relative clauses

Example: The dealer finally agreed to sell me the picture of the horses which hung from the ceiling.

EXPLANATION: As the sentence stands, the relative clause, *which hung from the ceiling,* is closest to *horses,* and therefore it appears to modify that word. However, the sentence then becomes one containing an absurd idea.

ACCEPTED FORM: The dealer finally agreed to sell me the picture of the horses. *This* is the *one which* hung from the ceiling.

Example: The teacher had the pamphlet on his desk which I had borrowed from the library.

ACCEPTED FORM: The teacher had on his desk the *pamphlet which* I had borrowed from the library.

2. Misplaced phrases

Example: We learned that no one had been injured by the next morning.

EXPLANATION: The phrase *by the next morning* seems to modify *had been injured.* The sense of the sentence is that it should modify *learned.* Therefore, the phrase must be put closer to the verb it really modifies.

ACCEPTED FORM: *By the next morning we learned* that no one had been injured.

or

We *learned by the next morning* that no one had been injured.

Example: They solemnly promised that they would be here the last time we saw them.

EXPLANATION: The phrase *the last time we saw them* belongs with *promised* and not with *would be.*

ACCEPTED FORM: *The last time we saw them, they solemnly promised* that . . .

3. Misplaced adverbs

Example: I almost saw the entire film.

EXPLANATION: The adverb *almost* does not modify the verb; it does modify the adjective *entire.* Therefore, it should be placed closer to the word it modifies. In this sentence *almost saw* would make no sense.

ACCEPTED FORM: I saw *almost the entire* film.

Example: He only sold two books during the entire week.

ACCEPTED FORM: He sold *only two* books during the entire week.

NOTE: There are seven adverbs that must be watched to prevent their being placed too close to a word that they do not modify. Such an incorrect placement could either change the meaning of the sentence or make the sentence meaningless. These seven adverbs are

almost   ever   even   just   merely   only   scarcely

4. Squinting modifiers

Example: He shouted that if we did not leave in five minutes we would be forcibly ejected.

EXPLANATION: The meaning intended by the speaker does not come through clearly. Did he mean that we had to leave in five minutes? Or did he mean that we would be thrown out in five minutes? The phrase *in five minutes* is a squinting modifier since it could modify either of the two subordinate verb forms. It must be relocated to make unambiguous the meaning intended.

ACCEPTED FORM: He shouted that if we did not leave we would be forcibly ejected *within five minutes*.

or

He shouted that if, *within five minutes,* we had not left, we would be forcibly ejected.

PRONOUN CASE

DEFINITION: *The troublesome pronouns are the ones that change their forms, depending upon their use in the sentence.* If the pronoun is the subject of the verb or is used as an appositive to the subject or as a predicate nominative, then it is in the subjective case.

Subjective Case: *I, he, she, we, they*

If the pronoun is used to show possession, then we must use the possessive case.

Possessive Case: *my, mine, your, yours, his, her, hers, its, our, ours, their, theirs, everyone's, somebody's*

If the pronoun is used as object of the verb, participle, gerund, infinitive or preposition or as appositive to an object than it must be in the objective case.

Objective Case: *me, him, her, us, them*

The problems dealing with case that arise and that are found on examinations range from those dealing with some of the crudest errors to some of the more subtle ones.

1. Problems involving the subjective case

Example: Lucy and (I, me) were chosen to be members of the varsity team.

EXPLANATION: Whether the pronoun is used alone or as part of a compound subject, when it is used as a subject, it must be in the subjective case. The pronoun in this example is part of a compound subject.

ACCEPTED FORM: *Lucy and I were chosen* to be members of the varsity team.

Example: (We, Us) seniors must assume the role of leadership.

EXPLANATION: The pronoun in this case is in apposition with the noun it is in close association with. It must be in the same case as that noun. The word *seniors* is the subject in this sentence. Therefore, the pronoun must be in the subjective form.

ACCEPTED FORM: *We seniors must assume* the role of leadership.

Example: They assumed that the culprit was (she, her).

EXPLANATION: A pronoun standing for the same person or thing as the subject and placed after a copulative verb is a predicate pronoun. The copulative verbs are principally *to be* and the following verbs when they are used to be synonymous with *to be: to seem, to grow, to appear, to become*. The pronoun in these cases renames the subject and is also in the subjective case.

ACCEPTED FORM: They assumed that the culprit *was she*.

NOTE: In colloquial usage, *It is me* has become an accepted form. However, *It is I* is still the accepted form in Standard Written English. In both colloquial and standard usage, you must use the subjective form for the other pronouns: It is (*she, he, we, they*).

Example: Helen knows more about that field than (we, us).

EXPLANATION: In sentences containing comparisons introduced by *than* or *as* the correct form of the pronoun can be determined by the simple device of adding the missing words.

EXPANDED SENTENCE: Helen knows more about that field than (we, us) do.

Obviously, we need a subject for the missing verb *do*.

ACCEPTED FORM: Helen knows more about that field *than we do*.

Example: The note was intended for the person (who, whom) is to address the meeting.

EXPLANATION: Many of the difficulties involved in deciding whether to use *who* or *whom* can be overcome if you test to see whether *he* or *him* can be fitted into the sentence without changing its meaning. If *he* fits, then we need the subjective form, *who*; if *him* fits, then we should use the objective form, *whom*. In the example just given, the key clause becomes *he is to address the meeting*. The pronoun then is the subject of the verb *is*,

ACCEPTED FORM: The note was intended for the person *who is to address the meeting*.

Example: Give the note to (whoever, whomever) is in the office.

EXPLANATION: The pronouns *whoever, whosoever, whomever, whomsoever* depend for their case on their use in the clause to which they belong. In the preceding example *whoever-whomever* is part of the clause . . . *is in the office*. The clause can be completed by *he* (*He is in the office*). Therefore *whoever* is correct.

ACCEPTED FORM: Give the note to *whoever is in the office*.

ACCEPTED FORM: Give the note to *whomever you meet*.

2. Problems involving the possessive case

Example: The manager announced that (your, you're) entry had won first place.

EXPLANATION: Personal pronouns have special forms for the possessive case. None of these forms therefore require an apostrophe: *mine, my, its, their, theirs, your, yours, his, her, hers, our, ours*. When personal pronouns contain an apostrophe, they stand for a contraction of a verb form plus the pronoun: *it's* (it is), *they're* (they are), *you're* (you are).

ACCEPTED FORM: The manager announced that *your* entry had won first place.

Example: We objected to (him, his) taking all of the credit.

EXPLANATION: The objection was not to the person, *him,* but to what he did, to the taking of all of the credit, to *his* taking all of the credit.

ACCEPTED FORM: We objected to *his taking* all of the credit.

3. Problems involving the objective case

Example: The bridge could never be built without (he, him).

EXPLANATION: The object of a preposition is in the objective case. Some of the prepositions causing difficulty are

except   with   but (meaning *except*)   between
among

ACCEPTED FORM: The bridge could never be built *without him.*

Example: They had notified everyone except Margie and (she, her).

EXPLANATION: When the object of a preposition is compound, both parts of that object are in the objective case.

ACCEPTED FORM: They had notified everyone *except Margie and her.*

TROUBLESOME FORM: Between you and (I, me) he's the one at fault.

ACCEPTED FORM: *Between you and me,* he's the one at fault.

TROUBLESOME FORM: No one but Henry or (we, us) could handle the machine.

ACCEPTED FORM: No one *but Henry or us* could handle the machine.

Example: The defeat did not hurt him as much as (they, them).

EXPLANATION: Since the sentence contains *as* in a comparison, it should be expanded:
The defeat did not hurt him as much as it hurt (they, them).
The pronoun in doubt is the object of the verb *hurt* and should be in the objective case.

ACCEPTED FORM: The defeat did not hurt him as much as it hurt *them.*

Example: The victim of the practical joke turned out to be (I, me).

EXPLANATION: Both the subject and the object of an infinitive are in the objective case.

ACCEPTED FORM: The victim of the practical joke turned out *to be me.*

Example: For (who, whom) was the gift intended?

EXPLANATION: Since the statement is in question form, it should be turned into a declarative sentence for the analysis.
The gift was intended for (who, whom).
Now, using the substitution method, we test *he-him* in place of the *who-whom* and discover that *him* is the correct form since we need an object of the preposition *for.* Therefore we must use the objective form, *whom.*

ACCEPTED FORM: *For whom* was the gift intended?

Example: The dean suspended Alex and (she, her) this afternoon.

EXPLANATION: Each element in a compound object of a verb must be in the objective case.
The dean suspended *Alex.*
The dean suspended *her.*

ACCEPTED FORM: The dean *suspended* Alex and *her* this afternoon.

VERB FORMS

The different forms of the verb are all derived from its principal parts. By knowing the principal parts, you can avoid some of the most costly errors, the ones that are usually labeled as *illiterate.*

Example: He had (chose, chosen) the latter.

EXPLANATION: Since there is an auxiliary verb (had) already present, the past participle must be used.

ACCEPTED FORM: He *had chosen* the latter.

Example: Yesterday I (drank, drunk) three glasses of well water.

EXPLANATION: Since there is no auxiliary verb present, the simple past tense is required.

ACCEPTED FORM: Yesterday I *drank* three glasses of well water.

Study the following list of troublesome verbs. Do not spend time on those that give you no trouble. Memorize the principal parts of verbs of which you are not certain.

Principal Parts of 53 Troublesome Verbs

PRESENT (Now I . . .)	PRESENT PARTICIPLE	PAST (Yesterday I . . .)	PAST PARTICIPLE I have, or I had . . .
arise	arising	arose	arisen
awake	awaking	awoke (awaked)	awoke (awaked, awoken)
bear	bearing	bore	borne
beat	beating	beat	beaten (beat)
bid	bidding	bade	bidden
[command]			
bid [offer]	bidding	bid	bid
bind	binding	bound	bound
bite	biting	bit	bitten (bit)
break	breaking	broke	broken
choose	choosing	chose	chosen
cling	clinging	clung	clung
drink	drinking	drank	drunk
drive	driving	drove	driven
eat	eating	ate	eaten
fall	falling	fell	fallen
fight	fighting	fought	fought
fly	flying	flew	flown
forbid	forbidding	forbade (forbad)	forbidden
forget	forgetting	forgot	forgotten (forgot)
freeze	freezing	froze	frozen
get	getting	got	gotten
go	going	went	gone
grow	growing	grew	grown
hang	hanging	hung	hung
hang	hanging	hanged	hanged

PRESENT (Now I . . .) [execute]	PRESENT PARTICIPLE	PAST (Yesterday I . . .)	PAST PARTICIPLE I have, or I had . . .
hide	hiding	hid	hidden
know	knowing	knew	known
lay	laying	laid	laid
lie	lying	lay	lain
ring	ringing	rang	rung
see	seeing	saw	seen
shoot	shooting	shot	shot
shrink	shrinking	shrank (shrunk)	shrunk (shrunken)
sing	singing	sang	sung
sit	sitting	sat	sat
slay	slaying	slew	slain
slide	sliding	slid	slid
spin	spinning	spun	spun
spring	springing	sprang (sprung)	sprung
steal	stealing	stole	stolen
sting	stinging	stung	stung
stride	striding	strode	stridden
strive	striving	strove	striven
swear	swearing	swore	sworn
swim	swimming	swam	swum
swing	swinging	swung	swung
take	taking	took	taken
tear	tearing	tore	torn
throw	throwing	threw	thrown
wake	waking	woke (waked)	waked (woken)
wear	wearing	wore	worn
wring	wringing	wrung	wrung
write	writing	wrote	written

IDIOMS

DEFINITION: *An idiomatic phrase is an expression peculiar to a language and not explainable through rules of logic or grammar. Custom, not principles of grammar, establishes its form and meaning.*

so long as = while

When used in an idiomatic phrase, a word loses its individual meaning; the expression or phrase takes on a meaning different from the literal meaning of the words involved.

1. Idiomatic phrases in compounds

If two idiomatic phrases are used in a compound construction, each phrase must be completed.

Example: He is as good if not better than the others.

ACCEPTED FORM: He is *as* good *as* . . .

Example: He was fully aware but not disturbed by the noise.

ACCEPTED FORM: He was fully aware *of* but not disturbed by the noise.

2. Fixed preposition in idiomatic phrases

The preposition that an idiom ends with is usually set by custom and should not be varied. Below are some of the accepted combinations.

Group One

agree *to* a proposal
    on a procedure
    with a person
argue *with* a person
    for, against, or *about* a measure
compare *to* a thing with a definite resemblance
    with something on the basis of similarities or dissimilarities
comply *with*
differ *with* a person in an opinion
    from in appearance
different *from*
identical *with*
independent *of*
in search *of*
show interest *in*
listen *to*
necessary *to*
plan *to*
required *of*
stay *at* home
superior *to*

Group Two

STANDARD	NONSTANDARD
accord with	accord to
according to	according with
acquitted of	acquitted from
aim to prove	aim at proving
as regards	as regards to
disdain for	disdain of
in accordance with	in accordance to
in search of	in search for
oblivious of	oblivious to
vie with	vie against
superior to	superior than
at home	to home
frightened by	frightened of
within a month	inside of a month
dissent from	dissent with

3. Synonymous pairs of idiomatic phrases

Custom often labels one of a pair of synonymous idioms standard and the other nonstandard. Here is a list of such pairs that you should have under complete control.

STANDARD	NONSTANDARD
as far as	all the farther
among all three	between the three
cannot help	cannot help but
blame us for it	blame it on us
doubt that	doubt if
in search of	in search for
within an hour	inside of an hour
kind of	kind of a
type of	type of a
try to see	try and see

4. With gerunds and infinitives

Certain words in idiomatic use are followed by gerunds and others by infinitives.

ACCEPTABLE	NOT ACCEPTABLE
like to go	like going
cannot help seeing	cannot help to see
hesitate to look	hesitate looking
enjoy seeing	enjoy to see
capable of doing	capable to do
intend to do	intend on doing

COMPARISON OF MODIFIERS

DEFINITION: *Most adjectives and adverbs have three forms: positive, comparative, and superlative.*

The positive form is the original adjective:
    beautiful young quiet harmful

The *comparative* form of the adjective is that form ending in *er* or preceded by *more*:
    more beautiful younger quieter more harmful

The *superlative* form of the adjective is that form ending in *est* or preceded by *most*:
    most beautiful youngest quietest most harmful

Example: Reenie is the (older, oldest) of the three.

EXPLANATION: The comparative form of the adjective is used when two are being compared. When three or more are in the comparison, then the superlative form of the adjective or adverb is used.

ACCEPTED FORM: Reenie is the oldest of the three.

Example: This vase is much more (lovelier, lovely) than the other one.

EXPLANATION: Since there are two ways of indicating the comparative and superlative degrees, when *one* method is used, the other should not be.

ACCEPTED FORM: This vase is much *more lovely* than the other one.

or

This vase is much *lovelier* than the other one.

SENTENCE FRAGMENT

DEFINITION: *A sentence fragment is a portion of a sentence treated as though it were complete.*

In practice, since the sentence fragment is a portion of a sentence, in order to correct this error, all that we have to do, in most cases, is not to add additional material, but to change the punctuation. The sentence fragment should be joined to the group of ideas from which it has been incorrectly separated.

In each of the following examples, the italicized sentence is the sentence fragment. The method of correction is to join it to the preceding or following sentence to which it grammatically belongs.

Typical Examples

1. Dependent clauses treated as independent

Adverb Clauses: The conditions are the same. *Although he thinks they have improved.*
If you listen to him. His arguments begin to seem logical.
The entire performance took on a vital liveliness. *Because Philip suddenly awakened to the requirements of his role.*

Relative Clause: Milton is the man. *Who claims to know the solution.*

ACCEPTED FORM:
The conditions are the same *although he thinks they have improved.*
If you listen to him, his arguments begin to seem logical.
The entire performance took on a vital liveliness *because Philip suddenly awakened to the requirements of his role.*
Milton is the man *who claims to know the solution.*

2. Verbal phrases treated as independent ideas

Infinitive: There was one thing he wanted above all. *To clear his name of this stigma.*

Participle: *Coming to the end of the road.* The old man sat down to rest.

Gerund: We intensified our understanding of the island culture. *By our learning much of its folklore.*

ACCEPTED FORM:
There was one thing he wanted above all, *to clear his name of this stigma.*
Coming to the end of the road, the old man sat down to rest.
We intensified our understanding of the island culture *by our learning much of its folklore.*

3. Prepositional phrases

They placed the formula in the safe. *On the morning of the third day.*
From every nook and cranny of the old house. Came groans and shrieks of despair.

ACCEPTED FORM:
They placed the formula in the safe *on the morning of the third day.*
From every nook and cranny of the old house came groans and shrieks of despair.

4. Appositives

I was proud to be introduced to Ben Edwards. *The champion chess player.*
There are certain things that I consider most necessary for successful living. *Such as adequate income, satisfying goals, and social approval.*

ACCEPTED FORM:
I was proud to be introduced to Ben Edwards, *the champion chess player.*
There are certain things that I consider most necessary for successful living—*such as, adequate income.*

5. Coordinating conjunctions

We tried every combination that came to our minds. *But we were unable to stumble on the correct one.*

EXPLANATION: The coordinating conjunctions, *and, but* or *or* logically *join* ideas; they do not separate ideas. Therefore, they should not be used to begin sentences—as a rule. However, many modern writers use them to introduce sentences when an unusual effect is desired. For examination purposes, such sentences are to be considered errors and are to be avoided.

ACCEPTED FORM:
We tried every combination that came to our minds, *but we were . . .*

DOUBLE NEGATIVE

DEFINITION: *A double negative is a construction that uses two negative terms when one would be sufficient. Current conventions have labeled three such uses as nonstandard.*

Example One: I do*n't* want *none* of it.

EXPLANATION: *No, nothing, not, none, nobody,* should not be used with another negative to convey a denial.

ACCEPTED FORM: I do*n't* want *any* of it. I want *none* of it.

Example Two: I ca*n't hardly (scarcely)* tell the difference.

EXPLANATION: Since *hardly* and *scarcely* are negatives, they do not require supporting negatives.

ACCEPTED FORM: I can *hardly (scarcely)* tell the difference.

Example Three: We had*n't* been there *but (only)* a few minutes.

EXPLANATION: Since the phrases *to have but* and *to have only* are considered negative, *not* is not required to modify *have.*

ACCEPTED FORM: We had been there *but (only)* a few minutes.

RECOGNIZING CORRECT SENTENCES

A run-on sentence should always be avoided; it is one in which two or more sentences are punctuated as though they were one.

Typical Examples

1. Those caused by the use of a comma in place of a period (These are sometimes called *comma-splice* or *comma sentences.*)

The error was unavoidable, it just could not be prevented at that time.

EXPLANATION: This unit consists of two complete ideas. They could have been separated by a period. A comma cannot be used to separate two complete ideas. A comma cannot take the place of a period.

METHODS OF CORRECTION:

There are three basic methods of correction:

a. Add a coordinating conjunction (*and, but, or, for, nor*).

The error was unavoidable, *and* it could not be prevented at that time.

b. Divide into two sentences, using a period and a capital letter.

The error was unavoidable. It could not be prevented at that time.

c. Subordinate one of the ideas, using one of the subordinating conjunctions (*after, although, because, if, since, unless, until, when, while, as if, where, whereas, though, so that*).

The error was unavoidable *because* it could not be prevented at that time.

NOTE: There is a fourth possible way of combining two complete ideas. This method involves the use of a semicolon. This method must not be overused. It is appropriate when the two ideas are very close to each other.

The room was filled with smoke; I could hardly breathe.

2. Those caused by conjunctive adverbs

Harold had lost his temper, nevertheless he was held responsible for his subsequent actions.

EXPLANATION: This unit consists of two complete ideas. Such ideas may be joined together by a coordinating conjunction—*and, but, or, for, nor.* (Some authorities include *so* and *yet* in this group. However, for this examination, it is better to avoid *so* as a conjunction and to consider *yet* as a conjunctive adverb.) Conjunctive adverbs do *not* have the privilege of being able to join two ideas together when they are preceded by a comma. The following conjunctive adverbs cannot do the work of a coordinating conjunction:

nevertheless hence also besides therefore then otherwise moreover consequently however meanwhile on the other hand in the meantime in fact accordingly indeed yet

METHODS OF CORRECTION:

Sentences containing conjunctive adverbs may be treated correctly in the following manner:

Add a conjunction:	Harold had lost his temper, but nevertheless he . . .
Use a semicolon:	Harold had lost hs temper; nevertheless, he . . .
Divide into two sentences:	Harold had lost his temper. Nevertheless, he . . .
Subordinate one of the ideas:	Since Harold had lost his temper, he was held . . .

3. Those caused by close ideas that are treated as one

Paul had one last desperate hope he could reach safety if his numbed mind could recall the combination of the safety factor.

EXPLANATION: Although these ideas flow into each other, only one of the three basic ideas has been subordinated. The one beginning with *if* has been treated correctly. The first two ideas, however, have been run together without a grammatical connection. *Paul had one last desperate hope* is one complete idea. *He could reach safety* is a second complete idea.

METHODS OF CORRECTION:

Separate with a period:	Paul had one last desperate hope. He could . . .
Join with a conjunction:	Paul had one last desperate hope, and he could . . .
Subordinate one of the ideas:	Paul had one last desperate hope that he could . . .
Use the semicolon:	Paul had one last desperate hope; he could . . .
Use a semicolon and a conjunctive adverb:	Paul had one last desperate hope; in fact, he could reach safety . . .

3. *Proper Punctuation and Capitalization*

Modern writing tends to follow specific rules for the use of punctuation marks. The day when students could be either generous or stingy in sprinkling commas or periods through their written themes is part of a past era.

This section is not an attempt to summarize all of the rules governing marks of punctuation. Rather it deals with the common errors found in student writing. The problems faced are those that students make in writing the essay and those that are usually used to test student ability in the objective questions.

USING THE APOSTROPHE

Most of the errors that occur in the use of the apostrophe occur because of carelessness. Since this is the mark of punctuation most frequently misused by high school seniors and college freshmen, the penalties for its misuse are severe and the apostrophe becomes a predictable item on examination papers.

With Pronouns

Example: The book is now (yours, your's).

EXPLANATION: The possessive pronouns are *my, mine, your, yours, his, its, her, hers, our, ours, their, theirs, whose*. These pronouns show possession in their own right. Therefore, they are *not* used with apostrophes.

ACCEPTED FORM: The book is now *yours*.

Example: (Its, It's) time for us to leave.

EXPLANATION: When one of the personal pronouns contains an apostrophe, the apostrophe stands for a missing letter or letters, usually missing from a verb form. The personal pronoun containing an apostrophe is always a contracted form. The test to discover whether such a pronoun belongs in the given sentence is to supply the missing letter or letters.

ACCEPTED FORM: *It is* time for us to leave. *It's* time for us to leave.

ACCEPTED FORM: Who's (Who is) to write the notice for the bulletin board?

ACCEPTED FORM: *Whose* (*Who is* does not fit) coat did he borrow?

With Nouns

Example: The president plans to speak to all of the (students, students', student's).

EXPLANATION: The apostrophe with nouns is usually used to indicate possession. It is not used as a sign of the plural. In the preceding example, *students* shows no ownership. Therefore, there should be no apostrophe in this plural form.

ACCEPTED FORM: The president plans to speak to all of the *students*.

Example: The teacher showed the completed project to the (childrens', children's) parents.

EXPLANATION: The rule is simple. If the noun showing possession ends in other than *s*, add *'s*; if the noun showing possession ends in *s*, then just add '. The application of the rule is just as simple, IF mentally you change the possessive phrase into the *of form*. For example, the above possessive phrase becomes *parents of the children*. We thus discover that the noun *children* ends in *n*; therefore, the correct form is *'s*.

ACCEPTED FORM: The teacher showed the completed project to the *children's* parents.

Example: The mothers were wheeling their (baby's, babies', babie's) carriages.

EXPLANATION: By changing the possessive phrase into the *of* form we discover *carriages of the babies*. Therefore the possessive noun ends in *s* and all we need add is the apostrophe. The word is written as is and the apostrophe is then added.

ACCEPTED FORM: The mothers were wheeling their *babies'* carriages.

Example: There was not a single (lady's, ladies', ladie's) voice raised in protest.

EXPLANATION: The *of* form is *voice of a single lady*. The possessive noun does not end in *s*, therefore the word is written as is and *'s* is added.

ACCEPTED FORM: There was not a single *lady's* voice raised in protest.

With Proper Names Ending in *s*

Example: May I introduce you to (Charles', Charles's) brother?

EXPLANATION: With names like *Harris, Thomas, Jones, Phyllis*, names ending in *s*, you may write *s'* or *s's*. The preferred American form at the present time is the *s's*.

ACCEPTED FORM: May I introduce you to *Charles's* (or *Charles'*) brother?

With Hyphenated Nouns

Example: Did Mr. Smith help build his (son's-in-law's, son-in-law's) new house?

EXPLANATION: While the sign of the plural will be placed usually on the important word in the compound (son-in-law), the sign of the possessive is always placed at the *end* of the compound word.

ACCEPTED FORM: Did Mr. Smith help build his *son-in-law's* new house?

With Letters, Numbers, and Words as Words

EXPLANATION: An apostrophe is generally used before an *s* to form the plurals of figures, letters of the alphabet, and words considered as words. However, where there can be no confusion, the apostrophe may be omitted.

ACCEPTED FORM: There are three *i*'s and two *s's* in *signifies*.
Eliminate all *y'see's* (or *y'sees*) from your conversation.
Give me no *and's* (or *ands*) or *but's* (or *buts*).
She carried two *.22's* (or *.22s*) during the raid.

USING THE COMMA

With Dependent Phrases and Clauses

EXPLANATION: When a dependent phrase or clause is in its natural order in the sentence, it is *not* separated from the rest of the sentence by a comma. Only when the phrase or clause is placed at the beginning of the sentence, before the main idea, is a separating comma needed.

ACCEPTED FORM: He did not see the error until I pointed it out to him.

Example: He did not see the error (,) ( ) until I pointed it out to him.

Example: When Margie saw the extent of the damage (,) ( ) she burst into tears.

EXPLANATION: The main clause is *she burst into tears*. This independent clause follows the dependent clause, *When Margie saw the extent of the damage*. Therefore the reader must be alerted to this inverted order.

ACCEPTED FORM: When Margie saw the extent of the damage, she burst . . .

Example: Far from the center of town (,) ( ) our cabin is hidden from view by a grove of towering pine trees.

EXPLANATION: The phrase *far from the center of town* is out of its natural order. To indicate that it is not the main idea, the writer must insert a comma.

ACCEPTED FORM: Far from the center of town, our cabin is . . .

ACCEPTED FORM: Our cabin is hidden from view by a grove of towering pine trees far from the center of town.

With Appositives

Example: Abel plans to spend the summer at Lake Luzerne (,) (.) (One) (one) of the quaint towns that stud the Adirondack region.

EXPLANATION: The group of words, *one of the quaint towns that stud the Adirondack region,* is not a complete thought. This group of words help to explain what Lake Luzerne is. Therefore they constitute an appositive phrase. Appositive phrases are set off by commas, not by periods.

ACCEPTED FORM: Abel plans to spend the summer at Lake Luzerne, *one of* . . .

With Words or Phrases in Series

Example: We followed the circus to the railroad station (,) ( ) to the center of town (,) ( ) to the suburbs (,) ( ) and finally to the Exhibition Field.

EXPLANATION: When two or more words or phrases of the same construction are joined by conjunctions, then no commas are needed. However, when the conjunctions are omitted, then commas are placed wherever the conjunction has been omitted. In the preceding example, there are four parallel phrases; the conjunction has been omitted between the first and second and the second and third. Therefore commas are needed at these points.

ACCEPTED FORM: We followed the circus *to the railroad station, to the center of town, to the suburbs and* finally *to the Exhibition Field.*

ACCEPTED FORM: I ordered peas and carrots and tomatoes and green beans.

ACCEPTED FORM: I ordered *peas, carrots, tomatoes and green beans.*

ACCEPTED FORM: *Max, Dan, and I* left for the trip to the ball field.

NOTE: The comma before the expressed conjunction (*and* in the last example) is an optional one. This means that it may or may not be used; however, modern usage prefers that it be used.

With Two Adjectives Modifying the Same Noun

Example: Tom has always been a cautious (,) ( ) accurate worker.

EXPLANATION: When both adjectives are of equal value and *and* can be inserted without changing the meaning, then a comma should be employed.

ACCEPTED FORM: Tom has always been a cautious, accurate worker.

ACCEPTED FORM: We learned to avoid the house guarded by that vicious barking dog.

EXPLANATION: The adjective *vicious* is not equal to *barking.* It is a *barking dog* that is vicious. Therefore no comma is used.

Restrictive and Nonrestrictive Modifiers

Example: Men (,) ( ) who have breathed free air (,) ( ) will never accept slavery.

EXPLANATION: A restrictive clause is one that so limits the meaning of the word it modifies that the entire meaning of the sentence is changed if the clause is removed. If the clause is removed in the preceding example, the sentence then becomes *Men will never accept slavery.* When a restrictive clause is used, then no commas must be employed to set that clause off from the rest of the sentence.

ACCEPTED FORM: Men *who have breathed free air* will never accept slavery.

Example: Edgar Zwilling (,) ( ) who had been my father's best friend (,) ( ) is professor of zoology in an Eastern college.

EXPLANATION: A nonrestrictive clause does not limit or restrict; it gives additional information. As with an appositive, it may be removed without destroying the original sense of the sentence. Such clauses are set off from the rest of the sentence by commas.

ACCEPTED FORM: Edgar Zwilling, *who had been my father's best friend,* is . . .

Example: All buildings (,) ( ) not mentioned specifically in the agreement (,) ( ) will be out of bounds for all soldiers.

EXPLANATION: With phrases, too, the test to decide whether they are restrictive or nonrestrictive rests on whether the meaning of the sentence is changed by their omission. If we omit the phrase in the example, then the rest of the sentence becomes *All buildings will be out of bounds for all soldiers,* a statement contrary to the intent of the original sentence. Therefore, the phrase is restrictive, and no commas should be used.

ACCEPTED FORM: All buildings not mentioned specifically in the agreement will be . . .

Example: The old house (,) ( ) filled with memories of days long since past (,) ( ) was a friendly refuge for the retired general.

EXPLANATION: The phrase *filled with memories of days long since past* merely adds additional information, and its omission does not alter the meaning of the sentence. Therefore commas should be used since the phrase is nonrestrictive.

ACCEPTED FORM: The old house, filled with memories of days long since past, was . . .

Between Verbs and Their Objects

Example: The leader of the group stated very emphatically (,) ( ) that he would not be responsible for our actions.

EXPLANATION: The object of the sentence is *that he would not be responsible for our actions*. Too many students confuse *that* with *and, but,* or *or*. This object should not be separated from its verb by a comma.

ACCEPTED FORM: The leader of the group stated very emphatically that he . . .

With Conjunctive Adverbs

Example: The course is a grueling one; however (,) (;) ( ) I expect to complete it!

EXPLANATION: With conjunctive adverbs used to join two independent ideas, a comma usually follows the conjunctive adverb when a semicolon precedes it. The principal conjunctive adverbs are

therefore hence moreover consequently nevertheless however then yet

ACCEPTED FORM: The course is a grueling one; however, . . .

USING THE SEMICOLON
After Salutations

Example: Dear Alice (;) (:) (,)

EXPLANATION: After the salutation in a friendly letter, the comma is the correct mark of punctuation. In a formal letter, the colon (:) or the comma may be used. In neither instance may you use the semicolon.

ACCEPTED FORM: Dear Alice,
ACCEPTED FORM: Dear Mr. Smith: (*or* Dear Mr. Smith,)

In Compound Sentences

Example: I really did not want to purchase that lamp (,) (:) (;) but I had no other choice.

EXPLANATION: The semicolon is used to separate two complete ideas when they are closely related and when the conjunction is omitted. When the conjunction is present and the two independent clauses contain no other commas, they should be separated by a comma. The colon cannot take the place of the comma.

ACCEPTED FORM: I really did not want to purchase that lamp, *but* I had no other choice.
ACCEPTED FORM: I really did not want to purchase that lamp; I had no other choice.

Example: Because the decision had to be made by Jack Rosenthal, our family lawyer, Pearl did not allow us to discuss the issue (,) (:) (;) and we waited impatiently until he had gathered all of the facts.

EXPLANATION: When a compound sentence contains ideas that require commas, then the conjunction that joins the two main thoughts may be preceded by a semicolon and not by a comma. In the example just given, the first independent idea contains necessary commas.

ACCEPTED FORM: Because the decision had to be made by Jack Rosenthal, our family lawyer, Pearl did not allow us to discuss the issue; and we waited . . .

Example: Denise followed my explanation (,) (;) ( ) and was able to do all of the practice problems.

EXPLANATION: The example does not contain two independent ideas (*was able to do all of the practice problems* is not a complete idea). This sentence contains a compound verb, two sentence elements joined by *and*. In this case, there should be no intervening mark of punctuation.

ACCEPTED FORM: Denise followed my explanation and was able to do . . .

With Conjunctive Adverbs

Example: Alexia had refused to see our side of the controversy (,) (;) (:) therefore, we saw no point in asking for her opinion.

EXPLANATION: The principal conjunctive adverbs are

therefore hence moreover consequently nevertheless however then yet

When these are used without a conjunction such as *and, but,* or *or*, they may *not* be preceded by a comma. They can begin a new sentence or be preceded by a semicolon and followed by a comma.

ACCEPTED FORM: Alexia had refused to see our side of the controversy; therefore, . . .
ACCEPTED FORM: Alexia had refused to see our side of the controversy. Therefore we . . .
ACCEPTED FORM: Alexia had refused to see our side of the controversy, and therefore we . . .

USING THE COLON

With Quotations

Example: Paul said (,) (:) (;) "Right should make might. Let me illustrate. . . ."

EXPLANATION: The quotation may be preceded by a comma or a colon. However modern usage prefers the comma.

ACCEPTED FORM: Paul said, "Right should make might. Let me . . ."
ACCEPTED FORM: Paul said: "Right should make might. Let me . . ."

In a Listing

Example: I have four reasons for considering this question. My reasons are (,) ( ) (:)

EXPLANATION: Even though an enumeration will follow, the preference of modern usage is to have *no* mark of punctuation follow *are* or *were*.

ACCEPTED FORM: My reasons are that he . . .

Example: We shall speak of three different types of drivers (,) (:) (;) namely (,) ( ) (:) . . .

EXPLANATION: When the series is introduced by expressions like

such as, namely, that is,

it is preceded by a colon and the introductory phrase is followed by a comma.

ACCEPTED FORM: We shall speak of three different types of drivers: namely, . . .

Example: The valise contained four items (;) (:) (,) the old gun, the note, a cuff-link, and a blood-stained handkerchief.

EXPLANATION: When a formal listing is not introduced by a form of *to be*, then it should be introduced by a colon.

ACCEPTED FORM: The valise contained four items: the old gun, . . .

USING QUOTATION MARKS

Setting off Titles

Example: She sang a selection from ("Lakme," *Lakme,* 'Lakme').

EXPLANATION: The preferred modern method of identifying titles is very definite. Main titles are underlined in themes (italicized in printed matter). Short compositions or parts of a larger work are set off by quotation marks.

ACCEPTED FORM: She sang a selection from *Lakme.*
ACCEPTED FORM: I have just finished reading the short story "My Old Man."
ACCEPTED FORM: I learned to respect Silas Marner in the novel *Silas Marner.*

NOTE: The name of the author is not set off. It requires neither underlining nor quotation marks.

ACCEPTED FORM: Our class is reading *The Return of the Native* by Thomas Hardy.

Accompanying Punctuation

Study the following examples. They illustrate the correct method of handling the various problems that arise in using quotations in themes.

ACCEPTED FORM: Helen asked, "Should we really accept his conclusions?"
ACCEPTED FORM: "Should we," Helen asked, "really accept his conclusions? I find him too self-seeking to be respected!
ACCEPTED FORM: "I had left at twelve," she said. "When did you?"
ACCEPTED FORM: Did Helen say, "I find him too self-seeking to be respected"?

NOTE: In handling sustained dialogue, a new paragraph is required for each change of speaker, regardless of the number of words each one says.

ACCEPTED FORM: "What did you say?"
    "Nothing!"
    "Nothing?"
    "Yes, nothing."

Position of Quotation Marks

Example: I have memorized the first stanza of "Song of Myself (.") (".)

EXPLANATION: The period and comma are always placed within the quotation marks.

ACCEPTED FORM: I have memorized the first stanza of "Song of Myself."

Example: I just did not understand Poe's "Bells (;") (";) then Jerry read it aloud to me.

EXPLANATION: The colon and the semicolon are placed outside the quotation marks.

ACCEPTED FORM: I just did not understand Poe's "Bells"; then . . .

Example: What is the meaning of "as slick as a skinned herring ("?) (?")

EXPLANATION: The question mark and the exclamation point are placed *within* the quoted material when the reference is to the quoted matter only. These marks are placed outside when they refer to the whole sentence.

ACCEPTED FORM: What is the meaning of "as slick as a skinned herring"?

ACCEPTED FORM: "When will the test be given?" Edna asked.

Indirect Quotations

Example: Milton said (, "That) (that) he would not visit the museum at all (.") (.)

EXPLANATION: Only the exact words of the speaker are set off in quotation marks. When the words are changed so that the quotation is not directly what had been said, no quotation marks must be used. In the example given, Milton had actually said, "*I* shall not visit the museum at all." Since the example does not contain his exact words, quotation marks should not be used. When *that* is a necessary introductory word, the statement that follows is usually not a direct quotation.

ACCEPTED FORM: Milton said that he would not visit the museum at all.

USING THE HYPHEN

With Numbers

Example: I saw twenty (-) ( ) one applicants in one hour!

EXPLANATION: The hyphen is used with compound numbers from twenty-one to ninety-nine.

ACCEPTED FORM: I saw *twenty-one* applicants in one hour!

With Fractions

Example: They gave us one (-) ( ) third of the winnings.

EXPLANATION: The hyphen is used to separate the numerator from the denominator in fractions that are spelled out.

ACCEPTED FORM: They gave us *one-third* of the winnings.

With Prefixes

Example: He solemnly swore that he would re (-) ( ) establish order.

EXPLANATION: Usually when the prefix will cause confusion because two vowels are placed next to each other, a hyphen is used unless the word has become part of long-established usage.

ACCEPTED FORM: The partners were *co-owners* of the business.

ACCEPTED FORM: We must *readjust* our clocks in October.

Example: I spoke to the ex (-) ( ) president of the local bank.

EXPLANATION: A hyphen is generally used with the prefixes *self-, post-, all-, ex-, anti-* when they are added to complete words.

> *self-centered anti-war all-American*
> *post-season ex-husband*

ACCEPTED FORM: I spoke to the *ex-president* of the local bank.

ACCEPTED FORM: He is a most *selfless* leader.

With Compound Modifiers

Example: He is an all (-) ( ) weather pilot.

EXPLANATION: A hyphen is used to join two or more words used as a single adjective preceding the noun.

ACCEPTED FORM: He is an *all-weather* pilot.

Example: The answer is well (-) ( ) known.

EXPLANATION: Since the compound modifier does *not* precede the noun, no hyphen is used.

ACCEPTED FORM: The answer is *well known*.

ACCEPTED FORM: Alex is a *well-known* referee.

Example: He insists that it is not an overly (-) ( ) complicated case.

EXPLANATION: If the first of the compound modifiers ends in *ly,* then *no* hyphen is used.

ACCEPTED FORM: He insists that it is not an *overly complicated* case.

USING ABBREVIATIONS

Example: 1416 East 26 (th) ( ) Street

EXPLANATION: Following the preference of the postal authorities, present usage requires the omission of *rd, st, th* after numbers.

ACCEPTED FORM: 1416 East 26 Street

Example: 1416 East 26 street
              B'klyn, NY 21210

EXPLANATION: The preferred form is to spell the word out rather than to abbreviate it. However, if in the abbreviation an apostrophe is used, then no period should be used. Therefore, if you must use the abbreviated form, use either *B'klyn* or Bklyn. and not both forms combined. The zone or zip code number is an integral part of the name. It is *not* an additional item. It is inseparable from the name.

ACCEPTED FORM: 1416 East 26 Street
                  Brooklyn, NY 21210

Example: ( ) (Dr.) Milton F. Gitlin, M.D.

EXPLANATION: The title can be given only once. Therefore if we use *Dr.,* we should not use *M.D.* If we use *M.D.,* we should not use *Dr.*

ACCEPTED FORM: Milton G. Gitlin, *M.D.* or *Dr.* Milton F. Gitlin

ACCEPTED FORM: *Mr.* George Getnick or George Getnick, *Esq.*

Example: I plan to visit the (U.N., UN) Building this Wednesday.

EXPLANATION: Most abbreviations are identified by terminal periods. However, the names of many governmental bureaus and agencies omit the periods.

ACCEPTED FORM: I plan to visit the *UN* Building this Wednesday.

ACCEPTED FORM: My father was able to obtain an *FHA* loan when he bought our house.

USING NUMERALS

Example: I spoke to all (five, 5) of my cousins.

EXPLANATION: Most textbooks agree that if the number is long, you can use the arabic form. They also agree that numbers from one to ten and the multiples of ten up to one hundred should be spelled out.

ACCEPTED FORM: I spoke to all *five* of my cousins.

ACCEPTED FORM: There were *115* candidates who showed up at practice.

Example: We shall meet promptly at (six-thirty P.M., 6:30 P.M.).

EXPLANATION: When time is expressed with A.M. or P.M., numbers are preferred.

ACCEPTED FORM: We shall meet promptly at *6:30* P.M.

Example: I finally sold 317 pens, 243 desks, and (forty, 40) pads.

EXPLANATION: In a series of numbers, consistency should be the guide.

ACCEPTED FORM: I finally sold *317* pens, *243* desks, and *40* pads.

Example: (Thirty-six, 36 seniors) were appointed to the staff.

EXPLANATION: When numbers must be used at the beginning of a sentence, they should be written out. If the number is very large, the sentence should be recast so that the number does not appear first in the sentence.

ACCEPTED FORM: *Thirty-six* seniors were appointed to the staff.

ACCEPTED FORM: We finally had accumulated *3,452* pennies.

USING SPECIAL TERMS

Example: We were able to avoid the mountain range by traveling due (North, north).

EXPLANATION: Points of the compass are not capitalized. However when *north, south, east, west* are used to refer to specific regions in our country, they are capitalized.

ACCEPTED FORM: We were able to avoid the mountain range by traveling due *north.*

ACCEPTED FORM: We plan to live in the *East* for the next few years.

Example: In order to be chosen for the honor course, I shall have to achieve 90% in (english, English) and (mathematics, Mathematics).

EXPLANATION: School subjects per se are *not* capitalized. However, we do capitalize the titles of those subjects whose names are derived from the names of languages.

ACCEPTED FORM: In order to be chosen for the honor course, I shall have to achieve 90% in *English* and *mathematics.*

Example: There are several groups of (jewish, Jewish) people who have lived among the (Chinese, chinese) for centuries.

EXPLANATION: Adjectives derived from the names of religions and countries are capitalized. Therefore *Protestant, Catholicism, Nigerian* should be capitalized.

ACCEPTED FORM: There are several groups of *Jewish* people who have lived among the *Chinese* for centuries.

Example: Ralph Bunche was one of the great (black, Black) leaders of the twentieth century.

EXPLANATION: Words that refer to race are capitalized. The word *Negro* is comparable to *Caucasian*; both are therefore capitalized. However, neither *black* nor *white* is capitalized.

ACCEPTED FORM: Ralph Bunche was one of the great *black* leaders . . .

Example: I had to telephone my (uncle, Uncle) three times today.

EXPLANATION: Names that denote close relationship unless they are used with a proper noun or stand alone are usually *not* capitalized.

ACCEPTED FORM: I had to telephone my *uncle* three times today.

ACCEPTED FORM: I had to telephone *Uncle Harold* three times today.

ACCEPTED FORM: Did you telephone *Mother* today?

ACCEPTED FORM: I had a long conversation with *Uncle* tonight.

The English Composition Test
(All Multiple-Choice Questions)

Section **T W O** : **Practice Tests for the English Composition Test (without Essay)**

1. *Typical Questions*

2. *Four Practice Tests*

3. *Answers to Practice Tests with Analyses of Answers*

To Do Your Best

1. The body of material being covered in the test remains the same, but the question items change. Therefore make certain that you read the directions before you begin to answer. Know what each of the letters in the Answer Key stands for before you mark any one of them.

2. The test must cover a wide range so that there can be a spread in student scores. Therefore, as you begin each set of choices, do not look for subtle variations first. Rather look for the obvious ones first! Unacceptable forms of agreement, incorrect tense, and confusion of common words will be much more frequent than stylistic changes. Only when you do not find the common blunder, then go toward the more sophisticated type of change.

3. Once you have found the "error" do not stop! Examine the other choices before you write your answer.

4. Do not mull over any one item. Remember the subtle is mixed with the obvious; you receive as much credit for one as the other. If you find one item difficult, skip it and then come back later if you have time.

5. Follow the suggested time schedule. It is better to go on to the next section when time is up. If you are permitted, you may be able to go back later.

6. You *can* guess. In fact, it is generally to your advantage to guess if you can eliminate one or more of the choices for a question. However, because of the way the tests are scored, guessing randomly is not likely to increase your score.

7. Rely upon your past training. Do not assume because it is a form that you normally use it must be unacceptable.

8. When in doubt, select the more formal item, the less colloquial choice. Remember that what is being tested is your control of Standard Written English.

NOTE: In College Board publications, the terms *correct* and *incorrect* are used interchangeably with *acceptable* and *not acceptable,* respectively, when referring to specific forms in usage, diction, and spelling. Thus, items labeled in this book as *acceptable* in current Standard Written English may be labeled as either *acceptable* or *correct* in directions and in test items of the English Composition Test; items labeled in this book as *not acceptable* may be identified as either *not acceptable* or *incorrect* in the explanatory material and directions of the English Composition Test.

1. *Typical Questions*

The multiple-choice questions that follow are the type found on recent examinations. Study the directions and then the analysis so that you will have full comprehension of the tasks ahead.

Type One: Underlined Choices

The sentences in this kind of question may contain problems in grammatical relationships, usage, diction (choice of words), or idiom.

DIRECTIONS: The following sentences contain problems in grammar, usage, diction (choice of words), and idiom.

Some sentences are correct.

No sentence contains more than one error.

You will find that the error, if there is one, is underlined and lettered. Assume that all other elements of the sentence are correct and cannot be changed. In choosing answers, follow the requirements of standard written English.

If there is an error, select the one underlined part that must be changed in order to make the sentence correct, and mark that on the answer sheet.

If there is no error, mark answer E.

SAMPLE ITEM ONE:

The record left by fossils, the ancient remains of plants and animals, provide scientists with their pri-
              A   B
mary source of knowledge about prehistoric life.
        C   D
No error
    E

(A) is definitely incorrect since the subject record is singular and should be followed by provides.
(B) Because the idiom is provide with, (B) is correct.
(C) Because the idiom is source of, (C) is correct.
(D) The idiom is knowledge about; (D) is correct.

SUMMARY: With this type of question, plan on being lucky. Look for the obvious first. But, after you have found an error, check off the others to avoid acting too hastily!

Type Two: Spotting the Error

DIRECTIONS: In each of the following sentences, some part of the sentence or the entire sentence is underlined. Beneath each sentence you will find five ways of phrasing the underlined part. The first of these repeats the original; the other four are different. If you think the original is better than any of the alternatives, choose answer A; otherwise choose one of the others.

This is a test of correctness and effectiveness of expression. In choosing answers, follow the requirements of standard written English; that is, pay at-

tention to grammar, choice of words, sentence construction and punctuation. Choose the answer that best expresses the meaning of the original sentence. Your choice should produce the most effective sentence—clear and precise, without awkwardness or ambiguity.

SAMPLE ITEM ONE:

Seeing how angry he had become, my fingers became more clumsy than ever, and I made a mess of the elements of the puzzle.

(A) Seeing how angry he had become,
(B) Seeing how angry he became,
(C) Having seen how angry he had become,
(D) Seeing as how he was becoming angry,
(E) When I saw how angry he had become,

ANALYSIS:

(A) is incorrect since it contains a dangling participle seeing which seems to modify fingers.
(B) is incorrect because seeing is a continuation of the dangling participle element.
(C) is incorrect because having seen is another dangling participle.
(D) is incorrect because not only is seeing dangling but seeing as how is unidiomatic.
(E) is correct because of the elimination of the dangling participle.

SAMPLE ITEM TWO:

Caution in leadership can sometimes be related more to intelligence than lack of forcefulness.

(A) sometimes be related more to intelligence than lack of forcefulness
(B) be related often to intelligence, not only to lack of forcefulness
(C) sometimes be related more to intelligence than to lack of forcefulness
(D) often be related to intelligence as to lack of forcefulness
(E) as sometimes be related more to intelligence as well as lack of forcefulness

ANALYSIS:

(B) and (D) change the meaning. Often does not mean sometimes.
(E) lacks syntactical balance and doesn't make sense.

(A) In the comparison, the preposition to must be repeated, as it is in (C). Therefore (C) is the answer.

SUMMARY: Very often a comparison of the suggested replacements points up the error. Rarely can this type of question be handled with the same speed as Type One. Knowing when to give up and go on to the next, hoping to come back later, is the name of the game!

Type Three: Editing

The third kind of question calls for editing or revising a correct and acceptable sentence. The revision should stay as close as possible to the meaning and language of the original. The traps planted in the unacceptable choices cover the errors found in each of the other types of questions, but the stress here is on the writing itself and not on the labels.

DIRECTIONS: Each of the following sentences is to be rephrased according to the directions that follow it. You should make only those changes that the directions require. Keep the meaning of the revised sentence as close to the meaning of the original sentence as the directions for that sentence permit.

If you think that more than one good sentence can be made according to the directions, select the sentence that
 retains, insofar as possible, the meaning of the original sentence;
 is most natural in phrasing and construction;
 meets the requirements of standard written English; and
 is the best sentence in terms of conciseness, idiom, logic and other qualities found in well-written sentences.

When you have thought out a good rephrasing of the original sentence, find in choices (A) through (E) the word or entire phrase that you have included in your revised sentence and blacken the corresponding space on your answer sheet. Be sure that the choice you select is the fullest expression of your revision available in the choices; that is, for example, if your revised sentence contains was playing and both was playing and playing are offered as choices, playing would not be an acceptable answer.

SAMPLE ITEM ONE:

When we approached the city, the stench of decaying flesh told us just where the ambush had occurred.

DIRECTIONS: Substitute *Approaching* for *When we approached*.
 (A) city, the stench
 (B) city the stench
 (C) could have told
 (D) ambush told
 (E) we were told

ANALYSIS:

Approaching is a participle and must have a noun or pronoun to modify.
 (A) and (B) would give us a dangling participle in *Approaching* the city(,) the *stench* . . .

 (C) and (D) make unnecessary changes.
 (E) supplies the pronoun for *approaching* to modify: *Approaching* the city, *we* were told by the stench . . .

SAMPLE ITEM TWO:

It seems to be inherent in human nature to want a deity to worship and a devil to abhor. Machinery has become the devil of a widespread cult.

DIRECTIONS: Begin with *Since machinery had become.*
 (A) cult. It seems
 (B) worship, and a devil
 (C) cult, it seemed
 (D) worship. A devil
 (E) cult; it had seemed

ANALYSIS:

Since introduces a subordinate clause that cannot be separated from the rest of the sentence.
 (A) and (D) create sentence fragments.
 (B) introduces an irrelevant error, a comma separating compound items joined by *and*.
 (E) uses a semicolon to separate the subordinate and the main clause.
 (C) has the necessary past tense for *seemed* and the comma to separate the introductory adverb clause from the main clause.

SAMPLE ITEM THREE:

A hero is no braver than an ordinary man, but he is brave for five minutes longer.

DIRECTIONS: Omit *but* and add *only*.
 (A) braver. Than an ordinary man, only
 (B) man; he is brave only
 (C) braver, than an ordinary man, only
 (D) man. He is only brave
 (E) man, only he is brave

ANALYSIS:

The adverb *only* must be placed as close as possible to the phrase *five minutes longer*. Without the conjunction *but*, the two clauses become independent and have to be so punctuated: either as two separate sentences or as one sentence containing a semicolon.

(A) introduces an irrelevant error with a meaningless period after *braver* and a capitalized *than*.

(B) uses an acceptable semicolon to separate the two independent clauses; *only* is placed close to *five minutes longer*.

(C) introduces an irrelevant error in its use of commas.

(D) misplaces the word *only,* changing the meaning of the sentence.

(E) misplaces the word *only*; a comma is misused to separate the two independent clauses.

SAMPLE ITEM FOUR:

Britain applied for membership in the European Economic Community, but that application was vetoed in 1963 by French President Charles de Gaulle.

DIRECTIONS: Begin with *French President Charles de Gaulle*.

(A) found its application vetoed
(B) to veto Britain's
(C) vetoed Britain's
(D) vetoed its
(E) had vetoed it

ANALYSIS:

The revision requires changing the direction of the action in the sentence. There does not seem to be an obvious grammatical trap. The best approach is to work out the editing as directed, with an eye on the choices. If necessary, begin to write the sentence:

French President Charles de Gaulle in 1963 *vetoed* Britain's application . . . Community.

This is a correct sentence grammatically and fits the requirements.

SUMMARY: If you can, follow the directions and evolve the sentence suggested. Then look through the choices for the one that fits. However, do not make your final selection before considering the other choices as well.

Not all possibilities of revision are included in the five choices. If you find that none of the choices fit your sentence, then rephrase it; begin your revision thinking with each of the choices offered.

PRACTICE TEST ONE

ANSWER SHEET

1	Ⓐ Ⓑ Ⓒ Ⓓ Ⓔ	31	Ⓐ Ⓑ Ⓒ Ⓓ Ⓔ	61	Ⓐ Ⓑ Ⓒ Ⓓ Ⓔ
2	Ⓐ Ⓑ Ⓒ Ⓓ Ⓔ	32	Ⓐ Ⓑ Ⓒ Ⓓ Ⓔ	62	Ⓐ Ⓑ Ⓒ Ⓓ Ⓔ
3	Ⓐ Ⓑ Ⓒ Ⓓ Ⓔ	33	Ⓐ Ⓑ Ⓒ Ⓓ Ⓔ	63	Ⓐ Ⓑ Ⓒ Ⓓ Ⓔ
4	Ⓐ Ⓑ Ⓒ Ⓓ Ⓔ	34	Ⓐ Ⓑ Ⓒ Ⓓ Ⓔ	64	Ⓐ Ⓑ Ⓒ Ⓓ Ⓔ
5	Ⓐ Ⓑ Ⓒ Ⓓ Ⓔ	35	Ⓐ Ⓑ Ⓒ Ⓓ Ⓔ	65	Ⓐ Ⓑ Ⓒ Ⓓ Ⓔ
6	Ⓐ Ⓑ Ⓒ Ⓓ Ⓔ	36	Ⓐ Ⓑ Ⓒ Ⓓ Ⓔ	66	Ⓐ Ⓑ Ⓒ Ⓓ Ⓔ
7	Ⓐ Ⓑ Ⓒ Ⓓ Ⓔ	37	Ⓐ Ⓑ Ⓒ Ⓓ Ⓔ	67	Ⓐ Ⓑ Ⓒ Ⓓ Ⓔ
8	Ⓐ Ⓑ Ⓒ Ⓓ Ⓔ	38	Ⓐ Ⓑ Ⓒ Ⓓ Ⓔ	68	Ⓐ Ⓑ Ⓒ Ⓓ Ⓔ
9	Ⓐ Ⓑ Ⓒ Ⓓ Ⓔ	39	Ⓐ Ⓑ Ⓒ Ⓓ Ⓔ	69	Ⓐ Ⓑ Ⓒ Ⓓ Ⓔ
10	Ⓐ Ⓑ Ⓒ Ⓓ Ⓔ	40	Ⓐ Ⓑ Ⓒ Ⓓ Ⓔ	70	Ⓐ Ⓑ Ⓒ Ⓓ Ⓔ
11	Ⓐ Ⓑ Ⓒ Ⓓ Ⓔ	41	Ⓐ Ⓑ Ⓒ Ⓓ Ⓔ	71	Ⓐ Ⓑ Ⓒ Ⓓ Ⓔ
12	Ⓐ Ⓑ Ⓒ Ⓓ Ⓔ	42	Ⓐ Ⓑ Ⓒ Ⓓ Ⓔ	72	Ⓐ Ⓑ Ⓒ Ⓓ Ⓔ
13	Ⓐ Ⓑ Ⓒ Ⓓ Ⓔ	43	Ⓐ Ⓑ Ⓒ Ⓓ Ⓔ	73	Ⓐ Ⓑ Ⓒ Ⓓ Ⓔ
14	Ⓐ Ⓑ Ⓒ Ⓓ Ⓔ	44	Ⓐ Ⓑ Ⓒ Ⓓ Ⓔ	74	Ⓐ Ⓑ Ⓒ Ⓓ Ⓔ
15	Ⓐ Ⓑ Ⓒ Ⓓ Ⓔ	45	Ⓐ Ⓑ Ⓒ Ⓓ Ⓔ	75	Ⓐ Ⓑ Ⓒ Ⓓ Ⓔ
16	Ⓐ Ⓑ Ⓒ Ⓓ Ⓔ	46	Ⓐ Ⓑ Ⓒ Ⓓ Ⓔ	76	Ⓐ Ⓑ Ⓒ Ⓓ Ⓔ
17	Ⓐ Ⓑ Ⓒ Ⓓ Ⓔ	47	Ⓐ Ⓑ Ⓒ Ⓓ Ⓔ	77	Ⓐ Ⓑ Ⓒ Ⓓ Ⓔ
18	Ⓐ Ⓑ Ⓒ Ⓓ Ⓔ	48	Ⓐ Ⓑ Ⓒ Ⓓ Ⓔ	78	Ⓐ Ⓑ Ⓒ Ⓓ Ⓔ
19	Ⓐ Ⓑ Ⓒ Ⓓ Ⓔ	49	Ⓐ Ⓑ Ⓒ Ⓓ Ⓔ	79	Ⓐ Ⓑ Ⓒ Ⓓ Ⓔ
20	Ⓐ Ⓑ Ⓒ Ⓓ Ⓔ	50	Ⓐ Ⓑ Ⓒ Ⓓ Ⓔ	80	Ⓐ Ⓑ Ⓒ Ⓓ Ⓔ
21	Ⓐ Ⓑ Ⓒ Ⓓ Ⓔ	51	Ⓐ Ⓑ Ⓒ Ⓓ Ⓔ	81	Ⓐ Ⓑ Ⓒ Ⓓ Ⓔ
22	Ⓐ Ⓑ Ⓒ Ⓓ Ⓔ	52	Ⓐ Ⓑ Ⓒ Ⓓ Ⓔ	82	Ⓐ Ⓑ Ⓒ Ⓓ Ⓔ
23	Ⓐ Ⓑ Ⓒ Ⓓ Ⓔ	53	Ⓐ Ⓑ Ⓒ Ⓓ Ⓔ	83	Ⓐ Ⓑ Ⓒ Ⓓ Ⓔ
24	Ⓐ Ⓑ Ⓒ Ⓓ Ⓔ	54	Ⓐ Ⓑ Ⓒ Ⓓ Ⓔ	84	Ⓐ Ⓑ Ⓒ Ⓓ Ⓔ
25	Ⓐ Ⓑ Ⓒ Ⓓ Ⓔ	55	Ⓐ Ⓑ Ⓒ Ⓓ Ⓔ	85	Ⓐ Ⓑ Ⓒ Ⓓ Ⓔ
26	Ⓐ Ⓑ Ⓒ Ⓓ Ⓔ	56	Ⓐ Ⓑ Ⓒ Ⓓ Ⓔ	86	Ⓐ Ⓑ Ⓒ Ⓓ Ⓔ
27	Ⓐ Ⓑ Ⓒ Ⓓ Ⓔ	57	Ⓐ Ⓑ Ⓒ Ⓓ Ⓔ	87	Ⓐ Ⓑ Ⓒ Ⓓ Ⓔ
28	Ⓐ Ⓑ Ⓒ Ⓓ Ⓔ	58	Ⓐ Ⓑ Ⓒ Ⓓ Ⓔ	88	Ⓐ Ⓑ Ⓒ Ⓓ Ⓔ
29	Ⓐ Ⓑ Ⓒ Ⓓ Ⓔ	59	Ⓐ Ⓑ Ⓒ Ⓓ Ⓔ	89	Ⓐ Ⓑ Ⓒ Ⓓ Ⓔ
30	Ⓐ Ⓑ Ⓒ Ⓓ Ⓔ	60	Ⓐ Ⓑ Ⓒ Ⓓ Ⓔ	90	Ⓐ Ⓑ Ⓒ Ⓓ Ⓔ

PRACTICE TEST ONE

Total Time: One Hour
PART 1 *Suggested Time: 20 Minutes*
Time begun .... Time ended .... Time used ....
Did you complete the section within the time limit? ..

DIRECTIONS: The following sentences contain problems in grammar, usage, diction (choice of words), and idiom.

Some sentences are correct.

No sentence contains more than one error.

You will find that the error, if there is one, is underlined and lettered. Assume that all other elements of the sentence are correct and cannot be changed. In choosing answers, follow the requirements of standard written English.

If there is an error, select the one underlined part that must be changed in order to make the sentence correct, and blacken the corresponding space on the answer sheet.

If there is no error, mark answer space E.

1. Everyone of us who <u>were</u> present <u>assumes</u> that
                        (A)   (B)
   the winner will be <u>she</u>, <u>barring</u> any unexpected
                      (C)   (D)
   turn of events. <u>No error</u>
                    (E)

2. Alfred is one <u>who</u> seems to like Helen better
                  (A)
   <u>than</u> <u>us</u>, <u>irregardless</u> of how much we try to
   (B) (C)   (D)
   please him. <u>No error</u>
               (E)

3. Statistics <u>can</u> be <u>cited</u> to prove that prices this
              (A)   (B)
   year <u>are</u> lower than <u>last year</u>. <u>No error</u>
        (C)   (D)   (E)

4. She <u>angered</u> him beyond <u>measure</u> when she <u>said</u>
        (A)   (B)   (C)
   he walks <u>like</u> his father does, slowly. <u>No error</u>
            (D)   (E)

5. If the loser in the contest turns out to be
   <u>him</u>, I <u>shall have had</u> hardly <u>no</u> opportunity
   (A)   (B)   (C)
   to speak <u>with</u> him. <u>No error</u>
            (D)   (E)

6. I just cannot <u>leave</u> the book <u>lie</u> on the floor
                  (A)   (B)
   without telling you and <u>her</u> that you
                           (C)
   <u>had better</u> pick it up immediately. <u>No error</u>
   (D)   (E)

7. <u>That there</u> is <u>a</u> army of ants sharing our lunch
   (A)   (B)
   with <u>us</u> would <u>have</u> come to my attention
        (C)   (D)
   sooner or later. <u>No error</u>
                    (E)

8. The clouds <u>obscured</u> <u>our view of</u> the earth
              (A)   (B)
   below; <u>consequently</u>, we had <u>to rely solely upon</u>
          (C)   (D)
   the instruments. <u>No error</u>
                    (E)

9. <u>Providing</u> you listen carefully, you <u>will</u> be able
   (A)   (B)
   to do the work as well as <u>I</u> without any assist-
                             (C)
   ance from <u>them</u>. <u>No error</u>
             (D)   (E)

10. <u>At that time</u> the United States <u>had appeared</u> to
    (A)   (B)
    be <u>more powerful</u> than <u>any country</u> in the
       (C)   (D)
    world. <u>No error</u>
           (E)

11. Worrying, <u>fretting</u>, and <u>unable</u> to stop talking,
             (A)   (B)
    Sara and George <u>had</u> paced the hospital cor-
                     (C)
    ridors <u>for</u> endless hours. <u>No error</u>
          (D)   (E)

12. Because I had scarcely <u>no</u> time to <u>lose</u>, Paula,
                     (A)   (B)
    along with the fourteen <u>other</u> members of the
                       (C)
    committee, <u>was</u> notified of our decision.
             (D)
    <u>No error</u>
     (E)

13. <u>Who</u> shall I blame when <u>it's</u> time for the group
     (A)   (B)
    and <u>us</u> to make our report , and we <u>shall</u> have
     (C)   (D)
    to report that we are unprepared? <u>No error</u>
                      (E)

14. My <u>brothers</u>-in-<u>law's</u> storage facilities far
        (A)   (B)
    <u>exceeds</u> <u>ours</u>. <u>No error</u>
     (C)   (D)   (E)

15. The leader of the <u>guerilla</u> band accompanied his
                 (A)
    demands <u>by</u> threats when we refused to <u>agree to</u>
          (B)   (C)
    his <u>proposal</u>. <u>No error</u>
        (D)   (E)

16. Since you will <u>be graduated from</u> high school
                 (A)
    <u>in</u> a few days, you <u>have been</u> granted the
     (B)   (C)
    <u>privilege to pay</u> adult admission prices.
          (D)
    <u>No error</u>
     (E)

17. <u>Let's</u> come to one basic conclusion: if <u>we're</u>
     (A)   (B)
    to put our savings <u>in</u> stocks and bonds, we
              (C)
    must first hire a <u>qualified</u> consultant. <u>No error</u>
              (D)   (E)

18. One of the workers <u>has</u> <u>accidently</u> overturned
               (A)   (B)
    the <u>pail</u> which was <u>lying</u> on the kitchen floor.
        (C)   (D)
    <u>No error</u>
     (E)

19. He spoke <u>out of turn</u> when he <u>allowed</u> that ex-
            (A)   (B)
    cept for you and <u>me</u> none of the members
               (C)
    <u>was</u> interested in the matter. <u>No error</u>
     (D)   (E)

20. Anyone who <u>asserts</u> that he <u>may</u> become <u>mad</u>
           (A)   (B)   (C)
    every time a friend disagrees with <u>him</u> will soon
                   (D)
    be without friends. <u>No error</u>
              (E)

21. My old, brown hat, <u>along with</u> several of my
               (A)
    sister's skirts, <u>were</u> badly soiled when the pack-
           (B)
    age fell <u>from</u> the <u>back of</u> the truck. <u>No error</u>
           (C)   (D)   (E)

22. I had worked alone <u>by myself</u> for hours, <u>trying</u>
              (A)   (B)
    to combine the <u>disparate</u> elements <u>in</u> this
            (C)   (D)
    puzzling case. <u>No error</u>
           (E)

23. My marks in English <u>was</u> higher <u>than</u> or equal
               (A)   (B)
    to <u>theirs</u>. <u>No error</u>
    (C) (D)   (E)

24. <u>Anywheres</u> you travel <u>in</u> this area you will
     (A)   (B)
    <u>lose</u> much time if you fail to read the road signs
    (C)
    <u>carefully</u>. <u>No error</u>
     (D)   (E)

25. Since they <u>had</u> arrived at <u>around</u> seven in the
           (A)   (B)
    evening, everybody but you and <u>us</u> <u>was</u> at the
                   (C) (D)
    station to greet them. <u>No error</u>
               (E)

26. I <u>may</u> not be <u>so</u> capable as you, but when I want
       (A)   (B)
    to do something <u>badly</u> enough, my work is su-
               (C)
    perior to <u>yours</u>. <u>No error</u>
          (D)   (E)

27. <u>Being that</u> neither Herbert <u>nor</u> I <u>am</u> scheduled
       (A)   (B) (C)
    to play in that game, the coach told Herbert and
    <u>me</u> that we were excused from the practice ses-
    (D)
    sions. <u>No error</u>
           (E)

28. I do not question <u>but what</u> he had made a se-
                 (A)
    rious error in <u>assuming</u> that the man <u>whom</u> we
             (B)   (C)
    had seen could be <u>responsible</u> for this confu-
               (D)
    sion. <u>No error</u>
         (E)

29. Is it <u>I</u> who <u>am</u> to <u>ever</u> stand between you and
         (A)   (B)   (C)
    <u>him</u>? <u>No error</u>
    (D)   (E)

30. Am I to <u>assume</u>, therefore, that it <u>is</u> the
         (A)   (B)
    <u>consensus of opinion</u> in this group that they are
         (C)
    more accurate than <u>we</u>? <u>No error</u>
               (D)   (E)

31. <u>Thomas'</u> method differs <u>with</u> yours in one very
     (A)   (B)
    important <u>aspect</u> — his greater <u>emphases</u> in the
           (C)   (D)
    fields of safety. <u>No error</u>
            (E)

32. Here <u>come</u> the group of astronauts who <u>are</u> to
       (A)   (B)
    lead <u>in man's</u> exploration of outer space.
        (D)
    <u>No error</u>
      (E)

33. The committee <u>are</u> unable to agree <u>on</u> <u>whom</u>
            (A)   (B) (C)
    they should elect to replace Jensen and <u>her</u>.
                             (D)
    <u>No error</u>
    (E)

34. If anyone is <u>interested</u>, it <u>has</u> been
              (A)   (B)
    <u>quite some time</u> since Henry and <u>I</u> had visited
        (C)   (D)
    the farm. <u>No error</u>
         (E)

35. Our old apartment is so large <u>in size</u> that we
                       (A)
    <u>may have</u> give away <u>much of</u> our furniture
      (B)   (C)
    when we <u>move</u>. <u>No error</u>
         (D)   (E)

36. His <u>conception</u> of the work <u>to be done</u> differs
       (A)   (B)
    so greatly <u>with mine</u> that I am <u>completely</u> per-
          (C)   (D)
    plexed. <u>No error</u>
        (E)

37. This <u>incredible</u> record had been compiled at a
       (A)
    <u>time when</u> the company <u>had</u> many <u>less</u> employ-
      (B)   (C)   (D)
    ees. <u>No error</u>
       (E)

38. You may <u>have a loan of</u> <u>these</u> data since
           (A)   (B)
    <u>they have</u> been adjusted for the <u>latest</u> changes.
     (C)   (D)
    <u>No error</u>
    (E)

39. The old car is <u>lying</u> <u>somewheres</u> on the <u>desert</u>
              (A)   (B)   (C)
    floor, turning <u>slowly</u> into red dust. <u>No error</u>
           (D)   (E)

PART 2   *Suggested Time: 25 Minutes*
Time begun .... Time ended .... Time used ....
Did you complete the section within the time limit? ..

DIRECTIONS: In each of the following sentences, some part of the sentence or the entire sentence is underlined. Beneath each sentence you will find five ways of phrasing the underlined part. The first of these repeats the original; the other four are different. If you think the original is better than any of the alternatives, choose answer A; otherwise choose one of the others. Select the best version and blacken the corresponding space on your answer sheet.

This is a test of correctness and effectiveness of expression. In choosing answers, follow the requirements of standard written English; that is, pay attention to grammar, choice of words, sentence construction and punctuation. Choose the answer that best expresses the meaning of the original sentence. Your choice should produce the most effective sentence—clear and precise, without awkwardness or ambiguity.

40. The young reporter went out on many routine assignments until his ability to grasp essentials was proved.

    (A) until his ability to grasp essentials was proved.
    (B) . Until his ability to grasp essentials was proved.
    (C) until his ability to grasp essentials was proven.
    (D) until he proved his ability to grasp essentials.
    (E) ; until his ability to grasp essentials was proven.

41. If the car would have been moved on time, we would not have received the ticket.

    (A) If the car would have been moved on time,
    (B) If the car could have been moved on time,
    (C) If the car had been moved on time,
    (D) If the car were moved on time,
    (E) If the car was moved on time,

42. Neither Janet nor Merwin have been in this office all day.

    (A) have been in this office
    (B) could have been in this office
    (C) has been in this office
    (D) have been in this here office
    (E) has been in this here office

43. The condenser was just installed, therefore it is the part to be checked first.

    (A) installed, therefore
    (B) installed therefore
    (C) installed, therefore,
    (D) installed and therefore
    (E) installed; therefore,

44. He answered me before I had completed my question, whch annoyed me very much.

    (A) question, which annoyed me very much.
    (B) question, which annoyed me muchly.
    (C) question which annoyed me muchly.
    (D) question. His impatience annoyed me very much.
    (E) question, this annoyed me very much.

45. The reason the machine failed is because the motor had overheated.

    (A) the machine failed is because
    (B) why the machine failed is because
    (C) the machine failed is that
    (D) that the machine failed is because
    (E) for the machine's failure is because

46. No sooner had the door opened than the nurse ordered us to close it.

    (A) than the nurse ordered us to close it.
    (B) when the nurse ordered us to close it.
    (C) when the nurse orders us to close it.
    (D) then the nurse ordered us to close it.
    (E) than the nurse orders us to close it.

47. To drive a tractor, your patience must match your skill.

    (A) To drive a tractor, your patience must match your skill.
    (B) When you drive a tractor, your patience must match your skill.
    (C) When driving a tractor, your patience must match your skill.
    (D) To drive a tractor; your patience must match your skill.
    (E) Driving a tractor, your patience must match your skill.

48. No one, including Harriet and I, have the right to make this decision for him,

    (A) one, including Harriet and I, have
    (B) one, including Harriet and me, have
    (C) one including Harriet and I have
    (D) one, including Harriet and me have
    (E) one, including Harriet and me, has

49. Your results <u>must be as good or even better than</u> those of your predecessor.

(A) must be as good or even better than
(B) must be as good as or even better then
(C) has to be as good or even better then
(D) must be as good as or even better than
(E) must be as good or better then

50. Not one of the <u>woman in the room smiled when the speaker used the phrase, "the man's world</u> of sports."

(A) woman in the room smiled when the speaker used the phrase, "the man's world
(B) women in the room smiles when the speaker used the phrase, "the man's world
(C) women in the room smiled when the speaker used the phrase, "the man's world
(D) woman in the room smiles when the speaker mentions, "the man's world
(E) woman in the room smiled when the speaker made mention of "the man's world

51. You must admit that he is by far a better passer <u>than any of the other players</u> on his squad.

(A) than any of the other players
(B) then any of the players
(C) then any of the other players
(D) than any of the players
(E) than any of the players'

52. <u>However difficult the task may be perseverance</u> is its own reward.

(A) However difficult the task may be perseverance
(B) However, difficult the task may be perseverance
(C) However, difficult the task may be, perseverance
(D) However difficult the task may be. Perseverance
(E) However difficult the task may be, perseverance

53. She is one of the delegates <u>who was chosen</u> to attend the convention.

(A) who was chosen
(B) who were chosen
(C) that was chosen
(D) whom was chosen
(E) which were chosen

54. <u>Because we saw the accident, the</u> judge ordered us to testify at the hearing.

(A) Because we saw the accident, the
(B) Because we saw the accident. The
(C) Because we saw the accident the
(D) Because we had seen the accident; the
(E) Because we had seen the accident, the

55. When I take into consideration all of the factors involved, I <u>neither have the inclination nor the insensitivity to interfere.</u>

(A) neither have the inclination nor the insensitivity to interfere.
(B) neither have the inclination or the insensitivity to interfere.
(C) have neither the inclination or the insensitivity to interfere.
(D) have neither the inclination nor the insensitivity to interfere.
(E) have neither inclination or the insensitivity to interfere.

56. <u>The state of the economy being what it is, I</u> feel that further commitment of fiduciary sums would be unwise at this time.

(A) The state of the economy being what it is, I
(B) The economy being what it is, I
(C) The state of the economy being what it is; I
(D) The economy being what it is I
(E) Thing being what they are. I

57. Ever since the reorganization was planned, <u>there has been too many promises made</u> and too few problems solved.

(A) there has been too many promises made
(B) there was to many promises made
(C) there had been too many promises
(D) there was too many promises made
(E) there have been too many promises made

58. After considering most carefully the arguments on both <u>sides there</u> is only one decision that could be reached.

(A) sides there
(B) sides, there
(C) sides. There
(D) sides, we realized that there
(E) sides. We concluded that there

59. The chief librarian as well as her student-aides was aware of your need for assistance.

    (A) was aware of your need for
    (B) were aware of your need for
    (C) have been aware of your need of
    (D) is aware of your need of
    (E) are aware of your need for

60. The intended victims of this crude practical joke seem to be Paul and I.

    (A) Paul and I.
    (B) I and Paul.
    (C) Paul and me.
    (D) me and Paul.
    (E) Paul or I.

61. Milton told me when I arrived I was to go directly to the office.

    (A) Milton told me when I arrived I was to go directly to the office.
    (B) Milton told me when I arrived, I was to go directly to the office.
    (C) Milton told me, when I arrived I was to go directly to the office.
    (D) Milton told me, "When I arrive I was to go directly to your office."
    (E) Milton told me I was to go directly to the office when I arrived.

62. Has any of our friends expressed his views in this matter?

    (A) Has any of our friends expressed his views in this matter?
    (B) Have any of our friends expressed his views, in this matter?
    (C) Have any of our friends expressed their views in this matter?
    (D) Has any of our friends expressed his views, in this matter?
    (E) Has any of our friends expressed views in this matter?

63. Upon receiving the letter of acceptance from the college of my choice my cup of happiness was filled to overflowing.

    (A) choice my cup of happiness was filled to overflowing.
    (B) choice. My cup of happiness was filled to overflowing.
    (C) choice, my cup of happiness was filled to overflowing.
    (D) choice, my happiness knew no bounds.
    (E) choice, I was overjoyed.

64. Marvin Aarons is the member of the group whom I think can best advise you.

    (A) whom I think can best advise you.
    (B) who I think can best advise you.
    (C) whom I think can best advice you.
    (D) whom, I think, can best advice you.
    (E) which, I think, can best advise you.

65. To be able to live with myself comfortably is more important than earning additional income.

    (A) than earning additional income.
    (B) then earning additional income.
    (C) then to earn additional income.
    (D) than earning some extra money.
    (E) than to earn additional income.

66. This fact shall remain a barrier in the way of a peaceful setting, irregardless of where the blame lays.

    (A) , irregardless of where the blame lays.
    (B) regardless of where the blame lays.
    (C) regardless of where the blame has been laid.
    (D) , regardless of where the blame lies.
    (E) irregardless of where the blame lies.

67. It is the kind of a argument that I find to painful to attempt to analyze or refute.

    (A) kind of argument that I find to painful
    (B) kind of a argument that I find too painful
    (C) kind of argument that I find too painful
    (D) kind of an argument that I find to painful
    (E) kind of an argument that I find too painful

68. "You cannot do that!" he exclaimed. "You are destroying public property!"

    (A) that!" he exclaimed. "You
    (B) that!" he exclaimed. "you
    (C) that," he exclaimed! "you
    (C) that," he exclaimed" "You
    (E) that"! he exclaimed. "You

69. Everybody except Alan and she knew the effect of the drug.

    (A) except Alan and she knew the effect
    (B) except Alan and her knew the affect
    (C) except Alan and she knew the affect
    (D) except Alan and her knew the effect
    (E) except Alan and her new the affect

70. You cannot claim that you knew nothing about this, moreover you will have to share the responsibility for affecting a cure.

    (A) , moreover
    (B) moreover
    (C) ; moreover
    (D) . However
    (E) ; moreover,

71. The set of documents that you must not loose is on the desk.

    (A) that you must not loose is on
    (B) which you must not loose is on
    (C) that you must not lose is on
    (D) that you must not lose are on
    (E) which you must not lose are on

72. I plan to bring these here notes with me to the counsel.

    (A) bring these here notes with me to the counsel.
    (B) take these notes with me to the council.
    (C) take these here notes with me to the council.
    (D) bring these notes with me to the consul.
    (E) transport these here notes with me to the council.

73. Dora is the sort of a secretary which I can trust.
    (A) sort of a secretary which I can trust.
    (B) sort of secretary who I can trust
    (C) sort of a secretary whom I can trust
    (D) sort of a secretary I can trust
    (E) sort of secretary I can trust

74. Knowing the cost of Tom's college education, his failure notice caused his parents untold anguish.

    (A) Knowing the cost of Tom's college education,
    (B) Knowing the cost of Tom's college education
    (C) Since we knew the cost of Tom's college education,
    (D) Knowing the cost of Tom's college education, we realized that
    (E) Knowing the cost of Toms' college education,

PART 3   Suggested Time: 15 Minutes
Time begun .... Time ended .... Time used ....
Did you complete the section within the time limit? ..

DIRECTIONS: Each of the following sentences is to be rephrased according to the directions that follow it. You should make only those changes that the directions require. Keep the meaning of the revised sentence as close to the meaning of the original sentence as the directions for that sentence permit.

75. To do good is merely to feed one's ego.
    Begin with *He insists that doing*.

    (A) to feed merely
    (B) merely to have fed
    (C) merely to have been feeding
    (D) feeding my ego merely
    (E) merely feeding

76. Giant turtles move so slowly on land that we often come to the conclusion that they are ill-adapted to their environment.
    Begin with *That they move so slowly*.

    (A) is the reason why
    (B) reason for our coming
    (C) conclusion; giant turtles
    (D) conclusion giant
    (E) environment, is

77. The performance scheduled for tonight may have to be postponed; the star performer was taken ill suddenly.
    Begin with *Because*.

    (A) had to be
    (B) postponing the performance
    (C) suddenly, the
    (D) would have been
    (E) ill, and the

78. If I am called in as a witness, I shall testify that no one of my friends has even seen a copy of the letter.
    Substitute *some* for *no one*.

    (A) friends, has even
    (B) friends have even
    (C) friends had even
    (D) friends even has
    (E) friends has even

79. With the approach of autumn, the nights have become cold and crisp, and the leaves of the surrounding forest are beginning to turn.
    Begin with *When the nights became*.

    (A) autumn, and the
    (B) turn with the approach
    (C) leaves began
    (D) crisp; with
    (E) autumn, the

80. We did not need an expensive survey team to tell us that Mr. Pollett is the most efficient diagnostician in our division.
Substitute *more efficient* for *the most efficient*.

(A) than any one
(B) than some of
(C) any diagnostician
(D) any other diagnostician
(E) diagnostician

81. I just do not know what he was referring to when he asked who can measure the worth of the dollars that are squandered in the name of vanity. Change *dollars* to *money*.

(A) that have been squandered
(B) squandering
(C) which has been squandered
(D) that is squandered
(E) money, which

82. It was evidenced in his disregard of our comfort that he was willing to be impatient with us.
Begin with *when*.

(A) us. It was
(B) us, and this was
(C) us and it was
(D) us; and it was
(E) us, it

83. These songs are the ones that we remember longest since they are the ones which were taught us in our childhood.
Begin with *These songs taught*.

(A) childhood are
(B) childhood; are
(C) ones. We
(D) ones, we
(E) longest are

84. Known for the excellence of its products, this fine small company employs only people living in the surrounding community.
Substitute *which is known* for *known*.

(A) company is
(B) company, which
(C) products. Employs
(D) has been employing
(E) company. Which

85. Harold insisted on continuing the journey even though he knew what my reaction would be.
Omit *even though,* and use *nevertheless*.

(A) journey, nevertheless,
(B) be; nevertheless,

(C) journey; nevertheless
(D) continuing, nevertheless,
(E) Nevertheless Harold

86. The Pulvers are the ones who will have to determine the lowest selling price since they are the owners of the property.
Omit *since they are.*

(A) price. The
(B) price, the
(C) property. The
(D) Pulvers, the
(E) ones, owners

87. Speaking before huge audiences of students, the Rhodes scholar tried to communicate to them his intense insights into world problems.
Substitute *The Rhodes scholar spoke* for *Speaking*.

(A) after he tried
(B) having tried
(C) and tried
(D) while he was trying
(E) since he tried

88. Mr. Arnold is my former college counselor, and I often turn to him for advice.
Begin with *Because*.

(A) advice, Mr. Arnold
(B) counselor, I
(C) Mr. Arnold, counselor
(D) Mr. Arnold, I
(E) advice. I

89. Fashions are not brought about by changes in man's needs, but they come about as the result of whim and chance.
Omit *they*.

(A) needs. But
(B) but coming
(C) needs, but
(D) needs, but
(E) but come

90. The task became an endless series of trials and errors when we tried to assemble the mechanism without resorting to the set of instructions.
Begin with *Without resorting*.

(A) instructions. We
(B) instructions. The
(C) errors, when
(D) mechanism when
(E) mechanism, the

PRACTICE TEST TWO

ANSWER SHEET

1 Ⓐ Ⓑ Ⓒ Ⓓ Ⓔ	31 Ⓐ Ⓑ Ⓒ Ⓓ Ⓔ	61 Ⓐ Ⓑ Ⓒ Ⓓ Ⓔ
2 Ⓐ Ⓑ Ⓒ Ⓓ Ⓔ	32 Ⓐ Ⓑ Ⓒ Ⓓ Ⓔ	62 Ⓐ Ⓑ Ⓒ Ⓓ Ⓔ
3 Ⓐ Ⓑ Ⓒ Ⓓ Ⓔ	33 Ⓐ Ⓑ Ⓒ Ⓓ Ⓔ	63 Ⓐ Ⓑ Ⓒ Ⓓ Ⓔ
4 Ⓐ Ⓑ Ⓒ Ⓓ Ⓔ	34 Ⓐ Ⓑ Ⓒ Ⓓ Ⓔ	64 Ⓐ Ⓑ Ⓒ Ⓓ Ⓔ
5 Ⓐ Ⓑ Ⓒ Ⓓ Ⓔ	35 Ⓐ Ⓑ Ⓒ Ⓓ Ⓔ	65 Ⓐ Ⓑ Ⓒ Ⓓ Ⓔ
6 Ⓐ Ⓑ Ⓒ Ⓓ Ⓔ	36 Ⓐ Ⓑ Ⓒ Ⓓ Ⓔ	66 Ⓐ Ⓑ Ⓒ Ⓓ Ⓔ
7 Ⓐ Ⓑ Ⓒ Ⓓ Ⓔ	37 Ⓐ Ⓑ Ⓒ Ⓓ Ⓔ	67 Ⓐ Ⓑ Ⓒ Ⓓ Ⓔ
8 Ⓐ Ⓑ Ⓒ Ⓓ Ⓔ	38 Ⓐ Ⓑ Ⓒ Ⓓ Ⓔ	68 Ⓐ Ⓑ Ⓒ Ⓓ Ⓔ
9 Ⓐ Ⓑ Ⓒ Ⓓ Ⓔ	39 Ⓐ Ⓑ Ⓒ Ⓓ Ⓔ	69 Ⓐ Ⓑ Ⓒ Ⓓ Ⓔ
10 Ⓐ Ⓑ Ⓒ Ⓓ Ⓔ	40 Ⓐ Ⓑ Ⓒ Ⓓ Ⓔ	70 Ⓐ Ⓑ Ⓒ Ⓓ Ⓔ
11 Ⓐ Ⓑ Ⓒ Ⓓ Ⓔ	41 Ⓐ Ⓑ Ⓒ Ⓓ Ⓔ	71 Ⓐ Ⓑ Ⓒ Ⓓ Ⓔ
12 Ⓐ Ⓑ Ⓒ Ⓓ Ⓔ	42 Ⓐ Ⓑ Ⓒ Ⓓ Ⓔ	72 Ⓐ Ⓑ Ⓒ Ⓓ Ⓔ
13 Ⓐ Ⓑ Ⓒ Ⓓ Ⓔ	43 Ⓐ Ⓑ Ⓒ Ⓓ Ⓔ	73 Ⓐ Ⓑ Ⓒ Ⓓ Ⓔ
14 Ⓐ Ⓑ Ⓒ Ⓓ Ⓔ	44 Ⓐ Ⓑ Ⓒ Ⓓ Ⓔ	74 Ⓐ Ⓑ Ⓒ Ⓓ Ⓔ
15 Ⓐ Ⓑ Ⓒ Ⓓ Ⓔ	45 Ⓐ Ⓑ Ⓒ Ⓓ Ⓔ	75 Ⓐ Ⓑ Ⓒ Ⓓ Ⓔ
16 Ⓐ Ⓑ Ⓒ Ⓓ Ⓔ	46 Ⓐ Ⓑ Ⓒ Ⓓ Ⓔ	76 Ⓐ Ⓑ Ⓒ Ⓓ Ⓔ
17 Ⓐ Ⓑ Ⓒ Ⓓ Ⓔ	47 Ⓐ Ⓑ Ⓒ Ⓓ Ⓔ	77 Ⓐ Ⓑ Ⓒ Ⓓ Ⓔ
18 Ⓐ Ⓑ Ⓒ Ⓓ Ⓔ	48 Ⓐ Ⓑ Ⓒ Ⓓ Ⓔ	78 Ⓐ Ⓑ Ⓒ Ⓓ Ⓔ
19 Ⓐ Ⓑ Ⓒ Ⓓ Ⓔ	49 Ⓐ Ⓑ Ⓒ Ⓓ Ⓔ	79 Ⓐ Ⓑ Ⓒ Ⓓ Ⓔ
20 Ⓐ Ⓑ Ⓒ Ⓓ Ⓔ	50 Ⓐ Ⓑ Ⓒ Ⓓ Ⓔ	80 Ⓐ Ⓑ Ⓒ Ⓓ Ⓔ
21 Ⓐ Ⓑ Ⓒ Ⓓ Ⓔ	51 Ⓐ Ⓑ Ⓒ Ⓓ Ⓔ	81 Ⓐ Ⓑ Ⓒ Ⓓ Ⓔ
22 Ⓐ Ⓑ Ⓒ Ⓓ Ⓔ	52 Ⓐ Ⓑ Ⓒ Ⓓ Ⓔ	82 Ⓐ Ⓑ Ⓒ Ⓓ Ⓔ
23 Ⓐ Ⓑ Ⓒ Ⓓ Ⓔ	53 Ⓐ Ⓑ Ⓒ Ⓓ Ⓔ	83 Ⓐ Ⓑ Ⓒ Ⓓ Ⓔ
24 Ⓐ Ⓑ Ⓒ Ⓓ Ⓔ	54 Ⓐ Ⓑ Ⓒ Ⓓ Ⓔ	84 Ⓐ Ⓑ Ⓒ Ⓓ Ⓔ
25 Ⓐ Ⓑ Ⓒ Ⓓ Ⓔ	55 Ⓐ Ⓑ Ⓒ Ⓓ Ⓔ	85 Ⓐ Ⓑ Ⓒ Ⓓ Ⓔ
26 Ⓐ Ⓑ Ⓒ Ⓓ Ⓔ	56 Ⓐ Ⓑ Ⓒ Ⓓ Ⓔ	86 Ⓐ Ⓑ Ⓒ Ⓓ Ⓔ
27 Ⓐ Ⓑ Ⓒ Ⓓ Ⓔ	57 Ⓐ Ⓑ Ⓒ Ⓓ Ⓔ	87 Ⓐ Ⓑ Ⓒ Ⓓ Ⓔ
28 Ⓐ Ⓑ Ⓒ Ⓓ Ⓔ	58 Ⓐ Ⓑ Ⓒ Ⓓ Ⓔ	88 Ⓐ Ⓑ Ⓒ Ⓓ Ⓔ
29 Ⓐ Ⓑ Ⓒ Ⓓ Ⓔ	59 Ⓐ Ⓑ Ⓒ Ⓓ Ⓔ	89 Ⓐ Ⓑ Ⓒ Ⓓ Ⓔ
30 Ⓐ Ⓑ Ⓒ Ⓓ Ⓔ	60 Ⓐ Ⓑ Ⓒ Ⓓ Ⓔ	90 Ⓐ Ⓑ Ⓒ Ⓓ Ⓔ

PRACTICE TEST TWO

Total Time: One Hour
PART 1   *Suggested Time:* **20** *Minutes*
Time begun .... Time ended .... Time used ....
Did you complete the section within the time limit? ..

DIRECTIONS: The following sentences contain problems in grammar, usage, diction (choice of words), and idiom.

Some sentences are correct.

No sentence contains more than one error.

You will find that the error, if there is one, is underlined and lettered. Assume that all other elements of the sentence are correct and cannot be changed. In choosing answers, follow the requirements of standard written English.

If there is an error, select the one underlined part that must be changed in order to make the sentence correct, and blacken the corresponding space on the answer sheet.

If there is no error, mark answer space E.

1. We felt like we had lost a friend when the fore-
   (A)   (B)
   man along with his four assistants was
                                      (C)
   summarily discharged. No error
   (D)   (E)

2. Except you follow directions, the set of books
   (A)   (B)
   which are now on the shelves is going to be as-
        (C)   (D)
   signed to another class. No error
                            (E)

3. I insist that there are less errors being made in
                      (A) (B)   (C)
   our division than in yours. No error
                        (D)   (E)

4. Coming into the room, we sensed quickly that
                          (A)   (B)
   they were sly, ignorant, and not to be depended
        (C)   (D)
   upon.

5. Anyone who thinks that I am in back of all of
                (A)   (B)
   this planning is reckoning in the wrong set of
                    (C)   (D)
   books. No error
          (E)

6. His contention is that clothes does not make
                  (A)   (B)
   the man; consequently, I do not see how
                (C)
   you can convince him to buy that new suit.
       (D)
   No error
   (E)

7. The moment at which Albert and she could
                                   (A)
   have interfered was when the car left
   (B)   (C)
   without us . No error
           (D)   (E)

8. I truly believe many aspects of witchcraft, but I
                       (A)
   doubt that they ride on broomsticks. No error
         (B) (C)   (D)   (E)

9. Either Jane or her brother is to be here
                              (A)
   inside of ten minutes to speak to you
   (B)
   in regard to the kind of reception we should be
   (C)   (D)
   planning. No error
             (E)

10. The summer residents of Luzerne, they told the
                                      (A)
    supervisor to let matters lie just as they are for
                     (B)   (C) (D)
    the time being. No error
                    (E)

11. All that they could see were their chances of
                             (A)   (B)
    losing out without support from you and us .
    (C)   (D)
    No error
    (E)

12. If they had only listened to me, we
             (A) (B)
    would have seen a most interesting film ,
    (C)   (D)
    because he was prepared to show it to us at that
    time. No error
          (E)

13. Helen, one of the women in the office, told
                                                    (A)
    Mrs. Mackey that she had mistakenly identified
                           (B)   (C)
    the wrong person. No error
              (D)   (E)

14. The advise that he gave us to accept your apol-
        (A)   (B)
    ogies was altogether unfortunate and should
                  (C)
    have in no way affected our decision.
               (D)
    No error
      (E)

15. Neither of the boys who have been helping us
                            (A)
    knows when this game will be over with.
     (B)   (C) (D)
    No error
      (E)

16. Standing beside the machine , we could not
              (A)   (B) (C)
    identify any of the occupants except Lucy and

    her. No error
    (D)   (E)

17. Whenever we watch an exciting television
    program , the main concern of my cousin is
                    (A)   (B)
    whether the advertisement will break in before
     (C)   (D)
    or after the big rescue scene. No error
                                    (E)

18. Neither of the applicants have the necessary tech-
                            (A)   (B)
    nical knowledge that would make accidents
                          (C)
    preventable. No error
      (D)   (E)

19. The counsel for the defense complemented
        (A)   (B)
    Joyce's father for his disinterested presentation
                      (C)   (D)
    when he was a witness giving testimony.
    No error
      (E)

20. The porter told us that he had not felt good when
                             (A)   (B)
    the effect of the injection finally wore off.
        (C)   (D)
    No error
      (E)

21. I shall repeat again the main point of my ar-
                    (A)
    gument: the danger that faces us can hardly be
                   (B)   (C)
    overcome by men of good will without training
     (D)
    in the tactics of modern warfare. No error
                                      (E)

22. This sort of nonsense usually appeals to those
         (A)
    students who I referred to earlier in this article.
             (B)   (C) (D)
    No error
      (E)

23. Please try and understand, there was so little
                (A)   (B) (C)
    that we guards were able to do to prevent such
         (D)
    an outbreak. No error
                  (E)

24. One of the workers has hung the curtains that
                        (A) (B)
    had been laying on the floor. No error
    (C)   (D)   (E)

25. This never would have happened if you
                       (A)
    would have given me the moment of advice that I
             (B)   (C)
    had asked for. No error
         (D)   (E)

26. Victor commented: "Let's end this petty
                        (A)
    quarreling ; there's so many things that we
                 (B)
    really have to be doing!" No error
     (C) (D)   (E)

27. Neither Edna nor her sisters knows to whom
                  (A)   (B)   (C)
    this kind of note must be sent. No error
         (D)   (E)

28. The ending is so different <u>from</u> the one that you
                              (A)
    and I <u>am</u> willing to <u>accept</u>, even in a
          (B)   (C)
    <u>third-rate</u> story. <u>No error</u>
        (D)   (E)

29. <u>Take</u> this book to the <u>principal</u>, <u>who</u> was so
    (A)   (B)   (C)
    <u>aggravated</u> when he discovered that it had been
       (D)
    borrowed without his permission. <u>No error</u>
                                       (E)

30. Since one of the teachers <u>has</u> objected to <u>him</u>
                              (A)   (B)
    having the <u>main</u> <u>role</u> in the varsity play, we have
               (C)   (D)
    had to make a last-minute substitution.
    <u>No error</u>
       (E)

31. If you <u>would have</u> listened, you <u>too</u> would have
           (A)   (B)
    concluded that Peter <u>is</u> more capable than <u>any</u>
                         (C)   (D)
    other boy in his class. <u>No error</u>
                              (E)

32. I had not <u>drank</u> more than <u>half</u> the coffee in the
              (A)   (B)
    container <u>when</u> the alarm sounded <u>,</u> sending
              (C)   (D)
    me hurtling through space! <u>No error</u>
                                 (E)

33. At forty, <u>his career</u> as an artist <u>had come</u> to an
             (A)   (B)
    abrupt end when he <u>suffered</u> severe injuries <u>in</u> a
                       (C)   (D)
    freak fall. <u>No error</u>
                  (E)

PART 2 *Suggested Time: 20 Minutes*
Time begun .... Time ended .... Time used ....
Did you complete the section within the time limit? ..

DIRECTIONS: In each of the following sentences,
some part of the sentence or the entire sentence is
underlined. Beneath each sentence you will find five
ways of phrasing the underlined part. The first of
these repeats the original; the other four are different. If you think the original is better than any of

the alternatives, choose answer A; otherwise
choose one of the others. Select the best version
and blacken the corresponding space on your answer sheet.

This is a test of correctness and effectiveness of
expression. In choosing answers, follow the requirements of standard written English; that is, pay attention to grammar, choice of words, sentence construction, and punctuation. Choose the answer that
best expresses the meaning of the original sentence.
Your choice should produce the most effective sentence—clear and precise, without awkwardness or
ambiguity.

34. They <u>must either choose the plans we proposed</u>
    or the ones approved by the preceding admin-
    istration.

    (A) must either choose the plans we proposed
    (B) either must choose the plans we proposed
    (C) must choose either the plans we proposed
    (D) either have to chose the plans we proposed
    (E) have either to choose the plans we pro-
        posed

35. <u>If the official would have consulted his staff, this</u>
    embarrassing situation would never have
    arisen.

    (A) If the official would have consulted his
        staff, this
    (B) If the official would have consulted his staff
        this
    (C) If the official would have consulted his
        staff. This
    (D) If the official were to consult his staff, this
    (E) If the official had consulted his staff, this

36. The contractor <u>hoped to have completed</u> the
    building on schedule, but the floods were dis-
    rupting deliveries of supplies.

    (A) hoped to have completed
    (B) had hoped to complete
    (C) had hoped to have completed
    (D) would have completed
    (E) could have completed

37. Due to his carelessness, the form of the data is
    <u>different from what</u> the computer can assimi-
    late.

    (A) Due to his carelessness, the form of the data
        is different from what
    (B) Because of his carelessness, the form of the
        data is different from what

(C) Due to his carelessness. The form of the data is different from what
(D) Due to his carelessness, the form of the data are different from that which
(E) Because of his carelessness, the form of the data is different than that which

38. They claimed that it was the responsibility of us students to see that no one of the intruders were admitted.

(A) us students to see that no one of the intruders were
(B) us students, to see that not one of the intruders were
(C) we students, to see that no one of the intruders were
(D) us students to see that no one of the intruders was
(E) we students to see that no one of the intruders was

39. My family lived in this town for three generations.

(A) lived in this town
(B) is living in this town
(C) is living in this here town
(D) has been living in this here town
(E) has lived in this town

40. The salesman assured us that if we placed the order by nine we could have the car fully equipped.

(A) that if we placed the order by nine
(B) that, if we placed the order by nine;
(C) that if we had placed the order by nine
(D) that if we were to place the order by nine
(E) that if by nine we had placed the order

41. The director stated that he had never been consulted on the changes before they were made.

(A) he had never been consulted on the changes before they were made.
(B) he was never consulted on the changes before they had been made.
(C) he had never been consulted on the changes before they had been made.
(D) he was never consulted on the changes before they were made.
(E) he was never consulted on the changes, before they were being made.

42. When in doubt, the best approach is to consult an expert.

(A) When in doubt, the
(B) When in doubt the
(C) When you are in doubt, the
(D) When you are in doubt the
(E) When one is in doubt; the

43. There must be a moral to this story, but somehow it eludes me.

(A) moral to this story, but somehow it
(B) moral to this story but somehow it
(C) moral to this story, however, it somehow
(D) moral to this story because it
(E) moral to this story. Since it somehow

44. Everyone of her classmates except Edna and me were invited to the gathering.

(A) except Edna and me were invited
(B) except Edna and I was invited
(C) except Edna and me was
(D) accept Edna and me were
(E) except Edna and I, were

45. Statistics the invention of devils and saints can easily confuse us into inactivity.

(A) Statistics the invention of devils and saints can
(B) Statistics, the invention of devils and saints, can
(C) Statistics are the invention of devils and saints, and can
(D) Statistics, the invention of devils and saints can
(E) Statistics—the invention of devils and saints, can

46. You hadn't ought to have said that the candidate must be him.

(A) You hadn't ought to have said that the candidate must be him.
(B) You hadn't ought to say that he must be the candidate.
(C) You shouldn't have said that the candidate must be him.
(D) You hadn't ought to have said that the candidate must be he.
(E) You should not have said that the candidate must be he.

47. At thirty, his reputation for honesty and forth-rightness was one of his most valuable business assets.

(A) At thirty, his reputation for honesty and forthrightness was
(B) On reaching thirty, his reputation for honesty and forthrightness was
(C) When he was thirty, his reputation for honesty and forthrightness was
(D) When he reached his thirtieth birthday, he was known for the honesty and forthrightness which were
(E) By the time he was thirty, his reputation for honesty and forthrightness were

48. If I was the chairperson, I would never have tolerated such rowdyism and flagrant disregard of decorum.

(A) If I was the chairperson, I
(B) If I were the chairperson. I
(C) If I had been the chairperson, I
(D) If I am chosen as chairperson, I
(E) If I was the chairperson; I

49. This pottery is better or at least equal to the very best that was produced in the last generation.

(A) better or at least equal to
(B) better than or at least equal to
(C) at least better than or equal to
(D) at least better or equal to
(E) better or at least the equal to

50. Having worked beside him for years, his decision to leave the firm does not surprise me.

(A) Having worked beside him for years, his
(B) Having worked beside him for years. His
(C) Having worked beside him for years his
(D) Since I had worked beside him for years, his
(E) Because of my having worked besides him for years, his

51. His reasoning during the discussion was logical, clear, and with much persuasive power.

(A) was logical, clear, and with much persuasive power.
(B) logical and clear and with much persuasive power.
(C) logical, clear, and highly persuasive.
(D) logical, clear; and highly persuasive power.
(E) logical, clear, and with much persuasion.

52. The slow solemn strains of the organ music flooded the room; it was a time for quiet meditation.

(A) room; it was
(B) room, and it was
(C) room, when it was
(D) room since it became
(E) room while it was

53. There never has been as far as I know any other short story collections to match these.

(A) There never has been as far as I know any
(B) Never has there been, as far as I know, any
(C) There never have been as far as I know
(D) Never has there been as far as I know any
(E) There never could have been—as far as I know—any

54. Without him helping us, everyone in our squad know that we could never have succeeded.

(A) Without him helping us, everyone in our squad know that
(B) Without him helping us everyone in our squad knows that
(C) Unless he helped, everyone in our squad know that
(D) Without help from him everyone in the squad knows that
(E) Without his help, everyone in our squad knows that

55. We not only enjoyed seeing our relatives but also visiting their homes.

(A) We not only enjoyed seeing our relatives but also visiting their homes.
(B) We not only enjoyed seeing our relatives but also to visit their homes.
(C) We not only enjoyed to see our relatives, but also to visit their homes.
(D) We enjoyed seeing our relatives and to visit their homes.
(E) We enjoyed not only seeing our relatives but also visiting their homes.

56. Because of the weakness of the UN, man's inhumanity to man reigns unabated.

(A) Because of the weakness of the UN, man's
(B) Because of the weakness of the UN. Man's
(C) Because of the weakness of the UN mans'
(D) Due to the weakness of the UN man's
(E) The weakness of the UN causes mans'

57. <u>Neither Sheldon nor I is</u> ready to decide who is to be the winner.

(A) Neither Sheldon nor I is ready to decide who is
(B) Neither Sheldon nor I is ready to decide whom is
(C) Neither Sheldon or I is ready to decide who is
(D) Neither Sheldon nor I am ready to decide who is
(E) Neither Sheldon or me is ready to decide who is

58. <u>He accepted full responsibility for something he had not done, which</u> surprised me very much.

(A) He accepted full responsibility for something he had not done, which
(B) His accepting full responsibility for something he had not done
(C) He excepted responsibility for something he had not done, which
(D) He accepted responsibility for something he had not done, this
(E) He accepted responsibility for something he had not done; which

59. <u>Had he spoken up, there</u> would have been no confusion.

(A) Had he spoken up, there
(B) He could have spoken up, so that there
(C) If he would have spoken up, there
(D) Had he spoken up; there
(E) If he were to speak up, there

60. The most exciting scene <u>is when the countdown begins.</u>

(A) is when the countdown begins.
(B) was when the countdown begins.
(C) occurs when the countdown begins.
(D) is where the countdown began.
(E) is where the countdown begins.

61. <u>My parents lived in that house before I was born!</u>

(A) My parents lived in that house before I was born!
(B) My parents had lived in that house before I was born!
(C) Before I was born my parents lived in that house!

(D) My parents lived in that house, before I was born!
(E) Before I was born, my parents lived in that house!

62. <u>Being Harriet had warned me, I was</u> not surprised by what I saw.

(A) Being Harriet had warned me, I was
(B) Being Harriet warned me, I am
(C) Since Harriet warned me, I am
(D) Since Harriet had warned me, I was
(E) Being Harriet warned me, I was

63. Feigning illness, procrastinating at every opportunity, and <u>without any of the controls that truth sets,</u> he amazed us by retaining the job for three whole days!

(A) without any of the controls that truth sets, he
(B) without the controls that truth sets. He
(C) prevaricating constantly, he
(D) without the controls the truth sets; he
(E) by lying, he

PART 3 *Suggested Time: 20 Minutes*
Time begun .... Time ended .... Time used ....
Did you complete the section within the time limit? ..

DIRECTIONS: Each of the following sentences is to be rephrased according to the directions that follow it. <u>You should make only those changes that the directions require.</u> Keep the meaning of the revised sentence as close to the meaning of the original sentence as the directions for that sentence permit.

If you think that more than one good sentence can be made according to the directions, select the sentence that

retains, insofar as possible, the meaning of the original sentence;

is most natural in phrasing and construction;

meets the requirements of standard written English; and is the best sentence in terms of conciseness, idiom, logic, and other qualities found in well-written sentences.

64. Everyone of the men caught in the deadly trap will be remembered as heroes who died for their countrymen.
Begin with We will remember.

(A) were caught
(B) men, who
(C) had been caught
(D) remember, everyone
(E) trap, as

65. Calling him a falsifier did not help to make our relationships any the more cordial.
Begin with I had not helped.

(A) by having called him
(B) by calling him
(C) falsifier I had
(D) because I could have called
(E) although I called

66. The new evidence along with the facts that had been gathered for the earlier trial is sufficient to free him.
Change along with to and.

(A) facts, that
(B) facts, which
(C) evidence, and
(D) trial, is
(E) trial are

67. Hoping to end the tournament quickly, the champion defeated his first opponent in straight sets.
Begin with His first opponent was defeated.

(A) champion, who
(B) who had hoped
(C) quickly in straight sets
(D) sets, by
(E) champion, he

68. Konner is one of those men who have devoted a lifetime to the study of past cultures.
Substitute a man for one of those men.

(A) to have devoted
(B) who has
(C) that have
(D) devoting
(E) , devoting

69. Paul and Dave have been selected to represent us at the conference.

Substitute Either Paul or Dave for Paul and Dave.

(A) have been selected
(B) had been selected
(C) were selected
(D) has been selected
(E) is selected

70. Bill told Margie, "You are to leave at ten to-night."
Substitute Margie that she for Margie, "You.

(A) is to leave
(B) could leave
(C) had to leave
(D) was leaving
(E) should have left

71. This model, like all the others that preceded it, is too bulky and fragile.
Substitute and its predecessors for like all the others that preceded it.

(A) model, and
(B) which are
(C) predecessors, is
(D) are too
(E) had been too

72. Mahogany is the best wood for making this type of castanet.
Substitute better than for the best.

(A) any other
(B) any wood
(C) could be
(D) type of a
(E) wood, for

73. I read all the directions, and I could find no mention of a set of gears.
Use the present thought sequence, and begin with Although.

(A) I read
(B) I would read
(C) I was reading
(D) I am reading
(E) directions I

74. To be able to sing like Joan Sutherland is beyond my wildest dream.
Begin with I cannot imagine.

(A) as Joan Sutherland
(B) ever being able

(C) never being able
(D) Sutherland's singing
(E) my having been able

75. He answered me in anger, a fact that irritated me very much.
Begin with His answering.

(A) which
(B) I was very much irritated
(C) anger he
(D) the fact
(E) anger irritated

76. They came into the house and were greeted by the visitor from their hometown.
Begin with The visitor who had just arrived.

(A) greeted from their hometown
(B) when they had come
(C) from his hometown
(D) when they did come
(E) greeted them

77. If you had listened to me, we could have completed the project in record time.
Change If to Because.

(A) completed
(B) should have completed
(C) had been completing
(D) would have been able to complete
(E) you would have listened

78. Both Edna and her sisters are insisting that we join them in the hike.
Change Both Edna and to Edna along with.

(A) had been insisting
(B) sisters,
(C) is insisting
(D) insisting. We
(E) insisting, we

79. They carried out 45 painstaking experiments, and then they finally succeeded in synthesizing the enzyme.
Begin with Only after.

(A) ; and then
(B) they carried
(C) , did they
(D) they had finally
(E) they synthesized

80. When we viewed the substance without the aid of the microscope, it seemed no different from any other colorless liquid.
Substitute Viewing for When we viewed.

(A) microscope, it
(B) microscope it
(C) different than
(D) it had seemed
(E) we found it

81. It turned out to be one of those toys that glut the market for a short while and then disappear.
Substitute a toy for one of those toys.

(A) disappears
(B) and then would disappear
(C) , and then they disappear
(D) glut the market
(E) could glut

82. It was a secret that was well kept, known to everyone except Edna and me.
Substitute but for except.

(A) well-kept
(B) everyone,
(C) and I
(D) me
(E) secret, that

83. The child whose personality traits do not match the values of his society is not likely to be well adjusted.
Substitute who has for whose.

(A) child, whose
(B) society, is
(C) who do not
(D) that have not
(E) which do not

84. Coming at the end of a long string of disappointments, this failure was more than I could bear. Begin with I could not bear.

(A) bear which
(B) failure, coming
(C) failure coming
(D) which could come
(E) more failure

85. A minority culture striving to maintain a viable and creative presence in the midst of a rich majority culture will inevitably find itself in a constant state of war.
Begin with A minority culture inevitably finds itself.

(A) majority culture striving
(B) when it strives
(C) if it would strive
(D) war striving
(E) war when striving

86. Except for the faded green of its foliage, the scenery is all in black and white in order to challenge the story's main characters with the cruelty of nature and the bleakness of death.
Begin with In order to challenge.

(A) challenge, except
(B) foliage the
(C) death, except
(D) which is all
(E) because it is all

87. Man with all the resources at his command is unable to prevent war from making a mockery of all of his pious utterings.
Begin with War still makes.

(A) despite
(B) man and all his resources
(C) man who has
(D) utterings;
(E) , considering

88. Many critics argue that the only sound criterion for banning strikes should be the essentiality of the service at stake, whether in the public or private sector.
Begin with The essentiality of the service.

(A) argue many critics
(B) sector is
(C) according to
(D) which is argued by
(E) could be considered

89. Interpolated into the main story is a set of lurid tales told by each of the major characters.
Begin with Each of the major characters.

(A) have told
(B) are interpolated
(C) that is
(D) which could have been
(E) are a

90. The two themes in this brief essay stress the dramatic psychological growth that occurs in the opening years and the importance of the parent-child relationship for that growth.
Substitute One of the two themes for The two themes.

(A) themes,
(B) that had occurred
(C) but the other
(D) years while
(E) years because

ANSWER KEY AND ANALYSIS OF ANSWERS / *Page 108*

PRACTICE TEST THREE

ANSWER SHEET

1	Ⓐ Ⓑ Ⓒ Ⓓ Ⓔ	31	Ⓐ Ⓑ Ⓒ Ⓓ Ⓔ	61	Ⓐ Ⓑ Ⓒ Ⓓ Ⓔ
2	Ⓐ Ⓑ Ⓒ Ⓓ Ⓔ	32	Ⓐ Ⓑ Ⓒ Ⓓ Ⓔ	62	Ⓐ Ⓑ Ⓒ Ⓓ Ⓔ
3	Ⓐ Ⓑ Ⓒ Ⓓ Ⓔ	33	Ⓐ Ⓑ Ⓒ Ⓓ Ⓔ	63	Ⓐ Ⓑ Ⓒ Ⓓ Ⓔ
4	Ⓐ Ⓑ Ⓒ Ⓓ Ⓔ	34	Ⓐ Ⓑ Ⓒ Ⓓ Ⓔ	64	Ⓐ Ⓑ Ⓒ Ⓓ Ⓔ
5	Ⓐ Ⓑ Ⓒ Ⓓ Ⓔ	35	Ⓐ Ⓑ Ⓒ Ⓓ Ⓔ	65	Ⓐ Ⓑ Ⓒ Ⓓ Ⓔ
6	Ⓐ Ⓑ Ⓒ Ⓓ Ⓔ	36	Ⓐ Ⓑ Ⓒ Ⓓ Ⓔ	66	Ⓐ Ⓑ Ⓒ Ⓓ Ⓔ
7	Ⓐ Ⓑ Ⓒ Ⓓ Ⓔ	37	Ⓐ Ⓑ Ⓒ Ⓓ Ⓔ	67	Ⓐ Ⓑ Ⓒ Ⓓ Ⓔ
8	Ⓐ Ⓑ Ⓒ Ⓓ Ⓔ	38	Ⓐ Ⓑ Ⓒ Ⓓ Ⓔ	68	Ⓐ Ⓑ Ⓒ Ⓓ Ⓔ
9	Ⓐ Ⓑ Ⓒ Ⓓ Ⓔ	39	Ⓐ Ⓑ Ⓒ Ⓓ Ⓔ	69	Ⓐ Ⓑ Ⓒ Ⓓ Ⓔ
10	Ⓐ Ⓑ Ⓒ Ⓓ Ⓔ	40	Ⓐ Ⓑ Ⓒ Ⓓ Ⓔ	70	Ⓐ Ⓑ Ⓒ Ⓓ Ⓔ
11	Ⓐ Ⓑ Ⓒ Ⓓ Ⓔ	41	Ⓐ Ⓑ Ⓒ Ⓓ Ⓔ	71	Ⓐ Ⓑ Ⓒ Ⓓ Ⓔ
12	Ⓐ Ⓑ Ⓒ Ⓓ Ⓔ	42	Ⓐ Ⓑ Ⓒ Ⓓ Ⓔ	72	Ⓐ Ⓑ Ⓒ Ⓓ Ⓔ
13	Ⓐ Ⓑ Ⓒ Ⓓ Ⓔ	43	Ⓐ Ⓑ Ⓒ Ⓓ Ⓔ	73	Ⓐ Ⓑ Ⓒ Ⓓ Ⓔ
14	Ⓐ Ⓑ Ⓒ Ⓓ Ⓔ	44	Ⓐ Ⓑ Ⓒ Ⓓ Ⓔ	74	Ⓐ Ⓑ Ⓒ Ⓓ Ⓔ
15	Ⓐ Ⓑ Ⓒ Ⓓ Ⓔ	45	Ⓐ Ⓑ Ⓒ Ⓓ Ⓔ	75	Ⓐ Ⓑ Ⓒ Ⓓ Ⓔ
16	Ⓐ Ⓑ Ⓒ Ⓓ Ⓔ	46	Ⓐ Ⓑ Ⓒ Ⓓ Ⓔ	76	Ⓐ Ⓑ Ⓒ Ⓓ Ⓔ
17	Ⓐ Ⓑ Ⓒ Ⓓ Ⓔ	47	Ⓐ Ⓑ Ⓒ Ⓓ Ⓔ	77	Ⓐ Ⓑ Ⓒ Ⓓ Ⓔ
18	Ⓐ Ⓑ Ⓒ Ⓓ Ⓔ	48	Ⓐ Ⓑ Ⓒ Ⓓ Ⓔ	78	Ⓐ Ⓑ Ⓒ Ⓓ Ⓔ
19	Ⓐ Ⓑ Ⓒ Ⓓ Ⓔ	49	Ⓐ Ⓑ Ⓒ Ⓓ Ⓔ	79	Ⓐ Ⓑ Ⓒ Ⓓ Ⓔ
20	Ⓐ Ⓑ Ⓒ Ⓓ Ⓔ	50	Ⓐ Ⓑ Ⓒ Ⓓ Ⓔ	80	Ⓐ Ⓑ Ⓒ Ⓓ Ⓔ
21	Ⓐ Ⓑ Ⓒ Ⓓ Ⓔ	51	Ⓐ Ⓑ Ⓒ Ⓓ Ⓔ	81	Ⓐ Ⓑ Ⓒ Ⓓ Ⓔ
22	Ⓐ Ⓑ Ⓒ Ⓓ Ⓔ	52	Ⓐ Ⓑ Ⓒ Ⓓ Ⓔ	82	Ⓐ Ⓑ Ⓒ Ⓓ Ⓔ
23	Ⓐ Ⓑ Ⓒ Ⓓ Ⓔ	53	Ⓐ Ⓑ Ⓒ Ⓓ Ⓔ	83	Ⓐ Ⓑ Ⓒ Ⓓ Ⓔ
24	Ⓐ Ⓑ Ⓒ Ⓓ Ⓔ	54	Ⓐ Ⓑ Ⓒ Ⓓ Ⓔ	84	Ⓐ Ⓑ Ⓒ Ⓓ Ⓔ
25	Ⓐ Ⓑ Ⓒ Ⓓ Ⓔ	55	Ⓐ Ⓑ Ⓒ Ⓓ Ⓔ	85	Ⓐ Ⓑ Ⓒ Ⓓ Ⓔ
26	Ⓐ Ⓑ Ⓒ Ⓓ Ⓔ	56	Ⓐ Ⓑ Ⓒ Ⓓ Ⓔ	86	Ⓐ Ⓑ Ⓒ Ⓓ Ⓔ
27	Ⓐ Ⓑ Ⓒ Ⓓ Ⓔ	57	Ⓐ Ⓑ Ⓒ Ⓓ Ⓔ	87	Ⓐ Ⓑ Ⓒ Ⓓ Ⓔ
28	Ⓐ Ⓑ Ⓒ Ⓓ Ⓔ	58	Ⓐ Ⓑ Ⓒ Ⓓ Ⓔ	88	Ⓐ Ⓑ Ⓒ Ⓓ Ⓔ
29	Ⓐ Ⓑ Ⓒ Ⓓ Ⓔ	59	Ⓐ Ⓑ Ⓒ Ⓓ Ⓔ	89	Ⓐ Ⓑ Ⓒ Ⓓ Ⓔ
30	Ⓐ Ⓑ Ⓒ Ⓓ Ⓔ	60	Ⓐ Ⓑ Ⓒ Ⓓ Ⓔ	90	Ⓐ Ⓑ Ⓒ Ⓓ Ⓔ

PRACTICE TEST THREE

Total Time: One Hour
PART 1   *Suggested Time: 25 Minutes*
Time begun .... Time ended .... Time used ....
Did you complete the section within the time limit? ..

DIRECTIONS: The following sentences contain problems in grammar, usage, diction (choice of words), and idiom.

  Some sentences are correct.

  No sentence contains more than one error.

  You will find that the error, if there is one, is underlined and lettered. Assume that all other elements of the sentence are correct and cannot be changed. In choosing answers, follow the requirements of standard written English.

  If there is an error, select the one underlined part that must be changed in order to make the sentence correct, and blacken the corresponding space on the answer sheet.

  If there is no error, mark answer space E.

1. Because we <u>had</u> left early , there <u>were</u> three
         (A)   (B)
   items included in the agenda <u>without</u> <u>us</u> having
                                    (C)   (D)
   a chance to vote for or against them. <u>No error</u>
                                              (E)

2. They are not <u>so</u> willing <u>as</u> <u>us</u> to have this pic-
                  (A)   (B) (C)
   ture <u>hung</u> in the corridor. <u>No error</u>
          (D)   (E)

3. Everyone <u>except</u> <u>her</u> realized that the data
                (A)   (B)
   <u>were</u> different <u>than</u> the professor had antici-
    (C)   (D)
   pated. <u>No error</u>
              (E)

4. Between you and <u>me</u>, neither Paul nor Frances
                      (A)
   <u>knows</u> to <u>whom</u> this letter should be
     (B)   (C)
   addressed <u>to</u> . <u>No error</u>
                (D)   (E)

5. I am <u>positive</u> that the cat had not <u>drank</u> all of
              (A)   (B)
   <u>its</u> milk before the alarm <u>was</u> sounded.
    (C)   (D)
   <u>No error</u>
      (E)

6. <u>All together</u> there <u>have</u> been three <u>cases</u> of ty-
      (A)   (B)   (C)
   phus reported during the <u>past</u> two weeks.
                                (D)
   <u>No error</u>
      (E)

7. They <u>reassured</u> us that it is <u>I</u> who <u>am</u> to be
             (A)   (B)   (C)
   <u>their</u> choice for candidate. <u>No error</u>
      (D)   (E)

8. The coach <u>emphasized</u> that all <u>we</u> varsity play-
                  (A)   (B)
   ers must <u>cooperate</u> with <u>each other</u>. <u>No error</u>
                (C)   (D)   (E)

9. <u>Regardless</u> of <u>whom</u> he thinks is guilty, I <u>shall</u>
      (A)   (B)   (C)
   never for a moment consider that it could be
   <u>she</u>. <u>No error</u>
    (D)   (E)

10. To read a poem well, <u>your</u> <u>attention</u> must
                            (A)   (B)
    <u>center</u> <u>upon</u> the mood created by the thought
      (C)   (D)
    patterns developed by the poet. <u>No error</u>
                                        (E)

11. <u>There</u> is no doubt <u>but</u> that ham and eggs <u>is</u> the
      (A)   (B)   (C)
    favorite <u>morning</u> food of many Americans.
                (D)
    <u>No error</u>
       (E)

12. <u>To me</u>, the <u>exercise</u> of my right to vote <u>has</u>
      (A)   (B)   (C)
    always been a responsibility and <u>necessary</u>.
                                         (D)
    <u>No error</u>
       (E)

13. The set of twelve books that <u>were</u> written in Erse
                                    (A)
    were <u>almost</u> <u>lost</u> <u>during</u> the moving. <u>No error</u>
           (B)   (C)   (D)   (E)

14. The <u>male</u> willingness to avoid foods with
           (A)
    <u>high-fat</u> content is a <u>healthful</u> sign in the
       (B)   (C)
    <u>national welfare</u> picture. <u>No error</u>
       (D)   (E)

15. Suzie, the tallest of the three speakers, was the
       (A) (B)   (C)
one who hadn't ought to be the first one called
          (D)
upon to address the group. No error
                            (E)

16. Whenever he comes into the room, his older sis-
              (A)   (B) (C)
ter finds any excuse to leave immediately.
                           (D)
No error
(E)

17. This group, among whom are Jean and
                  (A)   (B)
Eadie, certainly were the life of the party.
      (C)   (D)
No error
(E)

18. It's an occurrence most unique in the annals of
(A)   (B)   (C)
our club's long existence. No error
(D)   (E)

19. One must be very careful to do his work step
                (A)   (B)
by step lest you attempt more than can be done
      (C) (D)
within the given time limits. No error
                 (E)

20. "I have never before in my life," she
           (A)   (B)   (C)
shouted, "seen such a disregard of the rights
      (D)
of others!" No error
(E)

21. Neither Alan nor his classmates enjoy the
      (A)   (B)
kind of a display that you have been planning.
(C)   (D)
No error
(E)

22. The officer told the private that he would have
                  (A)
to lie where he had fallen until the arrival of
   (B)   (C)
an ambulance. No error
(D)   (E)

23. There is hardly any reason for you to feel
          (A)
badly and blame yourself for this mishap.
(B)   (C)   (D)
No error
(E)

24. Being that he is sensible, you're going to find
(A)   (B)
that it is he who will assume most of the re-
     (C)   (D)
sponsibility. No error
(E)

25. Put the book that is now lying on the shelf in the
            (A) (B)   (C)
closet before Edna returns. No error
          (D)   (E)

26. Of course, we shall have to agree with you
   (A)   (B)   (C)
when you say that he is taller than any boy in
                    (D)
his class. No error
(E)

27. Coming to the affects of the Civil War upon
      (A)
industry, I shall merely say in passing that
     (B)   (C)   (D)
much more research is needed in this area.
No error
(E)

28. Being tired, Herb listened heedlessly to the
(A)   (B)
words that had sounded so meaningfully to him
         (C)
only a brief two hours before. No error
(D)   (E)

29. We agreed that two thirds of the class suffers
                (A)
because their spelling and sentence structure are
                (B)
not good, but most of it is due to carelessness.
        (C)   (D)
No error
(E)

30. In the meantime, my brother and I, we
   (A)   (B) (C)
had attended to the most pressing of the matters
(D)
on hand. No error
(E)

31. Whoever has been responsible for this
    (A)
    mistake , regardless of who he is, shall be pun-
               (B)   (C)
    ished most severely by the provost and I .
                                            (D)

    No error
    (E)

32. Before baking a cake, you should list, gather, and
    (A)   (B)   (C)
    measure the ingredients. No error
    (D)   (E)

33. If you would have listened to me, no one but
          (A)
    me would have been involved in this experience
    (B)   (C)
    which has taken such a toll of our energy.
    (D)
    No error
    (E)

34. They had not come but once before; yet they
         (A)   (B)   (C)
    were able to negotiate the difficult trail without
                                      (D)

    difficulty. No error
                (E)

35. When the three brothers spoke to each other,
                            (A)   (B)
    there was only the highest respect in their
          (C)   (D)
    words. No error
           (E)

36. He never refused to help us when
              (A)   (B)
    every so often we had to turn to him for advice.
    (C)   (D)
    No error
    (E)

37. Not daring to challenge his statements, we
                                  (A)
    were completely overawed by the presence of
    (B)   (C)
    this eminent authority. No error
         (D)   (E)

38. Not one of the counselors who was there has
                    (A)   (B)   (C)

ever deduced fully the implications in that sim-
                      (D)
ple gesture. No error
             (E)

39. Without consulting the doctor or us, one of the
                                 (A)
    nurses who has been on the case revealed the
          (B)   (C)
    governor's true condition to the press.
    (D)
    No error
    (E)

40. In this televised series, they follow the age-old
                      (A)   (B)
    formula of romantic love, a formula that
                          (C)
    rarely ever fails. No error
    (D)   (E)

41. His principal concern were the rumors of im-
        (A)   (B)   (C)
    pending jurisdictional disputes between the un-
                                    (D)
    ions involved. No error
                   (E)

42. Here lie the ruins of hope destroyed by our
         (A)   (B)
    naive confidence in the integrity of our fellow
    (C)
    humans. No error
    (D)   (E)

43. Would that the judge had not raised these ques-
    (A)   (B)
    tions that have so upset all of our neighbors and
          (C)
    us . No error
    (D)   (E)

44. Even if the infantry were deployed
                         (A)
    properly, the concentrated mass of tanks
    (B)   (C)
    would have broken through the thin defenses.
    (D)
    No error
    (E)

PART 2 *Suggested Time: 15 Minutes*
Time begun .... Time ended .... Time used ....
Did you complete the section within the time limit? ..

DIRECTIONS: Each of the following sentences is to
be rephrased according to the directions that follow
it. You should make only those changes that the
directions require. Keep the meaning of the revised
sentence as close to the meaning of the original sentence as the directions for that sentence permit.

45. The depression seriously cut funds for medical
    research; nevertheless, the thirties were an-
    other decade of advance.
    Omit *nevertheless* and use *even though* instead.

    (A) advance; the
    (B) research, the
    (C) cutting funds
    (D) had been
    (E) advance, the

46. A peace which is merely founded on super-
    power military and economic equilibrium is nec-
    essarily put into question if the bases of that
    equilibrium undergo a change.
    Begin with *When a peace* and omit *necessarily*.

    (A) equilibrium, it
    (B) because the bases
    (C) which is necessarily
    (D) peace, which
    (E) will have undergone

47. The only people who buy and read first aid man-
    uals are the ones who already know what to do
    in an emergency and just want to reinforce their
    knowledge.
    Begin with *First aid manuals*.

    (A) only buy
    (B) who have known
    (C) emergency, and just wanted
    (D) only by the people
    (E) which are the ones

48. The World Trade Center when it is completely
    lighted up night after night probably consumes
    more of our energy resources than all the homes
    in a large-sized suburbia.
    Begin with *More of our energy resources*.

    (A) Center, when
    (B) night, than
    (C) than by all
    (D) had been consumed
    (E) were probably consumed

49. The political leaders face serious dilemmas
    when they attempt to control limited supplies
    of essential commodities in a vast continental
    country like the United States with its diverse
    climates and altitudes.
    Begin with *Had they attempted*.

    (A) would have faced
    (B) attitudes; the
    (C) attitudes. The
    (D) leaders faced
    (E) country. Like the

50. Lawyers in general do not look at their work as
    moral or immoral. That often allows them to act
    in a way that the rest of us would consider im-
    moral.
    Begin with *The fact that*.

    (A) allowing them
    (B) immoral often
    (C) way, that
    (D) allow them
    (E) immoral; that

51. Preliterate hunting and gathering tribes offer the
    best speculation on how our prehistoric fore-
    bears may have lived. They are highly pacific
    people by our "civilized standards."
    Change *offer* to *that offer*.

    (A) lived are
    (B) tribes; who
    (C) lived, they
    (D) tribes. Who
    (E) who are highly

52. No government office and especially not the
    highest in the land carries with it the right to
    ignore the law's command.
    Change *and especially* to *not even*.

    (A) command, not even
    (B) right not even
    (C) office, not
    (D) command; not even
    (E) office carries

53. National security has become a kind of talisman
    invoked by officials at widely disparate levels
    of government service to justify a wide range of
    apparently illegal activities.
    Begin with *Invoked by*.

    (A) service; national
    (B) service, which can justify
    (C) security would become

(D) talisman to justify
(E) service; to justify

54. The enormous scientific value of the achievements in space of the crews of Skylab was made abundantly evident years ago.
Begin with *That the achievements*.

(A) achievements were made
(B) have been made
(C) ago has
(D) value, was
(E) Skylab have

55. For nearly four decades, other American workers have had machinery for free elections and enforcement of fair labor practices. The basic need remained for passage by Congress of a law extending to farm workers the same machinery.
Omit the period after *the same machinery* and begin with *The basic need*.

(A) law; extending
(B) practices that other
(C) elections, enforcement
(D) machinery for nearly
(E) having had

56. All you hear are crisp leaves skittering or a few flakes nudging each other as they fall when winter comes over the hill and down the valley so quietly.
Begin with *So quietly does*.

(A) because all you
(B) valley that
(C) skittering, or a
(D) hills, and
(E) coming over

57. In asking us to consume less fuel in order to avert a real fuel crisis, the President has made a logical and reasonable request.
Begin with *In order to*.

(A) had made
(B) to make a logical
(C) request in asking
(D) who has made
(E) shortage. The

58. The United States is about to embark upon a momentous program to render itself independent of foreign energy supplies, by the end of a decade if possible.
Begin with *To render the United States*.

(A) possible, a
(B) supplies is about to be
(C) about to have been
(D) by the end is about
(E) embarked upon a momentous program

59. The two-party system has become a major stabilizing influence in the nation's conduct of Constitutional government; however, political parties are not mentioned in the written Constitution.
Change *however* to *although*.

(A) Constitution, the
(B) government; although
(C) not being mentioned
(D) parties, the
(E) government. Although

60. The first impression that one gets of a ruler and of his intelligence is from seeing the men he has about him.
Begin with *When we*.

(A) from getting
(B) him, we
(C) we seeing
(D) ruler, and
(E) men he had

61. Mao Tse-tung has set the stamp of his personality on modern China just as Lenin had set the stamp of his intellect on modern Russia.
Omit *just as*.

(A) Lenin setting
(B) Mao Tse-tung had set
(C) China; Lenin
(D) Lenin set
(E) China, Lenin

62. Yet we all should be reminded that the shock waves of change are not a sudden occurrence and not limited to the United States. Their origin was in World War II.
Change *Their origin* to *had their origin* and combine the sentences.

(A) States; had
(B) yet had
(C) change that had
(D) not being
(E) who are

63. Hoping that our political system will be stronger for the ordeal it has suffered, we Americans seem to like to put it to the test now and then. Change *Hoping* to *hope*.

(A) suffered we
(B) seeming to like
(C) hope now and then
(D) putting our
(E) then and

PART 3   *Suggested Time: 20 Minutes*
Time begun .... Time ended .... Time used ....
Did you complete the section within the time limit? ..

DIRECTIONS: In each of the following sentences, some part of the sentence or the entire sentence is underlined. Beneath each sentence you will find ways of phrasing the underlined part. The first of these repeats the original; the other four are different. If you think the original is better than any of the alternatives, choose answer A; otherwise choose one of the others. Select the best version and blacken the corresponding space on your answer sheet.

This is a test of correctness and effectiveness of expression. In choosing answers, follow the requirements of standard written English; that is, pay attention to grammar, choice of words, sentence construction, and punctuation. Choose the answer that best expresses the meaning of the original sentence. Your choice should produce the most effective sentence—clear and precise, without awkwardness or ambiguity.

64. We concluded that the amount of mistakes he made was almost equal to the maximum allowed by probability.

(A) the amount of mistakes he made was almost equal
(B) the amount of mistakes which he had made were almost equal
(C) the amount of mistakes made were almost equal
(D) the number of mistakes made were almost equal
(E) the number of mistakes he made was almost equal

65. Frances told her sister that she was scheduled to leave on the afternoon plane.

(A) sister that she was scheduled to leave on the afternoon plane.
(B) her sister, "You are scheduled to leave on the afternoon plane."
(C) her sister. That she was scheduled to leave on the afternoon plane.
(D) her sister she had been scheduled to leave on the afternoon plane.
(E) her sister, that she was scheduled to leave on the afternoon plane.

66. You can readily recognize the package since it is red in color and with exceptional bulk.

(A) package since it is red in color and with exceptional bulk.
(B) package. Since it is red in color and with exceptional bulk.
(C) package since it is red and exceptionally bulky.
(D) package since it is red and with exceptional bulk.
(E) package since it is red in color, and exceptionally bulky.

67. He has proven that the accused was seen placing the money in his pocket.

(A) proven that the accused was seen placing the money in his pocket.
(B) proved that the accused was seen placing the money in his pocket.
(C) proved that the accused was seen placing the money into his pocket.
(D) proven, that the accused was placing the money in his pocket when he was seen.
(E) proven that the accused was seen placing the money into his pocket.

68. He must either find a more economical way to produce his wares or a financial backer to pay for his subsequent losses.

(A) either find a more economical way to produce his wares
(B) either find a more economical way to produce his wares;
(C) be finding either a more economical way to produce his wares
(D) find either a more economical way to produce his wares
(E) have found either a more economical way to produce his wares,

69. We are compelled to conclude that he must respect them much more than me.

   (A) that he must respect them much more than me.
   (B) that he respects them much more than I.
   (C) that he has respected them more than I.
   (D) that he respects them much more than me.
   (E) that he has been respecting them much more than I.

70. My father worked in that factory until the year in which I was born.

   (A) worked in that factory until
   (B) worked in that factory; until
   (C) has been working in that factory, until
   (D) had been working in that factory; until
   (E) had worked in that factory until

71. The salesman spoke softly and with politeness to the group of potential customers.

   (A) spoke softly and with politeness to
   (B) spoke softly and politely to
   (D) had spoken softly and with politeness with
   (D) speaking softly and politely with
   (E) was speaking softly and with politeness with

72. Of the three men who had been working as coaches at that time—Grant, Smieds, and Lurie—only the latter is still working in this area.

   (A) time—Grant, Smieds, and Lurie—only the latter is
   (B) time, Grant, Smieds, and Lurie only the latter is
   (C) time. Grant, Smieds, and Lurie, only the latter is
   (D) time—Grant, Smieds, and Lurie—only the last is
   (E) time—Grant, Smieds, and Lurie—only the last had been

73. His sense of humor, together with his tact and ready wit, make him a deservedly popular leader.

   (A) humor, together with his fact and ready wit, make him
   (B) humor together with his tact and ready wit make him
   (C) humor, tact, and ready wit makes him
   (D) humor, together with his tact and ready wit, makes him
   (E) humor together with his tact and ready wit making him

74. The only logical solution to this dilema is to declare the winner to be her.

   (A) is to declare the winner to be her.
   (B) would be to declare the winner to be she.
   (C) is to declare she to be the winner.
   (D) would be to declare that the winner will be she.
   (E) should be to declare her to be the winner.

75. To be effective as a speaker, your message must have prime significance for your audience.

   (A) speaker, your message must have
   (B) speaker, you must deliver a message that has
   (C) speaker. You must deliver a message that has
   (D) speaker your message must have
   (E) speaker, what is said must have

76. I knew that I made a mistake when that peculiar smile spread across his face.

   (A) that I made a mistake when
   (B) that I made a mistake. When
   (C) that I made a mistake; when,
   (D) that I had made a mistake as
   (E) that I had made a mistake when

77. In this article it states that a strong UN is our only hope for peace in our time.

   (A) In this article it states
   (B) In this article, it states
   (C) In this article, the author states
   (D) In this article it is stated
   (E) In this article, they quote that

78. Between you and me, there is definitely fewer chances for survival than at any time since the end of World War II.

   (A) me, there is definitely fewer chances
   (B) me, there are definitely fewer chances
   (D) I, there is less chances
   (D) me, there are less chances
   (E) I, there are less chances

79. The counselor characterized Mr. Gardner <u>as being friendly, easygoing, and likely to be co-operative</u>.

   (A) as being friendly, easygoing, and likely to be cooperative,
   (B) as being friendly, easygoing and likely to be cooperative.
   (C) for being friendly, easygoing and likely to be cooperative.
   (D) by being friendly, easygoing, and likely to be cooperative.
   (E) as being friendly, easygoing, and potentially cooperative.

80. <u>No sooner had the truck arrived than the children</u> clamored for a ride.

   (A) No sooner had the truck arrived than the children
   (B) No sooner had the truck arrived when the children
   (C) Just as the truck was arriving, the children
   (D) No sooner had the truck arrived. When the children
   (E) Just as the truck arrived; the children

81. For many years now, the chances of a <u>war of annihilation erupting in the Middle East has filled</u> my dreams with nightmares.

   (A) war of annihilation erupting in the Middle East has filled
   (B) war of annihilation to erupt in the Middle East has filled
   (C) annihilating war erupting in the Middle East has filled
   (D) war of annihilation erupting in the Middle East have filled
   (E) war of annihilation that may erupt has filled

82. There is one cardinal rule of safety <u>involved here you must not allow</u> fear to be the decision-maker.

   (A) involved here you must not allow
   (B) involved, here you must not allow
   (C) involved, here, you must not let
   (D) involved here, you must not let
   (E) involved here: you must not allow

83. In the 1920s, there were very few business <u>machines; they did not have any cassette recorders</u>.

   (A) machines; they did not have any cassette recorders.
   (B) machines and no cassette recorders.
   (C) machines. They did not have any cassette recorders.
   (D) machines since they did not have any cassette recorders.
   (E) machines, and they did not have any cassette recorders.

84. We have the responsibility of choosing a representative <u>who will see that our needs are recognized and our point of view respected</u>.

   (A) who will see that our needs are recognized and our point of view respected.
   (B) to see that our needs are recognized and our point of view respected.
   (C) whom will see our needs recognized and point of view respected.
   (D) who will see that our needs are recognized and that our point of view is respected.
   (E) to see, our needs recognized, and our point of view respected.

85. I had been reading widely for years <u>which stood me in good stead when I went</u> for the college interview.

   (A) which stood me in good stead when I went
   (B) , which stood me in good stead when I went
   (C) , which stood me in good stead when I had gone
   (D) which stayed me in good stead when I went
   (E) , a fact which stood me in good stead when I went

86. <u>Henry's car is as good as if not better than</u> that of his neighbor.

   (A) Henry's car is as good as if not better than
   (B) Henry's car is as good if not better then
   (C) Henry's car is as good as if not better then
   (D) Henry's car is as good as if not better then
   (E) Henry's car is as good if not better than

87. Eating starchy foods, working long hours <u>and without recreation makes</u> any teenager much less efficient than he or she could be.

   (A) and without recreation makes
   (B) and without recreation make
   (C) without recreation makes
   (D) and avoiding recreation make
   (E) and avoiding recreation makes

PRACTICE TESTS FOR THE ENGLISH COMPOSITION TEST

88. The politician assured his constituents that their letters <u>may and had influenced his voting record</u>.

(A) may and had influenced his voting record.
(B) may, and had, influenced his voting record.
(C) may, and had influenced his voting record.
(D) may have and had, influenced his voting record.
(E) may have and had influenced his voting record.

89. To prove the effectiveness of the current <u>research, the death rate has been</u> lowered among those in the project.

(A) research, the death rate has been
(B) research, we can show that the death rate has been
(C) research. The death rate has been
(D) research, the death rate have been
(E) research we can show that the death rate have been

90. <u>The inspector announced after a thorough investigation he</u> would submit his report to his superiors.

(A) The inspector announced after a thorough investigation he
(B) The inspector announced, after a thorough investigation. He
(C) Investigating thoroughly, the inspector announced he
(D) After a thorough investigation, the inspector announced that he
(E) The announcement by the inspector stated after a thorough investigation he

ANSWER KEY AND ANALYSIS OF ANSWERS / *Page 110*

PRACTICE TEST FOUR

ANSWER SHEET

1	Ⓐ Ⓑ Ⓒ Ⓓ Ⓔ	31	Ⓐ Ⓑ Ⓒ Ⓓ Ⓔ	61	Ⓐ Ⓑ Ⓒ Ⓓ Ⓔ
2	Ⓐ Ⓑ Ⓒ Ⓓ Ⓔ	32	Ⓐ Ⓑ Ⓒ Ⓓ Ⓔ	62	Ⓐ Ⓑ Ⓒ Ⓓ Ⓔ
3	Ⓐ Ⓑ Ⓒ Ⓓ Ⓔ	33	Ⓐ Ⓑ Ⓒ Ⓓ Ⓔ	63	Ⓐ Ⓑ Ⓒ Ⓓ Ⓔ
4	Ⓐ Ⓑ Ⓒ Ⓓ Ⓔ	34	Ⓐ Ⓑ Ⓒ Ⓓ Ⓔ	64	Ⓐ Ⓑ Ⓒ Ⓓ Ⓔ
5	Ⓐ Ⓑ Ⓒ Ⓓ Ⓔ	35	Ⓐ Ⓑ Ⓒ Ⓓ Ⓔ	65	Ⓐ Ⓑ Ⓒ Ⓓ Ⓔ
6	Ⓐ Ⓑ Ⓒ Ⓓ Ⓔ	36	Ⓐ Ⓑ Ⓒ Ⓓ Ⓔ	66	Ⓐ Ⓑ Ⓒ Ⓓ Ⓔ
7	Ⓐ Ⓑ Ⓒ Ⓓ Ⓔ	37	Ⓐ Ⓑ Ⓒ Ⓓ Ⓔ	67	Ⓐ Ⓑ Ⓒ Ⓓ Ⓔ
8	Ⓐ Ⓑ Ⓒ Ⓓ Ⓔ	38	Ⓐ Ⓑ Ⓒ Ⓓ Ⓔ	68	Ⓐ Ⓑ Ⓒ Ⓓ Ⓔ
9	Ⓐ Ⓑ Ⓒ Ⓓ Ⓔ	39	Ⓐ Ⓑ Ⓒ Ⓓ Ⓔ	69	Ⓐ Ⓑ Ⓒ Ⓓ Ⓔ
10	Ⓐ Ⓑ Ⓒ Ⓓ Ⓔ	40	Ⓐ Ⓑ Ⓒ Ⓓ Ⓔ	70	Ⓐ Ⓑ Ⓒ Ⓓ Ⓔ
11	Ⓐ Ⓑ Ⓒ Ⓓ Ⓔ	41	Ⓐ Ⓑ Ⓒ Ⓓ Ⓔ	71	Ⓐ Ⓑ Ⓒ Ⓓ Ⓔ
12	Ⓐ Ⓑ Ⓒ Ⓓ Ⓔ	42	Ⓐ Ⓑ Ⓒ Ⓓ Ⓔ	72	Ⓐ Ⓑ Ⓒ Ⓓ Ⓔ
13	Ⓐ Ⓑ Ⓒ Ⓓ Ⓔ	43	Ⓐ Ⓑ Ⓒ Ⓓ Ⓔ	73	Ⓐ Ⓑ Ⓒ Ⓓ Ⓔ
14	Ⓐ Ⓑ Ⓒ Ⓓ Ⓔ	44	Ⓐ Ⓑ Ⓒ Ⓓ Ⓔ	74	Ⓐ Ⓑ Ⓒ Ⓓ Ⓔ
15	Ⓐ Ⓑ Ⓒ Ⓓ Ⓔ	45	Ⓐ Ⓑ Ⓒ Ⓓ Ⓔ	75	Ⓐ Ⓑ Ⓒ Ⓓ Ⓔ
16	Ⓐ Ⓑ Ⓒ Ⓓ Ⓔ	46	Ⓐ Ⓑ Ⓒ Ⓓ Ⓔ	76	Ⓐ Ⓑ Ⓒ Ⓓ Ⓔ
17	Ⓐ Ⓑ Ⓒ Ⓓ Ⓔ	47	Ⓐ Ⓑ Ⓒ Ⓓ Ⓔ	77	Ⓐ Ⓑ Ⓒ Ⓓ Ⓔ
18	Ⓐ Ⓑ Ⓒ Ⓓ Ⓔ	48	Ⓐ Ⓑ Ⓒ Ⓓ Ⓔ	78	Ⓐ Ⓑ Ⓒ Ⓓ Ⓔ
19	Ⓐ Ⓑ Ⓒ Ⓓ Ⓔ	49	Ⓐ Ⓑ Ⓒ Ⓓ Ⓔ	79	Ⓐ Ⓑ Ⓒ Ⓓ Ⓔ
20	Ⓐ Ⓑ Ⓒ Ⓓ Ⓔ	50	Ⓐ Ⓑ Ⓒ Ⓓ Ⓔ	80	Ⓐ Ⓑ Ⓒ Ⓓ Ⓔ
21	Ⓐ Ⓑ Ⓒ Ⓓ Ⓔ	51	Ⓐ Ⓑ Ⓒ Ⓓ Ⓔ	81	Ⓐ Ⓑ Ⓒ Ⓓ Ⓔ
22	Ⓐ Ⓑ Ⓒ Ⓓ Ⓔ	52	Ⓐ Ⓑ Ⓒ Ⓓ Ⓔ	82	Ⓐ Ⓑ Ⓒ Ⓓ Ⓔ
23	Ⓐ Ⓑ Ⓒ Ⓓ Ⓔ	53	Ⓐ Ⓑ Ⓒ Ⓓ Ⓔ	83	Ⓐ Ⓑ Ⓒ Ⓓ Ⓔ
24	Ⓐ Ⓑ Ⓒ Ⓓ Ⓔ	54	Ⓐ Ⓑ Ⓒ Ⓓ Ⓔ	84	Ⓐ Ⓑ Ⓒ Ⓓ Ⓔ
25	Ⓐ Ⓑ Ⓒ Ⓓ Ⓔ	55	Ⓐ Ⓑ Ⓒ Ⓓ Ⓔ	85	Ⓐ Ⓑ Ⓒ Ⓓ Ⓔ
26	Ⓐ Ⓑ Ⓒ Ⓓ Ⓔ	56	Ⓐ Ⓑ Ⓒ Ⓓ Ⓔ	86	Ⓐ Ⓑ Ⓒ Ⓓ Ⓔ
27	Ⓐ Ⓑ Ⓒ Ⓓ Ⓔ	57	Ⓐ Ⓑ Ⓒ Ⓓ Ⓔ	87	Ⓐ Ⓑ Ⓒ Ⓓ Ⓔ
28	Ⓐ Ⓑ Ⓒ Ⓓ Ⓔ	58	Ⓐ Ⓑ Ⓒ Ⓓ Ⓔ	88	Ⓐ Ⓑ Ⓒ Ⓓ Ⓔ
29	Ⓐ Ⓑ Ⓒ Ⓓ Ⓔ	59	Ⓐ Ⓑ Ⓒ Ⓓ Ⓔ	89	Ⓐ Ⓑ Ⓒ Ⓓ Ⓔ
30	Ⓐ Ⓑ Ⓒ Ⓓ Ⓔ	60	Ⓐ Ⓑ Ⓒ Ⓓ Ⓔ	90	Ⓐ Ⓑ Ⓒ Ⓓ Ⓔ

PRACTICE TEST FOUR

Total Time: One Hour
PART 1 *Suggested Time: 20 Minutes*
Time begun .... Time ended .... Time used ....
Did you complete the section within the time limit? ..

DIRECTIONS: The following sentences contain problems in grammar, usage, diction (choice of words), and idiom.
  Some sentences are correct.
  No sentence contains more than one error.
  You will find that the error, if there is one, is underlined and lettered. Assume that all other elements of the sentence are correct and cannot be changed. In choosing answers, follow the requirements of standard written English.
  If there is an error, select the one underlined part that must be changed in order to make the sentence correct, and blacken the corresponding space on the answer sheet.
  If there is no error, mark answer space E.

1. The percentages of saving is too slight in this
        (A)   (B)
   process ; moreover, the bookkeeping involved
          (C)
   becomes much more difficult for us to perform
     (D)
   accurately. No error
              (E)

2. May I have a loan of your book so that I can
         (A)   (B)
   study for the test on capitals of the world?
                    (C)   (D)
   No error
   (E)

3. Bring the results to his office so that the
   (A)
   council   can   examine   the   details   for
     (B)   (C)
   themselves. No error
     (D)   (E)

4. Arlene accompanied by her brother and sister
            (A)
   are in the foyer , waiting to discuss with you
   (B)   (C)
   the plans for the costume ball. No error
                      (D)   (E)

5. Not caring what happened to them,   I was
        (A)   (B)   (C)
   completely disinterested in their tale of woe.
                (D)
   No error
   (E)

6. The would-be rescuers formed a continuous
         (A)   (B)
   chain by holding hands; Henry , acting as lead
         (C)
   man , reached cautiously over the edge of the
                             (D)
   cliff. No error
          (E)

7. The laboratory practices of contemporary
                          (A)
   scientists relies heavily upon the results of
              (B)   (C)   (D)
   computer technology. No error
                          (E)

8. Is there no one among you to whom I can
   (A)   (B)
   turn to for advice and comfort? No error
        (C)   (D)   (E)

9. You're in eminent danger of being accused
   (A)   (B)
   of a crime you did not commit; therefore, you
   (C)   (D)
   must find out who is behind this foul plotting.
   No error
   (E)

10. The less mistakes one makes, the greater is
        (A)   (B)
    one's chance of unraveling this incredible mix-
          (C)   (D)
    up. No error
        (E)

11. Neither you nor I are capable of ridding the city
                (A) (B)   (C)
    of this unhealthful situation. No error
             (D)   (E)

12. A set of his fingerprints are on file in the
                          (A)   (B)
    office , and everyone of the officers of the
    law is able   to   examine it at   any   time.
        (C)   (D)
    No error
    (E)

13. Between you and <u>me</u>, he is <u>seldom ever</u> wrong
                    (A)   (B)
when he <u>decides on</u> <u>whom</u> to reject. <u>No error</u>
            (C)   (D)   (E)

14. I still think it would be <u>all right</u> if no one but
                                        (A)
<u>him</u> <u>was</u> permitted to eat <u>their</u> lunch in the of-
(B) (C)   (D)
fice. <u>No error</u>
          (E)

15. Bagels and lox <u>is</u> my favorite midnight snack
                        (A)
<u>due to</u> <u>my</u> having been <u>brought up</u> in Brooklyn,
  (B)   (C)   (D)
the home of wholesome foods. <u>No error</u>
                                        (E)

16. I read in the paper <u>that</u> the killer and his ac-
                            (A)
complices <u>are</u> to be <u>hung</u> at noon <u>by order</u> of
            (B)   (C)   (D)
the governor. <u>No error</u>
                    (E)

17. Do just <u>like</u> <u>I</u> , and you <u>will</u> have little <u>if any</u>
              (A)(B)   (C)   (D)
difficulty. <u>No error</u>
                  (E)

18. <u>Is</u> there any other set of tests that I could
(A)
<u>have</u> used to see the <u>affect</u> of tension on those
  (B)   (C)
<u>who</u> are involved in this project? <u>No error</u>
(D)   (E)

19. Is it <u>she</u> who spoke so <u>indistinct</u> that we did not
          (A)   (B)
know <u>whether</u> we were to <u>precede</u> or follow the
        (C)   (D)
procession? <u>No error</u>
                  (E)

20. Each of them <u>has</u> <u>ever</u> resented <u>you</u> daring to
                    (A) (B)   (C)
tell them what <u>had</u> to be done. <u>No error</u>
                    (D)   (E)

21. <u>Among</u> the three of them I would judge <u>him</u> to
    (A)   (B)
be the <u>more</u> intelligent, especially where ab-
          (C)
stract concepts <u>are</u> concerned. <u>No error</u>
                    (D)   (E)

22. Everyone of the boys in the class <u>who</u> <u>have</u>
                                        (A) (B)
<u>passed</u> the test <u>are</u> to receive certificates.
(C)   (D)
<u>No error</u>
  (E)

23. Larry <u>can</u> drive the car <u>as well as</u> you <u>or I</u>;
              (A)   (B)   (C)
therefore, he is permitted to <u>borrow</u> it. <u>No error</u>
                                (D)   (E)

24. To pass such a test, <u>it</u> is necessary that each
                          (A)
candidate <u>be</u> prepared to do <u>his</u> <u>utmost</u>.
            (B)   (C) (D)
<u>No error</u>
  (E)

25. He felt so <u>badly</u> that Ethel and <u>I</u> had to ask
              (A)   (B)
<u>whomever</u> we met to do the work for <u>him</u>.
(C)   (D)
<u>No error</u>
  (E)

26. <u>Whether</u> you agree or not, <u>this</u> was a
    (A)   (B)
<u>most perfect</u> arrangement for <u>him</u> and Paul
(C)   (D)
under the circumstances. <u>No error</u>
                                (E)

27. If you <u>would have</u> told me <u>just</u> what I was to
              (A)   (B)
do, they <u>would</u> never have found fault with
            (C)
<u>my</u> handling of the case. <u>No error</u>
(D)   (E)

28. <u>Somewheres</u> in my notes <u>there</u> is a statement
    (A)   (B)
that <u>we</u> seniors may use any of the lockers that
      (C)
<u>are</u> left open. <u>No error</u>
(D)   (E)

29. Every candidate who <u>has</u> <u>swam</u> the length of
                    (A)   (B)
the pool will be given a certificate stating that

<u>he</u> has <u>proved</u> his competence. <u>No error</u>
(C)   (D)   (E)

30. Neither of the drivers who <u>are</u> being held by the
                                (A)
police <u>knows</u> <u>whom</u> to blame for <u>his</u> plight.
        (B)   (C)   (D)
<u>No error</u>
(E)

31. He is the <u>sort</u> of <u>a</u> person <u>who</u> I suspect
              (A)   (B)   (C)
<u>would</u> be capable of making such a remark.
(D)
<u>No error</u>
(E)

32. The danger is <u>when</u> there <u>is</u> a series of cars that
                  (A)   (B)
<u>are</u> ready to cross an <u>obstructed</u> area.
(C)   (D)
<u>No error</u>
(E)

33. Without consulting Margie <u>or us</u>, Phyllis as-
                              (A)
serted that everyone <u>except her</u> had to contrib-
                     (B)
ute <u>one-tenth</u> of <u>his or her</u> earnings to the fund.
    (C)   (D)
<u>No error</u>
(E)

PART 2 *Suggested Time: 20 Minutes*
Time begun .... Time ended .... Time used ....
Did you complete the section within the time limit? ..

DIRECTIONS: Each of the following sentences is to be rephrased according to the directions that follow it. <u>You should make only those changes that the directions require.</u> Keep the meaning of the revised sentence as close to the meaning of the original sentence as the directions for that sentence permit.

34. The Navy had intercepted Japanese messages after the Battle of the Coral Sea, and it knew the next move and rushed every available plane and vessel into the Central Pacific.
Begin with *The Navy, having intercepted*.

(A) moved, and
(B) knowing the next
(C) vessel; into the
(D) messages. After the
(E) Sea, knew

35. The German's created a critical oil shortage by mid-January because they had moved so many submarines to the Atlantic Coast, where at night they torpedoed tankers silhouetted against the light of cities.
Begin with *By mid-January, the Germans had moved*.

(A) cities, that they created
(B) coast. Where
(C) tankers; silhouetted
(D) cities, that
(E) coast; where

36. Prophets have cried out in the wilderness, and they despaired of TV's lost opportunities during its first twenty-five years.
Omit *they*, and begin with *During*.

(A) wilderness; and
(B) opportunities prophets,
(C) wilderness. Despairing
(D) wilderness and despaired
(E) years. Prophets

37. All too often those who want to suppress a repugnant doctrine only succeed in giving it more notoriety.
Begin with *Those who would want*.

(A) succeed all too often
(B) doctrine all too often
(C) had only succeeded
(D) to suppress all too often
(E) only have succeeded

38. Moral issues can be debated endlessly with no resolution, but there is also a material side to this problem.
Substitute *even though* for *but*.

(A) resolution; even though
(B) there had been
(C) With no resolution
(D) resolution even
(E) would have been debated

39. Winter does not wait on the calendar. You need no almanac to recognize its coming.
Change *Winter does not* to *since it does not*.

    (A) needing no almanac
    (B) winter since
    (C) waiting on the calendar
    (D) recognize. The coming
    (E) calendar. You

40. John F. Kennedy considered the Test Ban Treaty not the most historic act since Creation but a single step on a journey of a thousand miles.
Begin with *The Test Ban Treaty*.

    (A) act, since Creation
    (B) step. On a journey
    (C) Kennedy as not the most
    (D) Kennedy. Not the most
    (E) Creation, but a single

41. We hesitate like Hamlet whipsawed by conflicting emotions of desire to avenge his father's death and guilt at having desired that very death.
Begin with *Like Hamlet*.

    (A) father's death; and guilt
    (B) guilt at desiring
    (C) death, we
    (D) father's death, and guilt
    (E) death; we

42. His skepticism, his sense of the absurd in life, his recognition of failure were all directed at himself as much as anyone.
Begin with *He directed*.

    (A) recognition of failure.
    (B) anyone: his
    (C) life; and his
    (D) skepticism; his
    (E) anyone; his

43. A quiet revolution in American life, the four-day week, could come to pass a decade before its time, hurried along by a sustained fuel shortage.
Begin with *Had a sustained fuel shortage resulted*.

    (A) life. The four-day week
    (B) could be coming to pass
    (C) life; the four-day week
    (D) resulted. A
    (E) week, could have come

44. There is no need for Americans to fear economic disaster when there is effective national leadership and a sustained and cooperative response from business and the public.
Change *when there is effective national leadership* to *Given effective national leadership*.

    (A) leadership, and a
    (B) public, there is
    (C) Americans. To fear
    (D) a sustaining and cooperative
    (E) there had been no need

45. The shot that claimed the life of John F. Kennedy will be remembered for more than the murder of a charismatic and promising young president; it marked the beginning of the end of an era filled with ebullient optimism and confidence.
Begin with *Having marked the beginning*.

    (A) confidence. The shot
    (B) shot that claims
    (C) remembered, for more
    (D) confidence, the shot
    (E) era, filled with

46. The old police headquarters on Centre Street is an architectural gem in an otherwise drab area. It should be preserved as an important New York City landmark.
Combine both sentences by eliminating *is* and *It*.

    (A) area, should be
    (B) Street an architectural gem
    (C) gem; in
    (D) area;
    (E) landmark should be

47. We must give up the demand for right answers and instead encourage students to explore many ways of viewing an issue or problem.
Eliminate *and instead* and begin with *Our obligation is to encourage*.

    (A) explore. Many ways
    (B) students exploring
    (C) problem; we
    (D) problem, nor must we
    (E) giving up the demand

48. That today's young people communicate more sensitively and more comfortably through visual media than through the printed page is one

of the obvious results of the massive, pervasive influence of television.
Begin with *Is it true that one of the obvious*.

(A) page, is
(B) television?
(C) television, is that
(D) media; rather than
(E) printed page?

49. The true genius of America lies in its ability to organize free and strong-minded men to solve great problems. It also lies in its ability to meet and overcome challenges.
Begin with *In its ability to meet* and combine the two sentences.

(A) problems is where
(B) problems are the true genius
(C) challenges; and
(D) problems lies
(E) America lie

50. In America our race relations are not perfect, but constructive processes are at work, and we are narrowing the gap in opportunity and in education, and in income, and in the day-to-day relations.
Omit *but* and all *and's*.

(A) gap, in
(B) perfect constructive
(C) work; we
(D) we will have narrowed
(E) education, in

51. When a train approaches a Paris subway station, gates at the ticket window automatically swing shut. Only those already on the platform may board the train.
Combine both sentences, and begin with *Because the gates*.

(A) approaches; only
(B) shut. When
(C) approaches, only
(D) the gates, at the
(E) shut when

52. It is an accepted fact that the rate of gasoline consumption increases with an increase in speed; and, therefore, over any given distance the higher the speed, the more gasoline will be used.

Change *It is an accepted fact that* to *Because*.

(A) gasoline could have been used
(B) given distance, the more
(C) speed; and therefore over any
(D) gasoline would have been used
(E) speed. Therefore, over any

53. The opportunity for a significant international effort at cooperation exists because of mutual need and shared emergency.
Change *because of* to *Since this is a time of*.

(A) need, and
(B) emergency the
(C) was this
(D) exists. Since this
(E) emergency, the

54. The chickadees and the juncos have come down from the woodlands and the hills, back to the dooryard feeders where they were welcomed last year. Change *have come* to *came*.

(A) year, the
(B) Welcomed last year,
(C) feeders; where
(D) had been welcomed
(E) feeders. Where

55. Political appeals to ignorance and selfishness needlessly divided the nation and thereby substituted neglect for compassion.
Change *thereby substituted* to *By substituting*.

(A) dividing needlessly
(B) compassion, political
(C) ignorance; and selfishness
(D) ignorance, and selfishness
(E) needlessly dividing

56. More of our people have lost their lives in automobile accidents than in all the wars in United States history.
Begin with *Automobile accidents have claimed*.

(A) claimed more of our people losing
(B) than have all the wars
(C) claimed. The lives of more
(D) people. Than
(E) lives than all

57. Consequently we cannot come to grips with the real issues until we first face the urgent need to make drastic changes in our energy economy. Begin with *First we had to face.*

    (A) Economy, coming to grips
    (B) economy; therefore, we cannot
    (C) economy before we could come to grips
    (D) economy, as we came
    (E) economy, as we come

58. Reports from transplant surgeons that immunosuppressive drugs given to patients to suppress organ rejection foster the rise of cancer are additional evidence of the relationship between cancer and immunity and the need for moderation in drug therapy.
    Begin with *Additional evidence.*

    (A) therapy, came from
    (B) drugs, given to patients
    (C) therapy comes from
    (D) cancer, and immunity, and the
    (E) surgeons. That

PART 3 Suggested Time: 20 *Minutes*
Time begun .... Time ended .... Time used ....
Did you complete the section within the time limit? ..

DIRECTIONS: In each of the following sentences, some part of the sentence or the entire sentence is underlined. Beneath each sentence you will find five ways of phrasing the underlined part. The first of these repeats the original; the other four are different. If you think the original is better than any of the alternatives, choose answer A; othewise choose one of the others. Select the best version and blacken the corresponding space on your answer sheet.
    This is a test of correctness and effectiveness of expression. In choosing answers, follow the requirements of standard written English; that is, pay attention to grammar, choice of words, sentence construction, and punctuation. Choose the answer that best expresses the meaning of the original sentence. Your choice should produce the most effective sentence—clear and recise, without awkwardness of ambiguity.

59. Seeing as how he disliked the camp site. I suggested that we repack and move.

    (A) Seeing as how he disliked the camp site, I
    (B) Seeing as how he had disliked the camp site, I
    (C) Seeing as he had disliked the camp site, I
    (D) Seeing as how he disliked the camp site. I
    (E) Since he disliked the camp site, I

60. She plowed through the vast heap of letters of complaint without respite, which pleased the supervisor no end.

    (A) , which pleased the supervisor no end
    (B) , which completely pleased the supervisor
    (C) , to the great satisfaction of her supervisor
    (D) . Which pleased the supervisor no end
    (E) , to the supervisor's complete satisfaction

61. Between you and I, there was no other books on the shelf.

    (A) Between you and I, there was
    (B) Between you and me, there was
    (C) Between us, there could not have been
    (D) Between you and me, there were
    (E) Between you and I there was

62. We should like to know whether he is one of the men, who are responsible for this confusion!

    (A) whether he is one of the men, who are
    (B) whether he is one of the men that has been
    (C) if he is one of the men which are
    (D) whether he is one of the men who are
    (E) if he is one of the men whose

63. In our city they are very much concerned over the increase in the number of street crimes.

    (A) In our city they are very much concerned
    (B) In our city the people are very much concerned
    (C) In our city people are very concerned
    (D) In our city they are much concerned
    (E) In our city, they are very concerned

64. If you would have listened to me, we could have prevented this mishap.

    (A) If you would have listened to me.
    (B) If you'd listened to me
    (C) If you would've listened to me
    (D) If you would of listened to me,
    (E) If you had listened to me,

65. She worked at the problem with renewed hope, completely oblivious to her surroundings.

(A) , completely oblivious to her surroundings
(B) . Completely oblivious to her surroundings
(C) , totally and completely oblivious to her surroundings
(D) , unaware of her surroundings
(E) completely oblivious of her surroundings

66. Being a sensible person, I did not argue with them at the time.

(A) Being a sensible person,
(B) Being that I am a sensible person,
(C) Being as I am a sensible person
(D) Because I am a sensible person
(E) Since I am a sensible person

67. They told me the entire story at that time, which surprised me very much.

(A) , which surprised me very much.
(B) which surprised me very much.
(C) ; a revelation which surprised me very much.
(D) . This revelation surprised me very much.
(E) . Which surprised me very much.

68. In our town they are very much interested in the current college crises.

(A) In our town they are very much interested in
(B) In our town they are very interested in
(C) The people who live in our town are very much interested in
(D) Our town is very interested in
(E) They are very much interested in our town in

69. He told Alex that he was foolish to become so angry.

(A) that he was foolish to become so angry.
(B) he was foolish to become so angry.
(C) , "That he was foolish to become so angry."
(D) "That he was foolish to become so angry."
(E) , "I was foolish to become so angry."

70. I bought a copy of the book of poems he had printed.

(A) book of poems he had printed
(B) book of poems that he had printed

(C) book of Poems that he had printed
(D) book of poems. He had printed
(E) poetry book he had printed

71. All of the possible angles having been explored, we sat by and waited for results.

(A) All of the possible angles having been explored, we
(B) When all of the possible angles would have been explored, we
(C) All of the possible angles having been explored. We
(D) All of the possible angles having been explored; we
(E) Since we were exploring all of the possible angles,

72. We plan to visit the house on the hill that she just bought.

(A) house on the hill that she just bought.
(B) house on the hill she just bought.
(C) house on the hill which she just bought.
(D) house she just bought on the hill.
(E) house on the hill. That she just bought.

73. The one is rounder than the others.

(A) rounder than the others.
(B) more round than the others.
(C) round.
(D) the roundest of them all.
(E) the most round.

74. He is as eligible or even more eligible than the other candidates.

(A) as eligible or even more eligible than
(B) as eligible or even more eligible as
(C) more eligible than
(D) as eligible or even more eligible then
(E) as eligible as or even more eligible than

75. He spoke ever so clearly and with emphasis.

(A) ever so clearly and with emphasis.
(B) ever so clearly and emphatically.
(C) never so clearly and with emphasis.
(D) never so clearly and emphatically.
(E) He spoke ever so clear and with emphasis.

76. We <u>lived on</u> Martense Street for seven years <u>before we moved</u> here.

   (A) We lived on . . . . before we moved
   (B) We would have lived on . . . . we had moved
   (C) We lived on . . . . before we had moved
   (D) We had lived on . . . . before moving
   (E) We lived on . . . . before we would have moved

77. <u>Everyone except you and me has been told</u> the formula.

   (A) Everyone except you and me has been told
   (B) Everyone except you and I has been told
   (C) Everyone except you and me have been told
   (D) Everyone except you and I have been told
   (E) Everyone except I and you have been told

78. There <u>isn't scarcely a penny left</u> in the larder.

   (A) isn't scarcely a penny left
   (B) is scarcely a penny left
   (C) is scarcely no pennies left
   (D) isn't scarcely no penny left
   (E) isn't a penny left

79. <u>Between you and I, nobody in this class knows</u> the right procedure.

   (A) Between you and I, nobody in this class knows
   (B) Between you and me, nobody in this class know
   (C) Between you and I, nobody in this class know
   (D) Between I and you, nobody in this class knows
   (E) Between you and me, nobody in this class knows

80. <u>Seeing as how they did not enjoy our company,</u> I soon excused myself and retired early.

   (A) Seeing as how they did not enjoy our company,
   (B) Seeing as how they did not enjoy our company.
   (C) Seeing as they did not enjoy our company,
   (D) Seeing as they did not enjoy our company.
   (E) Seeing that they did not enjoy our company,

81. We will have <u>to let it lie</u> just where it has fallen until we notify the police.

   (A) to let it lie
   (B) to leave it lay
   (C) to leave it lie
   (D) to let it lay
   (E) to have let it lay

82. <u>They stood on that farm for three weeks a year ago.</u>

   (A) They stood on that farm for three weeks a year ago.
   (B) A year ago they stood on that farm for three weeks.
   (C) For three weeks they had stood on that farm a year ago.
   (D) A year ago, they had stayed on that farm for three weeks.
   (E) A year ago, they stayed on that farm for three weeks.

83. <u>Take the package off of the shelf and put it in</u> the desk drawer.

   (A) Take the package off of the shelf and put it in
   (B) Take the package off the shelf and put it into
   (C) Take the package off the shelf, and put it in
   (D) Take the package off from the shelf and put it in
   (E) Take the package off of the shelf and put it in

84. <u>That there article is the type of a satire that</u> I enjoy least.

   (A) That there article is the type of a satire that
   (B) That there article is the type of a satire which
   (C) That article is the type of a satire that
   (D) That article is the type of a satire which
   (E) That article is the type of satire that

85. <u>They put on quite a act during their half hour on the stage.</u>

   (A) They put on quite a act during their half hour on the stage.
   (B) They put on quiet an act during there half-hour on the stage.
   (C) They put on quite a act during their half-hour on the stage.

(D) They put on quite an act during there half an hour on the stage.

(E) They put on quite an act during their half hour on the stage.

86. By the time he was thirty, Melvin Konner's prose style was ranked <u>with the greatest stylists of his generation</u>.

(A) with the greatest stylists of his generation

(B) at the top of his group

(C) with the stylists of his generation

(D) with that of the greatest stylists of his generation

(E) along with the great stylists of his generation

87. They say <u>were all together wrong in the advise</u> we plan to give the others.

(A) were all together wrong in the advise

(B) we're all together wrong in the advise

(C) we're altogether wrong in the advice

(D) we're all together wrong in the advise

(E) were altogether wrong in the advice

88. <u>Is anyone of the members of the committee able to loan us</u> a copy of the report?

(A) Is anyone of the members of the committee able to loan us

(B) Are anyone of the members of the committee able to loan us

(C) Is anyone of the members of the committee capable of loaning us

(D) Are anyone of the members of the committee able to lend us

(E) Is any one of the members of the committee able to lend us

89. Can you <u>learn me how to spill this liquid into the dish</u> without losing any of it?

(A) learn me how to spill this liquid into the dish

(B) teach me how to spill this liquid in the dish

(C) teach me how to pour this liquid into the dish

(D) learn me how to pour this liquid into the dish

(E) teach me to pour this liquid in the dish

90. He <u>read all of Dicken's works before writing</u> the report.

(A) read all of Dicken's works before writing

(B) had read all of Dicken's works before writing

(C) had read all of Dickens' works before he had written

(D) had read all of Dickens's works before writing.

(E) read all of Dickens' works before he had written

ANSWER KEY AND ANALYSIS OF ANSWERS / *Page 113*

3. *Answers to Practice Tests with Analyses of Answers*

ANSWER KEY: PRACTICE TEST ONE

Part 1			*Part 2*				*Part 3*	
1. (E)	16. (D)	31. (B)	40. (D)	49. (D)	58. (D)	67. (C)	75. (E)	83. (A)
2. (D)	17. (C)	32. (A)	41. (C)	50. (C)	59. (A)	68. (A)	76. (B)	84. (B)
3. (D)	18. (B)	33. (E)	42. (C)	51. (A)	60. (C)	69. (D)	77. (C)	85. (B)
4. (D)	19. (B)	34. (C)	43. (E)	52. (E)	61. (E)	70. (E)	78. (B)	86. (D)
5. (C)	20. (C)	35. (A)	44. (D)	53. (B)	62. (C)	71. (C)	79. (E)	87. (C)
6. (A)	21. (B)	36. (C)	45. (C)	54. (E)	63. (E)	72. (B)	80. (D)	88. (B)
7. (B)	22. (A)	37. (D)	46. (A)	55. (D)	64. (B)	73. (E)	81. (D)	89. (E)
8. (E)	23. (A)	38. (A)	47. (B)	56. (A)	65. (E)	74. (D)	82. (E)	90. (E)
9. (A)	24. (A)	39. (B)	48. (E)	57. (E)	66. (D)			
10. (D)	25. (B)							
11. (B)	26. (E)							
12. (A)	27. (A)							
13. (A)	28. (A)							
14. (C)	29. (C)							
15. (B)	30. (C)							

DETERMINING YOUR RAW SCORE

1. Tabulate Totals
   Number Right _____
   Number Wrong _____
   Number Omitted _____

2. Enter Number Right   A _____
   Divide Number Wrong by
   4 and put result here   B _____

3. **Subtract B from A. This
   results in your RAW SCORE** _____

> The subtraction of ¼ point for each incorrect answer adjusts for the effect of random guessing.

EVALUATING YOUR PERFORMANCE

Excellent	83–90
Very Good	59–82
Good	45–58
Average	31–44
Below Average	15–30
Unsatisfactory	14 or below

ANALYSIS OF ANSWERS: PRACTICE TEST ONE

Part 1

1. (E)   No error
2. (D)   The word *irregardless* is nonstandard for *regardless*.
3. (D)   The prices are lower than *last year's prices*.
4. (D)   *Like* should be followed by an object. *As* is followed by a clause.
5. (C)   The negative *hardly* is followed by *any*, not *no*.
6. (A)   The verb *let* (*allow*), not *leave* (*go*), is needed.
7. (B)   The noun *army* must be preceded by *an* since *army* has an initial vowel.
8. (E)   No error
9. (A)   The standard term is *provided*, not *providing*.
10. (D)   ...more powerful than any *other* country.
11. (B)   Parallel construction requires *being unable*.
12. (A)   Since *scarcely* has negative value, it is followed by *any* rather than *no*.
13. (A)   *Whom* is required as the object of the verb *shall blame*.
14. (C)   The plural *facilities* requires the plural *exceed*.
15. (B)   Accompanied *with* means *associated* with accompanied *by* means to be in the company of.
16. (D)   *Privilege of* (*paying*) is the idiom.
17. (C)   The preposition *into*, not *in*, is required in standard use.
18. (B)   The standard term is *accidentally*.

19. (B)   The verb *allowed* means *permitted* in standard usage.
20. (C)   The adjective *mad* is a nonstandard synonym for *angry*.
21. (B)   *Hat* is the subject of *was* soiled.
22. (A)   *By myself* repeats *alone*.
23. (A)   The plural *marks* requires *were*.
24. (A)   The adverb *anywheres* is nonstandard.
25. (B)   The word *around* is not a standard equivalent for *about*.
26. (E)   No error
27. (A)   The idiom *being that* is a nonstandard equivalent for *since* or *because*.
28. (A)   The term *but what* is not a standard equivalent for *that*.
29. (C)   There is no apparent reason for splitting the infinite *to stand*.
30. (C)   The nonstandard *consensus of opinion* should be replaced by *opinion* or by *consensus*.
31. (B)   The standard idiom is *differs from*.
32. (A)   The singular *group* requires the singular *comes*.
33. (E)   No error
34. (C)   The expression *quite some time* is nonstandard.
35. (A)   The terms *large* and *in size* repeat each other: omit *in size*.
36. (C)   The standard idiom is *differs from*.
37. (D)   The term *fewer* is required, not *less*, since units (*employees*) are involved.

38. (A) The idiom *have a loan of* is nonstandard as an equivalent for *borrow*.
39. (B) The term *somewheres* is nonstandard for *somewhere*.

Part 2
40. (D) Both verbs should be active.
41. (C) The subjunctive past is *had been* in this conditional clause.
42. (C) The verb is controlled by the singular noun *Merwin*.
43. (E) The conjunctive adverb *therefore* cannot be use as a coordinating conjunction.
44. (D) The pronoun *which* cannot be used to refer to the idea of the rest of the sentence.
45. (C) In standard usage *is because* cannot be used as an equivalent for *is that*.
46. (A) No error
47. (B) Patience cannot drive a tractor—dangling infinitive.
48. (E) The preposition *including* is followed by the object *me*; *no one* is the singular subject.
49. (D) The phrase *as good as* must be completed.
50. (C) The plural form is *women*.
51. (A) No error
52. (E) An introductory adverb clause is set off by a comma.
53. (B) The plural *delegates* requires the plural *were*; *who* refers to *delegates* and is the subject of *were chosen*.
54. (E) The introductory clause contains precedent action and therefore the past perfect *had seen* is required.
55. (D) The correlatives *neither . . . nor* must be placed before the words they balance.
56. (A) No error
57. (E) The plural *promises* requires the plural *have*.
58. (D) The introductory gerund phrase must have a noun or pronoun to modify.
59. (A) No error
60. (C) The subject of the infinitive *to be* is in the object form (*me*).
61. (E) In its given position, *when I arrived* could modify either clause.
62. (C) The pronoun *any* is plural and requires *have* and *their*.
63. (E) The ground phrase *upon receiving* requires a noun or pronoun to modify.
64. (B) Omission of the parenthetical *I think* uncovers *who* as the subject of *can advise*.

65. (E) Parallel construction requires *to be able* and *to earn*.
66. (D) The term *irregardless* is nonstandard. The form *lays* requires an object.
67. (C) The idiom *kind of a* is nonstandard. The form *too* is the adverb form.
68. (A) No error
69. (D) The pronoun *her* is the object of the preposition *except*; the noun *effect* is required in the phrase *the effect of*.
70. (E) The conjunctive adverb *moreover* cannot function as a coordinating conjunction.
71. (C) The singular *set* requires the singular *is*; *lose* (*misplace*) and not *loose* (*lax, free*) is required.
72. (B) The verb *take* is required since the action is not toward the speaker; *these here* is nonstandard. There is confusion of *council* (group), *counsel* (advice), and *consul* (government official).
73. (E) The idiom *sort of a* is nonstandard; as a pronoun *which* refers to things or ideas while *who* refers to people.
74. (D) The participle *knowing* requires a logical word for it to modify.

Part 3
75. (E) He insists that doing good is merely feeding one's ego.
76. (B) That they move so slowly on land is often the reason for our coming to the conclusion that giant turtles. . . .
77. (C) Because the star performer has been taken ill suddenly, the performance. . . .
78. (B) . . . some of my friends have. . . .
79. (E) When the nights became cold and crisp with the approach of autumn, the leaves of the surrounding forest began to turn.
80. (D) . . . Mr. Pollett is more efficient than any other diagnostician in our division.
81. (D) . . . money that is squandered . . .
82. (E) When he was willing to be impatient with us, it. . . .
83. (A) These songs taught us in our childhood are the ones we remember longest.
84. (B) This fine small company, which is known for the excellence of its products, employs. . . .
85. (B) Harold knew what my reaction would be; nevertheless, he insisted. . . .
86. (D) The Pulvers, the owners of the property, are the ones. . . .

87. (C)   The Rhodes scholar spoke before huge audiences of students and tried. . . .
88. (B)   Because Mr. Arnold is my former college counselor, I often. . . .

89. (E)   Fashions are not brought about by changes in man's needs but come about. . . .
90. (E)   Without resorting to the set of instructions when we tried to assemble the mechanism, the task became. . . .

ANSWER KEY: PRACTICE TEST TWO

Part 1

1. (A)	12. (D)	23. (A)
2. (A)	13. (B)	24. (D)
3. (B)	14. (A)	25. (B)
4. (D)	15. (D)	26. (B)
5. (B)	16. (E)	27. (B)
6. (B)	17. (B)	28. (B)
7. (C)	18. (A)	29. (D)
8. (C)	19. (B)	30. (B)
9. (B)	20. (B)	31. (A)
10. (A)	21. (A)	32. (A)
11. (C)	22. (B)	33. (A)

Part 2

34. (C)	44. (C)	54. (E)	
35. (E)	45. (B)	55. (E)	
36. (B)	46. (E)	56. (A)	
37. (B)	47. (C)	57. (D)	
38. (D)	48. (C)	58. (B)	
39. (E)	49. (B)	59. (A)	
40. (E)	50. (D)	60. (C)	
41. (A)	51. (C)	61. (B)	
42. (C)	52. (A)	62. (D)	
43. (A)	53. (C)	63. (C)	

Part 3

64. (C)	73. (D)	82. (D)
65. (B)	74. (B)	83. (E)
66. (E)	75. (E)	84. (C)
67. (A)	76. (E)	85. (B)
68. (B)	77. (A)	86. (C)
69. (D)	78. (C)	87. (A)
70. (D)	79. (C)	88. (C)
71. (D)	80. (E)	89. (B)
72. (A)	81. (A)	90. (D)

DETERMINING YOUR RAW SCORE

1. Tabulate Totals
   Number Right _____
   Number Wrong _____
   Number Omitted _____

2. Enter Number Right   A _____
   Divide Number Wrong by
   4 and put result here   B _____

3. Subtract B from A. This
   results in your RAW
   SCORE   _____

   The subtraction of ¼ point for each incorrect answer adjusts for the effect of random guessing.

EVALUATING YOUR PERFORMANCE

Excellent	83–90
Very Good	61–82
Good	42–60
Average	33–41
Below Average	15–32
Unsatisfactory	14 or below

ANALYSIS OF ANSWERS: PRACTICE TEST TWO

Part 1

1. (A)   The term *like* is not a standard equivalent for *as if*.
2. (A)   The term *except* is not a standard equivalent for *unless*.
3. (B)   The term *fewer*, not *less*, is required with units (errors).
4. (D)   Parallel structure requires *dependable*.
5. (B)   The idiom *in back of* is a nonstandard equivalent for *behind*.
6. (B)   The plural *clothes* requires the plural *do*.
7. (C)   The standard form is *occurred when*, not *was when*.

8. (C)   *They* has no word to refer to.
9. (B)   The phrase *inside of* is not a standard synonym for *within*.
10. (A)   The pronoun *they* is an unnecessary appositive.
11. (C)   The standard form is *losing*, not *losing out*.
12. (D)   The subordinating conjunction *because* should not be preceded by a comma when the clause it introduces is in its natural order.
13. (B)   The pronoun *she* has an ambiguous reference.

14. (A) The noun *advice*, not the verb *advise*, is needed.
15. (D) The term *over with* is nonstandard for *over*.
16. (E) No error
17. (B) The word *concern* is not in standard usage in this sentence.
18. (A) *Neither...has*.
19. (B) The term required is *complimented* (*praised*) and not *complemented* (*completed*).
20. (B) When referring to health, *well*, not *good*, is used.
21. (A) The word *again* is superfluous.
22. (B) I referred to him (*whom*).
23. (A) The standard idiom is *try to*.
24. (D) The particle *lying* (*resting*), *not laying* (*putting*), is required.
25. (B) *If you had given* is the correct idiomatic phrase.
26. (B) The plural *there are*, not the singular *there's* (*there is*), is required.
27. (B) The plural *sisters* requires *know*.
28. (B) Required is *you and I are*.
29. (D) The word *aggravated* is nonstandard as an equivalent for *annoyed*, *irritated*, or *exacerbated*.
30. (B) The possessive pronoun *his*, not *him*, is used to modify the gerund *having*.
31. (A) The past subjunctive form is *had*, not *would have*.
32. (A) The standard past perfect is *had drunk*.
33. (A) *He* and not *his career* reached forty.

Part 2
34. (C) Parallel construction requires *either the plans or the ones*.
35. (E) The standard form for the past subjunctive is *had consulted*.
36. (B) The past perfect *had hoped* is required for action precedent to past action (*were disrupting*).
37. (B) The standard idiom is *because of*, not *due to*; required is the standard *different from*, not *different than*.
38. (D) The pronoun *us* is required as object of *of*; *was* is required to follow the singular *no one*.
39. (E) The present perfect *has lived* is required for action begun in the past and carried into the present.
40. (E) The phrase *by nine* must be so placed that it can refer to only one of the three verbs in the sentence.

41. (A) No error
42. (C) The elliptical clause *When in doubt* must refer to a specific noun or pronoun.
43. (A) No error
44. (C) The pronoun *everyone* requires *was*; the preposition *except* should be followed by the object form (*me*).
45. (B) The nonrestrictive appositive phrase, *the invention of devils and saints*, should be set off by commas.
46. (E) The verb form *hadn't ought* is nonstandard for *ought not*; *he* is a predicate nominative after *must be*.
47. (C) Because *At thirty* dangles, *When he was thirty* is required; the singular *reputation* requires the singular *was*.
48. (C) The past subjunctive is required.
49. (B) The standard idiom is *better than*; *at least* should be close to the word modified (*equal*).
50. (D) The participle phrase *Having worked* dangles.
51. (C) Construction requires *persuasive* (adjective) to parallel *logical* (adjective) and *clear* (adjective).
52. (A) Two closely related independent clauses may be separated by a semicolon.
53. (C) The plural *collections* requires the plural *have*.
54. (E) The object form *him* cannot be used to modify the gerund *helping*; the possessive form *his* is required. The singular *everyone* requires the singular *knows*.
55. (E) Parallel construction requires *not only seeing but also visiting*.
56. (A) An introductory phrase is set off by a comma.
57. (D) With the correlatives *neither . . . nor*, the verb agrees with the noun or pronoun (*I*) following *nor*.
58. (B) The pronoun *which* cannot refer to the main idea in the rest of the sentence.
59. (A) An introductory clause is set off by a comma.
60. (C) The standard idiom is *occurs when*, not *is when*.
61. (B) The past perfect *had lived* is required for past action preceding past action (*was*).
62. (D) The expression *being that* is not a standard equivalent for *since* or *because*.
63. (C) Parallel construction requires the participle *prevaricating*.

Part 3

64. (C) We will remember as heroes who died for their countrymen everyone of the men who had been caught in the deadly trap.

65. (B) I had not helped to make our relationships any the more cordial by calling him a falsifier.

66. (E) The new evidence and the facts . . . are sufficient . . .

67. (A) His first opponent was defeated by the champion, who hoped . . .

68. (B) Konner is a man who has devoted . . .

69. (D) Either Paul or Dave has been selected . . .

70. (D) Bill told Margie that she was leaving . . .

71. (D) This model and its predecessors are too . . .

72. (A) Mahogany is better than any other wood for making . . .

73. (D) Although I am reading all the directions, I can . . .

74. (B) I cannot imagine my ever being able to sing like Joan . . .

75. (E) His answering me in anger irritated me very much.

76. (E) The visitor who had just arrived from their hometown greeted them as they came into the house.

77. (A) Because you had listened to me, we completed . . .

78. (C) Edna along with her sister is insisting that we . . .

79. (C) Only after they had carried out 45 painstaking experiments, did they. . . .

80. (E) Viewing the substance without the aid of a microscope, we found it no different from. . . .

81. (A) It turned out to be a toy that gluts the market for a short while and then disappears.

82. (D) . . . everyone but Edna and me.

83. (E) The child who has personality traits which do not match. . . .

84. (C) I could not bear this failure coming at the end. . . .

85. (B) A minority culture inevitably finds itself in a constant state of war when it strives to maintain. . . .

86. (C) In order to challenge the story's main characters with the cruelty of nature and the bleakness of death, except for the faded green of its foliage, the scenery is all in black and white.

87. (A) War still makes a mockery of all of man's pious utterings because, despite all his resources, he is unable to prevent it.

88. (C) The essentiality of the service at stake, whether in the public or private sector, should be the only sound criterion for banning strikes, according to the critics.

89. (B) Each of the major characters tells a set of lurid tales, which are interpolated into the main story.

90. (D) One of the two themes in this brief essay stresses the dramatic psychological growth that occurs in the opening years while the other theme emphasizes the importance. . . .

ANSWER KEY: PRACTICE TEST THREE

Part 1

1. (D)	16. (E)	31. (D)
2. (C)	17. (D)	32. (E)
3. (D)	18. (C)	33. (A)
4. (D)	19. (D)	34. (B)
5. (B)	20. (E)	35. (B)
6. (A)	21. (C)	36. (C)
7. (E)	22. (A)	37. (E)
8. (D)	23. (B)	38. (B)
9. (B)	24. (A)	39. (C)
10. (A)	25. (C)	40. (B)
11. (B)	26. (D)	41. (C)
12. (D)	27. (A)	42. (D)
13. (E)	28. (C)	43. (E)
14. (B)	29. (C)	44. (A)
15. (D)	30. (C)	

Part 2

45. (B)	55. (B)
46. (E)	56. (B)
47. (D)	57. (C)
48. (C)	58. (A)
49. (A)	59. (A)
50. (B)	60. (B)
51. (A)	61. (C)
52. (C)	62. (C)
53. (D)	63. (E)
54. (E)	

Part 3

64. (E)	78. (B)
65. (B)	79. (E)
66. (C)	80. (A)
67. (C)	81. (D)
68. (D)	82. (E)
69. (A)	83. (B)
70. (E)	84. (D)
71. (B)	85. (E)
72. (D)	86. (A)
73. (D)	87. (D)
74. (A)	88. (E)
75. (B)	89. (B)
76. (E)	90. (D)
77. (C)	

DETERMINING YOUR RAW SCORE

1. Tabulate Totals
   Number Right _____
   Number Wrong _____
   Number Omitted _____

2. Enter Number Right   A_____
   Divide Number Wrong by
   4 and put result here   B_____

3. Subtract B from A. This
   results in your RAW
   SCORE   _____

   The subtration of ¼ point for each incorrect answer adjusts for the effect of random guessing.

EVALUATING YOUR PERFORMANCE

Excellent	85–90
Very Good	62–84
Good	46–61
Average	34–45
Below Average	15–33
Unsatisfactory	14 or below

ANALYSIS OF ANSWERS: PRACTICE TEST THREE

Part 1

1. (D) The pronoun modifying the gerund *having* should be in the possessive case (*our*).
2. (C) . . . as *we* are. . . .
3. (D) The idiom is *different from*.
4. (D) The last *to* is repetitious.
5. (B) After the helping verb *had, drunk* is the required form.
6. (A) The adverb *altogether* is required.
7. (E) No error
8. (D) The phrase *each other* can refer to two only.
9. (B) . . . he thinks *he* (*who*) is guilty. . . .
10. (A) The infinitive phrase should modify the subject *you*: *To read a poem well, you*. . . .
11. (B) The term *but that* is in nonstandard use.
12. (D) Parallel structure requires *a necessity* instead of *necessary*.
13. (E) No error
14. (B) No hyphen is needed.
15. (D) The verb form *hadn't ought* is nonstandard.
16. (E) No error
17. (D) The singular subject (*group*) is followed by a singular verb (*was*).
18. (C) In standard use *unique* cannot be compared and cannot thus be used with *more* or *most*.
19. (D) The pronouns must be consistent: *You-your-you* or *One-one's-one*.
20. (E) No error
21. (C) The standard idiom is *kind of*.
22. (A) The pronoun *he* could refer to either the officer or the private.
23. (B) The standard idiom is *to feel bad*.
24. (A) The term *being that* is nonstandard when used as an equivalent of *since* or *because*.
25. (C) The standard phrase is *put into*.
26. (D) Logic requires *than any other*.
27. (A) The phrase to remember is *the effects of*.
28. (C) The adjective *meaningful* is required since the words did not make the sounds.
29. (C) *It* has no antecedent.
30. (C) The pronoun *we* is unnecessary.
31. (D) The objective *me* should follow the preposition *by*.
32. (E) No error
33. (A) The standard form for a condition contrary to fact is *If you had*.
34. (B) The negative *but* cannot follow the negative *not*.
35. (B) The phrase *each other* can refer to only two.
36. (C) The idiom *every so often* is nonstandard.
37. (E) No error
38. (B) The plural *counselors* is followed by *who were*.
39. (C) The plural *nurses* is followed by *who have been*.

40. (B)   The pronoun *they* lacks an antecedent.
41. (C)   The singular *concern* requires the singular verb *was*.
42. (D)   The standard term is *human beings,* not *humans.*
43. (E)   No error
44. (A)   The past perfect tense *had been deployed* is required.

Part 2
45. (B)   Even though the depression seriously cut funds for medical research, the thirties. . . .
46. (E)   When a peace . . . is put into question, the bases of that equilibrium will have undergone a change.
47. (D)   First aid manuals are bought and read only by the people who already know what to do in an emergency and just want. . . .
48. (C)   More of our energy resources are probably consumed by the World Trade Center when it is completely lighted up night after night than by all the homes in a large-sized suburbia.
49. (A)   Had they attempted to control . . . attitudes, the political leaders would have faced serious dilemmas.
50. (B)   The fact that lawyers in general . . . immoral often allows them to act. . . .
51. (A)   Preliterate hunting and gathering tribes that offer the best speculation . . . have lived are highly pacific people. . . .
52. (C)   No government office, not even the highest in the land, carries with it the right. . . .
53. (D)   Invoked by officials at widely disparate levels of government service, national security has become a kind of talisman to justify a wide range of apparently illegal activities.
54. (E)   That the achievements in space of the crews of Skylab have enormous scientific value was made abundantly evident years ago.
55. (B)   The basic need remained for passage by Congress of a law extending to farm workers the same machinery for free elections . . . practices that other American workers have had for nearly four decades.
56. (B)   So quietly does winter come over the hill and down the valley that all you hear are crisp leaves skittering or. . . .
57. (C)   In order to avert a real fuel crisis, the President has made a logical and reasonable request in asking us. . . .
58. (A)   To render the United States independent of foreign energy supplies, by the end of a decade if possible, a momentous program is about to be embarked upon.

59. (A)   Although political parties are not mentioned in the written Constitution, the two-party system has become. . . .
60. (B)   When we see the men about a ruler, we get our first impression of him and of his intelligence.
61. (C)   Mao Tse-tung . . . China; Lenin had set. . . .
62. (C)   Yet we all should be reminded that the shock waves of change that had their origin in World War II are not. . . .
63. (E)   We Americans seem to like to put our political system to the test now and then and hope that. . . .

Part 3
64. (E)   Required is *number* (units), not *amount* (quantity).
65. (B)   The pronoun *she* could refer to either *Frances* or her *sister.*
66. (C)   The phrase *in color* is unnecessary; the adjective *red* requires the adjective *bulky* for parallel construction.
67. (C)   *Place into,* not *place in,* is required. *Proved,* not *proven* is the acceptable past participle.
68. (D)   The parallel construction is *either a more economical way or a financial backer.*
69. (A)   No error
70. (E)   The past perfect *had worked* is required for past action preceding past action.
71. (B)   The adverb *softly* requires the adverb *politely* for parallel construction.
72. (D)   The noun *latter* refers to two only.
73. (D)   The singular *sense of humor* requires the singular verb *makes.*
74. (A)   No error
75. (B)   The phrase *To be effective* must have a noun or pronoun that it can modify logically.
76. (E)   The past perfect *had made* is required for action that preceded past action.
77. (C)   The pronoun *it* lacks a definite antecedent.
78. (B)   Required as a plural verb is *are* for the plural *fewer chances.*
79. (E)   The adjective *friendly* and the adjective *easygoing* require the adjective *cooperative* in parallel construction.
80. (A)   No error
81. (D)   The word *chances* (plural) requires *have* (plural).
82. (E)   Two closely related independent clauses can be separated by a semicolon.
83. (B)   In the 1920s there were very few business machines and no cassette recorders.

84. (D) The word *needs* should be followed by *are*; the singular *point of view* requires the singular *is*.

85. (E) The pronoun *which* must refer to a specific word.

86. (A) The expression *as good* requires *as*: *than*, not *then*, is used in comparisons.

87. (D) Parallel structure and compound subject require this answer.

88. (E) The completion of the helping verb is *may have*, not *may had*.

89. (B) The death rate is not being proved effective.

90. (D) The phrase *after a thorough investigation* must be so placed that it modifies only one part of the sentence.

ANSWER KEY: PRACTICE TEST FOUR

Part 1			Part 2			Part 3				
1. (B)	**12.** (A)	**23.** (E)	**34.** (E)	**43.** (E)	**52.** (B)	**59.** (E)	**67.** (D)	**75.** (B)	**83.** (B)
2. (A)	**13.** (B)	**24.** (A)	**35.** (D)	**44.** (B)	**53.** (E)	**60.** (E)	**68.** (C)	**76.** (D)	**84.** (E)
3. (A)	**14.** (D)	**25.** (A)	**36.** (D)	**45.** (D)	**54.** (D)	**61.** (D)	**69.** (E)	**77.** (A)	**85.** (E)
4. (B)	**15.** (B)	**26.** (C)	**37.** (A)	**46.** (A)	**55.** (B)	**62.** (D)	**70.** (E)	**78.** (B)	**86.** (D)
5. (D)	**16.** (C)	**27.** (A)	**38.** (D)	**47.** (C)	**56.** (B)	**63.** (E)	**71.** (A)	**79.** (E)	**87.** (C)
6. (E)	**17.** (A)	**28.** (A)	**39.** (B)	**48.** (E)	**57.** (C)	**64.** (E)	**72.** (D)	**80.** (E)	**88.** (E)
7. (B)	**18.** (C)	**29.** (B)	**40.** (C)	**49.** (D)	**58.** (C)	**65.** (E)	**73.** (C)	**81.** (A)	**89.** (C)
8. (C)	**19.** (B)	**30.** (E)	**41.** (C)	**50.** (E)		**66.** (A)	**74.** (E)	**82.** (D)	**90.** (D)
9. (B)	**20.** (C)	**31.** (B)	**42.** (A)	**51.** (E)					
10. (A)	**21.** (C)	**32.** (A)							
11. (B)	**22.** (D)	**33.** (B)							

DETERMINING YOUR RAW SCORE

1. Tabulate Totals

   Number Right _____

   Number Wrong _____

   Number Omitted _____

2. Enter Number Right   A _____
   Divide Number Wrong by
   4 and put result here   B _____

3. Subtract B from A. This
   results in your RAW
   SCORE   _____

The subtraction of ¼ point for each incorrect answer adjusts for the effect of random guessing.

EVALUATING YOUR PERFORMANCE

Excellent	82–90
Very Good	63–81
Good	45–62
Average	31–44
Below Average	15–30
Unsatisfactory	14 or below

ANALYSIS OF ANSWERS: PRACTICE TEST FOUR

Part 1

1. (B) The *percentages . . . are.*

2. (A) The idiom *have a loan of* is a nonstandard equivalent for *borrow*.

3. (A) The verb *bring* is used to convey action toward the speaker. *Take* should be used here.

4. (B) The subject is the singular *Arlene*.

5. (D) The term required is *uninterested* (*apathetic*), not *disinterested* (*impartial*).

6. (E) No error

7. (B) The plural subject *practices* requires *rely*.

8. (C) This *to* is repetitious.

9. (B) The adjective *imminent* (*about to happen*) is required.

10. (A) The term *less* refers to quantity; *fewer* refers to units.

11. (B) *. . . I am . . . .*

12. (A)   The singular noun *set* requires the singular verb *is*.
13. (B)   The term *ever* is superfluous.
14. (D)   The singular pronoun *one* requires the singular *his or her*.
15. (B)   The phrase *due to* is a nonstandard equivalent for *since* or *because*.
16. (C)   People are *hanged*.
17. (A)   . . . *just as I (do)*. . . .
18. (C)   The phrase to remember is *the effect (result) of*.
19. (B)   The adverb *indistinctly* is required to modify the verb *spoke*.
20. (C)   The pronoun subject of the gerund *daring* should be in the possessive case (*your*).
21. (C)   The adverb *most* is required when the reference is to three or more.
22. (D)   The pronoun *everyone* requires the singular *is*.
23. (E)   No error
24. (A)   The pronoun *it* cannot pass the test for dangling infinitive.
25. (A)   The standard idiom is *to feel bad*.
26. (C)   Something is *perfect* or *not perfect*; it cannot be *most perfect*.
27. (A)   The form of the past subjunctive is *If you had*.
28. (A)   The standard term is *somewhere*.
29. (B)   The standard present perfect is *has swum*.
30. (E)   No error
31. (B)   The standard idiom is *sort of*, not *sort of a*.
32. (A)   A clause beginning with *when* following *is* is a nonstandard synonym for *occurs when*.
33. (B)   The pronoun *her* can refer to either Margie or Phyllis.

Part 2

34. (E)   The Navy, having intercepted Japanese messages after the Battle of the Coral Sea, knew the next move and rushed. . . .
35. (D)   By mid-January the Germans had moved so many submarines to the Atlantic Coast, where at night they torpedoed tankers silhouetted against the light of the cities, that they created a critical oil shortage.
36. (D)   During its first twenty-five years, prophets have cried out in the wilderness and despaired of TV's lost opportunities.
37. (A)   Those who would want to suppress a repugnant doctrine only succeed all too often in giving it more notoriety.
38. (D)   Moral issues can be debated endlessly with no resolution even though there is. . . .

39. (B)   You need no almanac to recognize the coming of winter since it does not wait on the calendar.
40. (C)   The Test Ban Treaty was considered by John F. Kennedy as not the most historic act since Creation but as a single. . . .
41. (C)   Like Hamlet whipsawed by conflicting . . . death, we hesitate.
42. (A)   He directed at himself as much as anyone his skepticism . . . recognition of failure.
43. (E)   Had a sustained fuel shortage resulted, a quiet revolution in American life, the four-day week, could have come to pass. . . .
44. (B)   Given effective national leadership and a sustained and cooperative response from business and the public, there is no need for Americans to fear economic disaster.
45. (D)   Having marked the beginning of the end of an era filled with ebullient optimism and confidence, the shot that claimed the life of John F. Kennedy will be remembered for more. . . .
46. (A)   The old police headquarters on Centre Street, an architectural gem in an otherwise drab area, should be. . . .
47. (C)   Our obligation is to encourage students to explore many ways of viewing an issue or problem; we must give up. . . .
48. (E)   Is it true that one of the obvious results of the massive, pervasive influence of television is that today's . . . printed page?
49. (D)   In its ability to meet and overcome challenges and in its ability to organize free and strong-minded men to solve great problems lies the true genius of America.
50. (E)   In America our race relations are not perfect. Constructive processes are at work; we are narrowing the gap in opportunity, in education, in income, in the day-to-day relations.
51. (E)   Because the gates at the ticket window automatically swing shut when a train approaches a Paris subway station, only those. . . .
52. (B)   Because the rate of gasoline consumption . . . speed, the higher the speed over any given distance, the more. . . .
53. (E)   Since this is a time of mutual need and shared emergency, the opportunity. . . .
54. (D)   The chickadees . . . came . . . where they had been welcomed. . . .
55. (B)   By substituting neglect for compassion, political appeals to ignorance and selfishness needlessly divided the nation.
56. (B)   Automobile accidents have claimed more of the lives of our people than have all. . . .

57. (C) First we had to face the urgent need to make drastic changes in our energy economy before we could come. . . .

58. (C) Additional evidence . . . in drug therapy comes from the reports from. . . .

Part 3

59. (E) The term *Seeing as* is considered nonstandard usage.

60. (E) The pronoun *which* cannot refer to an idea, but to a specific word.

61. (D) The preposition *between* is followed by the objective *me*; the plural noun *books* requires the plural *were*.

62. (D) The plural *men* requires *who are*.

63. (B) The pronoun *they* lacks an antecedent.

64. (E) The past subjunctive form required is *If you had*.

65. (E) The idiom is *oblivious of*.

66. (A) No error

67. (D) The relative pronoun *which* lacks a stated antecedent.

68. (C) The pronoun *they* lacks an antecedent.

69. (E) The second pronoun *he* could refer to either the speaker or Alex.

70. (E) The clause *(that) he had printed* should follow the word it modifies (*book*).

71. (A) A clause in absolute construction needs no word for it to modify.

72. (D) She had not just bought the hill.

73. (C) In standard usage *round* is an absolute term.

74. (E) . . . *as eligible as*. . . .

75. (B) The adverbs *clearly* and *emphatically* are required for parallel construction.

76. (D) Action preceding past action requires the past perfect tense.

77. (A) No error

78. (B) In standard usage the adverb *scarcely* is not preceded by *not*.

79. (E) The preposition *between* is followed by the object form *me*. Since *nobody* is singular, the singular verb *knows* is required.

80. (E) The conjunctive *seeing as* is nonstandard.

81. (A) The standard phrase is *to let it lie*.

82. (D) The verb *stayed (remained)*, not *stood (on one's feet)*, is required; *had stayed* is required for completion on action in the past.

83. (B) The preposition *off of* is nonstandard; the idiom is *put into*, not *put in*.

84. (E) The additional *there* is unnecessary; the standard idiom is *type of*, not *type of a*.

85. (E) The one-syllable *quite* rather than the two-syllable *quiet* is required; the possessive *their* rather than the expletive *there* shows whose half hour it was; since *act* begins with a vowel sound, *an* rather than *a* is needed.

86. (D) Prose style cannot be compared to a stylist.

87. (C) The adverb *altogether* and the noun *advice* are required; *we are* contracts into *we're*.

88. (E) The verb *to loan* is a nonstandard equivalent of *to lend*. *Anyone* is spelled solid as a pronoun (*anyone can go*) and is spelled as two words when a prepositional phrase follows (*any one* of them can go).

89. (C) The phrase to remember is we *learn from and teach to*; *spill* implies an accidental act.

90. (D) Since the name *Dickens* ends in *s*, the possessive is *Dickens'* or *Dickens's*.

The English Composition Test with Essay

Section **THREE** : **Organization and Content of the Essay**

1. *Diagnostic Test*

2. *A Closer Look*

3. *Improving Prose Style and Organization*

4. *Writing the Essay*

5. *Additional Essay Assignments*

This section is planned primarily for those candidates scheduled to take the English Composition Test in December. In addition to the usual multiple-choice questions, this form of the examination requires the writing of a brief essay. The previous sections of this book review the aspects of writing tested in the approximately 70 multiple-choice questions that make up two-thirds of the test score, 40 minutes of the test time.

THE ESSAY

Although the following analyses and exercises can be helpful to all test candidates since they review the organization of topics covered in college-level expository writing courses, their main focus is on methods of handling ideas and putting them into an essay severely limited in length and to 20 minutes of preparation and writing time.

The essay question is a practical test of all aspects of writing covered in the objective questions. You must give evidence of your control of modern usage and your style of writing. In addition, the essay question measures your ability

- to express ideas clearly and effectively
- to organize ideas
- to marshal evidence and present proof to support opinions.

The type of question must be a general one. It must allow the candidates to present varied points of view. It must have sufficient scope to allow the candidates to react to it and begin to write almost immediately.

HOW THE ESSAYS ARE SCORED

Essays are scored on a four-point scale by each of two readers. Four is the highest score, and one is the lowest. The total essay score is the sum of the two readers' scores. The total is weighted to equal one-third of the total English Composition Achievement Test. The 70 multiple-choice questions are the basis for the other two-thirds.

The scorers do not mark a paper for errors. They look for what the student has done well rather than what the candidate failed to do. They read for the total impression made by the essay.

1. *Diagnostic Test*

The preparation for each of the reviews and drills for the three tests in English begins with a Diagnostic Test. This test has several purposes. First, it is a tool that will help you to discover strengths and weaknesses. It will aid you in setting up a realistic, practical study program to meet your particular needs. You will be able to check the efficiency of your studying by taking the Practice Tests in Section Four, beginning on page 171, and comparing the results with those of the Diagnostic Test.

Another purpose of the Diagnostic Tests is to give you familiarity with the format and level of difficulty of the English Composition multiple-choice questions. You will gain confidence and know-how by experiencing the "traps" set by the test-makers. You will learn to recognize your mistakes, especially if you study the reviews and explanations for the principles you did not know.

Finally, for those of you who still have a choice of which examination to take—all multiple-choice, multiple-choice with essay, or literature—taking the three Diagnostic Tests and comparing results may help you reach your decision.

DIAGNOSTIC TEST

ANSWER SHEET

1	Ⓐ Ⓑ Ⓒ Ⓓ Ⓔ	25	Ⓐ Ⓑ Ⓒ Ⓓ Ⓔ	48	Ⓐ Ⓑ Ⓒ Ⓓ Ⓔ
2	Ⓐ Ⓑ Ⓒ Ⓓ Ⓔ	26	Ⓐ Ⓑ Ⓒ Ⓓ Ⓔ	49	Ⓐ Ⓑ Ⓒ Ⓓ Ⓔ
3	Ⓐ Ⓑ Ⓒ Ⓓ Ⓔ	27	Ⓐ Ⓑ Ⓒ Ⓓ Ⓔ	50	Ⓐ Ⓑ Ⓒ Ⓓ Ⓔ
4	Ⓐ Ⓑ Ⓒ Ⓓ Ⓔ	28	Ⓐ Ⓑ Ⓒ Ⓓ Ⓔ	51	Ⓐ Ⓑ Ⓒ Ⓓ Ⓔ
5	Ⓐ Ⓑ Ⓒ Ⓓ Ⓔ	29	Ⓐ Ⓑ Ⓒ Ⓓ Ⓔ	52	Ⓐ Ⓑ Ⓒ Ⓓ Ⓔ
6	Ⓐ Ⓑ Ⓒ Ⓓ Ⓔ	30	Ⓐ Ⓑ Ⓒ Ⓓ Ⓔ	53	Ⓐ Ⓑ Ⓒ Ⓓ Ⓔ
7	Ⓐ Ⓑ Ⓒ Ⓓ Ⓔ	31	Ⓐ Ⓑ Ⓒ Ⓓ Ⓔ	54	Ⓐ Ⓑ Ⓒ Ⓓ Ⓔ
8	Ⓐ Ⓑ Ⓒ Ⓓ Ⓔ	32	Ⓐ Ⓑ Ⓒ Ⓓ Ⓔ	55	Ⓐ Ⓑ Ⓒ Ⓓ Ⓔ
9	Ⓐ Ⓑ Ⓒ Ⓓ Ⓔ	33	Ⓐ Ⓑ Ⓒ Ⓓ Ⓔ	56	Ⓐ Ⓑ Ⓒ Ⓓ Ⓔ
10	Ⓐ Ⓑ Ⓒ Ⓓ Ⓔ	34	Ⓐ Ⓑ Ⓒ Ⓓ Ⓔ	57	Ⓐ Ⓑ Ⓒ Ⓓ Ⓔ
11	Ⓐ Ⓑ Ⓒ Ⓓ Ⓔ	35	Ⓐ Ⓑ Ⓒ Ⓓ Ⓔ	58	Ⓐ Ⓑ Ⓒ Ⓓ Ⓔ
12	Ⓐ Ⓑ Ⓒ Ⓓ Ⓔ	36	Ⓐ Ⓑ Ⓒ Ⓓ Ⓔ	59	Ⓐ Ⓑ Ⓒ Ⓓ Ⓔ
13	Ⓐ Ⓑ Ⓒ Ⓓ Ⓔ	37	Ⓐ Ⓑ Ⓒ Ⓓ Ⓔ	60	Ⓐ Ⓑ Ⓒ Ⓓ Ⓔ
14	Ⓐ Ⓑ Ⓒ Ⓓ Ⓔ	38	Ⓐ Ⓑ Ⓒ Ⓓ Ⓔ	61	Ⓐ Ⓑ Ⓒ Ⓓ Ⓔ
15	Ⓐ Ⓑ Ⓒ Ⓓ Ⓔ	39	Ⓐ Ⓑ Ⓒ Ⓓ Ⓔ	62	Ⓐ Ⓑ Ⓒ Ⓓ Ⓔ
16	Ⓐ Ⓑ Ⓒ Ⓓ Ⓔ	40	Ⓐ Ⓑ Ⓒ Ⓓ Ⓔ	63	Ⓐ Ⓑ Ⓒ Ⓓ Ⓔ
17	Ⓐ Ⓑ Ⓒ Ⓓ Ⓔ	41	Ⓐ Ⓑ Ⓒ Ⓓ Ⓔ	64	Ⓐ Ⓑ Ⓒ Ⓓ Ⓔ
18	Ⓐ Ⓑ Ⓒ Ⓓ Ⓔ	42	Ⓐ Ⓑ Ⓒ Ⓓ Ⓔ	65	Ⓐ Ⓑ Ⓒ Ⓓ Ⓔ
19	Ⓐ Ⓑ Ⓒ Ⓓ Ⓔ	43	Ⓐ Ⓑ Ⓒ Ⓓ Ⓔ	66	Ⓐ Ⓑ Ⓒ Ⓓ Ⓔ
20	Ⓐ Ⓑ Ⓒ Ⓓ Ⓔ	44	Ⓐ Ⓑ Ⓒ Ⓓ Ⓔ	67	Ⓐ Ⓑ Ⓒ Ⓓ Ⓔ
21	Ⓐ Ⓑ Ⓒ Ⓓ Ⓔ	45	Ⓐ Ⓑ Ⓒ Ⓓ Ⓔ	68	Ⓐ Ⓑ Ⓒ Ⓓ Ⓔ
22	Ⓐ Ⓑ Ⓒ Ⓓ Ⓔ	46	Ⓐ Ⓑ Ⓒ Ⓓ Ⓔ	69	Ⓐ Ⓑ Ⓒ Ⓓ Ⓔ
23	Ⓐ Ⓑ Ⓒ Ⓓ Ⓔ	47	Ⓐ Ⓑ Ⓒ Ⓓ Ⓔ	70	Ⓐ Ⓑ Ⓒ Ⓓ Ⓔ
24	Ⓐ Ⓑ Ⓒ Ⓓ Ⓔ				

DIAGNOSTIC TEST

Total Time: One Hour
PART 1 *Suggested Time:* **20 *Minutes***
Time begun .... Time ended .... Time used ....
Did you complete the section within the time limit?...

DIRECTIONS: You have twenty minutes to plan and write an essay on the topic assigned below. DO NOT WRITE ON ANOTHER TOPIC. AN ESSAY ON ANOTHER TOPIC IS NOT ACCEPTABLE.

The essay is assigned to give you an opportunity to show how well you can write. You should, therefore, take care to express your thoughts on the topic clearly and effectively. How well you write is much more important than how much you write, but to cover the topic adequately you may want to write more than one paragraph. Be specific.

Your essay must be written on the lines provided on your answer sheet. You will receive no other paper on which to write. You will find that you have enough space if you write on every line, avoid wide margins, and keep your handwriting to a reasonable size. It is important to remember that what you write will be read by someone who is not familiar with your handwriting. Try to write or print so that what you are writing is legible.

Most people judge others only by success or by fortune.

ASSIGNMENT: To what extent do you agree with this statement? What does it tell us about ourselves? Use illustrations from your study or observation to support your opinion.

PART 2 *Suggested Time: 20 Minutes*
Time begun .... Time ended .... Time used ....
Did you complete the section within the time limit?...

DIRECTIONS: The following sentences contain problems in grammar, usage, diction (choice of words), and idiom.

Some sentences are correct.

No sentence contains more than one error.

You will find that the error, if there is one, is underlined and lettered. Assume that all other elements of the sentence are correct and cannot be changed. In choosing answers, follow the requirements of standard written English.

If there is an error, select the <u>one underlined part</u> that must be changed in order to make the sentence correct, and mark that on the answer sheet.

If there is no error, mark answer E.

1. Since I do not feel <u>well</u>, you <u>had ought not</u> to
 (A) (B)
 <u>expect</u> me to do <u>so much</u> of the organizing.
 (C) (D)
 <u>No error</u>
 (E)

2. A set of the company's books <u>is</u> in the safe so
 (A)
 that <u>everyone</u> of the officials <u>is</u> able to use <u>it</u> at
 (B) (C) (D)
 all times. <u>No error</u>
 (E)

3. Since there are <u>only</u> three to <u>choose from</u>,
 (A) (B)
 <u>may</u> I claim the <u>latter</u>. <u>No error</u>
 (C) (D) (E)

4. It does not <u>make sense</u> to me that <u>up until</u> yes-
 (A) (B)
 terday he <u>could have</u> been <u>jailed for life</u> for this
 (C) (D)
 act! <u>No error</u>
 (E)

5. To invest in a <u>mutual</u> fund as <u>a kind of a</u> forced
 (A) (B)
 savings, <u>you</u> must make arrangements with
 (C)
 your bank <u>for an</u> automatic withdrawal of
 (D)
 funds. <u>No error</u>
 (E)

6. The selfish acts <u>perpetrated</u> by Pauline and
 (A)
 <u>him</u> should have resulted in the <u>sort of</u> behavior
 (B) (C)
 that mirrors what they <u>have done</u>. <u>No error</u>
 (D) (E)

7. If they <u>had</u> <u>stayed at</u> home <u>more often</u>, the sit-
 (A) (B) (C)
 uation would be <u>far different than</u> it is.
 (D)
 <u>No error</u>
 (E)

8. This <u>is</u> my final reason: the solution <u>to</u> the puz-
 (A) (B)
 zle <u>lays</u> right <u>before</u> our eyes! <u>No error</u>
 (C) (D) (E)

9. There <u>is</u> hardly <u>no</u> reason that I can <u>think of</u>
 (A) (B) (C)
 for <u>his</u> refusing Dave's offer. <u>No error</u>
 (D) (E)

10. I <u>lived</u> <u>in</u> this neighborhood <u>for more than</u> 27
 (A) (B) (C)
 years, and I <u>will</u> not move now! <u>No error</u>
 (D) (E)

11. Go <u>slow</u>, <u>don't</u> be hasty; and <u>you</u> won't have
 (A) (B) (C)
 <u>no</u> regrets. <u>No error</u>
 (D) (E)

12. If <u>only</u> you <u>would have</u> listened to <u>me</u> then, we
 (A) (B) (C)
 <u>would</u> not be in danger now. <u>No error</u>
 (D) (E)

13. Before they had <u>began</u>, she <u>was</u> ready <u>to</u>
 (A) (B) (C)
 complain <u>to</u> the authorities. <u>No error</u>
 (D) (E)

14. Here <u>is</u> another one of those items <u>which</u>
 (A) (B)
 <u>have</u> been the <u>basis</u> of our weakness.
 (C) (D)
 <u>No error</u>
 (E)

15. People <u>must</u> not think that diversity is the rule <u>for</u>
      (A)   (B)
    every particle <u>in</u> the universe but <u>they</u>. <u>No error</u>
                    (C)   (D)   (E)

16. This <u>healthy</u> climate <u>will</u> restore not only
         (A)   (B)
    <u>his health</u> <u>but</u> his good nature as well.
      (C)   (D)
    <u>No error</u>
      (E)

17. He <u>pored</u> over the law books, <u>studying</u> each
        (A)   (B)
    <u>statue</u> and <u>hoping</u> to find the loophole that could
      (C)   (D)
    save his client. <u>No error</u>
                       (E)

18. Our mayor <u>has</u> <u>always</u> had a deep <u>interest for</u>
               (A)   (B)   (C)
    youth's <u>struggle for</u> identity. <u>No error</u>
             (D)   (E)

19. He was <u>formerly</u> introduced to the president of
            (A)
    the college <u>which</u> he had applied <u>to</u> <u>only</u> a few
                 (B)   (C) (D)
    days before. <u>No error</u>
                    (E)

20. In times <u>passed</u>, I <u>would have</u> refused to
              (A)   (B)
    <u>raise</u> a finger to help <u>them</u>. <u>No error</u>
      (C)   (D)   (E)

21. The bell had <u>rung</u> and the classes had <u>begun</u> <u>by</u>
                  (A)   (B)   (C)
    the time I <u>was reaching</u> the corner. <u>No error</u>
                (D)   (E)

22. <u>Somebody</u> <u>has gone and</u> left his hat <u>on</u> the rack
      (A)   (B)   (C)
    <u>without</u> asking permission. <u>No error</u>
      (D)   (E)

23. In our <u>city</u>, strangers <u>are</u> <u>customarily</u> treated
            (A)   (B)   (C)
    very <u>politely</u>. <u>No error</u>
          (D)   (E)

24. <u>They</u> said that I had <u>sung</u> a <u>song</u> in the wrong
      (A)   (B)   (C)
    key, <u>which</u> annoyed me very much.
          (D)
    <u>No error</u>
      (E)

25. I was not <u>so</u> willing <u>as</u> <u>he</u> to place blame in
               (A)   (B) (C)
    this <u>case</u>. <u>No error</u>
          (D)   (E)

26. They had <u>seen</u> all of <u>their</u> friends except Lucy
              (A)   (B)
    and <u>I</u> <u>at</u> the festival. <u>No error</u>
         (C)(D)   (E)

27. <u>It's</u> one of <u>them</u> things <u>that</u> I always find <u>so</u>
      (A)   (B)   (C)   (D)
    frightening. <u>No error</u>
                   (E)

28. These flowers do not <u>smell</u> <u>so</u> <u>sweetly</u> as <u>did</u>
                          (A)   (B)   (C)   (D)
    those we bought last night. <u>No error</u>
                                  (E)

29. You <u>will</u> have <u>to</u> settle this <u>issue</u> between
         (A)   (B)   (C)
    Henry and <u>me</u>. <u>No error</u>
               (D)   (E)

30. They had <u>brought</u> the picture of <u>a</u> <u>airplane</u>
              (A)   (B) (C)
    <u>into</u> the classroom. <u>No error</u>
      (D)   (E)

31. There <u>wasn't</u> <u>anything</u> I could do to help; we
            (A)   (B)
    were all <u>caught up</u> in that maze from which
              (C)
    there seemed to be <u>no</u> escape. <u>No error</u>
                         (D)   (E)

32. There <u>was</u> scarcely <u>no</u> time left for <u>them</u> to
            (A)   (B)   (C)
    leave before the fighting would <u>begin</u>.
                                      (D)
    <u>No error</u>
      (E)

33. <u>Have</u> there <u>ever</u> been any <u>others</u> just like you
      (A)   (B)   (C)
    and <u>me</u>? <u>No error</u>
         (D)   (E)

34. I had to <u>lay</u> down on the <u>couch</u> for ten minutes
      (A)   (B)
before <u>going into</u> the room in which the meeting
      (C) (D)
was being held. <u>No error</u>
            (E)

35. I <u>disapprove</u> of <u>your</u> <u>claiming</u> that the set of pa-
               (A)   (B)
pers   <u>were</u>   corrected   <u>with supervision</u>.
       (C)   (D)
<u>No error</u>
 (E)

PART 3 *Suggested Time:* **20** *Minutes*
Time begun .... Time ended .... Time used ....
Did you complete the section within the time limit?...

DIRECTIONS: In each of the following sentences, some part of the sentence or the entire sentence is underlined. Beneath each sentence you will find five ways of phrasing the underlined part. The first of these repeats the original; the other four are different. If you think the original is better than any of the alternatives, choose answer A; otherwise choose one of the others.

This is a test of correctness and effectiveness of expression. In choosing answers, follow the requirements of standard written English; that is, pay attention to grammar, choice of words, sentence construction and punctuation. Choose the answer that best expresses the meaning of the original sentence. Your choice should produce the most effective sentence—clear and precise, without awkwardness or ambiguity.

36. Whenever Alice feels tense, she has a frozen smile on her <u>face, which helps us</u> to understand her mood immediately.

  (A) face, which helps us
  (B) face which helps us
  (C) face. This helps us
  (D) face, a characteristic which helps us
  (E) face, helping us

37. Every book and magazine in the law <u>library have been processed</u> for borrowing.

  (A) library have been processed
  (B) library has been processed
  (C) library they processed
  (D) library were processed
  (E) library will have been processed

38. <u>Some members of the concern take their vacation in the fall, and this is better they think.</u>

  (A) Some members of the concern take their vacation in the fall, and this is better they think.
  (B) Some of the members of the concern take their vacation in the fall, which they think is better.
  (C) Some members of the concern prefer to take their vacation in the fall.
  (D) Some employees prefer fall vacations.
  (E) Some members of the concern take their vacation in the fall. This is better, they think.

39. He is sensitive, well <u>educated and has a wonderful sense of proportion</u>.

  (A) educated and has a wonderful sense of proportion.
  (B) educated and is well proportioned.
  (C) educated; and has a wonderful sense of proportion.
  (D) educated and able to see things in proper perspective.
  (E) educated, and flexible in his judgments.

40. The dissident students <u>not only demanded complete control</u> of the selection of courses to be offered but also the right to bring faculty members up on charges of incompetence.

  (A) not only demanded complete control
  (B) were not only demanding complete control
  (C) demanded not only complete control
  (D) were asking not only for absolute control
  (E) demanded complete control not only

41. <u>You will have to address yourself to the colonel in charge of this brigade who alone can give you permission to leave.</u>

  (A) You will have to address yourself to the colonel in charge of this brigade who alone can give you permission to leave.
  (B) Only the colonel can give you permission to leave.
  (C) Since the colonel is in command of this brigade, you will have to ask his permission to leave.
  (D) Because he is in charge of this brigade. Only the colonel can give you permission to leave.
  (E) Since only the colonel in charge of this brigade can give you permission to leave, you will have to send your request to him.

42. The salesman's impatience neither pleased the customers nor were the owners appreciative.

(A) customers nor were the owners appreciative.
(B) customers nor were the owners' appreciative.
(C) customers nor were the owner's appreciative.
(D) customers nor made the owners appreciative.
(E) customers. Nor made the owners appreciative.

43. By the end of Tom's first fishing trip he had mastered the art of netting minnows in a stream.

(A) Tom's first fishing trip he had mastered
(B) Tom's first fishing trip, he had mastered
(C) Tom's first fishing trip, having mastered
(D) Tom's first fishing trip. He had mastered
(E) Tom's first fishing trip, he mastered

44. The exhibition game lasted three hours which gave the children ample opportunity to renew their appetites.

(A) hours which gave the children
(B) hours which gave to the children
(C) hours. Which gave the children
(D) hours giving the children
(E) hours, a time interval which gave the children

45. It says in this paragraph that those who are eligible to fight for their country should be eligible to vote.

(A) It says in this paragraph that those
(B) In this paragraph the author states that those
(C) They say in this paragraph that those
(D) The author's main thesis in the paragraph under consideration is that those
(E) It says in this paragraph that, those

46. Sylvia and her sister went to see a revival of *Oklahoma* because she said that it was her favorite musical.

(A) *Oklahoma* because she said that it was her favorite musical.
(B) *Oklahoma* because she said, "It was my favorite musical."
(C) *Oklahoma* because she said it had always been her favorite musical.

(D) *Oklahoma* because it was the sister's favorite musical.
(E) *Oklahoma*, because she said that it was her favorite musical.

47. Before considering any of these proposals, a final disposition must be made on those in the preceding group.

(A) Before considering any of these proposals, a final
(B) Before we can consider any of these proposals, a final
(C) Before considering any of these proposals. A final
(D) Before considering any of these proposals a final
(E) Before we had considered these proposals, a final

48. The student who fails in nine cases out of ten has had excessive absences.

(A) The student who fails in nine cases out of ten has
(B) The student who fails, in nine cases out of ten has
(C) The student who fails in nine cases out of ten, has
(D) The student who fails, in nine cases out of ten, has
(E) In nine cases out of ten, the student who fails has

49. I handed my examination paper in after the composition had been proofread most carefully.

(A) I handed my examination paper in after the composition had been proofread most carefully.
(B) I handed my examination paper in. After the composition had been proofread most carefully.
(C) I handed my examination paper in, after a most careful rereading of the composition.
(D) I handed my examination paper in only after it was proofread most carefully.
(E) I handed in my examination paper after proofreading the composition most carefully.

50. When the committee of faculty members entered the room, the instructor was lecturing and the students taking notes.

(A) lecturing and the students taking notes.

(B) lecturing and the students were taking notes.

(C) lecturing; and the students taking notes.

(D) lecturing and the students had been taking notes.

(E) lecturing and the students' taking notes.

51. The new idol of the teenagers soon realized that he was being exploited by people who wanted to take advantage of him and use him.

(A) realized that he was being exploited by people who wanted to take advantage of him and use him.

(B) realized that he was being used by those whom he trusted.

(C) realized that he was being exploited.

(D) realized, that he was being taken advantage of.

(E) realized that people wanted to take advantage of him.

52. The twin towers of the World Trade Center are taller than any building in New York City.

(A) Center are taller than any building in New York City.

(B) Center are taller than any of the other buildings in New York City.

(C) Center, are taller than any building in New York City.

(D) Center are the tallest buildings in New York City.

(E) Center are the tallest of the buildings that are in New York City.

53. Stretched to the breaking point our budget is nevertheless the workhorse that will lead us into quieter waters.

(A) Stretched to the breaking point our budget is nevertheless the workhorse that will lead us into quieter waters.

(B) We must learn to rely upon our budget.

(C) If we want to have peace of mind, we must work within the tight limits of our budget.

(D) I am certain that we will be able to balance our budget regardless of how much strain we put on it.

(E) If we are to succeed, we must not misuse our budget.

54. When we made the costumes for the pageant that summer, we used whatever available clothing we could borrow which included dated cast-offs in large quantities.

(A) When we made costumes for the pageant that summer, we used whatever available clothing we could borrow which included dated cast-offs in large quantities.

(B) Making costumes for the pageant that summer, we borrowed many dated cast-offs from our friends.

(C) The costumes we had made for the pageant that summer came from many borrowed cast-offs.

(D) We made costumes for the pageant that summer from whatever clothing we could borrow, including many dated cast-offs.

(E) That summer for costumes for the pageant we borrowed dated cast-offs in large quantities.

55. As his parting gift to us, my cousin gave us a limited edition print by Picasso.

(A) gift to us, my cousin gave

(B) gift, my cousin gave

(C) gift. My cousin gave

(D) gift, my cousin presented to

(E) gift, my cousin bestowed on

56. The picnic was held in the grove, a small open area shaded by tall pines.

(A) grove, a small open area

(B) grove which is a small open area

(C) grove, which was a small open area

(D) grove. A small open area

(E) grove; this was a small open area

57. The Breath of Life Campaign was soon launched however it foundered from lack of funds.

(A) launched however it foundered from lack of funds.

(B) launched; however, it foundered from lack of funds.

(C) launched, however, it foundered from lack of funds.

(D) launched, but it soon failed.

(E) launched, but it stepped into trouble from lack of money.

58. <u>Legal terminology confuses me, I am unable</u> to follow even the simplest statements.

(A) Legal terminology confuses me, I am unable
(B) Legal terminology is confusing, being unable
(C) When legal terminology confuses me, I am unable
(D) Legal terminology sometimes confusing me, I am unable
(E) Legal terminology confuses me. I am unable

59. Because of the danger of plague, every man, woman, and child <u>in the village has been vaccinated</u>.

(A) in the village has been vaccinated.
(B) has been vaccinated in the village.
(C) in the village have been vaccinated.
(D) have been vaccinated in the village.
(E) must be vaccinated.

60. This is the only one of the television sets <u>that have been repaired</u>.

(A) that have been repaired.
(B) which have been repaired.
(C) that has been fixed.
(D) that has been repaired.
(E) that has had defective parts replaced and adjustments made.

61. During the years of my political career, <u>I always have and will continue to identify myself with</u> the needs of youth.

(A) I always have and will continue to identify myself with
(B) I have and will continue always to identify myself with
(C) I always have identified and will continue to identify myself with
(D) I have identified and will continue always to identify myself with
(E) I have and will continue to always identify myself with

62. <u>Only an ingenuous freshman would accept the bait offered by an instructor looking for a victim upon whom</u> he could vent the full force of his scathing witticisms.

(A) Only an ingenuous freshman would accept the bait offered by an instructor looking for a victim upon whom

(B) Only an ingenuous freshman would accept the bait offered by an instructor, looking for a victim upon whom
(C) Only an ingenious freshman would except the bait offered by the instructor looking for a victim upon whom
(D) Only an ingenious freshman would accept the bait offered by the instructor who is looking for a victim upon who
(E) Only an ingenuous freshman could accept the bait offered by the instructor looking for a victim upon whom

63. I have but one reaction when you say, "No one goes hungry in our <u>town," I wish it were true!</u>

(A) town," I wish it were true!
(B) town. I wish it were true!"
(C) town:" I wish it were true!
(D) town": I wish it were true!
(E) town;" I wish it was true!

64. <u>Although he is best known for his studies on megavitamins, like his brother, he</u> has hopes of winning the Nobel Prize for medicine.

(A) Although he is best known for his studies on megavitamins, like his brother, he
(B) Although he is best known for his studies on megavitamins. Like his brother, he
(C) Although best known for his studies on megavitamins, like his brother, he
(D) Although, like his brother, he is best known for his studies on megavitamins, he
(E) Like his brother, he is best known for his studies on megavitamins, and he

65. During her long hours of practice, the novice learned how to anticipate the strategy of her opponent, how to coordinate her own arm and leg movements, and <u>how important is frequent reviewing of fundamentals</u>.

(A) how important is frequent reviewing of fundamentals.
(B) how to emphasize frequent review of fundamentals.
(C) how important are frequent reviewing of fundamentals.
(D) how to review fundamentals frequently.
(E) the importance of frequent review of fundamentals.

66. The major discussion topic dealt with an aspect of my senior <u>thesis which added to my confidence</u> during the interview.

    (A) thesis which added to my confidence
    (B) thesis, thus giving me confidence
    (C) thesis. Which added to my confidence
    (D) thesis, this added to my confidence
    (E) thesis, a fact which added to my confidence

67. The purpose of this investigation of juvenile crime is to explore <u>the major causes which must be analyzed because of their importance</u>.

    (A) the major causes which must be analyzed because of their importance.
    (B) the major causes, which must be analyzed because of their importance.
    (C) the major causes.
    (D) the major causes that must be analyzed because of their importance.
    (E) the major causes to be analyzed because of their importance.

68. This is not the first of the generations to grow up with the fear that some careless finger could shatter the unstable cohesiveness of the <u>Earth's particles and disintegrate our atoms into interspace dust</u>.

    (A) Earth's particles and disintegrate our atoms into interspace dust.
    (B) Earth's particles and which would disintegrate our atoms into interspace dust.
    (C) Earth particles, and disintegrate our atoms into interspace dust.
    (D) Earth's particles disintegrating our atoms into interspace dust.
    (E) Earth's particles and disintegrate our atoms in interspace dust.

69. You must be pleased that your royalties have increased <u>sufficiently to make your income tax much higher than last year</u>.

    (A) sufficiently to make your income tax much higher than last year.
    (B) sufficiently, to make your income tax much higher than last year.
    (C) to make your income tax payments much higher.
    (D) sufficiently to make your income tax much higher than last years.
    (E) sufficiently to make your income tax much higher than last year's.

70. If you are to build within yourself the resilience necessary to overcome the blandishments <u>of cultism, you must believe firmly in the fundamental principles of egalitarianism</u>.

    (A) of cultism, you must believe firmly in the fundamental principles of egalitarianism.
    (B) of cultism, you must firmly believe in egalitarianism.
    (C) of cultism, you must believe firmly in egalitarianism.
    (D) of cultism, you must believe firmly in the principles of egalitarianism.
    (E) of cultism, you must firmly believe in fundamental egalitarianism.

ANALYSES AND ANSWER KEYS: DIAGNOSTIC TEST

ANALYSIS OF THE ESSAY QUESTION

Part 1

Answers to the essay question must vary greatly. However, as a guide to evaluating what you had written, four answers and their ratings follow.

To make the most effective use of your practice time:

1. Rate each of the following essays.
2. Compare your ratings with those found in this Analysis.
3. Compare your own essay with the ones you rated.
4. Rate your own essay.

While the results will lack absolute objectivity, for the sake of achieving a range that can lead to an evaluation, use the following rating system:

RATING SCALE	CHARACTERIZED BY	BASED ON A SCALE OF *1-6*
Superior	originality of thought freshness of expression aptness of illustrations	*6*
Above average	clarity of organization soundness of thought	*4-5*
Average	an attempt at a thesis fulfillment of the assignment	*3*
Below average	weak organization irrelevant arguments rambling style	*1-2*

Essay One

I find it very difficult to judge others. I suppose I feel this way because I resent being judged myself. I find it very unfair when what I do is considered mediocre or a failure. I can be depressed for days when that happens.

Some people are born with more assets than others. They are more beautiful or more intelligent. That doesn't mean that they are better than I am, or that what they do is more valuable than what I do. Neither success nor money, to me at least, are the criteria on which to judge us or our deeds. Quasimodo who was willing to give his life for another, as far as I am concerned accomplished more than did the robber barons of big industry, the men who exploited others to achieve huge fortunes and fame.

Most people may judge others by success or by fortune. As for me, these criteria are much too narrow.

ANALYSIS...
....
....
RATING...

Essay Two

I agree that most people judge others only by success or by fortune. They are willing to give fame and Nobel prizes to scientists who make the great discoveries. They are willing to be most respectful to those businessmen who amass millions, regardless of whom they exploit. What does this tell us about ourselves?

To me, it means that if we accept these standards, then most people agree with us—and they are right! On the other hand, if we feel that success and fortune are only two of the many accomplishments that help us to measure people, then it means that our judgments can be faulty and are not reliable, especially when considering people who achieve neither success nor wealth.

So you can see, I think that the quotation can be either right or wrong, depending on your point of view. Which side of the question do you favor?

ANALYSIS...
....
....
RATING...

Essay Three

There are many criteria for judging people and their accomplishments. These criteria range all the way from the idealistic to the self-fulfilling and materialistic.

Idealistic criteria center around what has been accomplished for the betterment of humanity. The greater the benefits for all, the greater the accomplishment. Moses, who gave hope and moral direction, is at the top of the pinnacle. Jay Gould, who made millions by exploiting underpaid workers, is rated low.

Another approach is through an evaluation of how close the person came to doing his best. The juggler in the Komroff short story had only one thing that he knew how to do well. He offered his juggling as his gift, and his prayer was acceptable. This type of evaluation is based on knowing that the person is not holding back, that the person's accomplishments were limited only by his limitations. The mentally retarded who achieve independence through satisfactory work and who thereby achieve self-dignity are rated higher than the brilliant people who work at one-fourth of capacity to achieve a high position in industry.

A third approach is the one basic to the quotation. You judge people only in terms of what success they achieve or in terms of how much money they have earned. This is the simplest of all approaches. While Uriah Heep had money, he was a success; when he was exposed and cast out penniless, he was a failure. The fact that he had cheated and robbed was immaterial. I often wonder why people take this approach. Is the reason that it is so simple to apply?

ANALYSIS...
....
....
RATING...

Essay Four

Even with things going so wrong in the world that we must be more and more part of as we grow into maturity, I am usually reluctant to listen to those who pontificate panaceas. Yet, I am firmly convinced that our tendency to judge others solely in terms of success and wealth is one of the basic causes of the predicament humanity is in, being on the brink of total destruction of all life on Earth.

The "have" nations enslaved and exploited the "have-nots" during the years of colonialization.

The heroes were the generals and industrialists who brought millions of square miles and countless people under the control of the British, French, Portuguese empires. The most respectable citizens were those who seized untold wealth from the natives. The oil-rich nations of today are following in the same pattern. They are not interested in humanity, global cooperation, the welfare of all human beings. They measure their success only in terms of the amount of money and power they can amass. The exploitation, the misery, the hatred, and the distrust they engender are none of their concern!

How different life could be if we measured people in terms of cooperation and self-fulfillment through bettering the lot of humanity, if we believed in global cooperation rather than in achievement of power. Then the welfare of all rather than the aggrandizement of the few would be the rule!

ANALYSIS...
....
....
RATING...

Ratings

Essay One
The thoughts are disconnected. They almost follow a stream-of-consciousness approach. The questions in the assignment were not answered.

RATING: Below Average—2

Essay Two
The essay does have three discernible parts, each in a separate paragraph. The first paragraph gives illustrations to justify a stand. A question is used as the transition to the development.

The development does attempt to show what the quotation tells us about ourselves. However, the observations are pedestrian; no illustrations are offered.

The conclusion does summarize, but it smacks of a formularized ending.

RATING: Average—3

Essay Three
The essay is clearly organized. The writer proves a thesis, that there are many criteria for judging people and their accomplishments. The writer designates three different sets of criteria and illustrates each from literature and studies.

Only in the last paragraph does the essay relate to the assignment. In it, the extent to which the writer agrees with the quotation is approached. The second part of the assignment becomes central. The main thrust of the essay is to prove that there are many criteria for judging people. A full treatment of the quotation is not approached.

RATING: Above Average—4

Essay Four
The essay is organized in a well-defined pattern. The author has a definite thesis, that world crises are caused by our stress on success and wealth. Although the thesis is dealt with in global terms, illustrations are presented. The vocabulary and sentence structure are on a mature level.

RATING: Superior—6

Your Own Essay
ANALYSIS...
....
....
It comes closest to Essay........ because ....
....
RATING (*1* to *6*).................................

ANSWER KEY, MULTIPLE-CHOICE QUESTIONS: DIAGNOSTIC TEST

Part 2				*Part 3*				
1. (B)	10. (A)	19. (A)	28. (C)	36. (D)	43. (B)	50. (B)	57. (B)	64. (D)
2. (E)	11. (D)	20. (A)	29. (E)	37. (B)	44. (E)	51. (C)	58. (E)	65. (B)
3. (D)	12. (B)	21. (D)	30. (B)	38. (C)	45. (B)	52. (D)	59. (A)	66. (E)
4. (B)	13. (A)	22. (B)	31. (E)	39. (E)	46. (D)	53. (C)	60. (D)	67. (C)
5. (B)	14. (E)	23. (E)	32. (B)	40. (C)	47. (B)	54. (D)	61. (C)	68. (A)
6. (D)	15. (D)	24. (D)	33. (E)	41. (E)	48. (E)	55. (B)	62. (A)	69. (E)
7. (D)	16. (A)	25. (E)	34. (A)	42. (D)	49. (E)	56. (A)	63. (D)	70. (D)
8. (C)	17. (C)	26. (C)	35. (C)					
9. (B)	18. (C)	27. (B)						

DETERMINING YOUR RAW SCORE

Multiple-Choice Questions

1. Tabulate Totals
   Number Right   _____
   Number Wrong   _____
   Number Omitted _____

2. Enter Number Right   A_____
   Divide Number Wrong by
   4 and put result here   B_____

3. Subtract B from A. This
   results in your
   MULTIPLE-CHOICE
   RAW SCORE   _____

   The subtraction of ¼ point for each
   incorrect answer adjusts for the effect
   of random guessing.

Essay Question

1. Compare your results
   with the models. Enter
   your own rating of your
   essay (1, 2, 3, 4, 5, or 6).   _____

2. Consult Conversion Chart
   below. Enter your
   CONVERTED SCORE
   here.   _____

3. Add total for
   MULTIPLE-CHOICE
   and CONVERTED
   SCORE for your essay.
         Total Raw Score   _____

EVALUATING YOUR PERFORMANCE

Excellent	94–100+
Very Good	81–94
Good	66–80
Average	47–65
Below Average	31–46
Unsatisfactory	30 or below

ESSAY CONVERSION CHART	
Score	Becomes
6	33
5	28
4	21
3	16
2	10
1	7

ANALYSIS OF ANSWERS, MULTIPLE-CHOICE QUESTIONS: DIAGNOSTIC TEST

Part 2

1. (B) The defective verb *ought* cannot be preceded by *had*. (*Ought* is known as a defective verb because it has only one form and cannot be used with an auxiliary.)

2. (E) No error

3. (D) The word *last* is required since *latter* can refer to two only.

4. (B) The term *up until* is not a standard equivalent for *until*.

5. (B) The idiom *kind of a* is nonstandard as an equivalent for *kind of*.

6. (D) Since action precedent to past action is described, the past perfect tense is required.

7. (D) The standard idiom is *different from*.

8. (C) *Lies* means rests and *lays* means puts.

9. (B) The term *hardly* is followed by any, not *no*.

10. (A) The present perfect *have lived* is required to describe action begun in the past and continued onto the present.

11. (D) *Any* not *no* is required to eliminate the double negative.

12. (B) The form for the past subjunctive is *had*, not *would have*.

13. (A) The past perfect is *had begun*.

14. (E) No error

15. (D) The preposition *but* is followed by the objective *them*.

16. (A) A person is *healthy*; climate is *healthful*.

17. (C) The term *statute* (*law*), not *statue* (*monument*) is required.

18. (C) *Interest in* is the idiom.

19. (A) The word *formally* (*in a formal manner*), and not *formerly* (*at one time*), is required.

20. (A) The form *past*, not *passed*, is required.

21. (D) Sequence of tense requires *had reached* for action completed in the past.

22. (B) The expression *has gone and* is nonstandard.

23. (E) No error

24. (D) The pronoun *which* lacks an antecedent.

25. (E) No error. In a negative, *so . . . as* replaces *as . . . as*.

26. (C) The preposition *except* should be followed by *me* as an object.

27. (B) The adjective *those*, and not the pronoun *them*, is required to modify the noun *things*.

28. (C) The predicate adjective form is *sweet*, not *sweetly*.

29. (E) No error

30. (B) . . . an airplane . . . .

31. (E) No error

32. (B) The team *scarcely* is followed by *any*, not *no*.

33. (E) No error

34. (A) The verb *lie* (*rest*), not *lay* (*put*), is required.

35. (C) The singular *set* requires the singular *was*.

Part 3

36. **D** (A) and (B) contain a relative clause that has no noun in the sentence for *which* to relate to. (C) changes *which* to *this* but does not correct the error in antecedent. (E) has the participle *helping* without a noun for it to modify.

37. **B** (A) has the plural verb *have* following the singular subject *every*. (D) and (E) incorrectly change the tense of the verb. (C) changes the meaning of the sentence.

38. **C** (A) and (E) have *this* with no antecedent. (B) changes *this* to *which* but does not correct the error in antecedent. (D), in changing *members of the concern* to *employees*, changes the meaning of the sentence.

39. **E** (A) incorrectly balances two adjectives and a verb in a series; strict parallelism is necessary. (B) and (D) change the meaning of the sentence. (C) incorrectly adds a semicolon without providing a parallel structure.

40. **C** The correlatives *not only* and *but also* require strictly parallel constructions following them; *complete control* is being correlated with *the right*. (A), (B), and (E) misplace the correlative *not only*; (D) unnecessarily changes the tense of the verb.

41. **E** In (A) the relative *who* clause is incorrectly placed next to *brigade*, rather than *colonel*, the word it modifies. (B) omits part of the meaning; (C) omits the emphasis of *alone*. (D) begins with a sentence fragment.

42. **D** Because the sentence has faulty parallelism following the correlatives *neither . . . nor*, (A) contains an unnecessary shift of subject from salesman to owner. (B) and (C) have an incorrectly used apostrophe. (E) creates a sentence fragment beginning with *Nor*.

43. **B** (A) omits a necessary comma following the introductory phrase. (C) is a sentence fragment. (D) has an introductory sentence fragment. (E) incorrectly changes the past perfect (*had mastered*) to the perfect (*mastered*).

44. **E** (A) and (B) contain a *which* clause with indefinite reference. (C) adds the error of a sentence fragment. In (D), *giving* is a dangling participle because it has no definite antecedent.

45. **B** (A) uses the pronoun *it* incorrectly, since *it* has no definite antecedent. (C) merely substitutes *they* for *it*. (D) is too wordy. (E) repeats the misused *it* and adds a superfluous comma.

46. **D** In (A), (B), (C), and (E), *she* is ambiguous—it could refer to either woman. (E) also adds a superfluous comma, and (C) changes the meaning of the sentence slightly.

47. **B** In (A) the initial gerund phrase dangles, since technically the sentence says the *disposition* will be doing the *considering*. (C) contains an initial sentence fragment. (D) continues to have the initial phrase incorrectly modifying *disposition*. In (E) the tense of the verb has been changed unnecessarily and incorrectly.

48. **E** In (A), (B), (C), and (D) *in nine cases out of ten* may refer to *fails* or *has had*. (B) and (C) are also incorrectly punctuated.

49. **E** (A) contains an unnecessary shift from active (*I handed*) to passive (*composition had been*). (B) adds a sentence fragment. (C) and (D) change the meaning of the sentence.

50. **B** (A) is incorrect because we cannot use the singular verb *was* for the plural subject *students*—it can properly apply only to the singular subject *instructor*. (C) adds an incorrectly used semicolon. (D) changes the tense unnecessarily. (E) has a misused apostrophe.

51. **C** (A) is verbose because *by . . . him* merely repeats the meaning of *exploited*. (B) and (E) change the meaning of the sentence. (D) adds a superfluous comma.

52. **D** Choice (A) omits a necessary *other* in the comparison. (B) corrects the error in comparison, but is not so effective as (D). (C) adds an unnecessary comma. (E) is wordy.

53. **C** (A) contains a triply mixed metaphor; (C) is the most concise statement that still retains any figurative force. (B), (D), and (E) change the meaning.

54. **D** (A) is wordy and contains a misplaced *which* clause. (B), (C), and (E) all change the meaning of the sentence.

55. **B** (A) has an unnecessary repetition of *us*. (C) creates an initial sentence fragment. By changing to more formal verbs, (D) and (E) alter the tone of the sentence.

56. **A** (B) makes the appositive into a restrictive relative clause by adding *which* and omitting the necessary comma. (C) uses the unnecessary *which* and incorrectly changes the tense of the verb. (D) creates a terminal sentence fragment. (E) *misuses the semicolon.*

57. **B** (A) incorrectly uses the adverb *however* as a conjunction. (C) creates a run-on sentence by preceding the second independent clause with a comma instead of a semicolon. (D) changes the tone with *failed*, as does (E) with *stepped into trouble . . . money*.

58. **E** (A) is a run-on sentence. (B) contains a dangling participle, *being*. (C) and (D) change the meaning of the sentence.

59. **A** The singular subject *every* is correctly followed by the singular verb *has* in (A). (B) and (E) change the meaning of the sentence. (C) and (D) have plural verbs; (D) also changes the meaning of the sentence.

60. **D** (A) and (B) incorrectly use the plural verb *have* for the singular subject *only one*. (C) changes the tone of the sentence with *fixed*, while (E) is wordy.

61. **C** (A), (B), and (E) omit *identified* after *have*. (D) has *always* modifying *continue* or *to identify* rather than *have identified* and *will continue* as in correct (C).

62. **A** In (B), the comma makes *looking* modify *freshman*. (C) and (D) confuse *ingenious* (crafty) and *ingenuous* (naive). (C) also confuses *except* and *accept*. (E) unnecessarily changes *would* to *could*.

63. **D** (A) creates a run-on sentence. *I wish it were true* is not part of the quotation, but in (B) the quotation marks include this statement. (C) is incorrect; the colon must be outside of the quotation marks. The semicolon in (E) is the wrong punctuation mark for the final summarizing statement; also, the subjunctive *were* is needed here.

64. **D** In (A) and (C) the phrase squints; *like his brother* could refer to either research or hopes. (B) contains an initial sentence fragment. (E) contains a change of meaning when *and* is substituted for *Although*.

65. **B** Since the three *how* phrases are parallel, they should be in similar construction. (A), (C), and (E) ignore the infinitives (*to anticipate* and *to coordinate*) that introduce action in the first two phrases. (D) unnecessarily changes the meaning of the last phrase by omitting the idea of *importance*.

66. **E** (A) contains a relative clause (*which . . . interview*) without a noun for it to modify logically. (C) converts this relative clause into a sentence fragment. (B) converts it into a participial phrase with a change in meaning. (D) converts the clause into a run-on sentence. In (E), *fact* is added for the clause to modify.

67. **C** The clause *which must be analyzed because of their importance* is a repetitious restatement of *major*. (B) merely attempts to correct it through an addition of a comma. In (D), *that* replaces *which* unnecessarily. (E) contains *because of their importance*, an unnecessary repetition of *major*.

68. **A** In (B) the addition of *which would* destroys the parallelism of *shatter* and *disintegrate*. In (D) the use of the participle *disintegrating* changes the meaning of the sentence. In (C), a comma is used improperly to separate the compound verbs *shatter* and *disintegrate*; since *all* of the participles are involved, *Earth's* is correct. Since action toward is implied, *into*, not *in* as in (E), is required.

69. **E** The income tax is not higher than last year, but it is higher than that of *last year* (year's); therefore (A), (B), and (D) are incorrect. (C) is incorrect because the meaning of the sentence has been changed.

70. **D** *Principles* are inherently *fundamental*; *fundamental* is unnecessary repetition; therefore, (A) is incorrect. (B), (C), and (E) have a change in meaning.

TAKING STOCK

Now that you have taken the Diagnostic Test, you should have a clearer idea of the scope of the examination and an assessment of your strengths and weaknesses in the areas tested. You are ready for the next step!

TO IMPROVE YOUR ESSAY SCORE

Most students are unaccustomed to writing an essay that must be completely written in 20 minutes. The digest that follows takes you through the steps that lead to mastery of the essay form unique to the Achievement Test.

1. Treat the explanations and exercises that follow in this section as you would the drills in a workbook. Do them!

2. Several shorter sessions are more productive than one cram session.

3. At intervals, take the Practice Tests that follow in order to assess your progress.

4. Reread the explanations and redo the exercises where necessary. Overlearning will give you the required speed and confidence.

TO IMPROVE YOUR MULTIPLE-CHOICE SCORES

The area of expertise is the same for the multiple-choice questions in both forms of the English Composition Achievement Tests. The tests vary in one question only. The all Multiple-Choice form contains three types of objective questions. The with-essay form has only Type One and Type Two, plus the essay. Type Three (Editing) will not be on the test you take. The writing of the essay replaces it.

Therefore, the preparation for this portion of the test is the same as for the All Multiple-Choice—except for the technique of mastering the essay type of question. To brush up on Type One and Type Two questions, review the Digest of Grammar and Usage in Section One.

2. *A Closer Look*

THE ACHIEVEMENT TEST ESSAY AND COLLEGE THEMES

A college theme differs in several important aspects from this essay. The typical college theme results from a unit of work during which the student is given time to select a topic, to think about its various ramifications, to write a rough outline, to write a rough draft, and then to plan the revision. The final copy is then prepared. The college theme may result from research or it may be based upon any analysis of one of the four basic types of writing—narration, description, exposition, argumentation.

The Achievement Test essay is written during a limited period of time. You do not have time to read widely or to weigh and consider for a length of time. All you have is 20 minutes! It resembles an impromptu theme given to test your ability to write a good answer to a question demanding a fairly extensive statement. It resembles exposition more than any other form of writing; it requires an explanation of why you think the way you do about a definite ideal or question of morality.

THE ACHIEVEMENT TEST ESSAY AND HIGH SCHOOL COMPOSITIONS

Many high school themes are of the narrative variety. You are required to recall an incident or retell a highlight in your experiences. The high school theme, then, tends to deal with concrete incidents or facts. It can be organized around the original timetable of the events you describe.

This essay, on the other hand, requires an ability to discuss ideas, generalizations, abstractions. Incidents and highlights from your own experiences are called in only briefly, as proof or support of a point of view. The essay focuses primarily on explanation and definition of an opinion. Development of your *thesis*, or main opinion, rather than chronological sequence becomes the basis for organization.

HOW THE ESSAY IS RATED

The essay will be read separately by *two* experienced high school and college instructors. They will judge the essays according to a set of criteria developed by the group from their pre-rating of several of the essays. Each reader will give your essay a numerical rating. Their ratings will be reconciled, when necessary, and the resulting grade will make up one-third of your total English Composition Test score. The score reported to the colleges of your choice will be on the same 200 to 800 scale as for all English Composition tests; however, the ATP Report will indicate that you took the test that included the writing of an essay. The following is a sample of the type of standards set. This is a scale recently adopted by several colleges.

5–6 *Generally Excellent:* Writing containing originality of thought, correctness of expression, and freshness of expression

3–4 *Competent:* Correct expression with soundness of thought and clear organization

2 *Interesting but incorrect:* Imagination and ability to think clearly combined with a lack of the formal requirements of correctness

1 *Inadequate:* Borderline in thought, content and organization; triteness of thought coupled with a lack of organization and errors typical of illiteracy

BASIS OF RATING

The rating of the essay is a composite result of negative and positive factors. Some errors cause greater deductions than others. For example, by the time a student becomes a candidate for admission to college, one sentence error can cause a theme to be lowered one or more complete grades.

Positive Factors

Content:

- development of ideas
- logical presentation
- appropriateness of examples

Technique:

- organization
- choice of words
- sentence structure
- punctuation

Negative Factors

Content:

- vagueness
- inconsistency
- undeveloped ideas
- inadequate development of basic argument

Technique:

- inexactness
- ineffectiveness of expression
- lack of variety in sentence structure
- inept choice of words
- misspelling

Technical Errors—In Order of Seriousness

1. Sentence errors—run-ons, comma splices, sentence fragments

2. Misspelling of common demons such as *to-too, their-there, than-then, separate, receive, doesn't*

3. Misuse of apostrophe—omission or addition

4. Word confusion: *altogether-all together, council-counsel, than-then*

5. Errors in case and agreement

6. Dangling elements

7. Vague reference

8. Misspelling of technical terms and words in general use

9. Additional errors in punctuation

10. Incorrect paragraphing: over- or under-paragraphing

11. Incorrect capitalization

12. Trite expressions

13. Mixed metaphors

14. Lack of sentence variety: too many simple or compound sentences

See Section One, "Correctness and Effectiveness of Expression," for a discussion of the preceding terms.

Errors in Content

These are the errors in what the student has to say. The major stress in college composition training is on developing the discipline that improves the content of themes.

1. Irrelevancies—additions to content that are not related to the ideas of the theme, lack of unity

2. Needless repetition of ideas

3. Superficiality—saying only the obvious

4. Incorrect statements of fact

5. Illogical deductions

6. Facile generalizations, overgeneralizing

The drills and tests in this section will not only help you to recognize these errors in your own writing but also help you to eliminate them.

Errors in Style and Organization

1. Lack of discernible three-part organization that includes an introduction, a development, and a conclusion

2. Incorrect level of diction or usage: for example, inappropriate inclusion of slang or nonstandard usage

3. Lack of coherence—lack of transitional words or phrases

4. Oversimplification or overelaborateness of sentence structure—overuse of short staccato sentences or pompous complex sentences

The drills and tests in Section One and in this section will not only help you to recognize these errors in your own writing but also help you to eliminate them.

3. Improving Prose Style and Organization

When writing the essay, you will probably be most aware of avoiding errors in usage, diction, and sentence structure. However, you should also attempt to display a sensitivity to the use of language and an effectiveness in organizing thoughts. Effective organization of thoughts comes through systematic consideration of the topic, compilation of evidence to support or attack the idea, and planned presentation of this evidence. Additional suggestions and practice material on planning your essay can be found in the following section. In this section, we consider the elements that go into producing varied, interesting prose style.

SENTENCE VARIETY

An experienced writer conveys a message most effectively by varying the types of sentences he or she uses. By varying your sentence types, you will achieve a certain rhythm and flow to your writing. Consider the following sentence patterns:

Simple Sentence: Maria walked to the store.

Simple Sentence with Compound Subject: *Maria and Sylvia* walked to the store.

Simple Sentence with Compound Verb: Maria *walked* to the store and *bought* two onions.

Simple Sentence with Compound Object: Maria walked to the store and bought two *onions* and three *potatoes*.

Compound Sentence: Maria walked to the store, and Sylvia followed her.

Complex Sentence: As soon as Maria left for the store, Sylvia began to follow her.

Compound-Complex Sentence: If Maria walks to the store, Sylvia will follow her; but Maria wants to be alone.

Practice changing simple sentences to complex; change compound sentences to complex. Remember that an essay with only simple sentences will sound immature, so vary your sentences!

PARAGRAPHS FOR PRACTICE

Using the various methods suggested in this book, recast the following paragraphs to gain maximum emphasis and variety.

1. Jonas Salk is a true hero in my opinion. He worked unselfishly. He worked for mankind. He wanted to better the lot of his fellow men. The grateful public showered honors on him. He avoided the limelight. He acknowledged the help he had received from others. He gave the money prizes to charity. His main request was a simple one. He wanted to continue to do his research in quiet and

without interruptions. He set a good example. Many young people will follow in his footsteps. He is a hero in the best sense.

....
....
....
....
....

2. Cowardice is considered as having many facets today. It was easier to define years ago. It meant not being able to face a situation. The coward ran away. The brave man stayed to face the consequences. The test was clearcut, and it was easy to apply. The word *foolhardy* was not used, but *rash* was used in its place. *Rash* was not correlated with being brave, nor was it connected with being a coward. We now realize more subtle values, and the picture changes. One man may run and be brave and another may stay and be a coward. The man may run, and he can plan to face the foe at a more advantageous position. The man may stay, and he may cover his cowardice by blustering and shouting. He may stay, and he can sacrifice the lives of others. This sacrifice may be unnecessary, but it could make the situation safer for the coward. We know more today, and we know that rashness and foolhardiness are not bravery. It is the motive and it is not the deed that should determine what is to be labeled cowardice.

....
....
....
....
....

3. The nineteenth century had its physical frontiers, and we today have political, social, scientific frontiers. The pioneers settled our country, and they faced the dangers on the frontiers of our land. The pioneers of today face similar dangers and these dangers require a similar courage. Some people see social injustice around us, and they devote their lives to fighting for equality for others. Some people see political tyranny, and they see others deprived of their right to vote by tricks. They plan long campaigns, and they try to educate the public. Freedom cannot belong to a few. Freedom must belong to all. These political and social frontiers are being explored, and others explore the frontiers of space and others explore the frontiers found in the laboratory. There are many frontiers today, and no one can say that frontiers no longer exist.

....
....
....
....
....

4. You can lead a horse to the well. You cannot make the horse drink. This is a homely analogy. It fits the present situation. Some colleges allow students very little choice of subjects to be taken, and other colleges give the students wide latitude. Some students are more advanced in their studies, and some students have to begin at the beginning. All students must take the same subjects in the tightly structured school. The advanced students learn bad habits, and the other students gain no advantage from having the advanced ones in their classes. The picture is almost the same in the more lax colleges, and the advanced student can go ahead on his own, and the undeveloped student still has little to guide him. There is a better procedure, and this could be a compromise between the two. The advanced could take some discussion seminars, and the undeveloped student could be in the course. The advanced would take electives, and the beginner could take the required, and each would then be developing at a pace best for him.

....
....
....
....
....

5. War is a costly luxury, and man must realize this. The winner loses, and so does the loser lose. There is no victor in a war, and we should realize it. Inflation eats away the life savings in the land of the winner, and it does the same in the land of the conquered. The men had been in the army, and they feel that they have been deprived. They become civilians, and they look for the good times that they had missed. Morality reaches a low ebb, and the winners talk about a lost generation, and the losers complain about a generation that is without moral fibers. Fads sweep the country, and worthwhile social advances are neglected. Money is spent on more and more armaments, and needed civic improvements are neglected. War does not end with the firing of the last gun, but it continues to wreak havoc for years afterward. We should realize this, and we should be resolved to fight war at all costs, and we should fight war at all turns. We should fight poverty, hunger, and ignorance, and we should not fight other human beings. The fight against other human beings is wasteful, and all who are in it suffer.

....
....
....
....
....

NOTE: *Answers to this exercise will vary too greatly to allow for an Answer Key.*

PROPER PARAGRAPHING

In writing the essay, the student faces a practical test of the ability to arrange ideas within a sentence and within a paragraph with appropriate connectives. The material that follows will give you practice in developing the correct habits for mature thought sequences. It will familiarize you with the level of development expected of you in your paragraph work on the college level.

Scan the following data. Do not spend much time on items that you already know. Concentrate on what you have to learn. The *Mastery Tests* that follow will help you to discover how effective your study has been.

Elements of Correct Paragraphing

Unity A theme has unity when each sentence and each paragraph in it is related to the topic under discussion. Sentences or paragraphs that are not related to the topic are *irrelevant*. Unity is obtained in a paragraph by excluding extraneous material.

Coherence Each part of a theme should lead logically to the next. Each thought should lead to the one that follows. Each sentence in a paragraph should follow this logical type of pattern. Coherence is gained by the logical arrangement of material, by the judicious use of transitional words and phrases, linking words and expressions.

Coherence is gained through the use of linking expressions such as

therefore, moreover, consequently, in addition to, furthermore, for example, for instance, as a result, nevertheless, obviously, first, on the whole, at any rate, naturally, of course, however, yet, at length, in conclusion, finally, next, first.

Length There is no prescribed length for a paragraph. The average paragraph length, however, is about 100 words. A theme should normally consist of more than one paragraph. A paragraph should normally consist of more than one sentence.

The rule of thumb used by most students is that a paragraph of more than a page in longhand is probably too long; a paragraph of two or three sentences is probably too brief.

Topic sentence The usual paragraph contains one sentence that summarizes the ideas of the paragraph. That sentence is called the topic sentence. If all of the ideas of the paragraph relate to that sentence, then the paragraph contains unity. If the ideas of the paragraph lead to or from that sentence then the paragraph contains coherence. The topic sentence is usually found at the beginning of the paragraph. It may be placed at the end or at any other point in the paragraph.

Developing the paragraph Although each of the parts of a composition serves varied purposes, typical paragraphs usually contain only one of the ideas to be developed in the theme. Each of these paragraphs may explain, develop, defend, attack, or illustrate one idea. The paragraph may be developed

1. by giving examples of the idea stated in the topic sentence

2. by defining one or more of the terms in the topic sentence

3. by giving details to support the topic sentence

4. by giving examples

5. by giving cause and effect

6. by giving the steps in a process

7. by using comparison and contrast

8. by presenting details or facts and also conclusions to be drawn from those details or facts

Introductory paragraph The introductory paragraph serves two main functions. The first is to delimit the topic, to explain just what the writer hopes to accomplish by writing the theme. The second is to interest the reader. Too often students are overconcerned with the need to interest the reader. If the introductory paragraph states the purpose of the theme succinctly, then that would be sufficient to create reader interest!

Concluding paragraph The final paragraph should *not* contain new ideas. It should serve to summarize the theme. It should also contain a concluding sentence that "clinches" the writer's main point.

Rhetorical question A rhetorical question is one that a writer uses in a theme for dramatic purposes but does not expect the reader to answer. A rhetorical question at the end of the introductory paragraph acts as an excellent connective. It joins the body of the composition to the introduction when the body of the composition actually is an answer to that question.

Transitions *Transitions* are words and expressions that make the direction and organization of the theme absolutely clear to the reader. A good example of a transitional phrase is the use of *in conclusion* or *therefore* as part of the topic sentence in the conclusion.

Emphasis Emphasis can be gained within a paragraph by employing the unexpected. Emphasis can be gained through the use of

Rhetorical Question: Who is responsible for the failure of the UN?

Repetition: His coach refused him. His teachers refused him. His parents had refused him. Now his best friend had just refused him!

Words Placed Out of Order: *Tired and frightened*, the prisoner was thrust into a cell.

In September, I expect to leave for Europe.

Whenever I come to that town, I visit my former colleague.

Swiftly came the night.

TEST OF MASTERY

I. Underline the irrelevant sentences in each of the following paragraphs.

1. I look forward to the time that I can retire. I shall seek a cabin somewhere and let others worry about budgets. He who has been gifted with the love of retirement possesses as it were another sense. I then shall do all the reading that I have missed for the past three years.

2. The wise disregard nothing that concerns the welfare of mankind. Proverbs are but rules, and rules do not create character. They prescribe conduct, but do not furnish a full and proper motive. They are usually but half-truths and seldom contain the principle of the action they teach.

3. The morality of an action depends upon the motive from which we act. Let us with caution indulge the supposition that morality can be maintained without religion. Let us suppose that I fling a few dollars to a beggar with the intention of breaking his head. He escapes my intention and picks the

money up. If he buys food with the money, the physical effect of my deed is good. However, with respect to me, the action was morally wrong.

4. Of course there is no one facet of a person's activities that can reveal him completely to others. However, what a person praises is perhaps a surer standard, even, than what he condemns. His praise can so often reveal his character, information, and abilities. No ashes are lighter than those of incense, and few burn out sooner. No wonder, then, that most people are so shy of praising anything.

5. Do not wait for a day of reckoning. Sum up at night what you have done by day. In the morning, plan reflectively what you are to do during that day. It is easier to enrich ourselves with a thousand virtues than to correct ourselves of a single fault. Dress and undress your inner being; mark well its decay and growth. You never know when your conscience will catch up with your deeds. Judged you will be, but by yourself, and on that day, beware of finding yourself wanting. There can be no sterner judge of your true accounts than you.

II. Underline the topic sentence in each of the following.

1. Hail can destroy one farmer's prospects of a harvest in a matter of seconds. It can leave his neighbor's unimpaired. It can slay a flock of sheep in one field, while the sun continues to shine in the next. To the harassed meteorologist its behavior is even more Machiavellian than that of the ice storm. He cannot predict the onset of a hailstorm, nor can he tell its course nor duration once it has started. He is not even too sure any more about the way in which hail forms. Hail is at once the cruelest weapon in Nature's armory, and the most incalculable.

2. The preservation of even small bits of marshlands or woods representing the last stands of irreplaceable biotic communities is interwoven with the red tape of law, conflicting local interests, the overlapping jurisdiction of governmental and private conservation bodies, and an intricate tangle of economic and social considerations. The problems we face in conserving natural resources are laborious and complex. During the time spent in desolving these factors, it often happens that the area to be preserved is swallowed up. Even more formidable is the broadscale conservation problem raised by the spread of urban belts. The pressures of human growth are so acute in such instances that they raise issues which would tax the wisdom of Solomon.

3. Farmers raising crops from the same type of seed will often band together into an association.

The purpose of the association is to spread the cost of advertising their product. The growers of navel oranges in California have helped to make Sunkist known in every home in the land. The American growers of one of the pima cottons have banded together in the SuPima Association of America, and garments made of this superior cotton often carry the SuPima label.

4. I have a rich neighbor who is always so busy that he has no leisure to laugh. The entire business of his life is to get money. The more money he amasses, the more he seems to want. He fails to consider that it is not in the power of riches to make a man happy. How wise were they that said, "There are as many miseries beyond riches as on this side of them." The search for happiness or contentment must not center upon worldly wealth.

5. I am so tired of having to argue with others on unequal terms. The moment my adversary centers his thoughts upon self-interest, how can I continue to discuss with him! I am lost from the start. He will never accept my premises as I cannot accept his. My facts are not facts to him. My conclusions are just as absurd when he weighs them in terms of only himself. Yet, how can humanity strive to reach a goal in which all will have an equal chance to live fully unless we keep our thoughts centered upon all and not one. We can march forward together only when we think of *we* and not *me*.

III. Rearrange the following sentences into logical order. In the space to the left, write the number that would represent that sentence's place in the paragraph.

. . . . **1.** (A) Great Britain declared war against the Netherlands a few months later.

. . . . (B) He was a former vice-president of South Carolina and president of the Continental Congress.

. . . . (C) Laurens was put into the Tower of London when the British discovered the projected treaty.

. . . . (D) In 1778 Henry Laurens was chosen to go to Holland to negotiate a $10,000,000 loan and a treaty of amity.

. . . . (E) He was captured off Newfoundland by the British frigate *Vestal*.

. . . . **2.** (A) For many years it was described as a hereditary disease, the result of some unknown defect in the germ plasm.

. . . . (B) Down's Syndrome is a congenital malformation that blights approximately one in 650 births.

. . . . (C) Proof is now at hand to show that the disease is neither typically hereditary nor environmental.

. . . . (D) Other investigators have often argued an opposite explanation, that the disease was environmental, caused by accidents during gestation.

. . . . (E) It arises from a defect in the mechanism by which the hereditary material is passed on from parent to offspring.

. . . . **3.** (A) One of the topics discussed was the development of methods that would elevate world fishing from a hunting industry to an agricultural technology.

. . . . (B) The group, known as the Conference of Science and World Affairs, convened for its seventh conference.

. . . . (C) Another topic discussed was the internationalization of the moon under the basic principles of the International Antarctic Treaty.

. . . . (D) The first conference had been held at Pugwash in Nova Scotia in 1957.

. . . . (E) In September 1961, 41 scientists from 12 countries met under skies darkened by distrust among nations.

. . . . (F) The purpose of these conferences is to foster the constructive use of science and help in preventing its destructive use.

. . . . **4.** (A) Its width varies from 1,200 miles to 2,500 miles.

. . . . (B) The waters of the Pacific off North and South America conceal a low bulge in the crust of the earth.

. . . . (C) The Rise runs roughly north and south for 8,000 miles.

. . . . (D) But it is not its size that is at present considered so significant; its crest is a region of high earthquake activity.

. . . . (E) This bulge is as extensive as both of the continents.

. . . . (F) The East Pacific Rise is the name given to this vast feature.

. . . . **5.** (A) They were supposed to live in the land of the Alps in houses built on silts out over the water of the lakes.

. . . . (B) Recent findings tend to disprove Keller.

. . . . (C) These dwellings seemed to resemble those of South Sea Islanders.

. . . . (D) For over a century anthropologists have believed that there were prehistoric Swiss lake dwellers.

. . . .   (E) This comparison resulted from the findings of Ferdinand Keller in 1854 along the shore of the Lake of Zurich.

. . . .   (F) Research seems to point to these houses having been built on the shores of lakes that have since grown larger.

ANSWER KEY: TEST OF MASTERY

I.

1. He who has been gifted with the love of retirement possesses as it were another sense.

2. The wise disregard nothing that concerns the welfare of mankind.

3. Let us with caution indulge the supposition that morality can be maintained without religion.

4. No ashes are lighter than those of incense, and few burn out sooner.

5. It is easier to enrich ourselves with a thousand virtues than to correct ourselves of a single fault.

II.

1. Hail is at once the cruelest weapon in Nature's armory, and the most incalculable.

2. The problems we face in conserving natural resources are laborious and complex.

3. Farmers raising crops from the same type of seed will often band together into an association.

4. The search for happiness or contentment must not center upon worldly wealth.

5. We can march forward together only when we think of *we* and not *me*.

III.

(1) 5, 2, 4, 1, 3   (4) 5, 1, 4, 6, 2, 3
(2) 3, 1, 5, 4, 2   (5) 2, 5, 3, 1, 4, 6
(3) 5, 2, 6, 3, 1, 4

PRACTICE IN ORGANIZATION

TEST 1   *Suggested Time:* **20** *Minutes*

The sentences in each of the following units belong to a well-organized paragraph. However, they are presented out of their correct order. You are to rearrange them into the best possible order. As you do the exercises, before you begin to answer the questions that follow, you should write in the margin the correct order of the sentences. In answering the questions, circle *N* if nothing follows the given sentence.

(A) The reaction of the American public to these disarmament proposals has ranged from great expectation to deep-seated lack of interest.

(B) Yet we know that if the United States and Russia were to fire all their weapons at each other, there would be over 90% population destruction in both countries.

(C) This is the grim fact that characterizes today's world.

(D) Disarmament discussions have been in the headlines perhaps more than any other issue ever since the cold war began.

(E) The failure of our leaders to inform and educate adequately on the complexities of this contemporary world problem has helped to cause the public mood.

1. Which sentence did you put first?   1. A B C D E N
2. Which sentence did you put after (A)?   2. A B C D E N
3. Which sentence did you put after (B)?   3. A B C D E N
4. Which sentence did you put after (C)?   4. A B C D E N
5. Which sentence did you put after (D)?   5. A B C D E N
6. Which sentence did you put after (E)?   6. A B C D E N

(A) The average number of moves is usually somewhere around forty-five, although the shortest game can consist of only two moves.

(B) A common saying among those who know the game best is that the winner of the game is the one who makes the next-to-the-last blunder.

(C) It is rare, therefore, that a game lasts for considerably more than 100 moves.

(D) The end of the game is heralded by the opponent's skillful exploitation of a mistake made at any point in the game.

(E) Even among grand masters the secret of success is not superior strategy but the persistent omission of tactical errors.

7. Which sentence did you put first?   7. A B C D E N
8. Which sentence did you put after (A)?   8. A B C D E N
9. Which sentence did you put after (B)?   9. A B C D E N
10. Which sentence did you put after (C)?   10. A B C D E N
11. Which sentence did you put after (D)?   11. A B C D E N
12. Which sentence did you put after (E)?   12. A B C D E N

(A) The early hunter could do little more than forage for berries, fruits, and edible animals.

(B) Later, agriculture emerged as man's dominant activity, and he learned to control and direct living matter around him.

(C) Primitive man lived in bondage to nature.

(D) This complex and broad interaction between man and nature is still going on today.

(E) He did nothing to interfere with the course of natural processes.

13. Which sentence did you put first?   **13.** A B C D E N

14. Which sentence did you put after (A)?   **14.** A B C D E N

15. Which sentence did you put after (B)?   **15.** A B C D E N

16. Which sentence did you put after (C)?   **16.** A B C D E N

17. Which sentence did you put after (D)?   **17.** A B C D E N

18. Which sentence did you put after (E)?   **18.** A B C D E N

(A) This procedure may lessen the number of freshmen who will be asked to leave, but it throws into the discard many who could have made the grade.

(B) The dropout rate has long been a major concern of most of our colleges.

(C) In addition to carrying only 12 instead of 16 credits, they are also enrolled in noncredit reading and study skills programs to help them improve their general academic competence.

(D) One way in which they have been facing the problem has been to restrict enrollments to those students whose previous academic record shows promise of success.

(E) A growing number of colleges have begun, instead, to offer marginal students a chance to prove themselves through restricted programs.

19. Which sentence did you put first?   **19.** A B C D E N

20. Which sentence did you put after (A)?   **20.** A B C D E N

21. Which sentence did you put after (B)?   **21.** A B C D E N

22. Which sentence did you put after (C)?   **22.** A B C D E N

23. Which sentence did you put after (D)?   **23.** A B C D E N

24. Which sentence did you put after (E)?   **24.** A B C D E N

(A) Our present research has enabled us to identify the sun as a large body of gas with a surface temperature of about 11,000 degrees F.

(B) Artificial satellites tell us that the corona envelops the earth and extends far out into the solar system.

(C) Above this visible sun is a thinner layer called the chromosphere where our rocket-directed cameras reveal the temperature rises to about 30,000 degrees F.

(D) Man's probing into space with rockets and satellites has helped to add much to his knowledge about the star nearest us, the sun.

(E) Beyond is the corona, an extremely hot region with a kinetic temperature measured in millions of degrees.

25. Which sentence did you put first?   **25.** A B C D E N

26. Which sentence did you put after (A)?   **26.** A B C D E N

27. Which sentence did you put after (B)?   **27.** A B C D E N

28. Which sentence did you put after (C)?   **28.** A B C D E N

29. Which sentence did you put after (D)?   **29.** A B C D E N

30. Which sentence did you put after (E)?   **30.** A B C D E N

(A) The great majority of bills die in committee.

(B) When a bill is introduced in either house, it is identified by a number and then referred to a committee.

(C) It may on the other hand decide to ignore the measure altogether.

(D) The committee may amend or even rewrite a bill before reporting it for final debate and vote.

31. Which sentence did you put first?   **31.** A B C D N

32. Which sentence did you put after (A)?   **32.** A B C D N

33. Which sentence did you put after (B)?   **33.** A B C D N

34. Which sentence did you put after (C)?   **34.** A B C D N

35. Which sentence did you put after (D)?   **35.** A B C D N

TEST 2   *Suggested Time: 15 Minutes*

The sentences in each of the following units belong to a well-organized paragraph. However, they are presented out of their correct order. You are to rearrange them into the best possible order. As you do the exercises, before you begin to answer the questions that follow, you should write in the margin the correct order of the sentences. In answering the questions, circle *N* if nothing follows the given sentence.

(A) One of the main arguments in support of the new plan is that unicameral legislature would centralize legislative responsibility.

(B) In 1934 Nebraska broke with a traditional feature of state as well as Federal government.

(C) However, although many states have evinced an interest in Nebraska's system, no other state has followed her lead.

(D) It replaced its bicameral legislature with an assembly of one house, with representatives chosen in a general election.

(E) It would also make the legislature less dependent upon professional politicians.

1. Which sentence did you put first?   1. A B C D E N
2. Which sentence did you put after (A)?   2. A B C D E N
3. Which sentence did you put after (B)?   3. A B C D E N
4. Which sentence did you put after (C)?   4. A B C D E N
5. Which sentence did you put after (D)?   5. A B C D E N
6. Which sentence did you put after (E)?   6. A B C D E N

(A) A shell of burning hydrogen encloses the helium core, allowing none of the energy released by the thermonuclear burning of the helium to escape from the star.

(B) At such temperatures, the star begins to expand and the runaway climb in temperature stops and reverses itself.

(C) The birth of a red giant star begins when the inner core of a star mass contains helium that has reached approximately 150 million degrees.

(D) As the star cools down, it becomes a red giant in a process that lasts a mere 3,000 years.

(E) The helium burning becomes more and more rapid with the temperature rising to about 630 million degrees.

7. Which sentence did you put first?   7. A B C D E N
8. Which sentence did you put after (A)?   8. A B C D E N
9. Which sentence did you put after (B)?   9. A B C D E N
10. Which sentence did you put after (C)?   10. A B C D E N
11. Which sentence did you put after (D)?   11. A B C D E N
12. Which sentence did you put after (E)?   12. A B C D E N

(A) He thus had to find his way from theatricalism to a purer and more simplified film style.

(B) He gives visible form to the inner conflicts of human beings in a genuine cinematic language.

(C) He rejected the theatrical tradition which for too long had dominated filmmaking with a consequent sterility in form.

(D) At his peak, now, the result is a clarity of both substance and form unrealized by any other film director.

(E) Films as an art form have achieved their highest peak to date under the direction of Sweden's Ingmar Bergman.

13. Which sentence did you put first?   13. A B C D E N
14. Which sentence did you put after (A)?   14. A B C D E N
15. Which sentence did you put after (B)?   15. A B C D E N
16. Which sentence did you put after (C)?   16. A B C D E N
17. Which sentence did you put after (D)?   17. A B C D E N
18. Which sentence did you put after (E)?   18. A B C D E N

(A) Wow is a slow waver of the pitch; flutter is a fast, stuttery tremolo resulting from rapid speed variations.

(B) At present there are varying and often opposing views of what constitutes the best in turntable design.

(C) Flutter and wow are pitch variations caused by inconstant turntable speed.

(D) Rumble, which sounds like distant rolling of thunder, is the result of vibration picked up by the phono cartridge.

(E) The common purpose of these differing design approaches is to banish rumble, flutter, and wow—the consequences of turntable malfunction.

19. Which sentence did you put first?   19. A B C D E N
20. Which sentence did you put after (A)?   20. A B C D E N
21. Which sentence did you put after (B)?   21. A B C D E N
22. Which sentence did you put after (C)?   22. A B C D E N
23. Which sentence did you put after (D)?   23. A B C D E N
24. Which sentence did you put after (E)?   24. A B C D E N

TEST 3 *Suggested Time:* **20** *Minutes*

The sentences in each of the following units belong to a well-organized paragraph. However, they are presented out of their correct order. You are to rearrange them into the best possible order. As you do the exercises, before you begin to answer the questions that follow, you should write in the margin the correct order of the sentences. In answering the questions, circle *N* if nothing follows the given sentence.

(A) This decline, which began in 1914, is attributed by some scholars to the failure of the alliance system which the political leaders had toiled to create.

(B) Gradually, before our very eyes Europe has disappeared as the overlord of the world.

(C) They claim that the nineteenth century was not a period of placidity and stability, as is commonly assumed, but one of deep and bitter discord.

(D) Its cultural, political, and economic achievements had been accepted universally as the measure of human progress.

(E) Others seem to feel that the basic cause lies in the undermining of traditional values by the intellectual giants of the preceding century—Darwin, Marx, Nietzsche.

1. Which sentence did you put first?   1. A B C D E N
2. Which sentence did you place after (A)?   2. A B C D E N
3. Which sentence did you place after (B)?   3. A B C D E N
4. Which sentence did you place after (C)?   4. A B C D E N
5. Which sentence did you place after (D)?   5. A B C D E N
6. Which sentence did you place after (E)?   6. A B C D E N

(A) Even among these large groupings called varieties there are subgroups that differ from other subgroups in many fundamental respects.

(B) Not only was this true, but when the experimenters tried to mate males of one kind with the females of another, they found sterility barriers in every case.

(C) Even among the anopheles mosquitoes, for example, there are some populations that do not bite man under any circumstances, with several preferring to bite cattle, pigs, or goats instead.

(D) Even though mosquitoes look the same everywhere, different varieties can be distinguished by microscopic examination of the patterns of spots on the eggs.

(E) One of the most striking discoveries was that each kind had characteristic mating habits.

7. Which sentence did you put first?   7. A B C D E N
8. Which sentence did you place after (A)?   8. A B C D E N
9. Which sentence did you place after (B)?   9. A B C D E N
10. Which sentence did you place after (C)?   10. A B C D E N
11. Which sentence did you place after (D)?   11. A B C D E N
12. Which sentence did you place after (E)?   12. A B C D E N

(A) When the rising cone of water and the cloud tip meet, a fountain of spray much wider than the spout itself is produced.

(B) The waterspout is a marine relative of the tornado although it is not so fierce as its unholy relative.

(C) As the lower tip of the cloud approaches the surface, the water churns and seems to boil upward.

(D) Despite this heavy spray and the accompanying average winds of one hundred miles an hour, the waterspout is much less dangerous than tornadoes since its energy is usually lost on the waves in the water wastes of the empty oceans.

(E) A snakelike cloud that writhes and dips toward the sea, it is in shape and appearance very much like a tornado.

13. Which sentence did you put first?   13. A B C D E N
14. Which sentence did you place after (A)?   14. A B C D E N
15. Which sentence did you place after (B)?   15. A B C D E N
16. Which sentence did you place after (C)?   16. A B C D E N
17. Which sentence did you place after (D)?   17. A B C D E N
18. Which sentence did you place after (E)?   18. A B C D E N

(A) When a proposal is introduced in either the House of Representatives or the Senate, it is called a bill.

(B) Once it has been passed by that House, it is reprinted as an act.

(C) It becomes a law when it has finally passed both Houses and has satisfactorily passed the scrutiny of the President and he has signed it.

(D) It remains a bill until it has been passed by that House.

(E) An act, therefore, means that it is a measure that has been enacted by one branch of the Legislature.

19. Which sentence did you put first?   19. A B C D E N
20. Which sentence did you place after (A)?   20. A B C D E N
21. Which sentence did you place after (B)?   21. A B C D E N
22. Which sentence did you place after (C)?   22. A B C D E N
23. Which sentence did you place after (D)?   23. A B C D E N
24. Which sentence did you place after (E)?   24. A B C D E N

(A) It furnished a faithful image of the deceased to aid his survival in the afterworld.
(B) Etruscan sculptors preferred to work in clay or bronze rather than in stone.
(C) The art of portraiture was deeply involved in their funeral rites.
(D) They were particularly fond of the bas-relief, in which they filled the scene with delightfully animated figures.
(E) They, however, did their best work in portraits.

25. Which sentence did you put first?   25. A B C D E N
26. Which sentence did you place after (A)?   26. A B C D E N
27. Which sentence did you place after (B)?   27. A B C D E N
28. Which sentence did you place after (C)?   28. A B C D E N
29. Which sentence did you place after (D)?   29. A B C D E N
30. Which sentence did you place after (E)?   30. A B C D E N

(A) Frequently the supply is limited by natural or social circumstances beyond the control of its users.
(B) Running the gamut of animal, vegetable, and mineral matter in the live, raw, and processed states, the forms of the currencies are as diverse as any of man's inventions.
(C) Often, however, scarcity must be maintained by some convention that through consumption or destruction renders the currency valueless and withdraws it from circulation.
(D) Many, but by no means all, primitive peoples have devised moneys of their own.
(E) The maintenance of these primitive monetary systems requires the same balancing of supply and demand that confronts the United States Treasury.

31. Which sentence did you put first?   31. A B C D E N
32. Which sentence did you place after (A)?   32. A B C D E N
33. Which sentence did you place after (B)?   33. A B C D E N
34. Which sentence did you place after (C)?   34. A B C D E N
35. Which sentence did you place after (D)?   35. A B C D E N
36. Which sentence did you place after (E)?   36. A B C D E N

TEST 4   *Suggested Time: 15 Minutes*

The sentences in each of the following units belong to a well-organized paragraph. However, they are presented out of their correct order. You are to rearrange them into the best possible order. As you do the exercises, before you begin to answer the questions that follow, you should write in the margin the correct order of the sentences. In answering the questions, circle *N* if nothing follows the given sentence.

(A) Because the pleuropneumonia organism passes through filters, it resembles viruses.
(B) It is, therefore, considered to be a bridge between these two large classes of organism.
(C) A laboratory rat is a billion times heavier than a protozoan; the latter is a billion times heavier than a pleuropneumonia organism.
(D) Since it can grow in non-living media, it is similar to bacteria.
(E) But because it shows obvious differences from both bacteria and viruses, it has been accorded the status of a separate and distinct order: *mycroplasmatales*.

1. Which sentence did you put first?   1. A B C D E N
2. Which sentence did you place after (A)?   2. A B C D E N
3. Which sentence did you place after (B)?   3. A B C D E N
4. Which sentence did you place after (C)?   4. A B C D E N
5. Which sentence did you place after (D)?   5. A B C D E N
6. Which sentence did you place after (E)?   6. A B C D E N

(A) This is the agent in the serum that brings about the transformation of fibrinogen to fibren.
(B) Of the ten or more clotting factors present in the serum, the best known is the protein, prothrombin.

(C) The latter is the material that forms one structure of the clot.

(D) When the blood leaves the circulation and comes in contact with the surface of the wound, this substance is converted into thrombin.

(E) It causes the independent molecules of fibrinogen to link up together in long fibers.

7. Which sentence did you put first?   7. A B C D E N
8. Which sentence did you place after (A)?   8. A B C D E N
9. Which sentence did you place after (B)?   9. A B C D E N
10. Which sentence did you place after (C)?   10. A B C D E N
11. Which sentence did you place after (D)?   11. A B C D E N
12. Which sentence did you place after (E)?   12. A B C D E N

(A) In 1959 one investigator set up a computer so that it not only played a fair game of checkers but was capable of looking over its past games and modifying its strategy in the light of this experience.

(B) Has man boasted for too long of his thinking ability as his biggest advantage over machines?

(C) Although at first the inventor was able to beat his machine with ease, it improved so rapidly that it soon reached the point at which it was beating him in every game.

(D) Such machines not only do what they have been told to do, but also what they have learned to do.

(E) The greatest threat to man comes from the learning machines, computers that improve with experience.

13. Which sentence did you place first?   13. A B C D E N
14. Which sentence did you place after (A)?   14. A B C D E N
15. Which sentence did you place after (B)?   15. A B C D E N
16. Which sentence did you place after (C)?   16. A B C D E N
17. Which sentence did you place after (D)?   17. A B C D E N
18. Which sentence did you place after (E)?   18. A B C D E N

(A) It also includes a brief summary of the Congressional activities of the previous day as well as a list of scheduled committee hearings.

(B) A bound edition is published for each session in volumes of convenient size for permanent preservation.

(C) The Congressional Record contains, in addition to an official record of everything said on the floors of both houses, the roll call on all questions.

(D) The appendix contains the extension of remarks, material not spoken on the floor but inserted by permission.

(E) Bimonthly, the daily records are bound in paper covers with an index covering the given period.

19. Which sentence did you place first?   19. A B C D E N
20. Which sentence did you place after (A)?   20. A B C D E N
21. Which sentence did you place after (B)?   21. A B C D E N
22. Which sentence did you place after (C)?   22. A B C D E N
23. Which sentence did you place after (D)?   23. A B C D E N
24. Which sentence did you place after (E)?   24. A B C D E N

TEST 5 *Suggested Time:* **15** *Minutes*

The sentences in each of the following units belong to a well-organized paragraph. However, they are presented out of their correct order. You are to rearrange them into the best possible order. As you do the exercises, before you begin to answer the questions that follow, you should write in the margin the correct order of the sentences. In answering the questions, circle N if nothing follows the given sentence.

(A) The snake overcomes the difficulty by throwing forward lateral loops of its body.

(B) However, it is the only way in which this snake can move satisfactorily over the yielding surfaces.

(C) One of the members of the rattlesnake family is called the sidewinder because of its method of traveling across the terrain in which it lives.

(D) It is an inhabitant of the southwestern United States, and it is usually found on soft soil or sand, bad surfaces for a thick-bodied snake to travel across if it uses the usual snake methods of progression.

(E) The effect of this "sidewinding" makes it appear as if the snake were trying to walk.

1. Which sentence did you place first?   1. A B C D E N
2. Which sentence did you place after (A)?   2. A B C D E N
3. Which sentence did you place after (B)?   3. A B C D E N
4. Which sentence did you place after (C)?   4. A B C D E N

5. Which sentence did you   5. A B C D E N
place after (D)?

6. Which sentence did you   6. A B C D E N
place after (E)?

(A) Spawned in the Sargasso Sea area, they soon become tiny, transparent eel larva, called *lepto cephali*, and are part of the ocean plankton.

(B) When they make their way up the rivers, they become darker and are called elvers.

(C) Eels show a pattern that is the reverse of the one followed by salmon and shad.

(D) As they grow in size, they collect around the estuaries of rivers in a form recognizable as that of an eel, the transparency still persisting in these *glass eels.*

(E) The life cycle is completed when they come down the streams and rivers to the ocean in a one-way journey to reach their spawning grounds thousands of miles away.

7. Which sentence did you   7. A B C D E N
put first?

8. Which sentence did you   8. A B C D E N
place after (A)?

9. Which sentence did you   9. A B C D E N
place after (B)?

10. Which sentence did you   10. A B C D E N
place after (C)?

11. Which sentence did you   11. A B C D E N
place after (D)?

12. Which sentence did you   12. A B C D E N
place after (E)?

(A) The Confederates almost succeeded in their plans, for on its first day as a destroyer of the old, the *Merrimac* quickly destroyed two wooden warships, and would have wiped out more of them if she had not met the *Monitor* the second day.

(B) For four hours the ironclads pounded each other with shot and shell, with little apparent damage.

(C) As an act of desperation in its attempt to end the Federal blockade that was strangling its commerce, the Confederacy placed all of its hopes in the *Merrimac.*

(D) However, the *Merrimac* left, leaking badly, unable to attack any more warships, thus failing to accomplish its primary mission.

(E) It was a 3,500-ton steam-propelled vessel that had been abandoned and then sunk by the Federals before it was refitted by the Southerners with a coating of four inches of railroad iron.

13. Which sentence did you   13. A B C D E N
place first?

14. Which sentence did you   14. A B C D E N
place after (A)?

15. Which sentence did you   15. A B C D E N
place after (B)?

16. Which sentence did you   16. A B C D E N
place after (C)?

17. Which sentence did you   17. A B C D E N
place after (D)?

18. Which sentence did you   18. A B C D E N
place after (E)?

(A) Many other postwar periods have been labeled "The Age of Anxiety," but the atom bomb, Communism, Asian and African self-assertion, and the downfall of Europe have given us an insecurity never felt before by man to the same depth as this.

(B) None of our old formulas seem capable of holding the powers of destruction in check: alliances, United Nations, arsenals, armies, religious revivals—all have failed to lessen our fear of the imminent downfall of man.

(C) Our basic premise has been that somehow each new invention and each new discovery was leading to progress, a desirable goal.

(D) Suddenly we awoke to discover that progress has brought us to the brink of self-destruction both as a basic civilization pattern based on European culture and as a species of animal life inhabiting a planet in the solar system.

(E) Without any foreplanning or vision on our part, we could create a better world for our children if we adjusted quickly to the latest advances.

19. Which sentence did you   19. A B C D E N
put first?

20. Which sentence did you   20. A B C D E N
place after (A)?

21. Which sentence did you   21. A B C D E N
place after (B)?

22. Which sentence did you   22. A B C D E N
place after (C)?

23. Which sentence did you   23. A B C D E N
place after (D)?

24. Which sentence did you   24. A B C D E N
place after (E)?

TEST 6 *Suggested Time:* **20 Minutes**

In each of the following exercises, the sentences form the sentence outline for a theme or composition. The sentences are out of their proper order. By circling the appropriate letter in the answer column, mark

(A) if the sentence contains the central idea of the theme

(B) if the sentence contains a main supporting idea that points directly to the central idea
(C) if the sentence contains an example or illustrative fact that acts as proof
(D) if the sentence contains a statement that is unrelated to the central idea

EXERCISE 1

1. The peasantry were overburdened by taxes from many sources. **1. A B C D**
2. Monarchs such as Peter the Great of Russia and Frederick II of Prussia supported the arts and sciences. **2. A B C D**
3. All men were subject to military duty in the destructive wars carried on by these rulers. **3. A B C D**
4. They spent millions of dollars in building magnificent palaces as monuments to remind people of their greatness. **4. A B C D**
5. While the Eighteenth Century saw many advances in literature, science, and art, the common people were oppressed by continuing burdens. **5. A B C D**
6. Voltaire was one of the intellectual leaders who revolted against the oppressive forces of the current rulers. **6. A B C D**
7. These enlightened despots sponsored writers and artists who praised their reigns. **7. A B C D**
8. They refused to change old, obsolete forms of government. **8. A B C D**

EXERCISE 2

9. The earth could be blanketed in the space of an hour with a deadly cloud of radioactive fall-out poisons. **9. A B C D**
10. Nearly half the population of America live or work in environments polluted to some degree by manmade fumes. **10. A B C D**
11. Unfriendly nations have at their disposal even more dangerous pollutive forces. **11. A B C D**
12. Bombs filled with bacterial agents can be exploded over vast areas, spreading disease and death for months and years. **12. A B C D**
13. Modern industrialized society has forced equally large segments of peoples of other countries to breathe in chemical fumes, from factories, automobile exhausts and processing plants. **13. A B C D**
14. Air pollution has become a social evil of widespread consequences. **14. A B C D**
15. The average person daily breathes about twenty pounds of air. **15. A B C D**
16. Airborne contaminants blanket large portions of the world. **16. A B C D**

EXERCISE 3

17. The reasons for public indifference reach deep into the private lives of the citizens. **17. A B C D**
18. In mid-term Congressional elections even fewer people take the trouble to cast their ballots. **18. A B C D**
19. The average person is so deeply absorbed in his personal affairs that he sees little connection between what he is doing and governmental operations. **19. A B C D**
20. Too often elections reveal an apathy on the part of the voters. **20. A B C D**
21. The strength of a democracy lies in the intelligence of its citizens. **21. A B C D**
22. America suffers from a widespread indifference to political affairs. **22. A B C D**
23. Fewer than 65% of those eligible to vote take the trouble to do so in important presidential election years. **23. A B C D**
24. Governmental agencies do not reach the people with the facts and figures needed to dispel ignorance of their principles and practices, so that the importance of their actions is unknown to the average voters. **24. A B C D**

EXERCISE 4

25. Silver and gold coins are milled around the edges because they contain valuable metal. **25. A B C D**
26. No one can pare a quarter or half-dollar without it being seen at once by anyone handling the coin. **26. A B C D**
27. Unless they were so treated, people could pare the edges of these coins and sell the precious metal. **27. A B C D**
28. Pennies and nickels have smooth edges, however. **28. A B C D**
29. Have you ever wondered why some coins have grooved edges while others do not? **29. A B C D**
30. Pennies and nickels are not milled because it would not be economically worthwhile to the thieves to pare the edges of these coins. **30. A B C D**
31. The cost of coinage is kept to a minimum because it is done exclusively by the government with no middleman to make a profit. **31. A B C D**

TEST 7 *Suggested Time: 20 Minutes*
In each of the following exercises, the sentences form the sentence outline for a theme or composition. The sentences are out of their proper order.

By circling the appropriate letter in the answer column, mark

(A) if the sentence contains the central idea of the theme

(B) if the sentence contains a main supporting idea that points directly to the central idea

(C) if the sentence contains an example or illustrative fact which acts as proof

(D) if the sentence contains a statement that is unrelated to the central idea

EXERCISE 1

1. The nuclear physicist holds a high priority in the group who center their interests in discovering more and more of the universe's until now unknown principles.　　　　　1. A B C D

2. The teacher of science and mathematics in the schools and colleges prepares the next generation for the tasks ahead of them.

2. A B C D

3. The man of science plays just as important a role in the practical world of everyday.

3. A B C D

4. The theoretical mathematician and the biochemist searching for the cure of man's physical ills meet here to exchange their ideas for the betterment of man.　　　　4. A B C D

5. The student interested in science and mathematics has many areas open to him, depending upon his interests and aptitudes.

5. A B C D

6. The technician, the pharmacist, the laboratory assistant, and the nurse have their roles to play in safeguarding man from physical ills.

6. A B C D

7. Those who decide to go into research may work in private or public laboratories.

7. A B C D

8. The paths that lead to science and mathematics begin in the earliest school grades.

8. A B C D

9. The physician makes his daily rounds, applying his knowledge to the immediate health problems that cannot wait for a future solution.

9. A B C D

EXERCISE 2

10. The bells also signified the passing of every half hour during each watch.　　10. A B C D

11. The time between four in the afternoon and eight in the early evening was often divided into two two-hour periods called dogwatches.

11. A B C D

12. Each watch consisted of four hours, and there were six watches in each day.

12. A B C D

13. One bell meant the passing of the first half hour in each watch.　　　　13. A B C D

14. Time on board ship was once based solely on the bell system.　　　　14. A B C D

15. Eight bells marked the end of each watch and the beginning of the next, when the man who was on duty departed and the next man came to relieve him.　　　　15. A B C D

16. Three bells would mean, for example, that an hour and a half had passed during the watch.

16. A B C D

17. The bells were used to signal the end of the watches.　　　　17. A B C D

18. Eight bells then meant that eight half hours had passed.　　　　18. A B C D

EXERCISE 3

19. The impermanence of Federal employment discouraged the more qualified and pressured them to seek employment elsewhere, where their salaries and position would depend more upon their ability as workers.　　19. A B C D

20. Before 1883 the spoils system prevailed, and nearly all positions in the Federal service were filled on the basis of political patronage.

20. A B C D

21. By 1933, nearly 80% of the positions in the executive branches of government were under the merit system.　　　　21. A B C D

22. To maintain his job, the officeholder had to contribute money and time to the political party in power.　　　　22. A B C D

23. It has only been within recent years that government service has attracted career men and highly qualified personnel.　23. A B C D

24. With the passage of the Pendleton Act and the establishment of the Civil Service Commission, the end of the spoils system began.

24. A B C D

25. Even then, when the party that had given him his job was defeated at the polls, he would most likely lose his job, regardless of how competent he might be.　　　　25. A B C D

26. In recent years there has been considerable criticism directed against the administration of the Federal civil service system.

26. A B C D

27. However, there are still thousands of positions that are filled by the politicians who are interested in votes and not in ability to produce on the job.　　　　27. A B C D

EXERCISE 4

28. Ability to receive sounds varies not only from person to person but from age group to age group.   28. A B C D
29. Sound is the result of air-molecule motion and cannot spread faster than the air's molecules move collectively.   29. A B C D
30. Sound waves are waves of energy that are received differently by different organisms.   30. A B C D
31. Sounds are audible to the average adult as continuous tones when they contain between twenty and thirty vibrations per second.   31. A B C D
32. Cats, small dogs, and guinea pigs detect better than thirty thousand vibrations per second.   32. A B C D
33. For ordinary sounds the energy involved is incredibly small.   33. A B C D
34. Brown bats have given evidence of hearing vibrations that are as high as a hundred thousand vibrations per second.   34. A B C D
35. Young children catch the more shrill sounds, sounds with the highest number of vibrations, much better than adults do.   35. A B C D
36. Five thousand people speaking over the telephone for one year would develop only enough energy to bring a gallon of water to boil.   36. A B C D
37. Animals, particularly the small mammals, hear sounds even higher than those heard by children.   37. A B C D

TEST 8   *Suggested Time: 15 Minutes*

In each of the following exercises, the sentences form the sentence outline for a theme or composition. The sentences are out of their proper order. By circling the appropriate letter in the answer column, mark

(A) if the sentence contains the central idea of the theme

(B) if the sentence contains a main supporting idea that points directly to the central idea

(C) if the sentence contains an example or illustrative fact that acts as proof

(D) if the sentence contains a statement that is unrelated to the central idea

EXERCISE 1

1. The lawyers, dentists, and doctors continue to receive their initial college training in the liberal arts.   1. A B C D
2. Other four-year institutions have been springing up.   2. A B C D
3. Parents have led their children to realize that within a rather short period of time the average white-collar worker will be college-trained.   3. A B C D
4. The liberal arts college is still a stepping-stone to traditional professional training.   4. A B C D
5. The many fields of business education can now be pursued following training in a college of business.   5. A B C D
6. Not only are there colleges of engineering, but some institutions now offer a four-year course in technology, the handmaiden to engineering.   6. A B C D
7. Formal education beyond high school has been undergoing a rapid change within recent years.   7. A B C D

EXERCISE 2

8. History has demonstrated that peace cannot be maintained by a combination of victorious powers.   8. A B C D
9. The rift between the Western nations and the Soviet Union has been widening through the years.   9. A B C D
10. Military alliances have invariably fallen apart.   10. A B C D
11. Peace in our time must rest upon the success or failure of the UN.   11. A B C D
12. Our former policy of isolation is outworn.   12. A B C D
13. The balance of power arrangement has inevitably led to an arms race.   13. A B C D
14. Science and invention have overcome the barriers of geography.   14. A B C D

EXERCISE 3

15. A jet pilot trying to leave a disabled plane has little chance of climbing out against the pressure of the hurricane of air rushing by.   15. A B C D
16. Ejecting him with a charge of gunpowder only partially solves the difficulties.   16. A B C D
17. Survival of man after a supersonic bail-out has been a serious problem when a failure occurs in jet planes.   17. A B C D
18. An unprotected man cannot depend on surviving the effects of being hit by the wind of present plane speeds.   18. A B C D
19. The speed generated by the plane is a basic cause of the difficulty.   19. A B C D
20. In February 1955, a test pilot was the first man to survive a forced bail-out while his plane was traveling at supersonic speeds.   20. A B C D

21. Even if he did succeed in getting out of the cabin, the tail assembly would most probably cut him in two. **21.** A B C D

EXERCISE 4

22. Hitler and his corps of followers destroyed the machinery that allowed nations to live at peace with each other. **22.** A B C D

23. Six million Jews were not their only victims. **23.** A B C D

24. Deceit and bullying, treachery and war replaced humanitarianism and Christian ethics as the principles the Nazis brought to the conference table when countries met to iron out their differences. **24.** A B C D

25. Each succeeding generation must be taught to recoil at the horror that was unleashed on the world by the forces of Nazism. **25.** A B C D

26. Many millions more from Russia, Poland, France and England were slaughtered like cattle and burned in ovens built to convert their bodies into fertilizer. **26.** A B C D

27. Innocent people throughout Europe were ground into slavery and dust because they stood in the path of these ruthless would-be conquerors of the world. **27.** A B C D

28. By January 1933, the Nazis had formed the largest single political party in Germany. **28.** A B C D

TEST 9 *Suggested Time:* **20** *Minutes*

In each of the following exercises, the sentences form the sentence outline for a theme or composition. The sentences are out of their proper order. By circling the appropriate letter in the answer column, mark

(A) if the sentence contains the central idea of the theme

(B) if the sentence contains a main supporting idea that points directly to the central idea

(C) if the sentence contains an example or illustrative fact which acts as proof

(D) if the sentence contains a statement that is unrelated to the central idea

EXERCISE 1

1. He hurried his family out of the house and into the cyclone cellar. **1.** A B C D

2. Before he realized what had happened, the great funnel was hanging directly over him. **2.** A B C D

3. Not many men have been as fortunate as the Kansas farmer, Will Keller, who escaped unharmed even though a tornado passed directly over him. **3.** A B C D

4. All wind had ceased, and he caught a very distinctive pungent odor. **4.** A B C D

5. He took one last look through the barn and hurried to the cellar himself. **5.** A B C D

6. When he saw a greenish black cloud in the southwest, Keller suspected a tornado. **6.** A B C D

7. A line of thunderheads, at first low on the horizon, soon appears in the west. **7.** A B C D

8. He looked directly into the circular opening of the tornado and saw small twisters form and writhe their way around inside the rim of the funnel. **8.** A B C D

9. He stopped at the cellar door before going down to safety. **9.** A B C D

EXERCISE 2

10. The late eighteenth and early nineteenth centuries were characterized by a relatively simple agricultural economy that did not require economic controls. **10.** A B C D

11. To outlaw practices which endangered the public health, Congress enacted the Meat Inspection Act. **11.** A B C D

12. The role of the government in assuring social justice for all has undergone marked changes during the last 75 years. **12.** A B C D

13. The important issues of that day seemed to be mainly political rather than in the area of the national economy. **13.** A B C D

14. The leaders felt that the government should try to encourage agriculture and commerce without restricting the individual farmer. **14.** A B C D

15. The earlier approach was based on the Jeffersonian idea that the best form of government is the one which disturbs the individual the least. **15.** A B C D

16. The government must exert controls in our social and economic organization to protect the individual. **16.** A B C D

17. The government must concern itself with everyday factors of living and earning a living. **17.** A B C D

18. The basic issues which confront the nation today are mainly economic, the outgrowth of a highly complex industrial civilization. **18.** A B C D

EXERCISE 3

19. The freshwater angler who enjoys walking along rocks or streambeds wanders with a box of flies into isolated areas in search of trout. **19.** A B C D

20. He casts his heavily weighted line out beyond the breakers and trolls it in, catching unwary fish that have come close to the beach in search of food.   20. A B C D
21. The fisherman of today has a variety of tackle and types of fishing activities to choose from.   21. A B C D
22. The surfcaster, equipped with heavy boots and the longest rod of them all, stands in the white water on the beach's edge.   22. A B C D
23. The sportsman with the big-game hunter instinct is usually attracted to the swivel chair and the deep-sea launches.   23. A B C D
24. The fly-fisherman can use either the traditional long bamboo pole or the modern spinning equipment with a spun-glass rod.   24. A B C D
25. The laker finds his fun and enjoyment by having a sport that has some of the characteristics usually found mainly among the other three types of fishing.   25. A B C D
26. The fishing widow is the wife who has resigned herself to being left stranded by her husband while he searches for the big one and for release of his tensions.   26. A B C D
27. The rod is secured to a harness that is part of the chair, and the line is usually of metal to give him a chance of bringing in a tarpon or sailfish if he is lucky enough to hook into one.
                                    27. A B C D

EXERCISE 4
28. Many seeds are water travelers, for those that are lighter than water are able to float.
                                    28. A B C D
29. Birds, tempted by pleasantly flavored fruit, feast and then drop and scatter the seeds.
                                    29. A B C D
30. Many seeds have wings that cause them to be carried by the wind.   30. A B C D
31. In the tumbleweeds, the whole plant breaks off from the roots when it stops growing.
                                    31. A B C D
32. Nature's means of seed dispersal are many and varied.   32. A B C D
33. Dandelion seeds sail long distances, wafted by the breeze on delicate parachutes composed of a crown of silky hairs.   33. A B C D
34. Although the dustlike seeds of the orchids have no special flying equipment, because of their small size, they are carried great distances by even gentle breezes.   34. A B C D
35. Coconuts can float many miles before the seed is landed on a distant shore.   35. A B C D

36. Fruits of the arrowhead have air chambers that help them on their voyage and enable the seeds to settle far from the parent plant.
                                    36. A B C D
37. For many seeds, birds serve as the means of transportation.   37. A B C D

TEST 10   *Suggested Time: 20 Minutes*
In each of the following exercises, the sentences form the sentence outline for a theme or composition. The sentences are out of their proper order. By circling the appropriate letter in the answer column, mark
(A) if the sentence contains the central idea of the theme
(B) if the sentence contains a main supporting idea that points directly to the central idea
(C) if the sentence contains an example or illustrative fact that acts as proof
(D) if the sentence contains a statement that is unrelated to the central idea

EXERCISE 1
1. Over 8,000,000 men died in battle or of wounds sustained in battle.   1. A B C D
2. Many cities and villages were destroyed completely.   2. A B C D
3. The loss in human life far exceeded that caused in all previous wars combined.
                                    3. A B C D
4. The immediate effects of World War I were almost unbelievable in their magnitude.
                                    4. A B C D
5. Material losses can be estimated only in billions of dollars.   5. A B C D
6. Over 22,000,000 soldiers were wounded.
                                    6. A B C D
7. Economic nationalism cut down world trade in a futile effort to rebuild destroyed manufacturing centers.   7. A B C D
8. Almost 20,000,000 civilians died because of the famine, disease, and the direct destructive forces of war.   8. A B C D
9. Trade and manufacturing as well as farming ceased in large areas.   9. A B C D

EXERCISE 2
10. At one time sponges were considered as worm houses built by worms much as bees build honeycombs.   10. A B C D
11. The skeleton, when the animal is alive, contains many tiny cells.   11. A B C D
12. The sponge is an intricate structure that once was regarded as one of nature's puzzles.
                                    12. A B C D

13. There are many mistaken beliefs about the sponge.   13. A B C D
14. The dry material that we buy is really a skeleton.   14. A B C D
15. One ancient writer asserted that sponges were from the foam of the sea.   15. A B C D
16. A stream of water carries food and oxygen around the cells.   16. A B C D
17. Actually the sponge is an animal.
                                                                                      17. A B C D
18. Some even consider the sponge a type of seaweed.   18. A B C D
19. The sponges are of many different colors.
                                                                                      19. A B C D

EXERCISE 3

20. Foreign governments could not deal with a government lacking this function.
                                                                                      20. A B C D
21. Any predatory group could attempt to seize power and run the government.
                                                                                      21. A B C D
22. The individual would be without protection for his personal liberties.   22. A B C D
23. The property of foreigners could not be protected, nor would their businessmen be able to deal with ours lest just debts be ignored by gangster groups.   23. A B C D
24. Criminal elements could seize from the weaker citizens their wealth and property.
                                                                                      24. A B C D
25. Policing is one of the chief functions of government.   25. A B C D

26. Anarchy is the type of social structure in which there are no governmental structures or restrictions.   26. A B C D
27. Organized group activities would be at a standstill if governments did not have this primary of policing.   27. A B C D

EXERCISE 4

28. The glands connected to the fang in the harmless snake look like those of the deadly snakes; yet they produce nothing to hurt anyone.
                                                                                      28. A B C D
29. The amount of poison is slight, but the venom of many of our poisonous snakes is among the most deadly of all poisons.   29. A B C D
30. The fang in the harmless snakes lacks the hollow slit.   30. A B C D
31. The snake's fang is an eye or canine tooth, corresponding to the sharp-pointed tooth that humans have between the front teeth and the back teeth.   31. A B C D
32. Those who fear snakes should learn to recognize the harmless ones that are beneficial to man.   32. A B C D
33. In poisonous snakes the fang has a hollow channel running through it.   33. A B C D
34. The fang in a poisonous snake has one significant difference from that found in the non-poisonous snakes.   34. A B C D
35. When the snake bites, drops of poison are forced through the channel and into the victim's body.   35. A B C D

ANSWER KEY: PRACTICE IN ORGANIZATION

TEST 1

1. (D)	6. (B)	11. (C)	16. (A)	21. (D)	25. (D)	29. (A)	33. (D)
2. (E)	7. (B)	12. (D)	17. (N)	22. (N)	26. (C)	30. (B)	34. (A)
3. (C)	8. (N)	13. (C)	18. (B)	23. (A)	27. (N)	31. (B)	35. (C)
4. (N)	9. (E)	14. (E)	19. (B)	24. (C)	28. (E)	32. (N)	
5. (A)	10. (A)	15. (D)	20. (E)				

TEST 2

1. (B)	4. (N)	7. (C)	10. (A)	13. (E)	16. (A)	19. (B)	22. (A)
2. (E)	5. (A)	8. (E)	11. (N)	14. (B)	17. (N)	20. (N)	23. (C)
3. (D)	6. (C)	9. (D)	12. (B)	15. (D)	18. (C)	21. (E)	24. (D)

TEST 3

1. (B)	6. (C)	11. (A)	16. (A)	21. (E)	25. (B)	29. (E)	33. (E)
2. (E)	7. (D)	12. (B)	17. (N)	22. (N)	26. (N)	30. (C)	34. (N)
3. (D)	8. (C)	13. (B)	18. (C)	23. (B)	27. (D)	31. (D)	35. (B)
4. (N)	9. (N)	14. (D)	19. (A)	24. (C)	28. (A)	32. (C)	36. (A)
5. (A)	10. (E)	15. (E)	20. (D)				

TEST 4

1. (C)	4. (A)	7. (B)	10. (E)	13. (B)	16. (N)	19. (C)	22. (A)
2. (D)	5. (B)	8. (C)	11. (A)	14. (C)	17. (A)	20. (D)	23. (E)
3. (E)	6. (N)	9. (D)	12. (N)	15. (E)	18. (D)	21. (N)	24. (B)

TEST 5

1. (C)	4. (D)	7. (C)	10. (A)	13. (C)	16. (E)	19. (D)	22. (E)
2. (E)	5. (A)	8. (D)	11. (B)	14. (B)	17. (N)	20. (C)	23. (A)
3. (N)	6. (B)	9. (E)	12. (N)	15. (D)	18. (A)	21. (N)	24. (B)

TEST 6

Exercise 1		Exercise 2		Exercise 3		Exercise 4	
1. (C)	5. (A)	9. (C)	13. (C)	17. (B)	21. (D)	25. (B)	29. (A)
2. (B)	6. (D)	10. (C)	14. (A)	18. (C)	22. (A)	26. (C)	30. (C)
3. (C)	7. (C)	11. (B)	15. (D)	19. (C)	23. (C)	27. (C)	31. (D)
4. (C)	8. (B)	12. (C)	16. (B)	20. (B)	24. (C)	28. (B)	

TEST 7

Exercise 1		Exercise 2		Exercise 3		Exercise 4	
1. (C)	6. (C)	10. (B)	15. (C)	19. (C)	24. (B)	28. (B)	33. (B)
2. (C)	7. (B)	11. (D)	16. (C)	20. (B)	25. (C)	29. (D)	34. (C)
3. (B)	8. (D)	12. (C)	17. (B)	21. (C)	26. (D)	30. (A)	35. (C)
4. (C)	9. (C)	13. (C)	18. (C)	22. (C)	27. (C)	31. (C)	36. (C)
5. (A)		14. (A)		23. (A)		32. (C)	37. (C)

TEST 8

Exercise 1		Exercise 2		Exercise 3		Exercise 4	
1. (C)	5. (C)	8. (B)	12. (B)	15. (C)	19. (B)	22. (B)	26. (C)
2. (B)	6. (C)	9. (D)	13. (C)	16. (B)	20. (D)	23. (C)	27. (B)
3. (D)	7. (A)	10. (C)	14. (C)	17. (A)	21. (C)	24. (C)	28. (D)
4. (B)		11. (A)		18. (C)		25. (A)	

TEST 9

Exercise 1		Exercise 2		Exercise 3		Exercise 4	
1. (C)	6. (B)	10. (C)	15. (B)	19. (B)	24. (C)	28. (B)	33. (C)
2. (B)	7. (D)	11. (D)	16. (C)	20. (C)	25. (B)	29. (C)	34. (B)
3. (A)	8. (C)	12. (A)	17. (C)	21. (A)	26. (D)	30. (B)	35. (C)
4. (C)	9. (C)	13. (C)	18. (B)	22. (B)	27. (C)	31. (D)	36. (C)
5. (C)		14. (C)		23. (B)		32. (A)	37. (B)

TEST 10

Exercise 1		Exercise 2		Exercise 3		Exercise 4	
1. (C)	6. (C)	10. (C)	15. (C)	20. (B)	24. (C)	28. (C)	32. (D)
2. (C)	7. (D)	11. (B)	16. (C)	21. (C)	25. (A)	29. (C)	33. (C)
3. (B)	8. (C)	12. (A)	17. (B)	22. (B)	26. (D)	30. (B)	34. (B)
4. (A)	9. (C)	13. (B)	18. (C)	23. (B)	27. (B)	31. (A)	35. (C)
5. (B)		14. (B)	19. (D)				

4. Writing the Essay

You are expected to do the essay question in the first 20 minutes of the test. You will need the full 20 minutes allotted to plan and write the essay assignment. You must resign yourself to stopping when time is up. You have to allow *full* time for the next two-thirds of the test! Of course, if you complete the multiple-choice questions in less than the allotted 40 minutes, you may go back to your essay; but don't rely on your finishing the short answer section ahead of time.

SOME QUESTIONS AND ANSWERS

How much time should I spend in planning? in writing? in proofreading?

You are allowed 20 minutes for the essay. How much of this time should you spend on each step? Of course there is no pat answer to this question.

However, you should know generally how much time you need to plan, to write, and then to proofread a one-page theme. The only way that you can find out is by timing yourself under practice examination conditions. The exercises and tests that follow will allow you to do just that so that you can discover how much of your time should be spent in becoming familiar with the directions, how much time you need to plan the paragraph-by-paragraph development of your ideas, how much time you need for the actual writing, and, equally important, how much time you will need for checking spelling, choice of words, punctuation, sentence structure, usage slips and how much time you will need for double-checking for errors of omission and carelessness.

Shall I plan a rough draft and then a finished copy?

In the 20 minutes allotted to you, you will not be able to write and then rewrite. Not only will you not have time, but you will not be given the paper to do such writing. If, however, you plan in advance the content of each paragraph or section, then you will not find the need for writing a rough draft.

Shall I write a formal outline, using the Harvard Outline System?

Your outline will not be rated. You will be given one special answer sheet. Your notes will have to be made in the examination booklet. Therefore, the outline or rough draft that you think through must be just that. If you are more comfortable in planning with a formal outline, then of course do so. If you have no preference, then you should train yourself to plan just what you want to say in each paragraph and then begin to write the essay.

Should I plan a title?

This item is usually not called for. Do not waste your time in trying to think of a title—unless the question requires you to plan one.

HOW CAN I DO MY BEST?

You cannot change yourself or your outlook for the moments of examination taking. Plan to express your own thoughts with honesty and sincerity. Do not try to guess what the markers would want you to say. You do *not* know what their opinions are. They are looking primarily for the method that you use to express your ideas, and for the basis of such ideas.

The material in the review section of this book will familiarize you with the errors in usage that you should avoid, the errors in diction that could lower their evaluation of your work. The exercises in this section will increase your ability to organize your ideas and to plan your paragraphs.

The ideal preparation takes time. The more time you can spend on each section of this book, the more effectively you will be able to express yourself. Do not waste time, however, in drilling yourself on the items you already know. Check for those that you do not have under control, and then review these until you know them thoroughly.

What shall I do if I make an error?

You will not be able to erase. Changes must be made by lining out and substituting. Do *not* block out or cross out. One line through the material to be omitted and then a neat interlinear change placed above will lead to no penalties.

Do handwriting and neatness count?

Usually, they are not taken into consideration; however, the reader will be inclined more favorably to a paper that is easier to read then he will be toward one that requires much time to decipher.

You cannot expect to change your handwriting overnight; yet, if you are careful, you can change a scrawl into a legible script. The following are some of the precautionary measures to be taken by those whose handwriting tends to be less than clear.

Letter formation

1. Dot your *i*'s and keep your *e*'s open.
   Illegible:
   Improved:
2. Close *a, d, b, q, o,* and *s*
   Confusing:
   Improved:
3. Close your *k* so that it is not confused with *h*.
   Confusing:
   Improved:
4. The *r* should not resemble *i*, nor should *m* look like *n*.
   Confusing:
   Improved:
5. The letters like *l, b, f, h,* and *y* should be looped, while *t* should be closed.
   Confusing:
   Improved:
6. The letters *g, q, f, y* should contain bottom loops.
   Confusing:
   Improved:
7. Letters like *m, n, u,* and *w* should be rounded, not pointed.
   Confusing:
   Improved:

Additional fundamentals

1. Keep your letters on the line; do not write uphill or downhill.
   Confusing:
   Improved:
2. Avoid flourishes at the beginning or end of words.
   Confusing:
   Improved:
3. The space between letters and the spaces between words should be kept uniform.
   Confusing:
   Improved:

Must I fill the entire page?

Some people can say much in little; others can never find enough words to express themselves. It is more important that you state clearly and forcefully what you have to say than that you completely fill the page. Only through practice will you be able to develop the skills necessary to encompass the beginning, development, and conclusion of an idea in the limits of one page.

Is it better to agree or disagree with the topic?

It is not your point of view that is being rated. The essay is planned to show how well you can express your thoughts. The subject of the essay is usually one that you can explore on the basis of your personal experience, observation, or reading. The specific details that you use to support your point of view are much more important than whether to agree or disagree.

If a quotation is included, shall I copy it?

Do not waste valuable space in copying verbatim. Try to reach your discussion as quickly as possible. If you need to quote from the question, try to limit this material.

May I both agree and disagree with the topic?

Here too, you are not being rated on your point of view. The clarity of your expression and the forcefulness of your statements are what count. Therefore, if you find that there are some aspects to agree with and some aspects to disagree with, good!

How many points should I make?

Remember, you are not being asked to write a book! You do not have time to explore all aspects of the topic. Choose a limited part; stick with what you think is most important—and then explain that clearly.

Shall I skip lines between paragraphs?

Since the amount of space offered you is limited to one page, do not skip lines. Begin to write on the first line and keep your margins very narrow.

ANALYSIS OF A TYPICAL ESSAY QUESTION

Typical Question

DIRECTIONS: You have twenty minutes to plan and write an essay on the topic assigned below. DO NOT WRITE ON ANOTHER TOPIC. AN ESSAY ON ANOTHER TOPIC IS NOT ACCEPTABLE.

The essay is assigned to give you an opportunity to show how well you can write. You should, therefore, take care to express your thoughts on the topic clearly and effectively. How well you write is much more important than how much you write, but to cover the topic adequately you may want to write more than one paragraph. Be specific.

Your essay must be written on the lines provided on your answer sheet. You will receive no other paper on which to write. You will find that you have enough space if you write on every line, avoid wide margins, and keep your handwriting to a reasonable size. It is important to remember that what you write will be read by someone who is not familiar with your handwriting. Try to write or print so that what you are writing is legible.

DO NOT WRITE IN YOUR TEST BOOK. You will receive credit only for what you write on your answer sheet.

Consider carefully the following quotation and the assignment following it. Then, plan and write your essay as directed.

The greatest need of a person is the need to be needed.

ASSIGNMENT: Do you agree or disagree with this statement? Write an essay in which you support your opinion with specific examples from history, contemporary affairs, literature, or personal observation.

The essay question usually consists of three parts: *directions*, a quotation or a statement, and an *assignment*.

Directions

The directions are the least productive part of the question. They are usually a generalized statement of procedure. However, you must not skip or skim through them. The directions on the form of the test that you take may differ significantly from those in the model or the samples in the official information bulletin.

Read the directions through quickly—with pen in hand for underlining statements that signal a change from the usual or that contain information that needs reinforcement for you.

Statement or Quotation

This sentence gives the subject that you are to write about. You are expected to discuss it from your experience, observations, or reading. This quotation or observation is planned to stimulate you to agree or disagree wholly or in part. It should lead you to explanations and generalizations supported by specific examples as you explore its implications according to your own knowledge or experience.

Before allowing your mind to explore, you must be able to answer:

What do the key words mean?
What is the literal meaning of the quotation?
What are some figurative meanings?
How do you react to its implications?
To what extent is the statement true?

With the given proverb, "The greatest need of a person is the need to be needed," for example:

A. You could disagree completely and show that the greatest need of a person could be satisfaction of physical needs, ambition, growth, self-fulfillment, etc. Unless people are good for themselves, they are not good for others. Without food, shelter, protection from harm for ourselves, we cannot think of the needs of others. We cannot be humanitarians when our own lives are in danger. You could use examples as the basis of your proof.

B. You could agree completely and show that although we have need of self-preservation, people will ignore their own welfare to meet the needs of others. You could use as examples Joan of Arc, police, firefighters, soldiers during wartime, parents in their relation to their children at times of crises. If you agree, then, you could define a hierarchy of needs and place the need to be needed at top.

C. You could agree in part and disagree in part. People who are aggressively self-seeking, who place personal ambition above all else, who measure life values in terms of material possessions disregard the needs of others and sublimate their own need to be needed. Macbeth, modern dictators, pirate leaders, hijackers are just a few possible examples.

People who are concerned about the welfare of others—their family, friends, neighbors, fellow human beings—find that the need to be needed gives their lives direction and purpose. Examples to prove this point of view could come from the ranks of teachers, doctors, religious workers, social workers, humanitarians.

However, once you have begun to explore the statement and have come up with some ideas, you are not ready to write your essay! You are ready to read the assignment.

Assignment

Given the bewildering flow of ideas that flood in when you begin to examine the quotation, the assignment becomes the key to your organization. It indicates which areas you are to explore and which type of conclusion you should reach.

Let us now return to the *Assignment*:

ASSIGNMENT: Do you agree or disagree with this statement? Write an essay in which you support your opinion with specific examples from history, contemporary affairs, literature, or personal observation.

As the assignment is worded, you are asked to decide to what extent and in which ways you agree or disagree with the statement. You are ready to return to your preliminary thinking on and reactions to the given quotation. Of all the arguments you mustered while reading the quotation, which seem most compelling? They do not have to be the ones you have always believed in or will believe in in the future. They should be ones that you presently accept.

Since the essay is necessarily a brief one, do not attempt an exhaustive listing. Limit yourself to the one or two arguments that you find most compelling at the time of the examination.

If you find yourself unable to be selective and too many ideas continue to churn around, imagine what the reaction to the task would be for some favorite personality—a teacher, friend, parent. Then write the response from that person's point of view.

When you have decided on the major thoughts you are planning to present, you are ready to formulate your *thesis*. Your *thesis* is the main point you want to bring out in your essay. It usually answers the question *why*, and it usually is formulated in a *because* sentence. For the given *Assignment,* the thesis could begin with:

The quotation is a justifiable generalization because . . .

The quotation is not justifiable because . . .

I both agree and disagree with the quotation because . . .

Remember, you are not going to be marked on the quality of the reason or proof. You do not have time to search for esoteric or highly original examples or arguments. The essay, at best, is a rough instrument for separating the candidates into groups, not a method for showing unique excellence. When you have selected your thesis, you are ready to organize and write your essay. The time for selection of your point of view and the major reasons for doing so has passed!

ORGANIZING YOUR ESSAY

You are not ready for this step until you have

1. understood the quotation

2. used the assignment to formulate your thesis

3. selected your explanation and illustrations

You will not have time to plan a formal outline. Your thinking, however, must be developed around three parts: introduction, development, conclusion. You should have a minimum, therefore, of three paragraphs.

The Introduction

Avoid elaborate flourishes. The introduction should point to the reader the direction of your theme. It may contain (a) a definition, (b) an example, (c) a statement of the problem, (d) a statement of the present situation, (e) a quotation, (f) a dramatization of the problem.

The transition from the introduction to the body can very well be a rhetorical question based on the topic being discussed. If you are discussing heroes of today, then the transitional sentence may be, "Is it true then, that there is no hero in our world of today?" The section of the essay that follows will be your answer to the question.

Do's and Don't's

1. Avoid the trite, the forced, the superfluous.

2. Be simple and direct.

3. Strive to be accurate, clear, emphatic.

4. Be modest, unassuming, and temperate.

5. Do not strive to be funny.

6. Be positive. Cynicism is to be avoided.

7. Try to achieve appropriate mood and manner.

PRACTICE EXERCISE

To obtain maximum learning, write, under simulated examination conditions, an introduction to the following practice essay question. Then compare what you have written with the five samples given. An evaluation of these introductions follows the samples.

DIRECTIONS: Following the given essay question are the beginning portions of essays typical of those submitted by college applicants. In the space provided, write your analysis of the strengths and weaknesses found in each. Confine your criticism to organization and content.

Our arguments often prove nothing but our wishes.

ASSIGNMENT: Comment on the validity of this statement. Explain and defend your answer, using illustrations from your observation or your reading.

1. Although I am not an expert psychologist, I think I can give good reasons to support my opinions. You do not need to be trained through college courses to be able to explain why people allow their feelings to decide their opinions.

ANALYSIS ....
....
....

2. In these troubled times, the multitude of issues that surround us can leave us torn by fears and doubts. We really do not know which way to turn. It is more important than ever that we amass facts, listen to varied opinions, and then reach logical conclusions based on the facts. Yet, all too often, our reasoning is so controlled by our wishful thinking that our conclusions reveal not truths but what we hoped would be true.

ANALYSIS ....
....
....

3. The word *often* takes the given sentence out of the realm of the controversial. What is given, then, is a truism that should be self-evident even to the slowest student in the class. All I can say is that someone must have erred when this quotation was chosen. However, since this is an examination process, I shall prove through example that the statement is true on the various occasions when it is true.

ANALYSIS ....
....
....

4. An argument is a verbal interchange between people on an issue in which there is disagreement. When we get into such conflict with other people, we often just don't listen to what the other person has to say because all we want to do is get our anger out. We can't convince the other person; the other person will not convince us. "Our arguments often prove nothing but our wishes."

ANALYSIS ....
....
....

5. My family has a saying that we inherited from my grandparents. "When a discussion becomes heated and the voices are raised, it becomes an argument; it should be ended at this moment because no one will win." However, I disagree that our arguments prove nothing but our wishes!

ANALYSIS ....
....
....

EVALUATION OF SAMPLE INTRODUCTIONS

1. The writer showed an awareness of the purpose of an introductory paragraph. While the opening statement may arouse reader interest, it is too self-conscious, directing attention unnecessarily to the writer rather than to the topic. In the second sentence, the writer attempted to present a thesis. However, the direction that the essay will take must be away from the meaning of the quotation if the thesis is followed up. The writer plans to explain *why* people allow their feelings to decide opinions; what has to be proved is that often our opinions are so dictated by our desires that we reveal not truths but only our own wishes.

2. The writer shows a firm grasp of the question. You can readily see the plan of organization. What will follow must be an illustration to prove the thesis stated in the last sentence. However, there is no justification for beginning with the old chestnut, "In these troubled times . . . ''! A less global approach would have been more effective.

3. The given paragraph has the basic characteristics of a superior essay. The first sentence could easily arouse the interest of the reader. The last sentence presents the thesis that the statement is true. This sentence shows the direction of the development; the proof will be in illustrations. *But*, the second and third sentences do not prove the conclusions stated in the first sentence; sarcasm and irrelevant accusations fill these sentences. The tone established by these sentences is unwarranted, impolitic—and costly in terms of rating!

4. The paragraph is well organized. It begins with a definition and ends with the quotation as a thesis sentence. The word *argument* is used in a sense different from that reached by the previous writers. Such an interpretation is completely acceptable. The major weakness in the paragraph is that the thought content is close to being a mere restatement of the question; the writer has said the obvious and added very little *opinion*.

5. The paragraph is well organized. It begins with a quotation and ends with a thesis sentence. The direction the essay will take is on target and clear to the reader.

EVALUATION OF YOUR OWN INTRODUCTION

Weakness ....
Strength ....
It is closest to number ....of the student introductions because ....
I would rate it ....
I could have improved it if I had ....
....

The Development

Don't attempt to turn the development into a listing of reasons, facts, illustrations; it is *not* a test of your memory. It is a test of your ability to explain and defend a point of view on a serious topic. The key to a mature development lies in your stressing the word *because*. The major portion of this section of your essay should consist of reasoning and selected examples or illustrations. You should support your statements by referring to your own experience or the world of literature.

PRACTICE EXERCISE

To obtain maximum learning, write, under simulated examination conditions, a development that could be evolved from the introduction given in the following question. Then compare what you have written with the five selections given. An evaluation of the selections follows on page 162.

DIRECTIONS: Following the given essay question is *one* introduction followed by *five* developments. In the space provided, write your analysis of the strengths and weaknesses in each of the developments. Confine your criticism to organization and content.

Good sportsmanship, doing unto others what you would have done unto yourself, is part of the ideals basic to the American way. Yet most businessmen do not hesitate to disregard these ideals when money is involved. Even our athletes often believe that winning is all that counts. Youth is rightfully confused about which moral standards to follow!

ASSIGNMENT: Are these statements justified? What do they tell us about our way of life? Explain and defend your answer, using illustrations from your observations, reading, or personal experience.

Introduction

No one can contradict the obvious evidence that reveals that, in many segments of our society, we do not practice what we preach. To make profit, business adds harmful adulterants to baby food, packages material in deceptive containers, charges as much as the traffic will bear. To win, athletes take drugs, injure opponents, break rules when the authorities are not looking. Yet, at the same time we pay lip service to high moral standards in our conduct toward others. What does this reveal about our way of life?

Student Developments

1. Greed is the cause of all the difficulties in our society. If people weren't so selfish, they would not disregard the welfare of others. We live in a world of dog eat dog and let the devil take the hindmost. If people weren't so greedy for wealth and power, this would be a much better world to live in. How can manufacturers live with themselves when they make and sell life-endangering products? Is it worth it when a young boy's entire future is ruined by an injury intentionally inflicted on the football field?

ANALYSIS ....
....
....

2. To me, the tragic conclusion is that after more than 200 years of existence our nation is showing signs of failing as the first noble experiment in democracy. Democracy is based on the belief that people can live together harmoniously as equals. It means that in the necessary division of labor required in our complex world, each of us must contribute to the welfare of the others while producing for our own benefit. Farming depends on the farmer's producing healthful foods for the manufacturer who will make the quality goods that the farmer's family needs. If neither is concerned about the welfare of the other, then some outside force must be used to regulate production. Democracy is eventually replaced by some form of dictatorship.

ANALYSIS ....
....
....

3. All societies have their contradictions. Such contradictions follow from the inevitable growth in our economy. Rules and regulations that were effective before international corporations, TV-dominated sports, and recent scientific discoveries may not be workable today. Rules made years ago to govern food products did not envisage chemical additives that could prevent aging of a product. Rules governing the sports world were not planned to regulate superstars and worldwide satellite TV broadcasts.

Yet, what this reveals to me is not the corruption of our society but the strength of our democratic system. Nondemocratic governments like Czarist Russia, or France under the Bourbons, fell because remedies for societal ills were not available. However, our government with its checks and balances can change regulations. The Food and Drug Administration is constantly upgrading the control of

chemical additives. I am certain that the evidences of moral disintegration are only symptoms of growing pains. Our government will pass regulations to correct these injustices!

ANALYSIS ....
....
....

4. Youth is confused about much more than good sportsmanship! Why do adults still act as though the very existence of the world is not on the line? At any minute, some country can decide to explode the nuclear weapon that could start a chain reaction of retaliation that would wipe out all of humanity and even blow up our planet into stardust! With such dire possibilities being ever present, how can we think in terms of trivia such as business profits or injuries in an athletic contest? We should put first things first! We must find some way to outlaw all nuclear weapons; nothing else really matters!

ANALYSIS ....
....
....

5. Our way of life is very complex, and as time goes on, it becomes even more so. The regulations passed by the government just add to the complications. As a result, not too many people really understand the factors involved in our way of life. I know that I, for one, find it very mystifying. I don't blame myself; if the experts don't know, how can I claim to know? Youth is rightfully confused about which moral standards to follow.

ANALYSIS ....
....
....

EVALUATION OF DEVELOPMENTS

1. The paragraph contains no direct answer to the question set in the assignment. It is, rather, a series of unconnected sentences. It does contain illustrations, but they are not explicitly associated with the assignment. This is an inadequate development.

2. The paragraph is developed in answer to the question in the introduction, "What does this reveal about our way of life?" The discussion tends toward the negative and the abstract, but an illustration is given and definite proof is presented. This is a superior development.

3. This is a more ambitious answer that only one who can think and write quickly can consider writing. In it the candidate proves through illustrations that the statement is justified and discusses what it

reveals about our way of life. This is a superior development.

4. This is a very dramatic plea for international control of nuclear weapons. It is clearly and effectively worded. However, it completely disregards the assignment. It could well have been written for any other assignment. This development must be given the lowest rating.

5. Only tangentially can this be said to tell what the quotation reveals about our way of life. Complexity is discussed in general terms. No illustrations are given. The sentences are not connected. Moral standards are not discussed. This is a most marginal answer.

EVALUATION OF YOUR OWN DEVELOPMENT

Weakness ....
Strength ....
It is closest to number . . . of the student developments because ....
I would rate it ....
I could have improved it if I had ....
....

PRACTICE EXERCISE

To obtain maximum learning, write, under simulated examination conditions, a conclusion that could be evolved from the introduction and development given in the following question. Then compare what you have written with the five conclusions given. An evaluation of the conclusions follows on page 164.

DIRECTIONS: Following the given essay question are an introduction and development followed by five conclusions. In the space provided, write your analysis of the strengths and weaknesses in each of the conclusions. Confine your criticism to organization and content.

TV viewing has become the opiate of the masses. It has turned us into a nation of flabby bodies overstuffed with junk food and a people with flabby minds overstuffed with repetitive stories of violence and endless series of athletic contests that require only passive watching.

ASSIGNMENT: Comment on this statement, using your personal experience or reading as the basis for your opinion. To what extent do you think the statement is correct or incorrect? Support your opinion by using specific illustrations.

Introduction and Development

Untold sets of statistics have been evolved to show how completely we as a nation have incorporated television viewing into our way of life. The direst of all analyses are those, like the quotation given for this essay, that view us as being converted into a nation of zombies. Is this a fair representation of the effect of television?

It is true that many people view the endless Kojak series and become involved in being glued to the viewing of the weekend football games, the evening baseball series, and basketball tournaments. Almost

The Conclusion

The conclusion should not introduce any new ideas. It should serve as a summary of what you had said before. It should end on a strong emotional note—if such a note is appropriate.

as bad are those addicted to the often repeated re-runs of old movies. But the picture is not so bad as the quotation suggests.

TV has helped to popularize jogging. The news programs and special series stress health topics, especially the recognition and prevention of disease. Such programming offsets somewhat the deleterious effects of too much sitting before the one-eyed monster's usual fare.

Then too, the Educational Television Network has expanded rapidly. Great literature, serious music, and expert discussion of timely topics form the major bill of fare offered. These channels show how television used effectively can raise the cultural level and social consciousness of the viewers. The commercial networks also have their share of simulcasts of opera, special musical spectaculars, weekly forums, and special coverage of outstanding events like the visit to our country of the Pope.

Student Conclusions

1. The biggest problem with television viewing is how to handle the conflicts of interest that arise in a family. In some homes, each member has a personal television set in addition to the one in the living room or playroom. Sometimes, usually not too often, all the individuals in the family get together and watch the same program. Most of the time, each goes a separate way. Sometimes, kindred souls who like the same program join the lone watcher. The alternatives to such compromise are violence, dictatorship, or even divorce!

ANALYSIS ....
....
....

2. I am always pleased when the mandated topic for an essay is on a timely issue that thinking people must be made aware of. The topic for this essay is just that kind. We were made aware of a problem that must be handled if we are to survive as a world leader. I offer you my sincerest congratulations for giving us this timely topic to write on. Thank you for giving me an opportunity to discuss how television has affected our lives.

ANALYSIS ....
....
....

3. It is true that too many of us spend too much of our time watching television programs that add nothing to our lives. Yet, television is only in its infancy. It has so many possibilities for being an effective force for improving our lives. Public Television in its entirety and network systems with their cultural and special events programs point up the fact that not all of television is bad even now. And as public television expands, the level of public interest will improve and so will the general run of programs. I have faith that television is a force for the good!

ANALYSIS ....
....
....

4. Therefore just saying that TV viewing has become an opiate of the masses tells only part of the story. The other part is much more encouraging. Selective TV viewing is possible. Junk TV can be limited or even eliminated. The educational system, therefore, along with parents and civic leaders, has an obvious obligation. The youth of today must be taught to shun programs that are sensational and overcommercialized. I am certain that our adult guides will show us the way!

ANALYSIS ....
....
....

5. As you can see, I believe that this condemnation of current TV fare has a large piece of the truth in it. However, not all is negative. Much of current programming, especially in Public Television, is wholesome, constructive, educational. As consumers, we must hope that the percentage of these better programs increases.

ANALYSIS ....
....
....

EVALUATION OF CONCLUSIONS

1. Another aspect of the effect of television is introduced in this paragraph. It effectively presents a serious problem that television has caused. However, this is not a summary of what has already been said. It is *not* a conclusion. A summarizing paragraph is still needed. This is an inadequate conclusion.

2. This generalized statement does include in the concluding sentence a reference to television. However, this is not a summary; it does not reinforce the thesis developed in the previous sections. Such a conclusion is given the lowest possible rating.

3. The paragraph begins with a summary of the aspects that the writer has discussed. It ends with a thesis-statement and a hope for the future. This is a superior conclusion.

4. The first two sentences begin as an effective summary even though the writer feels obligated to repeat the wording of the quotation. However, a new undeveloped aspect is introduced with the discussion of the role of educators, parents, and civil leaders, weakening the impact of the conclusion. This conclusion is barely adequate.

5. In the first three sentences, the paragraph summarizes the main ideas of the essay. The final sentence is an attempt to give an application of previous data. This conclusion is very good.

EVALUATION OF YOUR OWN CONCLUSION

Weakness ....
Strength ....
It is closest to number . . . of the student conclusions because ....
I would rate it ....
I could have improved it if I had ....
....

PRACTICE EXERCISE—THE COMPLETE ESSAY

To obtain maximum learning from the following exercise:

1. Write, under simulated examination conditions, a 20-minute essay based on the question.

2. Analyze the student responses.

3. Compare your analysis with the evaluation given.

4. Evaluate your own essay.

Time begun . . . . Time ended . . . . Time used . . . .

Did you complete the essay on time? . . . .

DIRECTIONS: You have twenty minutes to plan and write an essay on the topic assigned below. DO NOT WRITE ON ANOTHER TOPIC. AN ESSAY ON ANOTHER TOPIC IS NOT ACCEPTABLE.

The essay is assigned to give you an opportunity to show how well you can write. You should, therefore, take care to express your thoughts on the topic clearly and effectively. How well you write is much more important than how much you write, but to cover the topic adequately you may want to write more than one paragraph. Be specific.

Your essay must be written on the lines provided on your answer sheet. You will receive no other paper on which to write. You will find that you have enough space if you write on every line, avoid wide margins, and keep your handwriting to a reasonable size. It is important to remember that what you write will be read by someone who is not familiar with your handwriting. Try to write or print so that what you are writing is legible.

DO NOT WRITE IN YOUR TEST BOOK. You will receive credit only for what you write on your answer sheet.

Consider carefully the following quotation and the assignment following it. Then, plan and write your essay as directed.

The wise argue causes; fools decide them.

ASSIGNMENT: Do you agree or disagree with this statement? Write an essay in which you support your opinion with specific examples from history, contemporary affairs, literature, or personal observation.

The following essays are typical of those submitted by applicants. In the space below each, write your analysis of the strengths and weaknesses found in the essay. Confine your criticism to elements of content and organization. Rate each essay on this scale of 1 to 6:

5–6 *Generally excellent:* Writing contains originality of thought, freshness of expression
4–5 *Competent:* Soundness of thought and clear organization
3 *Interesting but flawed:* Imagination and ability to think clearly combined with irrelevancies, weakness in organization
1–2 *Inadequate:* Borderline in thought, content, and organization; triteness of thought coupled with a lack of organization

1. I find the given topic most provocative. It forces you to think about how people act and react in the world around us. If more people were to realize how important it is to allow wise sayings like this one to govern our lives, there would be fewer tensions in families and nations.

Wise sayings are the distillation of race experiences. They can serve as the touchstones for group reactions that are beneficial not only to the individual, but to the world of people around us.

It is only through a discussion of topics such as this one, "The wise argue causes; fools decide them," that we can come to grips with the problems that beset our world.

ANALYSIS ....
....
....
RATING ....

2. The given proverb contains a clever play on two of the meanings of *causes*. In the first half, *causes* means those aspects that bring about a given result. In the second half, *causes* means issues. To me, the saying means that the best approach to an issue is to find the underlying factors that brought it about; the worst way to handle a problem is to take sides before knowing what made it into a problem.

The world around us is filled with horrifying shadows. We seem to be rushing headlong into disaster. With the weapons we have perfected, we can wipe out all life from the surface of our planet; we can even destroy the planet itself. When will we learn that we are not masters of the Earth, but only a small part in an inexorable pattern that we cannot control!

ANALYSIS ....
....
....
RATING ....

3. "The wise argue causes; fools decide them." It is difficult under the stress of an examination to formulate my thoughts as clearly as I should like to. Yet in the world of responsibilities that surround us, we cannot stand still and let things just happen to us. We must rise to the occasion and do our best. Our best under such circumstances may prove inadequate, but the expectations of society cannot go beyond that.

Like all generalizations, the proverb given for this essay has a piece of the truth. When facing an issue, we are most prudent if we look for underlying causative factors before taking sides. Taking sides means that there must be a winner and a loser; but in controversial social issues, there cannot always be winners and losers. You cannot just be against slums, disease, poverty. You have to do more than just argue; you have to attack causes and try to overcome them through positive action.

Looking for causes is a constructive, beneficial approach, but if we stop there, nothing can be accomplished; we must take a firm stand and fight if necessary, once we have a clear idea of causes. We are not *fools* then! That is a piece of the truth that the quotation misses!

ANALYSIS ....
....
....
RATING ....

4. Proverbs have been fundamental guides to human action for thousands of years. They are truly distillations tested and proved by millions of people. Yet, we do not look to them for absolute truths. Like any generalization, we cannot expect them to be valid under all circumstances. Rather, we look to proverbs and folk sayings for insights that can help us to understand other people and ourselves. The saying "The wise argue causes; fools decide them" is an excellent illustration to prove my contention.

The proverb can be punched full of holes. It is not always wise to *argue causes*. When a child is drowning in a bathtub, you do not stand there arguing about what or who caused the accident. It is not *always* foolish to take a stand on an unresolved issue. If the blacks of Birmingham had not decided to act, instead of analyzing for causes of segregation, our march toward social and economic democracy would not have taken strides forward.

However, the proverb does contain a valuable insight. If we want to resolve an issue that has a solution, it is better to approach it through its causes and handle them. For example, when parents and children quarrel over curfew, chores, or allowances, the problems are more easily controlled when the family discusses the reasons for the rulings, the reasons for nonconformity. Nothing is truly resolved when each side takes a stand stating that one side is right and the other wrong; the reason for the position, rather than the rightness or wrongness, is the key to resolution.

ANALYSIS ....
....
....
RATING ....

5. We are beset on all sides by problems, personal, social, and economic. Proverbs can guide us through such difficulties.

Right now, my big problem is which college is going to accept me. If my first choice takes me, then I will be able to pursue the career of medicine. The cost of a medical education today is so high that my family just cannot afford to see me through. I really do not want to put such a burden on them. I do not think I have the right to do so. I have three brothers and sisters. They too should have the right to go to college. If the college I hope for gives me the nod, I will be able to work my way through my undergraduate years and save money for medical school.

By reading the proverb "The wise argue causes; fools decide them," I have been helped to see what my problem is and how I can resolve it. Proverbs can truly guide us through our difficulties.

ANALYSIS ....
....
....
RATING ....

EVALUATION OF ESSAYS

1. At no one point did the student discuss the given topic. The generalizations, while applicable, could be a form response to all similar topics. The answer contains no supportive illustrations. While the essay is divided into three paragraphs, the second is primarily a repetition of the first.

RATING: Inadequate—1

2. The essay is divided into two unconnected paragraphs. The first paragraph contains an excellent approach to the topic. A workable explanation of the proverb is presented. The second paragraph as given is completely unrelated to the first and apparently unrelated to the topic. The writer may have had a strong thread of connection planned, but it was never realized in the presentation.

RATING: Barely competent—3

3. There are two unrelated sections to the essay. The first paragraph begins with the proverb, but it is not related to the following sentences. What follows in the first paragraph is unrelated to the topic and to the next two paragraphs; it contains a self-conscious attempt at an introduction.

The second and third paragraphs are very well organized, and they deal cogently with the ideas the writer related to the quotation. More could have been done to illustrate the candidate's thesis that the proverb has only a piece of the truth.

RATING: Adequate—4

4. Although the introduction is long-winded, the organization of the essay is clear. The candidate presented a thesis: proverbs are valuable for the insights they give us, not for the validity of generalization. In the second paragraph, the writer showed a fallacy in the proverb. In the third paragraph, the writer presented proof of the insight obtained from the proverb.

RATING: Generally excellent—5–6

5. The essay has a three-part organization. The main idea in the first paragraph is repeated in the conclusion. But at no one point did the writer discuss the given assignment. There is no clarification of the quotation, presentation of a thesis, or proof to support a thesis.

RATING: Inadequate—2

EVALUATION OF YOUR OWN ESSAY

Weaknesses ....
Strengths ....
It is closest to number ....of the student essays because ....
I would rate it ....
I could have improved it if I had ....
....

5. Additional Essay Assignments

The following set of assignments is for those who have the time or need for additional practice in planning and organizing a 20-minute essay.

The assumption here, as throughout this section, is that you can write without making costly technical errors. If, however, you do need additional drill in that area, work on the material in Section One. Unless you have command of sentence structure, everyday spelling, word meanings, and grammatical usage, you are not ready to do the level of essay writing required to do well on this examination.

For each of the following topics, plan a three-part essay.

What will you put into the introduction? the development? the conclusion?

What will your thesis be?

What will be your major illustrations?

If time permits, you should write fully one or more of the three parts. If you complete the essay, limit yourself to about 1½ pages of 8½ by 11 paper, the usual size of theme paper.

DIRECTIONS: You have twenty minutes to plan and write an essay on the topic assigned below. DO NOT WRITE ON ANOTHER TOPIC. AN ESSAY ON ANOTHER TOPIC IS NOT ACCEPTABLE.

The essay is assigned to give you an opportunity to show how well you can write. You should, therefore, take care to express your thoughts on the topic clearly and effectively. How well you write is much more important than how much you write, but to cover the topic adequately you may want to write more than one paragraph. Be specific.

Your essay must be written on the lines provided on your answer sheet. You will receive no other paper on which to write. You will find that you have enough space if you write on every line, avoid wide margins, and keep your handwriting to a reasonable size. It is important to remember that what you write will be read by someone who is not familiar with your handwriting. Try to write or print so that what you are writing is legible.

DO NOT WRITE IN YOUR TEST BOOK. You will receive credit only for what you write on your answer sheet.

Consider carefully the following quotations and the assignment. Then, plan and write your essay as directed.

ASSIGNMENT: Do you agree or disagree with this statement? Write an essay in which you support your opinion with specific examples from history, contemporary affairs, literature, or personal observation.

ESSAY TOPICS
GROUP ONE

1. The best way to do good to ourselves is to do it to others; the right way to gather is to scatter.

2. Those who are just only are cruel. Who on earth could live were all judged justly?

3. Some will always be above others. Destroy the inequality today, and it will appear again tomorrow.

4. Where the press is free and every person is able to read, all is safe.

5. Liberty has restraints but no frontiers.

6. A map of the world that does not include Utopia is not worth glancing at.

7. White lies are but ushers to black ones.

8. Shallow people believe in luck; wise and strong people believe in cause and effect.

9. More firm and sure the hand of courage strikes when it obeys the watchful eye of caution.

10. Maxims are to the intellect what laws are to actions: they do not enlighten, but guide and direct, and though they themselves are blind, are protecting.

11. Prejudices are rarely overcome by argument; not being founded in reason, they cannot be destroyed by logic.

12. Master books, but do not let them master you. Read to live, not live to read.

13. The fire of anger that you kindle for your enemy often burns you more than him.

14. We have made a virtue of moderation to limit the ambition of the great and to console people of mediocrity for their want of fortune and of merit.

15. I am weary of hearing of the tremendous power of money. I will say to the contrary that for a genuine person it is no evil to be poor.

16. Our personal defects will commonly have, with the rest of the world, precisely that importance which they have for us. If we make light of them, so will other people.

17. It would be folly to argue that the people in a democracy cannot make political mistakes. They can and do make grave errors. They know it; they pay the penalty; but compared with the mistakes which have been made by every kind of dictatorship, they are unimportant.

18. Books are good enough in their own way, but they are a mighty bloodless substitute for life.

19. Boredom is a vital problem for the moralist, since at least half the sins of people are caused by the fear of it.

20. Opinions alter, manners change, creeds rise and fall, but the moral law is written on the tablet of eternity. For every false word or unrighteous deed, for cruelty and oppression, for lust or vanity, the price has to be paid at last, not always by the chief offender, but paid by someone.

21. People are valued not for what they are, but for what they seem to be.

22. We have no time to make allowances, and the graduation of punishment by the scale of guilt is a mere impossibility. Thieves are thieves in the law's eye even though they have been trained from their cradles in a den of thieves, and definite penalties must be attached to definite acts.

23. The wise learn through the experience of others; fools learn through their own experience.

24. The greatest challenge facing both the arts and education is how to respond to tradition without either rejecting it or becoming its slave.

25. Loyalty is *not* conformity.

GROUP TWO

1. Tradition can be both a liberator and a jailer.

2. Youth shows slavish conformity rather than rebellion or independence when following peer fashions.

3. All players on intercollegiate teams should receive compensation equivalent to that paid to professionals.

4. Reading is an obsolescent skill.

5. Experience is the best teacher.

6. Animated TV cartoons are harmful to the younger generation.

7. Outward appearance is as important as inner traits.

8. Parents have a right to feel disappointed and ashamed when their children are not perfect.

9. Career choice is usually an emotional rather than a logical function.

10. English should be made the official language of the United States.

11. Statewide lotteries have been a beneficial addition to our lives.

12. We are our brother's keepers.

13. Conformity or rebellion, which is the better way?

14. Planning to be second-best is the best strategy for survival.

15. People tend to choose pets that reflect their own personalities.

16. Those with physical or mental disabilities can fully experience life.

17. It is easier to love a person who seems perfect than one who seems imperfect.

18. There is no such thing as a totally normal person.

19. Beauty is in the eye of the beholder.

20. We need to feel needed.

The English Composition Test with Essay

Section F O U R : Practice Tests for the English Composition Test with Essay

1. *Practice Tests*

2. *Answers to Practice Tests with Analyses of Answers*

1. *Practice Tests*

The following practice examinations will help you to evaluate and improve both your timing and your control of the skills tested on the English Composition Test with Essay. Before you begin to take any of them, you should familiarize yourself with

- Section One and Section Two of this book; reviews and tests for multiple-choice questions
- The material in Section Three; review and drills for writing a 20-minute essay

After you have taken each of these practice examinations and have evaluated your results, turn to the preceding reviews for the knowledge your score revealed you lack. Take time out and redo the drills. By doing so, you will be making the best use of your study time. Use these examinations to help you achieve your maximum.

Simulate examination conditions as closely as you can when you do your practice.

1. Work alone—without distractions.
2. Take the entire examination in one sitting.
3. Allow 20 minutes for the essay and 40 minutes for the multiple-choice questions.

To Do Your Best in the Essay

1. Read the *Directions*. They may change from examination to examination.

2. Make certain that you comprehend both the literal and the figurative meaning of the quotation.

3. Read the *Assignment* with pen in hand to underline key phrases.

4. Do not begin to write before you have developed your thesis.

5. Do not change your thesis in midstream. Any topic can be approached from an endless variety of opinions. What you do with the opinion is more important than even the opinion!

6. *Stop at the end of 20 minutes.* When taking the actual examination, you would then proceed to the multiple-choice questions. If time permits, you could return to the essay after you have finished the multiple-choice exercises. Since this is a practice session, if you find that you need much more time, after a day or so *repeat* the same topic and delimit your discussion.

7. Remember that in 20 minutes you cannot be overly creative. The rating cannot be refined enough to allow for nuances of difference in candidate responses. The best response is well organized, free from technical errors, limited to one major idea; and it follows the direction given in the *Assignment*.

8. While waiting for an idea to jell, proofread the sections that you have completed. Errors that result from unintentional carelessness, pen slips, are as costly as those that are caused by lack of knowledge.

To Do Your Best on Multiple-Choice Questions

1. The body of material being covered in the test remains the same, but the question items change. Therefore make certain that you read the directions before you begin to answer. Know what each of the letters in the Answer Key stands for before you mark any one of them.

2. The test must cover a wide range so that there can be a spread in student scores. Therefore, do not look for subtle variations first. Rather look for the obvious ones first! Unacceptable forms of agreement, tense, use of the apostrophe, confusion of common words will be much more frequent than stylistic changes. Only when you do not find the common blunder, then go toward the more sophisticated type of change.

3. Once you have found the "error" do not stop! Examine the other choices before you write your answer.

4. Do not mull over any one item. Remember the subtle is mixed with the obvious; you receive as much credit for one as the other. If you find one item difficult, skip it and then come back later if you have time.

5. Follow the suggested time schedule. It is better to go on to the next section when time is up. If you are permitted, you may be able to go back later.

6. You *can* guess. In fact, it is generally to your advantage to guess if you can eliminate one or more of the choices for a question. However, because of the way the tests are scored, guessing randomly is not likely to increase your score.

7. Rely upon your past training. Do not assume because it is a form that you normally use it must be unacceptable.

8. When in doubt, select the more formal item, the less colloquial choice. Remember that what is being tested is your control of Standard Written English.

NOTE: In College Board publications, the terms *correct* and *incorrect* are used interchangeably with *acceptable* and *not acceptable,* respectively, when referring to specific forms in usage, diction, and spelling. Thus, items labeled in this book as *acceptable* in current Standard Written English may be labeled as either *acceptable* or *correct* in directions and in test items of the English Composition Test; items labeled in this book as *not acceptable* may be identified as either *not acceptable* or *incorrect* in the explanatory material and directions of the English Composition Test.

When Planning Your Essay

If you find that ideas do not come:

1. Look for both literal and figurative interpretations of the quotation.

2. Use examples to test the extent to which the quotation has a piece of the truth.

3. Re-read the *Assignment* and underline the phrases that tell you what is expected of you.

4. Begin by thinking in terms of the three-part development. Concentrate on an introduction.

5. Practice at this time in handling the following examinations will give you confidence in your ability to analyze the question and plan a satisfactory essay.

If you find that too many ideas crowd in:

1. List the key words of your ideas in the margin of the *Assignment*.

2. Re-read the *Assignment* and underline the phrases that tell you what is expected of you.

3. Arbitrarily pick the one or two ideas that fit best for you. Drop the others.

4. Begin to think in terms of the three-part development. Concentrate on the introduction.

If you find that you often miss the topic and go off into irrelevancies:

1. Develop the habit of reading the quotation and the *Assignment* together.

2. Underline in the *Assignment* what is expected of you. Then re-read the quotation.

3. Re-read the *Assignment* before you begin *each* part of the essay.

If you find that you need more than the allotted time of 20 minutes:

PRACTICE!

PRACTICE TEST ONE

ANSWER SHEET

1 Ⓐ Ⓑ Ⓒ Ⓓ Ⓔ   25 Ⓐ Ⓑ Ⓒ Ⓓ Ⓔ   48 Ⓐ Ⓑ Ⓒ Ⓓ Ⓔ
2 Ⓐ Ⓑ Ⓒ Ⓓ Ⓔ   26 Ⓐ Ⓑ Ⓒ Ⓓ Ⓔ   49 Ⓐ Ⓑ Ⓒ Ⓓ Ⓔ
3 Ⓐ Ⓑ Ⓒ Ⓓ Ⓔ   27 Ⓐ Ⓑ Ⓒ Ⓓ Ⓔ   50 Ⓐ Ⓑ Ⓒ Ⓓ Ⓔ
4 Ⓐ Ⓑ Ⓒ Ⓓ Ⓔ   28 Ⓐ Ⓑ Ⓒ Ⓓ Ⓔ   51 Ⓐ Ⓑ Ⓒ Ⓓ Ⓔ
5 Ⓐ Ⓑ Ⓒ Ⓓ Ⓔ   29 Ⓐ Ⓑ Ⓒ Ⓓ Ⓔ   52 Ⓐ Ⓑ Ⓒ Ⓓ Ⓔ
6 Ⓐ Ⓑ Ⓒ Ⓓ Ⓔ   30 Ⓐ Ⓑ Ⓒ Ⓓ Ⓔ   53 Ⓐ Ⓑ Ⓒ Ⓓ Ⓔ
7 Ⓐ Ⓑ Ⓒ Ⓓ Ⓔ   31 Ⓐ Ⓑ Ⓒ Ⓓ Ⓔ   54 Ⓐ Ⓑ Ⓒ Ⓓ Ⓔ
8 Ⓐ Ⓑ Ⓒ Ⓓ Ⓔ   32 Ⓐ Ⓑ Ⓒ Ⓓ Ⓔ   55 Ⓐ Ⓑ Ⓒ Ⓓ Ⓔ
9 Ⓐ Ⓑ Ⓒ Ⓓ Ⓔ   33 Ⓐ Ⓑ Ⓒ Ⓓ Ⓔ   56 Ⓐ Ⓑ Ⓒ Ⓓ Ⓔ
10 Ⓐ Ⓑ Ⓒ Ⓓ Ⓔ   34 Ⓐ Ⓑ Ⓒ Ⓓ Ⓔ   57 Ⓐ Ⓑ Ⓒ Ⓓ Ⓔ
11 Ⓐ Ⓑ Ⓒ Ⓓ Ⓔ   35 Ⓐ Ⓑ Ⓒ Ⓓ Ⓔ   58 Ⓐ Ⓑ Ⓒ Ⓓ Ⓔ
12 Ⓐ Ⓑ Ⓒ Ⓓ Ⓔ   36 Ⓐ Ⓑ Ⓒ Ⓓ Ⓔ   59 Ⓐ Ⓑ Ⓒ Ⓓ Ⓔ
13 Ⓐ Ⓑ Ⓒ Ⓓ Ⓔ   37 Ⓐ Ⓑ Ⓒ Ⓓ Ⓔ   60 Ⓐ Ⓑ Ⓒ Ⓓ Ⓔ
14 Ⓐ Ⓑ Ⓒ Ⓓ Ⓔ   38 Ⓐ Ⓑ Ⓒ Ⓓ Ⓔ   61 Ⓐ Ⓑ Ⓒ Ⓓ Ⓔ
15 Ⓐ Ⓑ Ⓒ Ⓓ Ⓔ   39 Ⓐ Ⓑ Ⓒ Ⓓ Ⓔ   62 Ⓐ Ⓑ Ⓒ Ⓓ Ⓔ
16 Ⓐ Ⓑ Ⓒ Ⓓ Ⓔ   40 Ⓐ Ⓑ Ⓒ Ⓓ Ⓔ   63 Ⓐ Ⓑ Ⓒ Ⓓ Ⓔ
17 Ⓐ Ⓑ Ⓒ Ⓓ Ⓔ   41 Ⓐ Ⓑ Ⓒ Ⓓ Ⓔ   64 Ⓐ Ⓑ Ⓒ Ⓓ Ⓔ
18 Ⓐ Ⓑ Ⓒ Ⓓ Ⓔ   42 Ⓐ Ⓑ Ⓒ Ⓓ Ⓔ   65 Ⓐ Ⓑ Ⓒ Ⓓ Ⓔ
19 Ⓐ Ⓑ Ⓒ Ⓓ Ⓔ   43 Ⓐ Ⓑ Ⓒ Ⓓ Ⓔ   66 Ⓐ Ⓑ Ⓒ Ⓓ Ⓔ
20 Ⓐ Ⓑ Ⓒ Ⓓ Ⓔ   44 Ⓐ Ⓑ Ⓒ Ⓓ Ⓔ   67 Ⓐ Ⓑ Ⓒ Ⓓ Ⓔ
21 Ⓐ Ⓑ Ⓒ Ⓓ Ⓔ   45 Ⓐ Ⓑ Ⓒ Ⓓ Ⓔ   68 Ⓐ Ⓑ Ⓒ Ⓓ Ⓔ
22 Ⓐ Ⓑ Ⓒ Ⓓ Ⓔ   46 Ⓐ Ⓑ Ⓒ Ⓓ Ⓔ   69 Ⓐ Ⓑ Ⓒ Ⓓ Ⓔ
23 Ⓐ Ⓑ Ⓒ Ⓓ Ⓔ   47 Ⓐ Ⓑ Ⓒ Ⓓ Ⓔ   70 Ⓐ Ⓑ Ⓒ Ⓓ Ⓔ
24 Ⓐ Ⓑ Ⓒ Ⓓ Ⓔ

PRACTICE TEST ONE

Total Time: One Hour
PART 1 *Suggested Time: 20 Minutes*
Time begin .... Time ended .... Time used ....
Did you complete the section within the time limit? ..

DIRECTIONS: You have twenty minutes to plan and write an essay on the topic assigned below. DO NOT WRITE ON ANOTHER TOPIC. AN ESSAY ON ANOTHER TOPIC IS NOT ACCEPTABLE.

The essay is assigned to give you an opportunity to show how well you can write. You should, therefore, take care to express your thoughts on the topic clearly and effectively. How well you write is much more important than how much you write, but to cover the topic adequately you may want to write more than one paragraph. Be specific.

Your essay must be written on the lines provided on your answer sheet. You will receive no other paper on which to write. You will find that you have enough space if you write on every line, avoid wide margins, and keep your handwriting to a reasonable size. It is important to remember that what you write will be read by someone who is not familiar with your handwriting. Try to write or print so that what you are writing is legible.

DO NOT WRITE IN YOUR TEST BOOK. You will receive credit only for what you write on your answer sheet.

Consider carefully the following quotation and the assignment following it. Then, plan and write your essay as directed.

> The printed page as a major means of preserving and transmitting knowledge is rapidly being replaced by electronic memories and devices.

ASSIGNMENT: Comment upon this statement. What are some of the implications for the educational system? Be specific. You should support your point of view with illustrations from your own experience or by references taken from your observations or readings.

PART 2 *Suggested Time:* **20** *Minutes*
Time begun .... Time ended .... Time used ....
Did you complete the section within the time limit? ..

DIRECTIONS: The following sentences contain problems in grammar, usage, diction (choice of words),
and idiom.
Some sentences are correct.
No sentence contains more than one error.
You will find that the error, if there is one, is
underlined and lettered. Assume that all other elements of the sentence are correct and cannot be
changed. In choosing answers, follow the requirements of standard written English.
If there is an error, select the <u>one underlined part</u>
that must be changed in order to make the sentence
correct, and mark that on the answer sheet.
If there is no error, mark answer E.

1. The <u>wear and tear</u> <u>on</u> the body <u>is</u> a
        (A)   (B)   (C)
   <u>medical problem</u>. <u>No error</u>
        (D)   (E)

2. The team <u>are</u> <u>waiting</u> behind the <u>main</u> grand-
              (A)   (B)   (C)
   stand next to the <u>playing field</u>. <u>No error</u>
                          (D)   (E)

3. The <u>firemen</u> <u>digged</u> out the victim <u>from under</u>
          (A)   (B)   (C)
   the <u>fallen debris</u>. <u>No error</u>
          (D)   (E)

4. The <u>First World War</u> <u>changed</u> the <u>major</u> inter-
              (A)   (B)   (C)
   national financial <u>relationships</u>. <u>No error</u>
                            (D)   (E)

5. A shot <u>was fired</u> in the dark but <u>a</u> policeman
              (A)   (B)
   <u>seen</u> where the bullet <u>came</u> from. <u>No error</u>
     (C)   (D)   (E)

6. He <u>plays</u> his violin every day <u>so that</u> he would
        (A)   (B)
   become <u>concertmaster</u> of the <u>orchestra</u>.
              (C)   (D)
   <u>No error</u>
      (E)

7. Humanity's <u>greatest</u> <u>source of</u> enlightenment
                (A)   (B)
   <u>lies in</u> the <u>printed word</u>. <u>No error</u>
     (C)   (D)   (E)

8. The <u>risk of</u> investors <u>in supplying capital</u> to de-
          (A)   (B)
   veloping countries <u>seem</u> <u>very great</u>. <u>No error</u>
                        (C)   (D)   (E)

9. The <u>museum</u> <u>where</u> we <u>visited</u> in Center City
          (A)   (B)   (C)
   <u>was</u> beautiful. <u>No error</u>
     (D)   (E)

10. After a <u>long and exhausting</u> trip <u>by car</u>, he ar-
                  (A)   (B)
    rived <u>at the river</u> and <u>pays</u> a toll to cross the
            (C)   (D)
    bridge. <u>No error</u>
                (E)

11. <u>After the battle</u> was over, the <u>soldiers</u>
        (A)   (B)
    <u>will advance</u> to <u>the front lines</u>. <u>No error</u>
        (C)   (D)   (E)

12. <u>I read</u> <u>in the newspaper</u> that in Nigeria <u>they</u>
        (A)   (B)   (C)
    grow <u>large tomatoes</u>. <u>No error</u>
            (D)   (E)

13. To   master   <u>the proper backstroke</u>,
                        (A)
    <u>the breathing</u> must <u>be</u> <u>carefully controlled</u>.
        (B)   (C)   (D)
    <u>No error</u>
        (E)

14. The key to <u>the persistence of the family farm</u> is
                            (B)
    the   <u>difficulty of</u>   routinizing
                (C)
    <u>agricultural operations</u>. <u>No error</u>
            (D)   (E)

15. <u>While one part</u> of the TV program carried the
        (A)
    football game, <u>the other part</u> <u>shows</u> the
                        (B)   (C)
    <u>training of the teams</u>. <u>No error</u>
            (D)   (E)

16. The parliamentarians cheered as the speaker
           (A)   (B)   (C)
    entered. No error
    (D)   (E)

17. Our favorite teacher and friend have gone.
    (A) (B)   (C)   (D)
    No error
    (E)

18. He told the teacher who had given him the cor-
    (A)   (B) (C)   (D)
    rect answers. No error
                  (E)

19. I had stopped playing ball three weeks ago
        (A)   (B)
    because I became ill. No error
    (C)   (D)   (E)

20. The plant manager, like many workers, were
                       (A)   (B)
    very experienced in safety precautions.
         (C)   (D)
    No error
    (E)

21. The entire community was saddened to hear of
         (A)   (B)   (C)
    the mayor's sudden resignation. No error
        (D)   (E)

22. Almost every day the laboratory assistant
    (A)   (B)
    helps Fred and I . No error
    (C)   (D)   (E)

23. He approached the counter and pays for
    (A)   (B)   (C)
    his meal. No error
    (D)   (E)

24. Economics is a subject which many students
              (A)   (B)   (C)
    take. No error
    (D)   (E)

25. The musician is a man with great promise and
                          (A)
    who should be encouraged to continue his
    (B)   (C)   (D)
    work. No error
          (E)

26. You have to remember that not all people
              (A)   (B)
    were honest and above reproach. No error
    (C)   (D)   (E)

27. Each supervisor and subordinate were to pre-
    (A)   (B)   (C)
    pare his or her reports independently.
         (D)
    No error
    (E)

28. It was he who traveled the distance in half
    (A) (B) (C) (D)
    the time. No error
              (E)

29. My wife and I travel by train many times in the
                (A) (B)   (C)
    past. No error
    (D)   (E)

30. Neither the teacher nor the students were in-
    (A)   (B)   (C)
    troduced to their dean. No error
                 (D)   (E)

31. The teacher appreciates whomever volunteers
                (A)   (B)   (C)
    in class. No error
    (D)   (E)

32. There is efficiency in the world for our needs
          (A) (B)   (C)
    but not for our greed. No error
                   (D)   (E)

33. When husbands and wives both work, they may
    (A)   (B)   (C)
    not have enough time for their children.
                              (D)
    No error
    (E)

34. My mathematics teacher is one person
    (A)   (B)
    who I shall always respect. No error
    (C) (D)   (E)

35. The day was very warm, so I hoped
                           (A) (B)
    to have played ball. No error
    (C)   (D)   (E)

PART 3 *Suggested Time:* **20** *Minutes*
Time begun .... Time ended .... Time used ....
Did you complete the section within the time limit? ..

DIRECTIONS: In each of the following sentences, some part of the sentence or the entire sentence is underlined. Beneath each sentence you will find five ways of phrasing the underlined part. The first of these repeats the original; the other four are different. If you think the original is better than any of the alternatives, choose answer A; otherwise choose one of the others.

This is a test of correctness and effectiveness of expression. In choosing answers, follow the requirements of standard written English; that is, pay attention to grammar, choice of words, sentence construction and punctuation. Choose the answer that best expresses the meaning of the original sentence. Your choice should produce the most effective sentence—clear and precise, without awkwardness or ambiguity.

36. Neither his choice of jacket nor the loud tone of his voice impress me.

    (A) Neither his choice of jacket nor the loud tone of his voice impress me.
    (B) Neither his jacket or his voice impresses me.
    (C) I am impressed by neither his choice of jacket or his voice.
    (D) Neither his choice of jacket nor his loud tones impress me.
    (E) Neither his choice of jacket nor the loud tone of his voice impresses me.

37. I do not know how many times I have tried to tell you that he dislikes you telling him what to do.

    (A) I have tried to tell you that he dislikes you telling him what to do.
    (B) I have told you, that he dislikes having you tell him what to do.
    (C) I have tried to let you know he doesn't want you to give him orders.
    (D) I told you not to order him around.
    (E) I have told you that he dislikes your telling him what to do.

38. Pedestrians who like to see squirrels, walk through the park with bags of peanuts in hand.

    (A) Pedestrians who like to see squirrels, walk through
    (B) Pedestrians, who like to see squirrels, walk into

    (C) Pedestrians, that like to see squirrels, walk
    (D) Pedestrians wishing to see squirrels walk through
    (E) Pedestrians who like to see squirrels walk through

39. I regret to report that neither of the microphones appear to be in working order.

    (A) neither of the microphones appear to be in working order.
    (B) neither microphone is working.
    (C) neither of the microphones appears to be in working order.
    (D) I cannot seem to get either of the microphones to work.
    (E) the microphones are dead.

40. I really like him better than any of the other students.

    (A) I really like him better than any of the other students.
    (B) Really, I like him better than any of the other students.
    (C) Of all the students I like him better.
    (D) I really like him better than I like any of the other students.
    (E) I like him best of the other students.

41. The gist of the report is that the commuters demand that the buses move passengers more rapidly and with greater economy.

    (A) buses move passengers more rapidly and with greater economy
    (B) buses be faster and cheaper.
    (C) buses go faster and at a lower cost.
    (D) buses move passengers more rapidly and more economically.
    (E) speed of buses be greater and that the cost of them be less.

42. The newcomer was put in charge of evening programs and the swimming pool.

    (A) put in charge of evening programs and the swimming pool.
    (B) in command of evening programs and the swimming pool.
    (C) placed over programs for the evening and the swimming pool.
    (D) in charge of programs of the evening and swimming pool.
    (E) put in charge of evening programs and the swimming pool schedule.

43. What do you accomplish by <u>announcing that you neither want his assistance nor his advice?</u>

    (A) announcing that you neither want his assistance nor his advice?
    (B) announcing, "You neither want his assistance nor advice"?
    (C) announcing you want neither his assistance or advice?
    (D) announcing that you want neither his assistance nor his advice?
    (E) announcing you don't want him to help you or tell you what to do?

44. We had a long talk with the coach in charge of <u>the soccer team who has been involved in this matter for a long time.</u>

    (A) We had a long talk with the coach in charge of the soccer team who has been involved in this matter for a long time.
    (B) We talked at length with the soccer coach who has long been involved in this matter.
    (C) We had a long talk with the soccer coach who has long been involved in this matter.
    (D) We had a long talk with the coach of the soccer team. He had been involved in this matter for a lengthy time.
    (E) Our long talk was with the soccer coach who has been in on this for a long time.

45. The critics all agreed that our senior show <u>was lively, colorful, and the entire production was well rehearsed.</u>

    (A) was lively, colorful, and the entire production was well rehearsed.
    (B) was lively, colorful and the entire production well rehearsed.
    (C) seemed lively, colorful, and with a well-rehearsed production.
    (D) was a lively, colorful, and well rehearsed production
    (E) was lively, colorful, and well rehearsed.

46. The neighborhood contains many nominal <u>religionists who follow its spirit rather than its tenets.</u>

    (A) religionists who follow its spirit rather than its tenets.
    (B) members of religious groups who follow the spirit rather than the tenets of their religion.
    (C) religionists who order their lives around the intentions of their religion rather than on rules and regulations.
    (D) worshipers who obey the spirit of their religious laws rather than the regulations issued by the clergy.
    (E) religionists following the spirit rather than its tenets.

47. The student <u>proudly told the visitors the classification of all the animals which pleased the instructor.</u>

    (A) proudly told the visitors the classification of all the animals which pleased the instructor.
    (B) told the visitors proudly the classification of all the animals, which pleased the instructor.
    (C) pleased the instructor when he proudly told the visitors the classification of all the animals.
    (D) pleased the instructor telling the visitors proudly the classification of all the animals.
    (E) pleased the instructor by telling the visitors the classification of all the animals proudly.

48. Forty years ago there was no such thing as <u>computers; they didn't even have tape recorders.</u>

    (A) computers; they didn't even have tape recorders.
    (B) computers when they didn't even have tape recorders.
    (C) computers because they didn't even have tape recorders.
    (D) as computers or tape recorders.
    (E) a computer, let alone a tape recorder.

49. In the past ten years more attention has been centered on social and economic <u>equality which led to changes in the lives of many members</u> of minority groups.

    (A) equality which led to changes in the lives of many members
    (B) equality leading to changes in members' lives
    (C) equality leading to changes in the lives of many members
    (D) equality. This interest has led to changes in the lives of many members
    (E) equality; which lead to changes in the lives of members

50. <u>The storm having abated, the</u> suburbanites began to assess the damages.

    (A) The storm having abated, the
    (B) When the storm was abated, the
    (C) After the storm abated the
    (D) The storm having abated; the
    (E) Because the storm abated, the

51. I do not recall whether <u>I had promised during the afternoon to call on him.</u>

(A) I had promised during the afternoon to call on him.
(B) I promised, during the afternoon, to call on him.
(C) I had promised to call on him during the afternoon.
(D) , "I promised to call on him in the afternoon."
(E) I had promised, during the afternoon to call on him.

52. Above all, don't <u>panic. You should keep your wits about you at all times.</u>

(A) panic. You should keep your wits about you at all times.
(B) panic. At all times, you are to keep your wits about you.
(C) panic, and you should keep cool at all times.
(D) panic. Always keep your wits about you.
(E) panic. Don't ever lose your cool.

53. To be nominated as the candidate of our <u>party, your record must bear close scrutiny.</u>

(A) party, your record must bear close scrutiny.
(B) party your past performance will be carefully evaluated.
(C) party, what you have done becomes of paramount importance.
(D) party, your past achievements will be studied.
(E) party, you must have a record that can pass close scrutiny.

54. Einstein was one of the <u>greatest if not the greatest</u> mathematicians of modern times.

(A) greatest if not the greatest
(B) greatest, if not the greatest
(C) greatest—if not the greatest
(D) greatest—if not the greatest—
(E) greatest mathematicians if not the greatest

55. The pianist <u>was oblivious and undisturbed by the impolite whispering in the front rows.</u>

(A) was oblivious and undisturbed by the impolite whispering in the front rows.
(B) seemed unaware of the talkers in the front rows.
(C) ignored the impolite whisperers in the front rows.

(D) was oblivious to and undisturbed by the impolite whispering in the front rows.
(E) was oblivious and undisturbed, by the impolite whispering in the front rows.

56. <u>The caretaker proudly announced that, at long last, the mats were scrubbed and the window washed.</u>

(A) The caretaker proudly announced that, at long last, the mats were scrubbed and the window washed.
(B) The proud caretaker announced that the mats were scrubbed and the window washed at long last.
(C) The caretaker proudly announced, "The mats have been scrubbed and the windows washed."
(D) The caretaker proudly announced that, at long last, the mats had been scrubbed and window washed.
(E) Proudly, at long last, the caretaker announced the successful scrubbing of the mats the and the washing of the window.

57. The principles we shall have to discuss first are the primary <u>ones which require careful consideration because of their importance.</u>

(A) ones which require careful consideration because of their importance.
(B) ones.
(C) ones, requiring careful consideration since they are important.
(D) ones of careful consideration and importance.
(E) ones, which need consideration because of their importance.

58. Swimming against the tide of popular <u>fashion, the designer soared to a high niche of acceptance among his clients.</u>

(A) fashion, the designer soared to a high niche of acceptance among his clients.
(B) fashion. The designer found ready acceptance among his clients.
(C) fashion, the designer made an enviable name for himself.
(D) fashion, the designer pleased his customers.
(E) fashion, the designer won full acceptance from his clients.

59. Ed <u>Reecks the community representative is also</u> a member of this impressive committee.

(A) Reecks the community representative is also

(B) Reecks, the community representative, is also

(C) Reecks, the community representative also is

(D) Reecks. The community representative was also

(E) Reecks—the community representative— has also been

60. The driver of the first car swerved off the road. In a vain attempt to avoid the head-on collision.

(A) road. In a vain attempt to avoid
(B) road, in a futile attempt at avoiding
(C) road in a vain attempt to avoid
(D) road as he tried in vain to head off
(E) road as he uselessly tried to prevent

61. Because of the enthusiasm the project generated, less working hours were needed to carry it to a successful conclusion.

(A) less working hours were needed to carry it to a successful conclusion.
(B) they required less working hours to succeed.
(C) less working hours were needed.
(D) the results were achieved through working less.
(E) fewer working hours were needed to carry it to a successful conclusion.

62. That the swimmer was in serious trouble was evident to most everyone on the beach.

(A) was evident to most everyone on the beach.
(B) was evident to most everyone who was on the beach.
(C) was evident to most everyone who were on the beach.
(D) was evident to almost everyone on the beach.
(E) was in evidence to most everyone who was on the beach.

63. In the Classics class we had to memorize the names of once famous personages, and very few of these people, if any, are referred to in current literature.

(A) and very few of these people, if any, are referred to in current literature.
(B) and very few, if any, are referred to in current literature.
(C) who are seldom, if ever, referred to in current literature.

(D) but very few are ever referred to in current literature.
(E) and very few, if any, are mentioned today.

64. In *Breakfast of Champions,* Vonnegut's style is ironic, and his characters are highly symbolic, so that it sometimes confuses or misleads his readers.

(A) so that it sometimes confuses or misleads his readers.
(B) which sometimes confuses or misleads his readers.
(C) confusing and misleading his readers.
(D) resulting in a combination that sometimes confuses or misleads his readers.
(E) thus confusing or misleading his readers.

65. She is usually so prudent that she is certain to purchase all the items necessary to complete the construction before she starts.

(A) all the items necessary to complete the construction before she starts.
(B) before she starts, all the items necessary to complete the construction.
(C) all the necessary items.
(D) , before completion, all the necessary items.
(E) whatever she will need.

66. During times of crisis, our physical selves are capable of surviving incredulous outbursts of energy.

(A) crisis, our physical selves are capable of surviving incredulous outbursts of energy.
(B) crises, incredulous outbursts of energy can be demanded of us.
(C) crisis, our physical selves are capable of surviving incredible outbursts of energy.
(D) crisis, our physical selves can sustain incredulous outbursts of energy.
(E) crises, our physical selves can generate incredible outbursts of energy.

67. How many years will you waste in search for the happiness that could be yours if only you would open your eyes!

(A) for the happiness that could be yours if only you would open your eyes!
(B) searching for happiness!
(C) for the happiness that could be yours if you would open your eyes only!

P R A C T I C E   T E S T S   F O R   T H E   E N G L I S H   C O M P O S I T I O N   T E S T

(D) of the happiness that could only be yours if you would open your eyes!

(E) in search of the happiness that could be yours if only you would open your eyes!

68. The trivia that crowded the display areas in the flea market were purchased by tourists who bought on impulse and dealers who were in search of bargains.

(A) were purchased by tourists who bought on impulse and dealers who were in search of bargains.

(B) was purchased by impulsive tourists and dealers.

(C) were purchased by tourists buying on impulse and by dealers searching for bargains.

(D) was purchased by tourists buying on impulse and dealers who were in search of bargains.

(E) were purchased by tourists who bought on impulse and bargain-hunting dealers.

69. With great fanfare, the traditional quadrennial debate between the major presidential candidates forces two very weary men to put forth superhuman efforts at the end of a grueling campaign.

(A) the traditional quadrennial debate between the major presidential candidates forces

(B) the traditional debate among the major presidential candidates forces

(C) the traditional quadrennial debate between the major presidential candidates force

(D) the quadrennial debate between the major presidential candidates obligates

(E) the quadrennial debate among the major presidential candidates force

70. In order to fit everything into his crowded schedule, a detailed weekly calendar was kept by the district manager.

(A) schedule, a detailed weekly calendar was kept by the district manager.

(B) schedule; a detailed weekly calendar was kept by the district manager.

(C) schedule, the district manager would keep a weekly calendar.

(D) schedule, the district manager kept a detailed weekly calendar.

(E) schedule, a detailed weekly calendar was kept by the district manager.

ANSWER KEY AND ANALYSIS OF ANSWERS / *Page 198*

PRACTICE TEST TWO

ANSWER SHEET

1	Ⓐ Ⓑ Ⓒ Ⓓ Ⓔ	25	Ⓐ Ⓑ Ⓒ Ⓓ Ⓔ	48	Ⓐ Ⓑ Ⓒ Ⓓ Ⓔ
2	Ⓐ Ⓑ Ⓒ Ⓓ Ⓔ	26	Ⓐ Ⓑ Ⓒ Ⓓ Ⓔ	49	Ⓐ Ⓑ Ⓒ Ⓓ Ⓔ
3	Ⓐ Ⓑ Ⓒ Ⓓ Ⓔ	27	Ⓐ Ⓑ Ⓒ Ⓓ Ⓔ	50	Ⓐ Ⓑ Ⓒ Ⓓ Ⓔ
4	Ⓐ Ⓑ Ⓒ Ⓓ Ⓔ	28	Ⓐ Ⓑ Ⓒ Ⓓ Ⓔ	51	Ⓐ Ⓑ Ⓒ Ⓓ Ⓔ
5	Ⓐ Ⓑ Ⓒ Ⓓ Ⓔ	29	Ⓐ Ⓑ Ⓒ Ⓓ Ⓔ	52	Ⓐ Ⓑ Ⓒ Ⓓ Ⓔ
6	Ⓐ Ⓑ Ⓒ Ⓓ Ⓔ	30	Ⓐ Ⓑ Ⓒ Ⓓ Ⓔ	53	Ⓐ Ⓑ Ⓒ Ⓓ Ⓔ
7	Ⓐ Ⓑ Ⓒ Ⓓ Ⓔ	31	Ⓐ Ⓑ Ⓒ Ⓓ Ⓔ	54	Ⓐ Ⓑ Ⓒ Ⓓ Ⓔ
8	Ⓐ Ⓑ Ⓒ Ⓓ Ⓔ	32	Ⓐ Ⓑ Ⓒ Ⓓ Ⓔ	55	Ⓐ Ⓑ Ⓒ Ⓓ Ⓔ
9	Ⓐ Ⓑ Ⓒ Ⓓ Ⓔ	33	Ⓐ Ⓑ Ⓒ Ⓓ Ⓔ	56	Ⓐ Ⓑ Ⓒ Ⓓ Ⓔ
10	Ⓐ Ⓑ Ⓒ Ⓓ Ⓔ	34	Ⓐ Ⓑ Ⓒ Ⓓ Ⓔ	57	Ⓐ Ⓑ Ⓒ Ⓓ Ⓔ
11	Ⓐ Ⓑ Ⓒ Ⓓ Ⓔ	35	Ⓐ Ⓑ Ⓒ Ⓓ Ⓔ	58	Ⓐ Ⓑ Ⓒ Ⓓ Ⓔ
12	Ⓐ Ⓑ Ⓒ Ⓓ Ⓔ	36	Ⓐ Ⓑ Ⓒ Ⓓ Ⓔ	59	Ⓐ Ⓑ Ⓒ Ⓓ Ⓔ
13	Ⓐ Ⓑ Ⓒ Ⓓ Ⓔ	37	Ⓐ Ⓑ Ⓒ Ⓓ Ⓔ	60	Ⓐ Ⓑ Ⓒ Ⓓ Ⓔ
14	Ⓐ Ⓑ Ⓒ Ⓓ Ⓔ	38	Ⓐ Ⓑ Ⓒ Ⓓ Ⓔ	61	Ⓐ Ⓑ Ⓒ Ⓓ Ⓔ
15	Ⓐ Ⓑ Ⓒ Ⓓ Ⓔ	39	Ⓐ Ⓑ Ⓒ Ⓓ Ⓔ	62	Ⓐ Ⓑ Ⓒ Ⓓ Ⓔ
16	Ⓐ Ⓑ Ⓒ Ⓓ Ⓔ	40	Ⓐ Ⓑ Ⓒ Ⓓ Ⓔ	63	Ⓐ Ⓑ Ⓒ Ⓓ Ⓔ
17	Ⓐ Ⓑ Ⓒ Ⓓ Ⓔ	41	Ⓐ Ⓑ Ⓒ Ⓓ Ⓔ	64	Ⓐ Ⓑ Ⓒ Ⓓ Ⓔ
18	Ⓐ Ⓑ Ⓒ Ⓓ Ⓔ	42	Ⓐ Ⓑ Ⓒ Ⓓ Ⓔ	65	Ⓐ Ⓑ Ⓒ Ⓓ Ⓔ
19	Ⓐ Ⓑ Ⓒ Ⓓ Ⓔ	43	Ⓐ Ⓑ Ⓒ Ⓓ Ⓔ	66	Ⓐ Ⓑ Ⓒ Ⓓ Ⓔ
20	Ⓐ Ⓑ Ⓒ Ⓓ Ⓔ	44	Ⓐ Ⓑ Ⓒ Ⓓ Ⓔ	67	Ⓐ Ⓑ Ⓒ Ⓓ Ⓔ
21	Ⓐ Ⓑ Ⓒ Ⓓ Ⓔ	45	Ⓐ Ⓑ Ⓒ Ⓓ Ⓔ	68	Ⓐ Ⓑ Ⓒ Ⓓ Ⓔ
22	Ⓐ Ⓑ Ⓒ Ⓓ Ⓔ	46	Ⓐ Ⓑ Ⓒ Ⓓ Ⓔ	69	Ⓐ Ⓑ Ⓒ Ⓓ Ⓔ
23	Ⓐ Ⓑ Ⓒ Ⓓ Ⓔ	47	Ⓐ Ⓑ Ⓒ Ⓓ Ⓔ	70	Ⓐ Ⓑ Ⓒ Ⓓ Ⓔ
24	Ⓐ Ⓑ Ⓒ Ⓓ Ⓔ				

PRACTICE TEST TWO

Total Time: One Hour
PART 1 *Suggested Time:* **20** *Minutes*
Time begun .... Time ended .... Time used ....
Did you complete the section within the time limit? ..

DIRECTIONS: You have twenty minutes to plan and write an essay on the topic assigned below. DO NOT WRITE ON ANOTHER TOPIC. AN ESSAY ON ANOTHER TOPIC IS NOT ACCEPTABLE.

The essay is assigned to give you an opportunity to show how well you can write. You should, therefore, take care to express your thoughts on the topic clearly and effectively. How well you write is much more important than how much you write, but to cover the topic adequately you may want to write more than one paragraph. Be specific.

Your essay must be written on the lines provided on your answer sheet. You will receive no other paper on which to write. You will find that you have enough space if you write on every line, avoid wide margins, and keep your handwriting to a reasonable size. It is important to remember that what you write will be read by someone who is not familiar with your handwriting. Try to write or print so that what you are writing is legible.

DO NOT WRITE IN YOUR TEST BOOK. You will receive credit only for what you write on your answer sheet.

Consider carefully the following quotation and the assignment following it. Then, plan and write your essay as directed.

> As I view the world around me, I see a significant change in the moral standards. You hear only infrequently, "I practice what I preach." Instead, the expression often uttered is, "Do what I say, not what I do."

ASSIGNMENT: Organize your comments around the following questions: What significance is implied in the contrast of proverbs? Is the statement justified? What does it tell us about ourselves?

PART 2 *Suggested Time: 20 Minutes*
Time begun .... Time ended .... Time used ....
Did you complete the section within the time limit? ..

DIRECTIONS: In each of the following sentences, some part of the sentence or the entire sentence is underlined. Beneath each sentence you will five ways of phrasing the underlined part. The first of these repeats the original; the other four are different. If you think the original is better than any of the alternatives, choose answer A; otherwise choose one of the others.

   This is a test of correctness and effectiveness of expression. In choosing answers, follow the requirements of standard written English; that is, pay attention to grammar, choice of words, sentence construction and punctuation. Choose the answer that best expresses the meaning of the original sentence. Your choice should produce the most effective sentence—clear and precise, without awkwardness or ambiguity.

1. From all the major highways of the state come the multitude who overflow our metropolitan area.

   (A) highways of the state come the multitude who overflow
   (B) highways of the state comes the multitude that overflows
   (C) highways of the state comes the multitude which overflow
   (D) highways of the state come the multitude which overflows
   (E) highways of the state come the multitude overflowing

2. The recipient of the award could so easily have been I—or you!

   (A) could so easily have been I—or you!
   (B) could so easily have been any one of us!
   (C) could have so easily been I—or you!
   (D) could have been so easily me—or you!
   (E) so easily could have been me—or you!

3. No one, but him and me knew, the combination to the strongbox.

   (A) No one, but him and me knew, the
   (B) No one but he and me knew the
   (C) No one but him and me knew the
   (D) No one but he and I knew the
   (E) No one, but he and I, knew the

4. It was one of those ideas that is ignored because it was proposed before its time.

   (A) that is ignored because it was proposed
   (B) which is ignored because it was proposed
   (C) that are ignored, because it was proposed
   (D) that was ignored because it was proposed
   (E) that are ignored because it had been proposed

5. Being it was Saturday night, the shopping center did not close until midnight.

   (A) Being it was Saturday night, the
   (B) Being Saturday night, the
   (C) Since it was Saturday night, the
   (D) Being that it was Saturday night, the
   (E) Being it was Saturday night. The

6. Not one of the soldiers that were called up was aware of the gravity of the situation.

   (A) soldiers that were called up was
   (B) soldiers which were called up was
   (C) soldiers that was called up were
   (D) soldiers that were called up were
   (E) soldiers being called up were

7. Things being the way they are, we shall have to be satisfied with crumbs and not feasts from now on.

   (A) they are, we shall have to be
   (B) they are. We shall have to be
   (C) they are; we shall have to be
   (D) they are we shall have to be
   (E) that they are we shall have to be

8. He readily accepted my offer to help him, which pleased me greatly.

   (A) He readily accepted my offer to help him, which
   (B) That he readily accepted my offer to help him
   (C) He readily accepted my offer to help him. Which
   (D) He readily accepted my offer to help him, this
   (E) He excepted readily my offer to help him; which

9. It is the sort of a bargain that no one except him could resist.

   (A) the sort of a bargain that no one except him
   (B) a bargain that no one
   (C) the sort of bargain that no one except him
   (D) the sort of a bargain that no one except he
   (E) the sort of bargain that no one except he

10. I had to drive to town <u>immediately, otherwise</u> I would never meet him.

   (A) immediately, otherwise
   (B) immediately: otherwise
   (C) immediately. Otherwise
   (D) immediately otherwise
   (E) immediately. Otherwise,

11. I knew <u>I made my offer out of turn when</u> the chairman ignored my remarks.

   (A) I made my offer out of turn when
   (B) I made my offer out of turn. When
   (C) I had made my offer out of turn when
   (D) I made my offer out of turn since
   (E) I made my offer out of turn; however,

12. Will you please send me a list of the <u>pamphlets which deals with this topic.</u>

   (A) pamphlets which deals with this topic.
   (B) pamphlets which deal with this topic.
   (C) pamphlets which deal on this topic.
   (D) pamphlets which is relevant.
   (E) pamphlets which deals with this here topic.

13. I still do not see the <u>reason for him being released on parole.</u>

   (A) reason for him being released on parole.
   (A) why he is being released on parole:
   (C) for his having been released on parole.
   (D) for him having been released on parole.
   (E) for his being released on parole.

14. I found the cruel narrative <u>excruciating; it was</u> more than I could endure.

   (A) excruciating; it was
   (B) tortuous. It was
   (C) excruciating, it was
   (D) excruciating it was
   (E) tortuous; it was

15. Paula is <u>more sensitive by far than any girl</u> in her sorority.

   (A) more sensitive by far than any girl
   (B) by far more sensitive then any other girl
   (C) more sensitive, by far, then any girl
   (D) more sensitive by far than any other girl
   (E) more sensitive by far than any of the girls

16. When you <u>have raised the necessary capitol, the offer</u> will be renewed.

   (A) have raised the necessary capitol, the offer
   (B) have raised the necessary capitol the offer

   (C) have raised the necessary capital, the offer
   (D) raised the necessary capital the offer
   (E) raised the necessary capitol; the offer

17. <u>Having taken a firm stand, we</u> were reluctant to reopen the issue.

   (A) Having taken a firm stand, we
   (B) Because we were taking a firm stand we
   (C) Having taken a firm stand. We
   (D) Because we had taken a firm stand. We
   (E) Because our stand was firm; we

18. The seer <u>prophesied dire events to follow if</u> his warnings were ignored.

   (A) prophesied dire events to follow if
   (B) prophesied dire events to follow, if
   (C) prophesied dire events to follow. If
   (D) prophecied dire events to follow when
   (E) prophecied dire events to follow if

19. Although many of the larger trees survived, the fire destroyed much of the overhead canopy, <u>which opened the forest floor</u> to the sky and sunlight.

   (A) which opened the forest floor
   (B) having opened the forest floor
   (C) opening the forest floor
   (D) after baring the forest floor
   (E) after it had exposed the forest floor

20. An idealist is one <u>who notices that a rose smells better than a cabbage and who</u> concludes that it will also make better soup.

   (A) who notices that a rose smells better than a cabbage and who
   (B) who on noticing that a rose smells better than a cabbage
   (C) who, when he notices that roses smell better than cabbages,
   (D) who, while notating that a rose smells better than a cabbage,
   (E) of those who upon noticing that a rose smells better than a cabbage

21. Until recently any history of art of the 19th century could reasonably have been expected to follow a familiar line, <u>concentrating on art that was bold, experimental, French.</u>

   (A) concentrating on art that was bold, experimental, French.
   (B) where they concentrated on bold, experimental French art.

(C) having concentrated on art that was bold, experimental, and with its origin in France.

(D) with an emphasis on the works of boldly experimental French artisans.

(E) and concentrated on bold, experimental French art.

22. The lecturer repeatedly brought on the issue of the propriety of killing animals to learn about them.

(A) brought on the issue of the propriety of killing animals to learn

(B) homing in on the issue of the moral rightness in killing animals to learn

(C) focused on the issue of the propriety in their killing animals to learn

(D) discussed the morality in killing animals and learning

(E) raised the issue of the propriety of killing animals to learn

23. Sea snakes, a recent evolutionary phenomenon, have descended from Australian tiger snakes— whose venom is so poisonous that they have no aquatic predators whatsoever.

(A) Sea snakes, a recent evolutionary phenomenon, have descended from Australian tiger snakes

(B) A recent evolutionary phenomenon, sea snakes, descended from Australian tiger snakes

(C) Sea snakes by descending from Australian tiger snakes are a recent phenomenon

(D) A recent evolutionary phenomenon descended from Australian tiger snakes is the sea snakes

(E) Sea snakes, descended from Australian tiger snakes, are a recent evolutionary phenomenon.

24. We must constantly seek a form of faith adapted to a world that is being continually renewed.

(A) We must constantly seek a form of faith adapted to a world that is being continually renewed.

(B) Adapted to a renewing world, we must constantly seek a viable form of faith.

(C) Our constant search must be for a form of faith that is continuously renewable since the world is ever changing.

(D) In a world that is inconstant, we must search for a faith that conforms to changes.

(E) To adapt to an ever-changing world, the faith we seek must be ever renewed.

25. Humanity's capacity for justice makes democracy possible, but the inclination of humanity toward injustice makes democracy necessary.

(A) but the inclination of humanity toward injustice makes

(B) and the inclination of humanity to injustice makes

(C) but democracy is made imperative because the injustice in humanity makes

(D) but humanity's inclination to injustice makes democracy necessary

(E) but humanity's predilection for injustice which makes

26. The visibility of the mentally ill on the streets of American cities, although they make up only a fraction of the homeless, are the legacy of decades of squabbling among governmental agencies.

(A) are the legacy of decades of squabbling among governmental agencies.

(B) is the result of years or rivalry between governmental agencies.

(C) results from disagreements about mental health.

(D) had been caused by years of quarreling by federal and state agencies.

(E) is the legacy of decades of infighting among factions in government.

27. Because no single system of dance notation is universally accepted and some of the company's ballets have never been video-taped, is why any work not being danced can easily be forgotten.

(A) is why any work not being danced can easily be forgotten.

(B) this is the reason any works not being danced can easily be forgotten.

(C) any work not in current programs can easily be lost.

(D) any dance not in concurrent repertory can easily be forgotten.

(E) accounts for the fact that dances are easily forgotten.

28. As words hiss out like dueling rapiers, swish, clang, the high ceilings of the committee rooms have moods of rage and disgust bounce off them, and the intellect becomes dull and insulted.

(A) the high ceilings of the committee rooms have moods of rage and disgust bounce off them

(B) moods of rage and disgust bounce off the lofty heights of committee rooms

(C) tempers are razed beyond the levels of polite controls

(D) moods of rage and disgust resounding throughout the vast committee rooms

(E) with rage and disgust voiced by the aroused participants.

29. This volume maps the life of a unique American writer, and many of today's writers still reveal his influence in plain talk and straightforward fiction.

(A) and many of today's writers still reveal his influence in plain talk and straightforward fiction.

(B) and many of today's writers in plain talk and straightforward narrative reveal his influence.

(C) influencing many of today's writers in their plain talk and straightforward narratives.

(D) one who has influenced the vocabulary and style of many contemporary writers of today.

(E) one whose presence is still felt in the plain talk and straightforward fiction of many of today's writers.

30. I have written a few stories that are like the stones laid along the highway which have solidity and will stay there.

(A) the highway which have solidity and will stay there.

(B) the highway which has solidity and will stay there.

(C) the highway; they have solidity and will stay there.

(D) the highway and have solidity but will stay there.

(E) the highway, having solidity, will stay there.

31. Termites can be detected by trained dogs who have a sense of smell sharp enough to pick up the pheronomes, minute doses of chemicals that termites use to communicate with each other.

(A) who have a sense of smell sharp enough to pick up the pheronomes

(B) that can detect pheronomes by their distinct odor

(C) which can find pheronomes through their sense of smell

(D) honed to pick up pheronomes

(E) who have noses sharp enough to pick up the pheronomes

32. In the nineteenth century, Fanny Wright was the first to argue that women were not only men's equals but also that they must be granted equal roles in all the business of public life.

(A) women were not only men's equals but also that they must be granted equal roles

(B) men and women have equity and therefore must be granted equal roles

(C) women are men's equals and equal roles must be granted them

(D) women were men's equals and must be granted equal roles

(E) women had been men's equals and should be granted equal roles

33. To be sure, these are not letters written in the grand tradition of letters, with one eye aimed at the recipient and the other at posterity.

(A) with one eye aimed at the recipient and the other at posterity.

(B) planned to please all their tastes.

(C) and aimed at the readers of all ages.

(D) with one eye aimed at the receiver and the other to future readers.

(E) with an eye for the receiver and an eyeful for posterity.

34. Whether he had agreed or did not is irrelevant to the solution may be Ann's basic contention, but it certainly is not one that I can accept.

(A) Whether he had agreed or did not is irrelevant

(B) That he had agreed or did not is irrelevant

(C) That his agreement or lack of it is irrelevant

(D) That his acceptation is irrelevant

(E) Him agreeing or not agreeing is irrelevant

35. Given to fearsome tantrums and quick to hand out wounding personal abuse, his correspondence reveals him as an unlikely candidate for a popularity award.

(A) Given to fearsome tantrums and quick to hand out wounding personal abuse, his correspondence reveals him

(B) He was given to fearsome tantrums and was quick to insult others, his correspondence reveals him

(C) Given to tantrums and insulting others, his correspondence reveals him

(D) Given to fearsome tantrums and quick to hand out wounding personal abuse, he emerges from his correspondence

(E) Although he threw tantrums and was quick to insult others, his correspondence reveals him

PART 3 *Suggested Time: 20 Minutes*
Time begun .... Time ended .... Time used ....

DIRECTIONS: The following sentences contain problems in grammar, usage, diction (choice of words),
and idioms.
  Some sentences are correct.
  No sentence contains more than one error.
  You will find that the error, if there is one, is
underlined and lettered. Assume that all other elements of the sentence are correct and cannot be
changed. In choosing answers, follow the requirements of standard written English.
  If there is an error, select the <u>one underlined part</u>
that must be changed in order to make the sentence
correct, and blacken the corresponding space on the
answer sheet.
  If there is no error, mark answer space E.

36. If history repeats itself and the unexpected

    always <u>happens</u>, how <u>incapacitated</u> must people
              (A)   (B)
    <u>be</u> <u>of learning</u> from experience! <u>No error</u>
    (C)   (D)   (E)

37. Treat people <u>as if they</u> are <u>what</u> they <u>ought to</u>
                     (A)   (B)   (C)
    be, and you help them to become what they are
    <u>capable to be</u>. <u>No error</u>
    (D)   (E)

38. Who was the <u>ingenuous</u> wordmaster who said
                    (A)
    that many problems the world faces <u>today are</u>
                                         (B)
    the <u>eventual result</u> of <u>short-term</u> measures
        (C)   (D)
    taken in the last century? <u>No error</u>
                                (E)

39. <u>Being that</u> all of us <u>are creatures</u> of the age in
       (A)   (B)
    which we live, very few are <u>able to</u>
                                 (C)
    <u>raise ourselves</u> above the ideas of the time.
    (D)
    <u>No error</u>
    (E)

40. The universe is not <u>hostile</u>, <u>nor yet</u> is it <u>friendly</u>;
                        (A)   (B)   (C)
    it is simply <u>a case of indifference</u>. <u>No error</u>
                 (D)   (E)

41. The <u>group that</u> had gathered <u>around us</u>
          (A)   (B)
    <u>quietly watched</u> the <u>proceedings</u>. <u>No error</u>
    (C)   (D)   (E)

42. Faith means <u>intense</u>, <u>usually confident belief</u>
                 (A)   (B)
    that is not based on evidence sufficient to com-
    mand <u>assent</u> <u>from</u> every reasonable person.
          (C)   (D)
    <u>No error</u>
    (E)

43. I know <u>how badly</u> you feel. I
             (A)
    <u>had to go through</u> the same <u>torment when</u> Har-
    (B)   (C)
    old was <u>injured playing</u> tennis with me.
              (D)
    <u>No error</u>
    (E)

44. They objected <u>to you giving</u> free advice to their
                  (A)
    <u>clients</u>, <u>especially when</u> they have a
    (B)   (C)
    <u>contractual obligation</u> and a retainer. <u>No error</u>
    (D)   (E)

45. If you steal from <u>another, it's</u> labeled
                      (A)
    <u>as plagiarism</u>, but if you steal <u>from many</u>,
    (B)   (C)
    <u>it's research</u>. <u>No error</u>
    (D)   (E)

46. <u>Three-year old</u> children are <u>beings who</u> get as
       (A)   (B)
    much <u>pleasure almost</u> <u>out of a</u> $98 set of swings ·
          (C)   (D)
    as they get out of a green worm. <u>No error</u>
                                      (E)

47. Adults who <u>cease after youth</u> to unlearn and
                (A)
    <u>relearn their</u> facts and <u>reconsideration</u> of their
    (B)   (C)
    opinions <u>are a menace</u> to their democratic com-
              (D)
    munity. <u>No error</u>
             (E)

48. When <u>he painted</u> the series of <u>pictures</u>, this
           (A)   (B)

leader <u>of the avant-garde</u> had used his parents
         (C)
<u>as models</u>. <u>No error</u>
 (D)   (E)

49. Listen to <u>the enormity of</u> this <u>achievement</u>: at
            (A)   (B)
the age of 12, <u>Rossini wrote</u> <u>four concerti</u> in
           (C)   (D)
three days. <u>No error</u>
        (E)

50. <u>An advantage of</u> a bad memory <u>is that one</u>
    (A)   (B)
<u>enjoys several times</u> the same good things
       (C)
<u>for the first time</u>. <u>No error</u>
    (D)   (E)

51. He learned <u>from previous experience</u> that
                (A)
<u>it requires</u> a very unusual mind to
 (B)
<u>make an analysis</u> <u>of the obvious</u>. <u>No error</u>
   (C)   (D)   (E)

52. No other factor <u>in history</u>, not even religion,
           (A)
has produced the <u>incredulous number of wars</u>
            (B)
<u>as has</u> the class of national egotism
 (C)
<u>sanctified by the name</u> of patriotism. <u>No error</u>
   (D)   (E)

53. The discussion group reached
<u>a mutual agreement</u>: <u>capital punishment</u> is
    (A)   (B)
<u>as fundamentally wrong as</u> a cure <u>for crimes</u>,
        (C)   (D)
as charity is wrong as a cure for poverty.
<u>No error</u>
 (E)

54. I still <u>question her contention</u> that it was
        (A)
<u>their mother</u> and <u>not her</u> that answered the tele-
   (B)   (C)
phone <u>when I called</u>. <u>No error</u>
     (D)   (E)

55. At this <u>time, there</u> is <u>no universal panacea</u> that
     (A)   (B)

<u>can prevent</u> <u>or cure</u> the common cold.
  (C)   (D)
<u>No error</u>
 (E)

56. Since her parents <u>are both</u> <u>lawyers, it</u> is not sur-
            (A)   (B)
prising <u>that she chose</u> <u>that for a career</u>.
      (C)   (D)
<u>No error</u>
 (E)

57. It was this <u>deeply profound religious</u> experi-
          (A)
ence that <u>altered</u> <u>my basic concepts</u> of
      (B)   (C)
<u>life many years ago</u>. <u>No error</u>
    (D)   (E)

58. <u>It is a program</u> <u>instituted by</u> concerned physi-
   (A)   (B)
cians to <u>prevent successful suicides</u> among
      (C)
<u>despondent patients</u> of all ages. <u>No error</u>
   (D)   (E)

59. In his <u>present mood, he</u> is <u>capable to do</u> any
      (A)   (B)
rash thing <u>that will endanger</u> our
       (C)
<u>entire movement</u>. <u>No error</u>
   (D)   (E)

60. <u>To be misunderstood</u> <u>often</u> is the fate of mum-
   (A)   (B)
blers and <u>mutterers</u>, <u>regardless of</u> their status.
     (C)   (D)
<u>No error</u>
 (E)

61. The <u>irrevocable conclusion</u> of the dissident
     (A)
<u>group is that</u> <u>they will</u> never <u>accede with</u> the
  (B)   (C)   (D)
leader's outrageous demands. <u>No error</u>
            (E)

62. The <u>essential purpose</u> of the course is to
    (A)
<u>train consumers</u> to <u>get more</u> for
 (B)   (C)
<u>their money's worth</u>. <u>No error</u>
   (D)   (E)

63. Some <u>nonverbal messages</u> are so <u>necessary to</u>
         (A)   (B)

language that they must be <u>inclusive</u> in
                            (C)

<u>descriptions of it.</u> <u>No error</u>
         (D)   (E)

64. Susanna told Sarah <u>that she</u> did not
                          (A)

<u>know the intricacies</u> of the game <u>well enough</u>
         (B)   (C)

<u>to teach it.</u> <u>No error</u>
      (D)   (E)

65. I <u>heartily</u> <u>agree with</u> your contention that sales-
         (A)   (B)

people often earn <u>as much if not more</u> than
                         (C)

plant <u>supervisors.</u> <u>No error</u>
         (D)   (E)

66. <u>None</u> of us <u>anticipated</u> the difficulty
      (A)   (B)

<u>of the ascent</u>   or   <u>how long it would take.</u>
      (C)   (D)

<u>No error</u>
   (E)

67. The   bulletin   <u>briefly stated</u>   that   he
                          (A)

<u>had been recovering</u> <u>at the hospital</u> when   he
         (B)   (C)

suffered   his   <u>second fatal heart attack.</u>
                            (D)

<u>No error</u>
   (E)

68. I   <u>did see</u>   a   performance   at   the
           (A)

<u>beautiful new playhouse,</u>   but
            (B)

<u>now I just cannot</u>   <u>remember it</u>   very   well.
         (C)   (D)

<u>No error</u>
   (E)

69. How can she <u>pretend to be</u> so <u>oblivious to</u> to
                        (A)   (B)

public   opinion!   She   <u>surely</u>   must   be   more
                              (C)

<u>aware than she</u> reveals. <u>No error</u>
      (D)   (E)

70. <u>Multitudes of people</u> <u>swarmed into</u> the streets
            (A)   (B)

<u>along</u> the lengthy <u>parade route</u> to welcome the
   (C)   (D)

returning heroes. <u>No error</u>
                      (E)

ANSWER KEY AND ANALYSIS OF ANSWERS   /   *Page 204*

ANALYSES AND ANSWER KEYS: PRACTICE TEST ONE

ANALYSIS OF THE ESSAY QUESTION

Part 1

Answers to the essay question must vary greatly. However, as a guide to evaluating what you had written, four answers and their ratings follow.

To make the most effective use of your practice time:

1. Rate each of the following essays.

2. Compare your ratings with those found in this Analysis.

3. Compare your own essay with the ones you rated.

4. Rate your own essay.

While the results will lack absolute objectivity, for the sake of achieving a range that can lead to an evaluation, use the following rating system:

RATING SCALE	CHARACTERIZED BY	BASED ON A SCALE OF 1-6
Superior	originality of thought freshness of expression aptness of illustrations	6
Above average	clarity of organization soundness of thought	4-5
Average	an attempt at a thesis fulfillment of the assignment	3
Below average	weak organization irrelevant arguments rambling style	1-2

Essay One

One of the reasons for the lowered reading ability of recent high school students is that the youth growing up today was born into a world dominated by electronic devices for viewing and hearing.

No longer are children read to during eating time and rest periods. Instead, the TV is turned on, and they are immersed in pictures and sounds. They are not exposed to models of adults reading from the printed page. When they are not watching TV, then the radio or record players fill their ears with music. They do not have the opportunity to sit quietly and thumb through a book, looking at pictures and familiarizing themselves with the printed words in the captions.

The printed page is no longer a means of preserving and transmitting knowledge. The day of electronic devices has arrived!

ANALYSIS ....
....
....
RATING ....

Essay Two

Long before the invention of the printing press, people had learned that the superiority of our species could be increased by developing writing as a means of passing on knowledge from one generation to another. Preserved in the archeological findings are many handwritten records that transmit records of the past. From these written documents we learn lessons that have helped us to assess our own efforts.

With the invention of the printing press, the amount of knowledge that could be preserved was increased many times. In that there were so many more books available, the information spread to many people.

Now that electronic devices have found their place in so many homes, the lessons of the past are reaching even more people than ever. We now have the ability to make people everywhere on the face of the earth aware of events as they happen. A good example to prove this is the viewing of athletic contests as they occur during the Olympic Games. Millions of people view the running of the race while it is actually occurring.

What are the implications of this for education? As I see it, we should no longer stress reading and learning how to read. We should make the children of today more critical viewers and listeners so that they can better cope with the problems that will arise in their world of tomorrow.

ANALYSIS ....
....
....
RATING ....

Essay Three

For hundreds of years, people have relied on the printed page to transmit knowledge from one generation to another. Today, many electronic devices—television, radio, phonographs, tape recorders, computers—are being used to store and transmit the same knowledge. What are the implications for educators?

Reading has always been an imperfect instrument. The skills necessary to master the printed page have required a high level of intelligence and a well-disciplined approach to learning mastery of reading; many hours of practice are required. Too many people never gained competency, and therefore reading has never been the ideal way to educate, especially in a democracy where the people need the knowledge in order to vote wisely.

Because of its multisensory appeal, TV, for example, is an excellent way of presenting facts to millions of people. It is far superior to reading in its ability to reach quickly and widely. However, in that its presentation is instant—and once—the viewer is not given a full opportunity to review and mull over. The printed page can be re-read as often as necessary; the printed page can be approached at the rate best suited for each person.

Therefore, as I see it, the electronic miracles of today cannot and should not replace the printed page. Both have their place in our world. TV can let us see for ourselves; books can let us think for ourselves. Teachers must continue to teach children how to read; teachers must continue to teach children how to view TV critically. The person who can read well and view TV critically and selectively can be the informed person so necessary in our complex and fast-moving society.

ANALYSIS ....
....
....
RATING ....

Essay Four

The educational system has always been a dilatory lagger. The generation of teachers presently educating the next generation is more interested in preserving and passing on their own adjustment to our culture than in preparing the children for their world of tomorrow. The present all-out stress on teaching children how to read rather than how to make full use of electronic memories is a case in point.

Endless school hours are now spent in teaching children to reach perfection in the skills of reading;

most of them will make little use of most of these skills. Hundreds of thousands of students who resist learning skills of little value in their lives fail to master the intricacies of reading; these students are labeled as handicapped, retarded, special cases, and are so branded for life.

The main source of communication for these children is and will continue to be electronic equipment like TV, radio, computers, tape recorders. Why not spend the invaluable school time in teaching them to react better to these devices! Teach them to enjoy better programs. Teach them to listen and view critically. They must learn how to select the significant from the misleading and trivial. There is so much that the schools could teach them to make their lives fuller and more meaningful through wise use of their viewing and listening time! Our educational system is once again missing an opportunity to focus on the needs of the children of tomorrow!

ANALYSIS ....
....
....
RATING ....

Ratings

Essay One
The essay is organized into three units of thought. The first paragraph presents the thesis that children are born into a world dominated by electronic devices for viewing and hearing. The second paragraph illustrates the thesis by describing generalized TV viewing, listening to radio programs and recordings. The third paragraph summarizes by referring to the quotation in the assignment.

However, the candidate ignored the directive given in the Assignment. The essay should have answered the question, "What are the implications for our educational system?" Instead, the candidate wrote on the assumption that proof of the quotation had been presented.

RATING: Below average—1–2

Essay Two
The essay reveals an awareness of the need for a three-phase development of a topic. However, the first two paragraphs are unrelated to the third and fourth. The candidate attempted an historical survey as the introduction. The result reveals the danger of such an approach when writing a 20-minute essay. Too many words and too much space become involved in the introduction. The essay could well have begun with the third paragraph! The question in the Assignment is answered in part in the fourth paragraph, but necessary illustrations are lacking.

RATING: Average—3

Essay Three
The introduction focuses on the question in the Assignment: "What are the educational implications?" In the development, the candidate comments on the given quotation, showing both agreement and disagreement. In the conclusion, the implications for education are given. A negative aspect of the essay is that the only electronic device illustrated is television although other devices have been mentioned. However, other than that, the essay is definitely on target.

RATING: Above average—**4–5**

Essay Four
The essay follows a clear three-part development.

The candidate develops a thesis, our schools are teaching how to read instead of how to learn through electronic devices. The implications are clearly defined. The candidates does take an extreme point of view that would be hard to maintain, but it is documented and logically defended.

RATING: Superior—**6**

Your Own Essay
ANALYSIS ....
....
....
It comes closest to Essay ....because ....
....
RATING ....

ANSWER KEY, MULTIPLE-CHOICE QUESTIONS: PRACTICE TEST ONE

Part 2

1. (E)	**6.** (A)	**11.** (C)	**16.** (E)	**21.** (E)	**26.** (C)	**31.** (B)
2. (A)	**7.** (E)	**12.** (C)	**17.** (C)	**22.** (D)	**27.** (C)	**32.** (B)
3. (B)	**8.** (C)	**13.** (B)	**18.** (E)	**23.** (C)	**28.** (E)	**33.** (E)
4. (E)	**9.** (B)	**14.** (E)	**19.** (E)	**24.** (E)	**29.** (B)	**34.** (C)
5. (C)	**10.** (D)	**15.** (C)	**20.** (B)	**25.** (A)	**30.** (E)	**35.** (C)

Part 3

36. (E)	**41.** (D)	**46.** (B)	**51.** (C)	**56.** (D)	**61.** (E)	**66.** (C)
37. (E)	**42.** (E)	**47.** (C)	**52.** (D)	**57.** (B)	**62.** (D)	**67.** (E)
38. (A)	**43.** (D)	**48.** (D)	**53.** (E)	**58.** (E)	**63.** (D)	**68.** (C)
39. (C)	**44.** (B)	**49.** (D)	**54.** (E)	**59.** (B)	**64.** (D)	**69.** (A)
40. (D)	**45.** (E)	**50.** (A)	**55.** (D)	**60.** (C)	**65.** (B)	**70.** (D)

DETERMINING YOUR RAW SCORE

Multiple-Choice Questions

1. Tabulate Totals
     Number Right   _____
     Number Wrong   _____
     Number Omitted _____

2. Enter Number Right   A _____
   Divide Number Wrong by
   4 and put result here   B _____

3. Subtract B from A. This
   results in your

   MULTIPLE-CHOICE
   RAW SCORE   _____

   The subtraction of ¼ point for each incorrect answer adjusts for the effect of random guessing.

Essay Question

1. Compare your results
   with the models. Enter
   your own rating of your
   essay (1, 2, 3, 4, 5, or 6).   _____

2. Consult Conversion Chart
   below. Enter your
   CONVERTED SCORE
   here   _____

3. Add total for
   MULTIPLE-CHOICE
   and CONVERTED
   SCORE for essay.

       Total Raw Score   _____

EVALUATING YOUR PERFORMANCE

Excellent	82–100+
Very Good	64–81
Good	46–63
Average	31–45
Below Average	15–30
Unsatisfactory	29 or below

ESSAY CONVERSION CHART	
Score	Becomes
6	30
5	24
4	19
3	15
2	11
1	8

ANALYSIS OF ANSWERS, MULTIPLE-CHOICE QUESTIONS: PRACTICE TEST ONE

Part 2

1. **E** No error. Since both subjects are joined by the word *and,* and since they are considered as a single thing, we use the single verb form *is.*

2. **A** The word *team* is a collective noun and is considered singular when the group is regarded as a unit. Therefore, the singular form *is* should be used.

3. **B** *Dig* is an irregular verb, and its past tense is *dug.*

4. **E** No error.

5. **C** *Seen* is the wrong tense; *saw* is the correct form.

6. **A** *Plays* is an illogical time form. The verb tense should be *played.*

7. **E** No error.

8. **C** The singular subject *risk* requires a singular verb (*seems*).

9. **B** The word *where* is redundant and is not needed as a connective between the two clauses of the sentence.

10. **D** The verb *pays* (present tense) must agree with the first verb of the compound predicate, *arrived.* The correct form is *paid.*

11. **C** *After the battle was over* is the past tense, while the rest of the sentence is in the future tense. Part C should read *advanced.*

12. **C** The use of a personal pronoun *they* in an impersonal sense (as in this sentence) should be avoided. The sentence should read: "I read in the newspaper that large tomatoes are grown in Nigeria."

13. **B** In this sentence, it seems as if *the breathing* is doing the swimming. The problem here is the dangling phrase which must be given a word to modify: "To master the proper backstroke, the swimmer must carefully control his or her breathing."

14. **E** No error.

15. **C** This is a complex sentence with one subordinate clause (about the football game) and one main clause (about the training sequence). However, the error is in tense. The subordinate clause is in the past tense, while the main clause is in the present. This main clause should also be in the past tense: "the other part *showed.* . . ."

16. **E** No error. The past tense *entered* is correct, following *cheered.*

17. **C** In this sentence there is only one person or subject—*teacher and friend.* This is a compound subject that is treated as singular since it is only one person. The correct form of the verb is *has.*

18. **E** No error. *Who* is the subject of the verb *had given* and is in the nominative case.

19. **E** No error. The verb tense (past) in the subordinate clause indicates a time period before the main verb, *had stopped,* which is in the past perfect tense.

20. **B** Since the subject of the sentence, *plant manager,* is singular, the verb should be singular too—*was.* Do not be confused by the plural *workers* in the parenthetical expression following the subject.

21. **E** No error. Collective nouns such as *community, group,* or *family,* if regarded as a unit, take singular verbs.

22. **D** Since the pronoun is the object of the verb *helps,* it takes the objective form *me.*

23. **C** Tenses do not agree in this sentence. *Pays* is in the present tense but should agree with the

past tense *approached*. The correct form is *paid*.

24. E No error. Nouns representing an organized field of knowledge ending in *-ics* (*statistics, ergonomics,* etc.) take the singular form. If these same nouns refer to an activity, they are considered plural: "The economics of the proposed building site *were* satisfactory."

25. A The pronoun *who* is not parallel to the word *with*. The sentence should read: "The musician is a man *who has* great promise and who should be encouraged. . . ."

26. C Inconsistent shift of tense from present in the main clause to past in the subordinate clause. A better structure is: "You have to remember that not all people *are honest* and above reproach."

27. C When a singular subject is preceded by *each* and joined by *and* to another singular subject, they are treated as singular units and the verb in the sentence is singular (to agree with *each*). This is an exception to the rule that subjects joined by *and* are usually plural. The correct verb form is *was*.

28. E No error. *He* is the subject complement, and *who* is the subject of *traveled*.

29. B Since the action took place in the past, the past tense (*traveled*) or the present perfect tense (*have traveled*) would be correct.

30. E No error. In this sentence, two antecedents, *teacher* and *students*, are joined by the word *nor*. Since one antecedent is singular and the other plural, the question is whether the pronoun should be the plural *their* or the singular *his*. In such a sentence structure, the rule is that the pronoun agrees with the number of the *nearest* antecedent (*students*).

31. B The subject of a clause is written in the nominative case. Therefore, *whomever* should be *whoever*.

32. B The word *sufficiency* (enough) rather than *efficiency* (effectiveness) is required.

33. E No error. The plural pronoun *their* agrees with its antecedent *husbands and wives*.

34. C The pronoun *who* is the object of *respect* and should take the objective form *whom*.

35. C *To play* is the correct form of the verb. The subject is hoping to do something (*play*) in the future. *Have played* indicates a past action preceding the *hoping*.

Part 3

36. E (A) is incorrect because the correlatives *neither . . . nor* join singular nouns (*choice* and *tone*) and take the singular verb *impresses*. (B) and (C) use the incorrect correlative *or*. (D) changes the meaning of the sentence.

37. E (A) is incorrect because the gerund *telling* requires a possessive pronoun as its modifier; *your,* not *you.* (B) has a superfluous comma; (C) is wordy; (D) changes the sentence meaning.

38. A The comma is necessary to prevent confusion because of the juxtaposition of *squirrels* and *walk.* (B) has an unnecessary comma before *who,* making the relative clause incorrectly nonrestrictive, as does (C). (D) and (E) omit the comma separating *squirrels* and *walk.*

39. C (A) is incorrect because the pronoun *neither* takes the singular verb *appears.* (B), (D), and (E) change the sense of the sentence.

40. D (A) is confusing: do *you* like him better or do the *other* students like him better? (B) causes the same confusion as (A). (C) would require the superlative *best,* since more than two are being compared. (E) is incorrect because the category "other students" is not defined, thus changing the sense of the sentence.

41. D (A) has faulty parallelism when it balances an adverb with a prepositional phrase, as does (C). (B) changes the tonal value of the sentence. (E) is parallel but wordy.

42. E (A), (B), (C), and (D) all balance *programs* with *pool.* (E) balances *programs* with *schedule,* a correct parallel structure.

43. D (A) and (B) have faulty parallelism because they place *neither* incorrectly before *want,* when *assistance* is the noun being contrasted with *advice.* (C) uses the *or* as the incorrect correlative for *neither.* (E) changes the sentence's tonal value when it concludes on too informal a note.

44. B (A) places the relative clause so that it modifies *team* rather than *coach.* (C) unnecessarily repeats *long.* (D) has an error in tense in *had been involved.* (E) changes the sentence tone by emphasizing the talk rather than the coach and by switching to the colloquial *in on this.*

45. E (A) and (B) incorrectly shift the series from parallel adjectives—*lively, colorful*—to a complete clause. (C) changes the clause to a phrase without correcting the lack of parallelism. (D) requires a hyphen in *well-rehearsed* because the compound adjective precedes the noun it modifies.

46. **B** (A) and (E) are incorrect because *its* has no antecedent (the antecedent should be *religion*). (C) is wordy; (D) changes the meaning of the sentence.

47. **C** (A) makes the relative clause say that the student *only* discussed animals the instructor liked. (B) contains a *which* clause with indefinite reference. (D) and (E) misplace *proudly*.

48. **D** (A), (B), and (C) have *they* with no antecedent. (E) changes the tone of the sentence with *let alone*.

49. **D** (A) contains a *which* clause that incorrectly refers to the entire idea of the sentence, not to a single word. (B) and (C) change the meaning of the sentence. (D) adds *This interest* to avoid the antecedent problem. (E) incorrectly adds a semicolon.

50. **A** The introductory absolute construction in (A) is correct. (B) and (C) have errors in tense. (D) incorrectly adds a semicolon. (E) changes the meaning of the sentence.

51. **C** (A) and (B) contain the "squinting modifier" *during the afternoon*; (C) resets the modifier correctly; (D) incorrectly introduces quotation marks for a statement that is not a direct quotation; (E) retains the squinting modifier and is incorrectly punctuated.

52. **D** (A) and (B) shift unnecessarily from the imperative mood. (C) and (E) change the language level.

53. **E** (A), (B), (C), and (D) do not contain a word for the infinitive *to be nominated* to modify.

54. **E** (A), (B), (C), and (D) omit the necessary *mathematicians* which should follow the first *greatest,* since *mathematicians* cannot be understood to follow *one of the greatest.*

55. **D** (A) omits the *to* which must follow *oblivious.* (B) and (C) change the meaning of the sentence, while (E) adds an unnecessary comma.

56. **D** The verb *were* cannot be understood for *window,* which should be followed by the singular *was.* Therefore, (A) and (B) are incorrect. In (C), *has been* must follow *window.* (E) is verbose.

57. **B** *Primary* means *require careful consideration because of their importance,* so (A), (C), (D), and (E) are verbose.

58. **E** (A) contains a mixed metaphor. (B) contains an initial sentence fragment. (C) and (D) change the meaning of the sentence.

59. **B** The appositive *the community representative* is nonrestrictive and should be set off by commas. (A) lacks the commas; (C) supplies only one of them. (D) has an initial sentence fragment, while (E) makes an unnecessary change in tense.

60. **C** As the example now stands, the second portion is a sentence fragment, so (A) is wrong; (C) corrects that fault by making a subordinate prepositional phrase. Although (B) corrects the sentence fragment, it introduces a superfluous comma; (D) is verbose, and (E) makes an unnecessary substitution of *uselessly* for *in vain.*

61. **E** *Fewer* involves units; *less* involves total quantity. Since units are discussed (*hours*), *fewer* is required; therefore (A), (B), and (C) are eliminated. (D) contains a change in meaning.

62. **D** *Almost* means *very nearly*; *most* means the *greater* or *greatest number, very.* Since *almost* is required in the given sentence, (A), (B), (C), and (E), are eliminated.

63. **D** The two main ideas are contrastive, not equal; therefore, *and* is incorrect, eliminating (A), (B), and (E). (C) contains a change in meaning (D) contains the conjunction *but* to indicate the inequality.

64. **D** The pronoun *it* can refer to style or the book. The confusion is eliminated in (D). (A) retains the confusion; (B) substitutes *which,* but that pronoun also has a vague reference. (C) and (E) substitute a participle construction (*confusing* and *misleading*), a construction that is just as ambiguous.

65. **B** In (A), the clause *before she starts* squints because it can modify either *purchase* or *complete,* the latter being an absurdity. In (B) the clause is shifted to make its dependency clear. (C), (D), and (E) contain changes in meaning.

66. **C** *Incredible* means unbelievable; *incredulous* means unbelieving. Since *incredible* is required, (A), (B), and (D) are eliminated. In (E) the meaning is changed.

67. **E** The idiom is *in search of*; therefore, (A) and (C) are incorrect. (B) contains a change in meaning. In (D) *only* is too close to *be* and too far from *would open,* which it modifies.

68. **C** Because of the intervening clause *by* must be repeated before *dealers*; therefore (A), (D), and (E) are incorrect. (B) contains a change in meaning.

69. **A** Since *two very weary men* are involved, *between* (two) and not *among* (more than two) is required; therefore (B) and (E) are eliminated.

The subject of *forces* is the singular *debate*; therefore, (C) and (E) are incorrect. (D) contains a change in meaning.

70. D The initial phrase, *In . . . schedule,* cannot logically modify *calendar,* the nearest noun; therefore, (A) and (E) are incorrect. Substitu- tion of a semicolon for the comma does not correct the error in (B). The unnecessary change of *was* to *would* eliminates (C). In (D) the phrase is placed immediately before *manager,* the logical noun to be modified.

ANALYSES AND ANSWER KEYS: PRACTICE TEST TWO

ANALYSIS OF THE ESSAY QUESTION

Part 1

Answers to the essay question must vary greatly. However, as a guide to evaluating what you had written, four answers and their ratings follow.

To make the most effective use of your practice time:

1. Rate each of the following essays.

2. Compare your ratings with those found in this Analysis.

3. Compare your own essay with the ones you rated.

4. Rate your own essay.

While the results will lack absolute objectivity, for the sake of achieving a range that can lead to an evaluation, use the following rating system:

RATING SCALE	CHARACTERIZED BY	BASED ON A SCALE OF 1–6
Superior	originality of thought freshness of expression aptness of illustrations	6
Above average	clarity of organization soundness of thought	4–5
Average	an attempt at a thesis fulfillment of the assignment	3
Below average	weak organization irrelevant arguments rambling style	1–2

Essay One

I really see no contrast between the two proverbs. The first one is used by people who do not have double standards. They act according to their moral principles. They do not have one set of standards in their thoughts and discussions and another when they have to translate their thoughts into action. They do not affirm the Ten Commandments in one breath and then cheat their neighbors and lie blatantly in the next.

The second proverb is a much more sophisticated one. It really says that I have certain experiences. As a result, I have learned from my mistakes. I don't want you to fall into the same traps that I did. Therefore, I am telling you what to do in order to avoid making the same errors that I did.

As you can see, I do not find anything in common in these proverbs. The users of both proverbs are both honorable people with high moral standards in a confusing world.

ANALYSIS ....

RATING ....

Essay Two

"Practice what you preach" has long been a proverb passed down from generation to generation. It was a favorite of my grandparents. They were proud of the fact that the moral standards they instilled in their children were the very ones that had guided their own lives. Their children were never confused by finding that their parents told them to be honest in their dealings with others while the parents themselves made money by selling inferior items to the unsuspecting public.

One of the troubles with the world today is that people are selfish and self-centered. They don't care about what happens to others. They are concerned only with their own welfare. They will be hypocritical and cheat at the very first opportunity that presents itself.

The result is that nations react the same way. They do not concern themselves with the misery prevalent in countries throughout our world. The only thing that counts is to see that the powerful become more powerful. The fact that people are starving and being deprived of all human dignity is completely ignored.

If the leaders of the nations would only follow the example set by my grandparents, there would be more hope in the lives of millions of people. These leaders must learn to practice what they preach!

ANALYSIS ....
....
....
RATING ....

Essay Three

The writer of the quotation contends that at one time people's standards of conduct were so high that their actions were guided at all times by their moral principles. In business, for example, they did not exploit others or misrepresent for their own profit. On the other hand, the writer feels that people today knowingly live on a double standard. They mouth high-minded principles that they ignore in their daily practices. They tell the young to be considerate and honest while they themselves act as though they are above the standards they have set.

I am always suspicious of the validity of any generalization. When two generalizations are used, as in this case, my acceptance becomes even more dubious. We can think of endless examples to show that many people in the past were hypocritical and had double standards. The philanthropic Rockefeller Foundation was built with money made through many sharp practices. Fortunes in the food industry, especially meat packing, grew from practices dangerous to the health of the consumers.

In the present, there are so many instances that I can think of to prove that people still follow their principles: religious leaders like the Pope and Albert Schweitzer, scientists like the Nobel Prize winners,

etc. These people do not have to hide behind a hypocritical mouthing of "Do as I say, not as I do."

We have always had self-centered, grasping people who disregarded the welfare of others for their own aggrandizement. We have always had altruistic people motivated by a desire to help others. There may be a lowering in the moral standards of our world, but, to me, the writer offers no substantial proof in the proverbs offered to us.

ANALYSIS ....
....
....
RATING ....

Essay Four

During the past decade, there has been a multifold increase in violent crimes throughout the world. Not only has there been a frightening increase of murders and rapes, but chances of being attacked and robbed have grown so that the elderly avoid leaving their apartments.

The exact cause of this horrifying development has not been found. Some sociologists feel that the growth of crime on TV correlates with the growth of violence on our streets. Others blame the constant threat of annihilation from nuclear-explosives. If the world is going to be blown up, why not enjoy yourself fully!

Regardless of the cause or causes, a fundamental change in attitude among people is discernible. Years back, the adage "Practice what you preach" was a prevalent one. People had moral standards that they could follow; people were concerned about their fellow human beings.

Today, people have become "I-centered." They are more interested in achieving immediate, selfish pleasures. The best advice they can give—in the rare instances when they do—is, "Do what I say, not what I do." They are saying, "There are moral principles to follow if you want to, but don't use me as a guide since I no longer follow them."

The major difference that I see in the quotations points out the tragic change in our morality and social ways. Until people once more learn to replace "I" with "we," we shall continue to move toward destructive self-centeredness.

ANALYSIS ....
....
....
RATING ....

Ratings

Essay One

The candidate's thesis is that there is no significance in the contrasting of the two proverbs. An illustration is given in handling the first proverb. No example is given for the second. The discussion is too general. The point of view taken is an unusual one, but the candidate proves it feasible.

RATING: Average—3

Essay Two

The first paragraph explains through illustration the meaning of "Practice what you preach." The second paragraph inveighs against self-centeredness and cheating; it is not related to the first paragraph. The third paragraph amplifies on selfishness. The last paragraph makes summary sentences—without giving reasons. None of the material is related to the Assignment.

RATING: Inadequate—2

Essay Three

The candidate overlooked the author's contention that the change in frequency of use of the proverbs is significant. Instead, the candidate set out to prove that both proverbs have exceptions. This approach is only slightly tangential to the Assignment. The first paragraph is an excellent beginning that was never developed.

RATING: Average—4

Essay Four

The first two paragraphs present the candidate's thesis of violence. In the third and fourth paragraphs, the connection between the proverbs and the thesis is explained and documented with examples. The final paragraph is a summary one.

RATING: Superior—6

Your Own Essay

ANALYSIS ....
....
....
It comes closest to Essay .... because ....
....
RATING: ....

ANSWER KEY, MULTIPLE-CHOICE QUESTIONS: PRACTICE EXAMINATION TWO

Part 2 / Page 189

1. (B)	6. (A)	11. (C)	16. (C)	21. (A)	26. (E)	31. (A)
2. (A)	7. (A)	12. (B)	17. (A)	22. (E)	27. (C)	32. (D)
3. (C)	8. (B)	13. (E)	18. (A)	23. (E)	28. (B)	33. (A)
4. (E)	9. (C)	14. (A)	19. (C)	24. (A)	29. (E)	34. (C)
5. (C)	10. (E)	15. (D)	20. (B)	25. (D)	30. (C)	35. (D)

Part 3 / Page 193

36. (C)	41. (C)	46. (C)	51. (A)	56. (D)	61. (D)	66. (D)
37. (D)	42. (E)	47. (C)	52. (B)	57. (A)	62. (D)	67. (D)
38. (C)	43. (A)	48. (A)	53. (A)	58. (C)	63. (C)	68. (D)
39. (A)	44. (A)	49. (A)	54. (C)	59. (B)	64. (A)	69. (B)
40. (D)	45. (B)	50. (E)	55. (B)	60. (A)	65. (C)	70. (A)

DETERMINING YOUR RAW SCORE

Multiple Choice Questions

1. Tabulate Totals
   Number Right   _____
   Number Wrong   _____
   Number Omitted _____

2. Enter Number Right   A _____
   Divide Number Wrong by
   4 and put result here   B _____

3. Subtract B from A. This results in your MULTIPLE-CHOICE RAW SCORE   _____

The subtraction of ¼ point for each incorrect answer adjusts for the effect of random guessing.

Essay Question

1. Compare your results with the models. Enter your own rating of your essay (1, 2, 3, 4, 5, or 6).   _____

2. Consult Conversion Chart below. Enter your converted score here. _____

3. Add total for MULTIPLE-CHOICE and CONVERTED SCORE for your essay.
   TOTAL RAW SCORE _____

EVALUATING YOUR PERFORMANCE

Excellent	93–100+
Very Good	80–92
Good	65–79
Average	48–64
Below Average	31–47
Unsatisfactory	30 or below

ESSAY CONVERSION CHART	
Score	**Becomes**
6	30
5	26
4	20
3	15
2	11
1	6

ANALYSIS OF ANSWERS, MULTIPLE-CHOICE QUESTIONS: PRACTICE EXAMINATION TWO

Part 2

1. (B) The singular *multitude* requires the singular *comes* and *overflows*.
2. (A) No error
3. (C) The preposition *but* requires the objective *me*.
4. (E) Action precedent to past action requires the past perfect *had been proposed*. The clause *that is ignored* modifies *ideas,* a plural noun, and should contain a plural verb, *are*.
5. (C) *Being* is a nonstandard equivalent for *since* or *because*.
6. (A) No error
7. (A) The nominative absolute *things being the way they are* is an independent construction.
8. (B) The pronoun *which* lacks a definite antecedent.
9. (C) The standard idiom is *sort of*.
10. (E) Example (E) is standard when *otherwise* connects two independent ideas.
11. (C) The past perfect *had made* is required for action preceding past action (*ignored*).
12. (B) The plural *pamphlets* requires the plural *deal*.
13. (E) The pronoun modifying the gerund (*being released*) should be in the possessive case (*his*).
14. (A) No error
15. (D) *. . . than any other girl. . . .*
16. (C) The term *capital* (money) is required.
17. (A) No error
18. (A) The verb *prophesy* is required.
19. (C) (B) and (D) change the original meaning; (A) *which* can refer to canopy or fire; (E) changes the original meaning and contains *it* which could refer to *canopy* or *fire*; (C) is the correct answer.
20. (A) lacks subordination of *concludes* to *notices*; (C) has *it* referring to *roses*; (D) has *notating* misused; (E) has *concludes,* a singular verb for the plural *those*; (B) is the correct answer.
21. (B) *with its origin in France* destroys the adjective parallelism; (C) *they* has no referent; *artisans* is misused; (D) leaves *line* unmodified or explained; (A) is the correct answer.
22. (A) uses idiom *brought on* incorrectly; (B) is a sentence fragment; (C) *their* has no referent; (D) causal relationship between *killing* and *learning* is lost; (E) is the correct answer.
23. (A) and (B) have the venom belonging to the wrong snakes; (C) creates a causality that does not exist in the original; (D) misuses *are* as the verb to refer to singular *phenomenon*; (E) is correct.
24. (B) In the original *faith* is *adapted*, not *we*; (C) is wordy and contains a misused word, *continuously*; (D) *inconstant* is misused; (E) *faith* does not do the adapting; (A) is the correct answer.
25. (A) and (C) lack parallelism in use of *humanity*; (B) through use of *and* lacks original's contrast; (E) is a sentence fragment; (D) is the correct answer.

26. (A) *are* is incorrectly used to follow *visibility*; (B) has *between* used incorrectly; (C) changes the meaning of the original; (D) contains an error in tense in *had been caused*; (E) is the correct answer.

27. (A) *is why* is unidiomatic; (B) *this is* is superfluous; (D) *concurrent* is misused; (E) is wordy; (C) is correct.

28. (A) lacks parallelism; (C) *razed* is misused; (D) and (E) are sentence fragments; (B) is the correct answer.

29. (A) lacks subordination; (B) is involuted with phrase in wrong place; (C) changes meaning of original; (D) contains *of today* as an unnecessary repetition; (E) is correct.

30. (A) *which* is too far from *stones*; (B) and (E) the solidity of the highway is not what is being talked about; (D) lacks subordination of ideas; (C) is the correct answer.

31. Both (B) and (C) place the wrong noun before the appositive *minute doses*; (D) contains *honed* used incorrectly; (E) presents a ludicrous literal image of noses sharpened; (A) is the correct answer.

32. (A) has a misplaced *not only*; (B) *equity* is misused; (C) lacks parallelism in the balancing clauses joined by *and*; (E) has a misused past perfect tense in *had been*; (D) is the correct answer.

33. (B) *their* is too vague since it lacks an antecedent; (C) *all ages* is ambiguous; (D) *aimed to* is misused; (E) is clever but changes the meaning; (A) is the correct answer.

34. Both (A) and (B) omit a necessary *agree*; (D) has *acceptation* misused; (E) requires *His* rather than *Him* as subject of *agreeing*; (C) is the correct answer.

35. Both (A) and (D) have *given* as a dangling participle modifying *correspondence*; (B) contains a run-on sentence; (D) changes the meaning of the sentence with *although*; (D) is the correct answer.

36. (B) *Incapable* not *incapacitated* is the required term.

37. (D) The idiom is *capable of being*.

38. (C) The phrase *eventual result* is redundant; the word *result* contains the sense of *eventual*.

39. (A) *Being that* cannot be used as a substitute for *since* or *because*.

40. (D) Parallel structure requires the adjective *indifferent*.

41. (C) The adverb *quietly* squints; it could modify either *gathered* or *watched*. It must be moved closer to the verb it is intended to modify.

42. (E) No error

43. (A) The adjective and not the adverb is required; *bad* should replace *badly* because *feel* describes a condition and not an action.

44. (A) The gerund *giving* requires the possessive case for its subject. (They do not object to *you* but to *your* giving.)

45. (B) The *as* is redundant and must be omitted. (Because *it is* was meant, *it's* is the correct form.)

46. (C) The adverb *almost* must be placed closer to the word it is intended to modify. . . . *get almost* . . .

47. (C) Parallel structure is violated. . . . *and to reconsider their opinions* . . .

48. (A) The painting and the modeling occurred at the same time. The two verbs should be in the same tense: *painted . . . used* or had *painted . . . had used*.

49. (A) *Enormity* has a negative connotation. The better word would be *enormousness*, which involves only *bigness*.

50. (E) No error

51. (A) *Experience* is always *previous* and does not require reinforcement in this sentence.

52. (B) *Incredible* means *beyond belief*. *Incredulous* means *not believing*. The word required in this sentence is *incredible*.

53. (A) When *agreement* is preceded and modified by *mutual*, the phrase is redundant because *agreement* implies mutuality.

54. (C) After the verb *to be,* the noun in the predicate should be subjective case to agree with the subject *it*. (*It was she*.)

55. (B) A panacea is a universal cure-all; *universal* is redundant.

56. (D) The relative pronoun *that* requires a word in the sentence to which it refers. . . . she chose *to follow the same career*.

57. (A) The redundant *deeply* repeats the basic idea of *profound*.

58. (C) A *suicide,* unfortunately, is always successful.

59. (B) The idiom is *capable of doing*.

60. (A) *Often* squints. Does it mean to be misunderstood often or does it mean is the fate often? It must be placed closer to the word it is intended to modify.

61. (D) The idiom is *accede to*.

62. (D) The word worth is redundant. . . . for *their money* . . .

63. (C) *Included* (verb) not *inclusive* (adjective) is required.

64. (A) The pronoun *she* could refer either to Sarah or to Susanna. The sentence must be recast. *Susanna said to Sarah, "I . . ."*

65. (C) The phrase must be completed: . . . earn *as much as . . .*

66. (D) There is a lack of parallelism. . . . *the length of its duration.*

67. (D) One can suffer only one *fatal* attack. The sentence must be recast. . . . *suffered a second heart attack that proved fatal.*

68. (D) Does *it* refer to *performance* or *playhouse*? The sentence must be recast to clarify.

69. (B) The idiom is *oblivious of.*

70. (A) *Multitudes* are people. The redundance can be eliminated by dropping *of people.*

The Literature Test

Section F I V E : Improving Your Ability to Read Critically

1. *Diagnostic Test*

2. *The Nature of the Achievement Test in Literature*

3. *Taste and Sensitivity in Poetry*

4. *Terms of Literary Analysis*

There are three Achievement Tests in English: the English Composition Test (all multiple-choice questions), the English Composition Test with Essay, and the Literature Test. Some colleges require both the English Composition Test (and may specify which form) and the Literature Test; other schools require only one of these tests. Before attempting to master the material in this part of the book, make certain that the college or colleges of your choice request that you take the Literature Test.

The information, examination techniques, practice exercises, and practice tests that follow will sharpen your ability to interpret works of literature, a skill invaluable for entering college freshmen. These pages, however, will do little toward acquainting you with the skills required for doing your best on either form of the English Composition Test. Turn to the practice material for that test and see the difference!

Each examination has different emphases; practice for one may be unrelated to the practice required for the other. Be positive that you are studying for the required examination.

If you are in doubt, check with the office of admissions. If the choice is yours, then spend some time examining each section and take one of the Diagnostic Tests in each. This procedure will help you to discover objectively which examination will center on your greater strengths—writing or reading critically. If you have to take both, then study separately for each examination for best results.

1. *Diagnostic Test*

The preparation for each of the reviews and drills for the three tests in English begins with a Diagnostic Test. This test has several purposes. First, it is a tool that will help you to discover strengths and weaknesses. It will aid you in setting up a realistic, practical study program to meet your particular needs. You will be able to check the efficiency of your studying by taking the Practice Tests in Section Six on page 248 and comparing the results with those of the Diagnostic Test.

Another purpose of the Diagnostic Tests is to give you familiarity with the format and level of difficulty of the literature multiple-choice questions. You will gain confidence and know-how by experiencing the "traps" set by the test-makers. You will learn to recognize your mistakes, especially if you study the reviews and explanations for the principles you did not know.

Finally, for those of you who still have a choice of which examination they will take—all multiple-choice, with essay, or literature—taking the three Diagnostic Tests and comparing results will help them reach their decision.

DIAGNOSTIC TEST

ANSWER SHEET

1 Ⓐ Ⓑ Ⓒ Ⓓ Ⓔ		31 Ⓐ Ⓑ Ⓒ Ⓓ Ⓔ	
2 Ⓐ Ⓑ Ⓒ Ⓓ Ⓔ		32 Ⓐ Ⓑ Ⓒ Ⓓ Ⓔ	
3 Ⓐ Ⓑ Ⓒ Ⓓ Ⓔ		33 Ⓐ Ⓑ Ⓒ Ⓓ Ⓔ	
4 Ⓐ Ⓑ Ⓒ Ⓓ Ⓔ		34 Ⓐ Ⓑ Ⓒ Ⓓ Ⓔ	
5 Ⓐ Ⓑ Ⓒ Ⓓ Ⓔ		35 Ⓐ Ⓑ Ⓒ Ⓓ Ⓔ	
6 Ⓐ Ⓑ Ⓒ Ⓓ Ⓔ		36 Ⓐ Ⓑ Ⓒ Ⓓ Ⓔ	
7 Ⓐ Ⓑ Ⓒ Ⓓ Ⓔ		37 Ⓐ Ⓑ Ⓒ Ⓓ Ⓔ	
8 Ⓐ Ⓑ Ⓒ Ⓓ Ⓔ		38 Ⓐ Ⓑ Ⓒ Ⓓ Ⓔ	
9 Ⓐ Ⓑ Ⓒ Ⓓ Ⓔ		39 Ⓐ Ⓑ Ⓒ Ⓓ Ⓔ	
10 Ⓐ Ⓑ Ⓒ Ⓓ Ⓔ		40 Ⓐ Ⓑ Ⓒ Ⓓ Ⓔ	
11 Ⓐ Ⓑ Ⓒ Ⓓ Ⓔ		41 Ⓐ Ⓑ Ⓒ Ⓓ Ⓔ	
12 Ⓐ Ⓑ Ⓒ Ⓓ Ⓔ		42 Ⓐ Ⓑ Ⓒ Ⓓ Ⓔ	
13 Ⓐ Ⓑ Ⓒ Ⓓ Ⓔ		43 Ⓐ Ⓑ Ⓒ Ⓓ Ⓔ	
14 Ⓐ Ⓑ Ⓒ Ⓓ Ⓔ		44 Ⓐ Ⓑ Ⓒ Ⓓ Ⓔ	
15 Ⓐ Ⓑ Ⓒ Ⓓ Ⓔ		45 Ⓐ Ⓑ Ⓒ Ⓓ Ⓔ	
16 Ⓐ Ⓑ Ⓒ Ⓓ Ⓔ		46 Ⓐ Ⓑ Ⓒ Ⓓ Ⓔ	
17 Ⓐ Ⓑ Ⓒ Ⓓ Ⓔ		47 Ⓐ Ⓑ Ⓒ Ⓓ Ⓔ	
18 Ⓐ Ⓑ Ⓒ Ⓓ Ⓔ		48 Ⓐ Ⓑ Ⓒ Ⓓ Ⓔ	
19 Ⓐ Ⓑ Ⓒ Ⓓ Ⓔ		49 Ⓐ Ⓑ Ⓒ Ⓓ Ⓔ	
20 Ⓐ Ⓑ Ⓒ Ⓓ Ⓔ		50 Ⓐ Ⓑ Ⓒ Ⓓ Ⓔ	
21 Ⓐ Ⓑ Ⓒ Ⓓ Ⓔ		51 Ⓐ Ⓑ Ⓒ Ⓓ Ⓔ	
22 Ⓐ Ⓑ Ⓒ Ⓓ Ⓔ		52 Ⓐ Ⓑ Ⓒ Ⓓ Ⓔ	
23 Ⓐ Ⓑ Ⓒ Ⓓ Ⓔ		53 Ⓐ Ⓑ Ⓒ Ⓓ Ⓔ	
24 Ⓐ Ⓑ Ⓒ Ⓓ Ⓔ		54 Ⓐ Ⓑ Ⓒ Ⓓ Ⓔ	
25 Ⓐ Ⓑ Ⓒ Ⓓ Ⓔ		55 Ⓐ Ⓑ Ⓒ Ⓓ Ⓔ	
26 Ⓐ Ⓑ Ⓒ Ⓓ Ⓔ		56 Ⓐ Ⓑ Ⓒ Ⓓ Ⓔ	
27 Ⓐ Ⓑ Ⓒ Ⓓ Ⓔ		57 Ⓐ Ⓑ Ⓒ Ⓓ Ⓔ	
28 Ⓐ Ⓑ Ⓒ Ⓓ Ⓔ		58 Ⓐ Ⓑ Ⓒ Ⓓ Ⓔ	
29 Ⓐ Ⓑ Ⓒ Ⓓ Ⓔ		59 Ⓐ Ⓑ Ⓒ Ⓓ Ⓔ	
30 Ⓐ Ⓑ Ⓒ Ⓓ Ⓔ		60 Ⓐ Ⓑ Ⓒ Ⓓ Ⓔ	

DIAGNOSTIC TEST

Total Time: One Hour
Time begun .... Time ended .... Time used ....

DIRECTIONS: This test consists of selections from literary works and questions on their content, form, and style. After reading each passage or poem, choose the best answer to each question and blacken the corresponding space on the answer sheet.

NOTE: Pay particular attention to the requirement of questions that contain the words NOT, LEAST, or EXCEPT.

Questions 1–6: Read the following passage carefully before you choose your answers.

The value of philosophy is to be sought largely in its very uncertainty. He who has no tincture of philosophy goes through life imprisoned in the prejudices derived from common
(5) sense, from the habitual beliefs of his age or his nation, and from convictions that have grown up in his mind without the cooperation or consent of his deliberate reason. As soon as we begin to philosophize, on the contrary, we find
(10) that even the most everyday things lead to problems to which only very incomplete answers can be given. Philosophy, though unable to tell us with certainty what is the true answer to the doubts that it raises, is able to suggest many possibilities that enlarge our thoughts and free them from the tyranny of custom.

1. This paragraph is organized primarily according to the principle of

(A) partition in that the author begins with a large idea and then explains its subdivisions
(B) cause and effect in that the author describes an effect and then relates it to its causes
(C) chronology in that the author presents events in the order in which they occurred
(D) explication in that he begins with a large idea and then explains it through expansion
(E) exemplification in that he gives examples to clarify his main idea

2. A person who does not allow philosophy to help shape his life lacks

(A) convictions based on prejudices
(B) ability to think about the social issues of his time

(C) beliefs of his age as reflected in the principles of his nation
(D) knowledge of the rights of man
(E) opinions arrived at by his independent thinking

3. Philosophy allows us to

(A) question our doubts in the terms of our certainties
(B) become leaders of the age
(C) examine man's efforts through the ages
(D) follow the true thinking of our leaders
(E) have faith in our own ability to think

4. This selection lacks

(A) generalizations
(B) abstract terms
(C) specific examples
(D) a topic sentence
(E) a summarizing sentence

5. Philosophy has uncertainty because

(A) it deals with complex problems
(B) it questions accepted beliefs
(C) it strikes out for new solutions
(D) its concern is inquiry and not solutions
(E) it is a way of life

6. The tone of the passage is best termed

(A) scornful
(B) amused
(C) meditative
(D) impassioned
(E) judgmental

Questions 7–11: Read the following poem carefully before you choose your answers.

Bright be the place of thy soul!
　　No lovelier spirit than thine
E'er burst from its mortal control,
　　In the orbs of the blessed to shine.
(5) On earth thou wert all but divine,
　　As thy soul shall immortally be;
And our sorrow may cease to repine
　　When we know that thy God is with thee.
Light be the turf of thy tomb!
(10)　　May its verdure like emeralds be!
There should not be the shadow of gloom
　　In aught that reminds us of thee.
Young flowers and an evergreen tree
　　May spring from the spot of thy rest:
(15) But nor cypress nor yew let us see;
　　For why should we mourn for the blest?

7. This poem does NOT contain

    (A) traditional expressions of sorrow
    (B) belief in immortality of the soul
    (C) personal sorrow
    (D) religious faith
    (E) an evaluation of the deceased

8. Which of the following is NOT true of this selection?

    (A) In it resignation replaces fear of death
    (B) It leaves little time for weeping
    (C) It was intended for a country tombstone
    (D) Its naiveté gives it everyday universality
    (E) It justifies the ways of God to man

9. In its context the phrase "Bright be the place of thy soul" refers to

    I. the orbs of the blessed
    II. the final resting place on the hillside
    III. the hearts of friends
    (A) I only
    (B) II only
    (C) III only
    (D) I and II only
    (E) I, II, and III

10. Cypress should be absent from the spot because

    (A) it is a symbol of joy
    (B) it would destroy the beauty of the place
    (C) it would compete with the beauty of the place
    (D) it is too symmetrical
    (E) it is a symbol of sorrow

11. The criteria used to evaluate this poem must be similar to those used in judging

    (A) Victorian poetry
    (B) Elizabethan comedies
    (C) Greek tragedies
    (D) the modern novel
    (E) Norse folk tales

Questions 12–21: Read the following passage carefully before you choose your answers.

Thus we feed on genius, and refresh ourselves from too much conversation with our mates, and exult in the depth of nature in that direction in which he leads us. What indemnification is (5) one great man for populations of pigmies! Every mother wishes one son a genius, though all the rest should be mediocre. But a new danger appears in the excess of influence of the great man. His attractions warp us from our place. We have (10) become underlings and intellectual suicides. Ah! yonder in the horizon is our help; other great men, new qualities, counterweights and checks on each other. We cloy of the honey of each peculiar greatness. Every hero becomes a (15) bore at last. Perhaps Voltaire was not bad-hearted, yet he said of the good Jesus, even, "I pray you, let me never hear that man's name again." They cry up the virtues of George Washington—"Damn George Washington!" is (20) the poor Jacobin's whole speech and confutation. But it is human nature's indispensable defence. The centripetence augments the centrifugence. We balance one man with his opposite, and the health of the state depends on the see- (25) saw.

There is however a speedy limit to the use of heroes. Every genius is defended from approach by quantities of unavailableness. They are very attractive, and seem at a distance our (30) own: but we are hindered on all sides from approach. The more we are drawn, the more we are repelled. There is something not solid in the good that is done for us. The best discovery the discoverer makes for himself. It has something (35) unreal for his companion until he too has substantiated it. It seems as if the Deity dressed each soul, which he sends into nature in certain virtues and powers not communicable to other men, and sending it to perform one more turn (40) through the circle of beings, wrote "*Not transferable*" and "*Good for this trip only*," on these garments of the soul. There is something deceptive about the intercourse of minds. The boundaries are invisible, but they are never (45) crossed. There is such good will to impart, and such good will to receive, that each threatens to become the other; but the law of individuality collects its secret strength: you are you, and I am I, so we remain.

12. The selection is organized primarily according to the principle of

    (A) saturation; that is, the author develops an idea, gives an example, and then attacks and defends it throughout the rest of the selection
    (B) ambiguity; that is, the author hints at an idea through the development of a topic sentence and then avoids specific examples and concrete terms so that the writer is compelled to think in and around his idea
    (C) insightfulness; that is, the author suggests one facet of an unprovable truth and then

goes to another without attempting to link his concepts into a meaningful unit

(D) spatiality, in that the author moves from the most narrowest confines of an idea out to its daring implications

(E) counterbalance; each facet of his thesis is presented in the order of an idea followed by its countereffect

13. The poor Jacobin (line 20) was

(A) Jesus
(B) Voltaire
(C) George Washington
(D) The author
(E) the population of pigmies

14. Which of the following defines the relationship of the last sentence in paragraph one to the rest of the paragraph?

(A) It contains an example to prove the preceding sentence.
(B) It summarizes the meaning of the entire paragraph.
(C) It serves as a transition to the next paragraph.
(D) It raises the problem that is discussed further in the next paragraph.
(E) It presents the counter-arguments to strengthen the author's thesis.

15. In his evaluation of the influence of geniuses, the author claims that

(A) the genius could convert us into automatons, without minds of our own
(B) geniuses can destroy progress
(C) mediocre people do not admire geniuses
(D) geniuses are a threat to the democratic processes
(E) the genius is power hungry

16. The author tries to convince us that

(A) we should be suspicious of geniuses
(B) we should be suspicious of our own intuitions
(C) geniuses cause waste and destruction in this world
(D) counterforces prevent geniuses from carrying mankind to excesses
(E) certain rights are not transferable

17. In our contacts with other people we should

(A) select our leaders carefully
(B) trust our leaders completely
(C) be glad to follow our leaders
(D) be suspicious of people who attack our leaders
(E) look for direction from everyone

18. We should not fear being misled by our leaders because

(A) they are all men of good will
(B) our intuitions will warn us in time
(C) they are essentially bores
(D) we shall tire of them quickly
(E) their mistakes become known quickly

19. "Every hero becomes a bore at last" is an example of a(n)

(A) truism
(B) epigram
(C) blurb
(D) caricature
(E) conceit

20. The tone of the passage is best termed

(A) cynical
(B) amused
(C) detached
(D) scornful
(E) optimistic

21. The author explores all of the following facets, EXCEPT

(A) the causes of progress
(B) why geniuses want to become heroes
(C) why we follow leaders
(D) why leaders are deposed
(E) why we never identify completely with a leader

Questions 22–29: Read the following poem carefully before you choose your answers.

To fight aloud is very brave,
But gallanter, I know,
Who charge within the bosom,
The cavalry of woe.

(5) Who win, and nations do not see,
Who fall, and none observe,
Whose dying eyes no country
Regards with patriot love.

We trust, in plumed procession,
(10) For such the angels go,
Rank after rank, with even feet
And uniforms of snow.

22. Which of the following best expresses the main idea of the selection?

    (A) The angels are on the side of the brave.
    (B) Life for the unknowns requires more courage than life does for the leaders.
    (C) Angels set the example for us in our lives.
    (D) Heroes' medals are always deserved.
    (E) Misfortunes will always beset the common man.

23. *Charge* in line three contains the image of

    (A) the debits and credits of a business account
    (B) the accusations made by a lawyer for the defense
    (C) payments due for an installment account
    (D) the rush to enter into battle with an enemy
    (E) the accusation one has to face in court in the presence of a judge

24. The second stanza forwards the poet's ideas by

    (A) giving examples of the cavalry of woe
    (B) showing those who can and do fight aloud
    (C) explaining what is meant by patriotic love
    (D) explaining why these people are angels
    (E) giving examples of those referred to in lines two and three

25. "Uniforms of snow" in the last line is an example of

    (A) a metaphor
    (B) literal use
    (C) litotes
    (D) irony
    (E) epigram

26. Which of the following is NOT implied in the final comparison?

    (A) God's will is in evidence even in the actions of the ordinary people in their moments of trial.
    (B) The universality of suffering among men is symbolized by the multitudes of angels.
    (C) The suffering we all face in life should not fill us with feelings of guilt.
    (D) As men suffer so do the angels.
    (E) We must take comfort from the very fact that we are suffering.

27. The tone of the poem is best termed

    (A) joyful
    (B) pessimistic
    (C) resentful

    (D) complacent
    (E) understanding

28. The diction of this passage is best defined as

    (A) oratorical and dogmatic
    (B) philosophical and abstract
    (C) charged and metaphoric
    (D) allegorical and figurative
    (E) simple and ordinary

29. The sentence structure and flow of ideas of this passage are best defined as

    (A) inverted
    (B) direct and simple
    (C) complex and abstruse
    (D) complicated but natural
    (E) dramatic and direct

Questions 30–36: Read the following poem carefully before you choose your answers.

> He that loves a rosy cheek,
>   Or a coral lip admires,
> Or from star-like eyes doth seek
>   Fuel to maintain his fires:
> (5) As old Time makes these decay,
> So his flames must waste away.
>
> But a smooth and steadfast mind,
>   Gentle thought and calm desires,
> Hearts with equal love combined,
> (10)   Kindle never-dying fires.
> Where these are not, I despise
> Lovely cheeks or lips or eyes.

30. The underlying subject of the passage is

    (A) beauty is skin deep
    (B) mental stability is the basis of true love
    (C) mental and psychological compatibility are the true basis of love
    (D) physical attraction is not the basis of love
    (E) time conquers all regardless of whether physical or mental or emotional compatibility is present

31. Which of the following best explains the function of the versification of the poem?

    (A) The regularity of the rhythms emphasizes the truth in the conclusion.
    (B) The regularity of the rhymes emphasizes the flow of ideas.
    (C) The rhyming of the last two lines in each

stanza serves to help these lines serve as summaries of the thought.

(D) The lack of variations in rhythm tends to dull the reader's attention.

(E) The simplicity of the rhymed pairs is in contrast to the complexity of the author's message.

32. Line five contains an example of

(A) allusion
(B) alliteration
(C) oxymoron
(D) conceit
(E) personification

33. The effect of the style is best explained as one that

(A) reveals how certain the poet was that he was right
(B) reinforces the complexity of his thought pattern
(C) reveals how uncertain he was
(D) proves how deep his distrust for beauty was
(E) how much he exalted intelligence

34. The third line contains

(A) a metaphor
(B) a simile
(C) comic relief
(D) a malapropism
(E) a maxim

35. The first line contains

(A) dramatic irony
(B) an epitaph
(C) a euphemism
(D) irony
(E) a cliché

36. The mood of the poet is best interpreted as one of

(A) awe
(B) doubt
(C) excitement
(D) conviction
(E) horror

Questions 37–44: Read the following passage carefully before you choose your answers.

A true classic, as I should like to hear it defined, is an author who has enriched the human mind, increased its treasure and caused it to ad-

vance a step; who has discovered some moral
(5) and not equivocal truth, or revealed some eternal passion in that heart where all seemed known and discovered; who has expressed his thought, observation, or invention, in no matter what form, only provided it be broad and great,
(10) refined and sensible, sane and beautiful in itself; who has spoken to all in his own peculiar style, a style which is found to be also that of the whole world, a style new without neologism, new and old, easily contemporary with all time.
(15)   Such a classic may for a moment have been revolutionary; it may at least have seemed so, but it is not; it only lashed and subverted whatever prevented the restoration of the balance of order and beauty.

37. The tone of the passage is best defined as

(A) joyful
(B) cynical
(C) confused
(D) didactic
(E) scornful

38. A true classic need not

(A) contain moral values
(B) expose the weakness in older ways
(C) deal with emotional values
(D) reveal man's self to man
(E) employ new techniques of writing

39. The test of a true classic is that

(A) it revealed truth to one generation
(B) it made the world a better place to live in
(C) it has historical significance
(D) it fills with pride the hearts of the countrymen of the author
(E) it continues to be read throughout the world

40. A true class is revolutionary because

(A) it clears away styles and ideas that confused men
(B) it brings new techniques into fields of expression
(C) it contains moral values
(D) it is understood by so many people
(E) it defies time

41. The author of this selection proves his points by

(A) giving examples

(B) citing authorities
(C) developing his ideas logically
(D) disproving false ideas
(E) stating his opinions

42. An author who reveals "some eternal passion in that heart where all seemed known and discovered"

    (A) must develop a new vocabulary
    (B) distorts accepted reality
    (C) reveals new insights into man's reasons for behavior
    (D) develops a style of his own
    (E) puts old ideas into new forms

43. The diction and style of this passage are best defined as

    (A) emotional and allegorical
    (B) poetic and oratorical
    (C) abstract and philosophical
    (D) direct and moralistic
    (E) oratorical and prophetic

44. A treasure of the human mind

    (A) reveals moral truth
    (B) reveals truth, order, and beauty
    (C) contains universal passion, moral values, and mental worth
    (D) is based on observation, invention, and insights
    (E) is based on enrichment, advancement, and discovery

Questions 45-49: Read the following passage carefully before you choose your answers.

It is not only what we have inherited from our fathers that exists again in us, but all sorts of old, dead ideas and all kinds of old, dead beliefs, and things of that kind. They are not actually alive in us; but they are there, dormant all the same, and we can never be rid of them. Whenever I take up a newspaper and read it, I fancy I see ghosts creeping between the lines. There must be ghosts all over the world.

45. The author is suspicious of

    (A) our inheritance
    (B) old ideas
    (C) whatever is not new
    (D) ideas that are not fully accepted
    (E) ways of life based on dated traditions

46. The author condemns men who

    (A) are uncritical
    (B) are cruel and merciless
    (C) condemn others for acts that they themselves have done
    (D) judge others by their inheritances
    (E) read newspapers carelessly

47. The tone of the passage is best termed

    (A) hopeful
    (B) pessimistic
    (C) romantic
    (D) cynical
    (E) didactic

48. All of the following statements are true of the selection EXCEPT

    (A) the artful simplicity in the first sentence is emphasized by the phrase "and things of that kind"
    (B) "ghosts" were intended to be interpreted literally
    (C) the lack of abstract terms and long words is in contrast to the sophistication of the message
    (D) to test the validity of the message, the readers feel called upon to supply their own examples
    (E) the single concrete example supplied by the author gives the paragraph a poetic tone

49. Emphasis is achieved in this selection through

    (A) logical piling up of details
    (B) imagery and oxymoron
    (C) repetition of single words
    (D) rhetorical questions
    (E) argumentation and exposition

Questions 50-56: Read the following passage carefully before you choose your answers.

All the philanthropists in the world, and all the legislators, meeting to advocate and decree the total abolition of corporal punishment, will never persuade me to the contrary! There is
(5) something even more disgraceful than what I have just mentioned. Often enough you may see a carter walking along the street, quite alone, without any horses, and still cracking away incessantly; so accustomed has the wretch be-
(10) come to it in consequence of the unwarrantable toleration of this practice. A man's body and

the needs of his body are now everywhere treated with a tender indulgence. Is the thinking mind then, to be the only thing that is never to (15) obtain the slightest measure of consideration or protection, to say nothing of respect? Carters, porters, messengers—these are the beasts of burden amongst mankind; by all means let them be treated justly, fairly, indulgently, and with (20) forethought; but they must not be permitted to stand in the way of the higher endeavors of humanity by wantonly making a noise. How many great and splendid thoughts, I should like to know, have been lost to the world by the crack (25) of a whip? If I had the upper hand, I should soon produce in the heads of these people an indissoluble association of ideas between cracking a whip and getting a whipping.

50. The underlying subject of this selection is that

(A) man is fundamentally bad and must be punished in order to know right from wrong
(B) poetic justice can never operate in the world of carters, porters, and messengers
(C) philanthropy can often commit grave errors in helping wrong group sections of society
(D) brute force rather than reason is the effective control in society
(E) no man can escape the social consequences of his acts

51. The writer of this article can best be characterized as

(A) democratic in his desire to see that all segments of society have equal privileges when in the streets
(B) autocratic because of his concern over the few rather than the many
(C) democratic because he is willing to discuss calmly in this selection an injustice in our society
(D) autocratic because of his condescending attitude toward people engaged in the service trades
(E) totalitarian because of his advocacy of corporal punishment and desire for noise abatement

52. Which of the following best expresses the reaction of a modern reader?

(A) Because of its stress on something so trivial, there must be some hidden meaning
(B) The article deals with a social problem and admirably suggests a positive solution

(C) While his solution may be practical, the problem dealt with is too insignificant
(D) Stratification of society has its merits; it allows some men to improve the manners of others through threats or fear of threats
(E) The carters, porters, and messengers appreciated the writer's willingness to help them realize faults

53. The first sentence is an example of

(A) fable
(B) parody
(C) generalization
(D) caricature
(E) paradox

54. The author does not explain

(A) why corporal punishment should not be abolished
(B) why the thinking minds must be protected against noise
(C) why the carters crack their whips when walking down the streets
(D) why whipping these men would be effective
(E) why he advocates corporal punishment

55. The author's main objection to the cracking of the whip was

(A) it was a cruel way to treat animals
(B) the noise brutalized the city atmosphere
(C) the men might hurt a passerby
(D) the whip is a symbol of oppression
(E) the noise bothered him

56. The diction and style of this passage are best defined as

(A) abstract and philosophical
(B) legal and argumentative
(C) emotional and figurative
(D) ordinary and serious
(E) allegorical and didactic

Questions 57–60: Read the following poem carefully before you choose your answers.

Each seed is a fulfilling dream,
    Stretched horizons
    To other worlds.
Yet we sit by the fire,
(5)   Smug and earnest;
Snapping peanuts between
    Gulps of beer.

57. Another writer communicated a similar insight in the line

(A) "Man's inhumanity to man"
(B) "What fools these mortals be"
(C) "What care I for whom she be"
(D) "Hoisted by his own petard"
(E) "This lives on and this gives life to thee"

58. Each of the following is true of the poet's intent, EXCEPT

(A) "gulps of beer" was chosen for its staccato and stark contrasts with "stretched horizons"
(B) the living seed with its potential was intentionally paired with the sterile peanuts
(C) the "stretched horizon" stands for the poet's own ideals
(D) the warmth of the fire makes even more cold and uninspired those who sit before it
(E) our lack of ambition is highlighted by our being smug and earnest while doing trivial things

59. The "seed" mentioned in line 1 could not represent

I. humanity's potential
II. reach rather than grasp
III. survival of the fittest
(A) I only
(B) II only
(C) III only
(D) II and III only
(E) I, II, and III

60. By using "we" and not "you" the poet

(A) condemns the living for not accomplishing great deeds
(B) reveals our lack of imagination
(C) lessens the value of her message
(D) accepts our limitations
(E) attacks disdain and cruelty

ANSWER KEY: DIAGNOSTIC TEST

1. (D)	11. (E)	21. (B)	31. (C)	41. (E)	51. (D)
2. (E)	12. (E)	22. (B)	32. (E)	42. (C)	52. (A)
3. (E)	13. (B)	23. (D)	33. (A)	43. (D)	53. (C)
4. (C)	14. (A)	24. (E)	34. (B)	44. (B)	54. (D)
5. (D)	15. (D)	25. (A)	35. (E)	45. (E)	55. (E)
6. (C)	16. (D)	26. (D)	36. (D)	46. (A)	56. (D)
7. (C)	17. (C)	27. (E)	37. (D)	47. (B)	57. (D)
8. (E)	18. (B)	28. (E)	38. (E)	48. (B)	58. (B)
9. (E)	19. (B)	29. (A)	39. (E)	49. (C)	59. (C)
10. (E)	20. (E)	30. (C)	40. (A)	50. (D)	60. (D)

DETERMINING YOUR RAW SCORE

1. Tabulate Totals

Number Right _____
Number Wrong _____
Number Omitted _____

2. Enter Number Right   A_____
Divide Number Wrong by
4 and put result here   B_____

3. Subtract B from A. This
results in your RAW
SCORE   _____

The subtraction of ¼ point for each incorrect answer adjusts for the effect of random guessing.

EVALUATING YOUR PERFORMANCE

Excellent	55–60
Very Good	45–54
Good	34–44
Average	24–33
Below Average	16–23
Unsatisfactory	15 or Below

HOW TO MAKE THE BEST USE OF YOUR STUDY TIME

The material that follows in this chapter is a digest of basic concepts and terms. It is the key to maximum results, if used judiciously.

STEPS TO A HIGH SCORE

1. Use the results of the Diagnostic Test to assess your strengths and weaknesses.

2. Scan through each group in the units that follow and check the items to review or learn. Do *not* spend time in going over items you have already mastered.

3. Space your learning. Frequent short sessions are more productive than long cram periods. The more frequent the periods of learning, the greater the mastery.

4. Use the exercises for both overlearning and gaining speed in handling questions.

5. After your study sessions, take one of the Practice Tests. Simulate the actual examination in time and privacy and evaluate your progress and discover the areas requiring additional review. These Practice Tests will help you gain confidence by familiarizing you with the style and types of questions to be found on the exam. Your speed and control will increase as the result of the continued practice. Use the scoring results to judge your progress.

2. *The Nature of the Achievement Test in Literature*

The Literature Test consists of approximately 60 multiple-choice questions based on six to eight reading selections. About half of the selections are prose and half are poetry. The passages selected may be

- complete poems
- portions of poems
- excerpts from dialogue in short stories or novels
- brief thoughts in paragraph form, usually taken from essays
- longer selections from plays, novels, stories, essays.

The selections are taken from works written in English, from the Renaissance to the present.

SCOPE

The test is planned to measure your skill in reading literary works. It does *not* measure your knowledge of the life of the author, the literary background of the period, or critical opinions about the work. You are not expected to be familiar with the selections included on the test.

Extensive knowledge of literary terms is not essential, but you should be aware of basic terminology. Your comprehension will be tested in three areas: meaning, form, and style.

MEANING

- parts of the passage (specific words, phrases, lines, denotation, syntax)
- entire passage (theme, argument)
- implications (effect, connotation)
- author's point of view
- allusions

FORM

- structure of the passage (stanza)
- method of organization (development of thesis, how one part develops from or differs from another)

STYLE

- literary terms and devices (alliteration, simile)
- rhetorical devices (irony)
- tone (irate, dispassionate, sympathetic)
- imagery
- narrative voice (characterization of the speaker)
- mood

You are not expected to be familiar with more obscure terms such as assonance, alexandrine, syncope, metonymy. There is no prescribed or suggested reading list for this test. The best long-term preparation involves the development of the habit of reading extensively.

How This Section Can Help You

Control of literary terms and the ability to meet the range of literature come from reading regularly and widely over a period of years. This book cannot be a substitute for such experiencing. However, it will help you to review the technical terms and concepts you should know and then give you the practice that will lead you to maximum results in reading for comprehension and appreciation.

So that you can concentrate your efforts more effectively, the review material has been divided into poetry and prose. Each unit begins with a review of the terms and concepts that are basic to critical understanding. These are followed by practice exercises to help you evaluate your control of these terms and concepts. The combined Practice Tests will help you reach your maximum level of speed and accuracy.

3. Taste and Sensitivity in Poetry

Candidates taking the Literature Test must have a developed realization of the appropriateness of sound and sense not only in prose but also in poetry. The material in this section will review for you the terms and concepts involved in achieving an understanding of the tonal values of poetry. However, once again, unless you have experienced poetry, unless you are willing to accustom yourself through exposure to poetry, learning the terms that follow will not give you the maturity of approach being sought in the questions in this area. Once you have mastered the concepts involved, you must put to use the skills developed. You must read sufficiently to be able to agree that poetry is the best that man has thought and said, presented in condensed form.

BASIC CHARACTERISTICS OF THE BEST IN POETRY

1. Recurrent rhythms: Although the rhythm of a poem will vary from the mechanical beat of its meter, there is always a recurring beat that unifies the poem and makes it one. This rhythm is in harmony with the thought. Sadness and contemplation, for example, demand a slower beat.

> Break, break, break,
>   Oh thy cold gray stones, O Sea!

Happiness and swiftness on the other hand demand rapid movement.

> The road was a ribbon of moonlight over
>   the purple moor,
> And the highwayman came riding—

2. Imaginative use of language: Prose is used basically to communicate ideas and facts. Poetry stirs our feelings and imaginations. It shows us relationships that we had never dreamed existed. It puts into words that which we have often felt but have never before expressed.

> I never saw a moor,
> I never saw the sea;
> Yet know I how the heather looks,
> And what a wave must be.
>
> I never spoke with God,
> Nor visited in Heaven;
> Yet certain am I of the spot
> As if the chart were given.

3. Poetic machinery: The poet takes full advantage of the less subtle aspects of poetry such as rhymes, figures of speech and stanzaic patterns to emphasize his imagery, pinpoint the emotional reactions sought, and increase the pleasure of the reader.

4. Condensed utterance: The poet will express his thoughts in a minimum of words. He requires concentration on the part of the reader, a willingness to re-read and re-read until the full import of the words is realized. He makes each word carry a much heavier load of meaning than can be expected of the same word in prose. He expects a word or phrase to evoke a vivid mental image or specific emotional reaction.

After the reader has read the best in poetry, he feels that he has grown mentally and emotionally. He feels that he has met man and understood.

BASIC CHARACTERISTICS OF VERSE AND POOR POETRY

1. Obvious meter: Instead of the rhythms subtly harmonizing with the thought pattern, the meter in these poems drowns all else out and the regular beat of the lines comes through without variation.

And now I see the end of all I sought
Of why, Oh why should it have come to nought!

2. Sentimentality: A poem should contain sentiment, true feeling, but when the poet pulls at our heart strings and brings forth sorrow or sympathy beyond that called for by the situation, the poem suffers—as does the reader.

Stay awhile and shed two dozen tears
For this poor thief o'ercome with fears
That any one of a number of ills
Could rob him so quickly of his skills.

3. Sermonizing: A poem should help to make the reader a better person through leading him to a more sensitive understanding of men and ideals. The moment the poet, however, delivers a lethal blow and then makes certain that the reader understands by drawing the obvious moral, the poet has killed the suggestiveness that must be part of a poem for it to be good.

Therefore dear reader now you know
A truth that has ever been so—
The hopes of those that practice sin
Must ever be found among the might have been.

4. False images: The poet can convey much through the pictures he evokes in the minds of his reader. These images, however, must harmonize with the thought, the mood, the sentiment. Unless the poet is deliberately planning to evoke laughter, he can easily cause a reader to smile instead of feel sad by bringing forth the wrong type of imagery.

Like poor fish turning brown in the frying pan
Jerry allowed the sun to turn his pallor to tan.

5. Prosy lines: Instead of the lines singing as in great poetry or even following a too regular beat as in limericks or verse, too often the lines in poor poetry will lose all meter and sound like prose.

Therefore dear reader I know what I say
Allan fought much too hard on that Monday

6. Trite rhymes: Even in his use of words to be rhymed, the poet must be fully aware of the lift that his lines must give the reader's spirit. If he uses too many obvious rhymes, the reader soon feels that the thought is just as obvious. He must learn to use very sparingly

love—above moon—June day—say might—right

7. Wordiness: The essence of poetry is its economy of words. If the poet uses too many words to express an idea, if he repeats himself needlessly, or if he adds words to fill out a line, he is not writing at the highest levels.

THE DEVICES OF POETRY

Figures of Speech

The figures of speech are those forms of expression that are different from the ordinary modes in order to emphasize or make the meaning more effective. In the hands of a skilled craftsman these devices can enhance the value of the written material. When misused these devices can destroy the worth of the material. The following are the figures of speech most frequently used in poetry.

1. The simile: A directly expressed comparison. It usually contains the words *like* or *as*. The successful simile can evoke an ever-expanding, vivid image in the mind of the reader. An effective simile must have an element of surprise in it; it must be appropriate; it should realize the emotional reaction anticipated by the poet.

as idle as "a painted ship upon a painted ocean"

Similes, however, may be misused.

Trite (Commonplace) Simile: red as a rose innocent as a child
Exaggerated Simile: as powerful as ten men
Inappropriate Simile: As silently as a ghoul, my love glided into my heart.

Her hair drooped round her pallid cheeks, like seaweed on a clam.

2. The metaphor: A comparison which is implied rather than stated. It does not contain the words *like* or *as*.

Trite Metaphor: pearly teeth, icy stare, clammy hands

Exaggerated Metaphor: one who is *the right hand of justice*

Appropriate Metaphor: The Lord is my shepherd.
  A spring of love gushes from his heart.

Mixed Metaphor: The bitter taste of her remarks acted as a fuse that set off my anger.

This is a big step forward in our jet-propelled push forward.

He will take a backseat in our eyes if he remains forever self-centered.

You will have to learn to steer a steady course as the sands of time fly by.

3. Personification: The figure of speech in which we give human qualities to inhuman things or objects.

The wind sings a varied song.

This intensifier must be used with caution by the poet. Too often it can lead to sentimentalism rather than heightened reality.

Inappropriate Personification: Nature cried in torrents when I failed the test.

4. Hyperbole: Intentional exaggeration. In the hands of a skilled humorist, this can be a most powerful device. Used occasionally, it can involve the reader very quickly in the author's ideas.

My thoughts threaten to shake down the goodness that is left in the world and leave all to evil and ruin.

5. Apostrophe: The figure of speech in which the absent are addressed as though they were present, the living as well as the dead, objects as well as human beings. Again, this can be a device highly charged with emotion.

Blow, blow thou winter wind
Thou art not so unkind
As man's ingratitude

This device can be so easily abused, leading to overcharged words that do not arouse the reader's imagination.

Come forth, all former graduates of
  Lafayette High . . .
Kindness, fill her heart with goodness, not fear.

6. Inversion: The figure of speech in which words are presented out of their natural or expected order.

Of arms and a man I sing

This device is frowned upon by most modern serious poets. However, it is a crutch that is much overused by the beginner and those who are striving for effects that are beyond the words and thoughts that they are using.

7. Onomatopoeia: Formation of words to represent natural sounds. A most effective device in appealing to the sense of sound.

shrill bugles   *buzzing* of the bees   *whirring* wings

As with the other figures of speech, this device can be effective or most inappropriate.

Inappropriate: The buzzing of the babies in their cribs

8. Alliteration: Repetition of initial consonant sounds, rhyming of initial consonants.

furrow   followed   free

Alliteration gives a sense of continuity. It is one of the oldest devices in the language and one that is most effective if it is not overused.

9. Assonance: Repetition of vowel sounds, the pairing of the same vowel sounds without regard for consonants.

and *screen* from *seeing* and *leave* in sight

This is a device used to give tonal values to lines. It is difficult to introduce and not easily sensed by the reader.

10. Rhyme: The word reserved for rhymes occurring at the end of lines.

To the seas and the *streams*
In their noonday *dreams*

Masculine Rhyme: The rhyme ends with accented syllables.

She tried and tried in *vain*
To bring that ease from *pain* . . .

Feminine Rhyme: A rhyme in two syllables, the first of which is accented.

sweater—letter

Rhymes add music to the lines and are a source of pleasure for the reader if the poet does not resort to misuse. The major fault is found in hackneyed rhymes, ones that have been much overused

bright—light   flower—hour   gold—old

11. Poetic language: The fashion has long since come and gone, but many writers don't seem to be aware of this change in styles. They still insist on using old-fashioned words that were once considered elegant and poetic. Some such words are

ope for open   *oft* for often   *yclept* (called)

Sometimes in the Literature Test one of the choices offered for the missing line of poetry can be eliminated because it relies on these words whereas the other three choices use more modern, direct words.

THE RHYTHMS OF POETRY

The basic of poetry rhythm is in the repetition of accented syllables. These syllables are followed by unaccented ones in an ordered fashion to create the tempo of the lines. For the sake of identification, a line of poetry has been arbitrarily said to consist of a number of feet.

Feet of Two Syllables

1. The iambus: The iambic foot contains an unaccented first syllable and an accented second syllable.

 de táil   con fér

2. The trochee: The trochaic foot contains an accented first syllable and an unaccented second syllable.

spéll ing   màs ter

Feet of Three Syllables

1. The dactyl: The dactylic foot begins with an accented syllable which is followed by two unaccented syllables.

fá mi ly̆   téch ni căl

2. The anapest: The anapestic foot begins with two unaccented syllables which are followed by the accented syllable.

un re fórmed   non be líef

THE LINES OF POETRY

Poetic lines are named according to the number of feet they contain. The most common ones follow.

Dimeter   A line of two feet
Raise her | gently |

Trimeter   A line of three feet
On high | our flag | is flown |

Tetrameter   A line of four feet
Of all | the men | I e'er | have known |

Pentameter   A line of five feet
When I | consi | der how | my light | is spent |

Hexameter   A line of six feet
When I | have felt | the weight | of days | and
years | pushing |

The lines of poetry are usually named after the type of foot that is found most frequently in it. Therefore we speak of an iambic pentameter or a trochaic trimeter. The most common line in the English language is the iambic pentameter. The diactylic hexameter, while much used in Latin and French, has proved too long for English.

You should be able to identify lines in this fashion since very often on the Literature Test you are asked to choose a missing line of poetry and one or more of those suggested may be defective, lacking a foot or using a different type of foot.

THE PATTERNS OF POETRY

Free Verse

The rhythm is determined by the subject matter. The lines do not follow a regular meter but vary from thought to thought. Rhyme is usually not used.

Pile the bodies high at Austerlitz and Waterloo.
Shovel them under and let me work—
I am the grass; I cover all.

Walt Whitman and Carl Sandburg have helped to establish this as a staple in the repertory of the modern poet. Free verse is a modern form and therefore the images and the language used by the poet tend to be modern.

Blank Verse

Each line contains ten syllables. The predominant beat is iambic. The lines are unrhymed. Blank verse is written in unrhymed iambic pentameter. This has been most popular among the best and the poorest technicians. If each line is a complete thought, then it is *end stop*. If the ideas flow from one line to the next, then it is *enjambed*. The pause within the line is called the *caesura*.

> Here we may reign secure, and in my choice
> When I was young and thought I knew all truths

Heroic Couplet

Two lines of rhymed iambic pentameter.

> Know then thy self, presume not God to scan;
> The proper study of mankind is man.

Quatrain

Any four-line stanza. The best known of the quatrains is in the old English ballads. The most frequent ballad quatrain consisted of alternating iambic tetrameter and iambic trimeter lines rhyming *xaya*; that is, the second and fourth lines only would usually rhyme.

> The king sits in Dumferling town,
>   Drinking the blood-red wine:
> "Oh where will I get a good sailor,
>   To sail this ship of mine."

Sonnet

A 14-line stanza usually in iambic pentameter. The Italian sonnet has a thought division. The first eight lines, the octave, will present an idea or state a thesis; the last six lines, the sestet, will apply the idea or give the example that proves the truth in the thesis. The Italian sonnet is also called the Petrarchan or the Miltonic after the Italian master who originated the form and the great English writer who used it as the vehicle for some of his greatest poetic realizations. The Shakespearean sonnet consists of three quatrains and a concluding, summarizing couplet.

TEST OF MASTERY

I.   Below is a series of paired alternatives. In the space to the left, place a check before the better alternative.

1. (A) _____ How like a winter has my absence been

(B) _____ I know I've been away for a week or so

2. (A) _____ She's a doll as all can see
   (B) _____ How sweet and fair she seems to be

3. (A) _____ The balding trees will soon be bare
   (B) _____ The trees are in their autumn beauty

4. (A) _____ Drive my dead thoughts over the universe,
   (B) _____ Send my televised message abroad

5. (A) _____ I'll fight no more like cat and dog with you
   (B) _____ Since there's no help, come let us kiss and part—

6. (A) _____ As silent as death the city is at night
   (B) _____ Dear God! The very houses seem asleep

7. (A) _____ Time cannot take one drop of your beauty from me
   (B) _____ To me, fair friend, you can never be old

8. (A) _____ Thus conscience does make cowards of us all
   (B) _____ Because we feel we therefore fear

9. (A) _____ Oft is the iris born in lands unknown
   (B) _____ Full many a flower is born to blush unseen

10. (A) _____ Thy soul was like a star, and dwelt apart:
    (B) _____ How like a star in a comet-filled sky thou art

II.   In the space to the left write *Yes* if the line contains five feet; write *No* if it is not a pentameter line.

_____ 11. He walked as one who is done with fear
_____ 12. To strive, to seek, to find, and not to yield
_____ 13. The King sits in Dumferling Town
_____ 14. The drooping of the daylight in the West
_____ 15. No longer mourn for me when I am dead
_____ 16. The lone and level sands stretch far away
_____ 17. Gather ye rosebuds while ye may,
_____ 18. And down the path they roamed with hand in hand forever more
_____ 19. A Sonnet is a moment's monument
_____ 20. Memorial from the Soul's eternity

III.   In the space provided to the left, write *No* if the line is not one that has a poetic beat; write *Yes* if it is predominantly poetic.

_____ 21. In me thou seest the glowing of such fire
_____ 22. Friend, thou are not ready to partake of this meal
_____ 23. The lights began to twinkle from the rocks
_____ 24. Before you could say "Jack Robinson," the lawyer had trapped the defendant

_____ 25. The buzz-saw snarled and rattled in the yard

_____ 26. My clumsiest dear, whose hands ship-wreck vases

_____ 27. The trapped weasel snarled at us even though its leg was broken.

_____ 28. I met an old man near a darkened house

_____ 29. I am part of all that I have met

_____ 30. We must share and share alike when the profits come in

IV. In the space provided to the left, write the name of a figure of speech found in each of the following.

_____ 31. All the world's a stage

_____ 32. How dull it is to pause, to make an end, To rust unburnished, not to shine with use!

_____ 33. There is no frigate like a book To take us lands away

_____ 34. The moon was a ghostly gallon tossed upon cloudy seas

_____ 35. Then felt I like some watcher of the skies.

_____ 36. Go forth—and Virtue, ever in your sight, Shall be your guide. . . .

_____ 37. Look how the pale Queen of the silent night Doth cause the ocean to attend upon her

_____ 38. Oh God! that food should be so dear and life so cheap!

_____ 39. Daughters of Time, the hypocritic Days

_____ 40. For skies of couple-color as a brindled cow

V. One line in each of the following selections has been omitted. Below are four choices to complete the selection. In the space to the left, label the line
  Correct if the line is appropriate
  Rhythm if the line is inappropriate because of rhythm or meter
  Tone if the line is inappropriate because of tone or style
  Meaning if it is inappropriate because of ideas or content

A.   My candle burns at both ends;
        It will not last the night;
      But ah, my foes, and oh, my friends—

      _____

_____ 41. No one knows just where it tends

_____ 42. Thou canst not miss its sight

_____ 43. Doctor Frank says it's too bright

_____ 44. It gives a lovely light

B.   As a rule, man is a fool,
      When it's hot, he wants it cool;
      When it's cool, he wants it hot,

      _____

_____ 45. Whether it's cool or can't be got.

_____ 46. Always wanting what is not.

_____ 47. He just can't make his mind up.

_____ 48. I say it's all a lot of tommyrot!

C.   There was a faith-healer in Deal
      Who said, "Although pain isn't real,
        If I sit on a pin
        And it punctures my skin,

      _____

_____ 49. I dislike what I fancy I feel."

_____ 50. My epidermis is like that of a seal.

_____ 51. I miss the pain that I feel

_____ 52. The pain of ache is my spiel.

D.   Yes, I'm in love, I feel it now,
        And Celia has undone me;
      And yet I'll swear I can't tell how

      _____

_____ 53. She was able to bewitch me.

_____ 54. The fears of death and woe are on my brow.

_____ 55. The pleasing plague stole on me.

_____ 56. Why my enemies do not shun me.

E.   To Mercy, Pity, Peace, and Love
      All pray in their distress;
      And to these virtues of delight

      _____

_____ 57. Their eternal thanks impress.

_____ 58. Return their thankfulness.

_____ 59. In the hours of night their truth express.

_____ 60. Conmen and yeggs their fears express.

ANSWER KEY: TEST OF MASTERY / *Page 213*

I. The better lines are

1. (A)	**4.** (A)	**7.** (B)	**9.** (B)
2. (B)	**5.** (B)	**8.** (A)	**10.** (A)
3. (B)	**6.** (B)		

II.

11. No	**14.** Yes	**17.** No	**19.** Yes
12. Yes	**15.** Yes	**18.** No	**20.** Yes
13. No	**16.** Yes		

III.

21. Yes	**24.** No	**27.** No	**29.** Yes
22. No	**25.** Yes	**28.** Yes	**30.** No
23. Yes	**26.** Yes		

IV.

31. metaphor	**36.** personifica-tion
32. metaphor	**37.** personifica-tion
33. simile	**38.** apostrophe
34. metaphor	**39.** personification
35. simile	**40.** simile

V.

41. meaning	**48.** tone	**55.** correct
42. tone	**49.** correct	**56.** meaning
43. rhythm	**50.** rhythm	**57.** meaning
44. correct	**51.** meaning	**58.** correct
45. meaning	**52.** tone	**59.** rhythm
46. correct	**53.** rhythm	**60.** tone
47. rhythm	**54.** tone	

ADDITIONAL MASTERY TESTS

TEST 1   *Suggested Time:* **20** *Minutes*

Each of the following selections contains a missing line. Beneath each are four lines that could complete the passage. Only one of the four is entirely satisfactory. The others all have a definite deficiency.

By circling the letters provided to the right, for each of the four lines, mark

(A) if the line is acceptable
(B) if the line is not satisfactory because of a defect in rhythm or meter
(C) if the line is not acceptable because of style or tone
(D) if the line is inappropriate in meaning

Trochee trips from long to short
From long to long in solemn sort
Slow Spondee stalks; strong foot! yet ill able
Ever to come up with Dactyl trisyllable

_____

With a leap and a bound the swift Anapests throng.

1. To be or not to be is iam's song but not for long.   **1.** A B C D

2. In the book from each page come the iam's strong.   **2.** A B C D

3. Iambics march from short to long.   **3.** A B C D

4. Then do indite iams in running song.   **4.** A B C D

Charge once more, then, and be dumb!
Let the victors, when they come,
When the forts of folly fall,

_____

5. Shout with triumph through thy hall.   **5.** A B C D

6. Find thy body by the wall.   **6.** A B C D

7. Give you credit in the ledger for the sum.   **7.** A B C D

8. Shout aloud, "Don't stall!"   **8.** A B C D

To me, fair friend, you never can be old;
For as you were when first your eye I eyed,
Such seems your beauty still. Three Winters cold

_____

9. Have been our keepsake with you by my side;   **9.** A B C D

10. Have from the forests shook three Summers' pride;   **10.** A B C D

11. In the flight of our time for your love has vied.   **11.** A B C D

12. Doth with thy love within my heart for e'er abide.   **12.** A B C D

My pictures blacken in their frames
    As night comes on,
And youthful maids and wrinkled dames

_____

13. Sit in tear-filled silence.   **13.** A B C D

14. Steal away in mocking thoughts.   **14.** A B C D

15. Understandeth the frightening dark.   **15.** A B C D

16. Are now all one.   **16.** A B C D

Ask me no more where Jove bestows,
When June is past, the fading rose;
For in your beauty's orient deep

17. Man will ever find eternal sleep.

                          17. A B C D

18. Roses stay in radiant heap.   **18.** A B C D

19. These flowers, as in their causes, sleep.

                          19. A B C D

20. With the light of true beauty they sleep.

                          20. A B C D

The breezy call of incense-bearing morn,
   The swallow twittering from the straw-built shed,
The cock's shrill clarion, or the echoing horn,

       ———————————————

21. No more shall rouse them from their lowly bed.

                          21. A B C D

22. Will find them slightly withered in their stead.

                          22. A B C D

23. Blow the bugle; cattle must be fed.

                          23. A B C D

24. Do chide, 'tis time to arise from bed.

                          24. A B C D

     In every cry of every man,

      ———————————————

     In every voice; in every ban,
     The mind-forged manacles I hear.

25. When every boy is filled with fear,

                          25. A B C D

26. That freedom's coming near, **26.** A B C D

27. In every infant's cry of fear, **27.** A B C D

28. O ye gods on high, please hear

                          28. A B C D

   In the world's broad field of battle,
     In the bivouac of Life,
   Be not like dumb, driven cattle!

      ———————————————

29. Be a hero in the strife!   **29.** A B C D

30. Let us marry, be my wife!   **30.** A B C D

31. Dance a down-beat to the fife

                          31. A B C D

32. Let us drive and push and win the strife!

                          32. A B C D

TEST 2 *Suggested Time: 15 Minutes*

The stanzas of the poem that follows are in scrambled order. Read the poem first and then decide which would be the best order. If you number the stanzas in correct order, you will find it easier to answer the questions that follow. In answering the questions (E) stands for nothing follows.

(A)   Small is the worth
         Of beauty from the light retired:
         Bid her come forth

         Suffer her self to be desired,
         And not blush so to be admired.

(B)   Tell her that's young,
         And shuns to have her graces spied,
          That hadst thou sprung
         In deserts where no men abide,
         Thou must have uncommended died.

(C)   Then die, that she
         The common fate of all things rare
          May read in thee,
         How small a part of time they share,
         That are so wondrous sweet and fair.

(D)   Go, lovely Rose,
         Tell her that wastes her time and me,
          That now she knows,
         When I resemble her to thee,
         How sweet and fair she seems to be.

1. Which stanza did you put first?   **1.** A B C D E

2. Which stanza did you put after (A)?   **2.** A B C D E

3. Which stanza did you put after (B)?   **3.** A B C D E

4. Which stanza did you put after (C)?   **4.** A B C D E

5. Which stanza did you put after (D)?   **5.** A B C D E

(A)   My horse moved on; hoof after hoof
        He raised, and never stopped:
        When down behind the cottage roof,
        At once the bright moon dropped.

(B)   Strange fits of passion have I known:
        And I will dare to tell,
        But in a lover's car alone,
        What once to me befell.

(C)   What fond and wayward thoughts will slide
        Into a lover's head!
        "O mercy!" to myself I cried,
        "If Lucy should be dead!"

(D)   When she I loved looked every day
        Fresh as a rose in June,
        I to her cottage bent my way,
        Beneath an evening moon.

6. Which stanza did you put first?   **6.** A B C D E

7. Which stanza did you put after (A)?   **7.** A B C D E

8. Which stanza did you put after (B)?   **8.** A B C D E

9. Which stanza did you   9. A B C D E
   put after (C)?
10. Which stanza did you   10. A B C D E
    put after (D)?

(A)   Shake hands for ever! Cancel all our vows!
      And when we meet at any time again,
      Be it not seen in either of our brows
      That we one jot of former love retain.

(B)   Now, if thou would'st, when all have given
      him over,
      From death to life thou might'st him yet
      recover!

(C)   Now at the last gasp of Love's latest
      breath,
      When his pulse failing, Passion speechless
      lies,
      When Faith is kneeling by his bed of death,
      And Innocence is closing up his eyes—

(D)   Since there's no help, come let us kiss and
      part.
      Nay, I have done, you get no more of me!
      And I am glad, yea, glad with all my heart,
      That thus so cleanly I myself can free.

11. Which stanza did you   11. A B C D E
    put first?
12. Which stanza did you   12. A B C D E
    put after (A)?
13. Which stanza did you   13. A B C D E
    put after (B)?
14. Which stanza did you   14. A B C D E
    put after (C)?
15. Which stanza did you   15. A B C D E
    put after (D)?

(A)   I walked, with other souls in pain,
      Within another ring.
      And was wondering if the man had done
      A great or little thing.
      When a voice behind me whispered low,
      "That fellow's got to swing."

(B)   He did not wear his scarlet coat,
      For blood and wine are red,
      And blood and wine were on his hands
      When they found him with the dead.
      The poor dead woman whom he loved,
      And murdered in her bed.

(C)   I only knew what hunted thought
      Quickened his step, and why
      He looked upon the garish day
      With such a wistful eye:
      The man had killed the thing he loved,
      And so he had to die.

(D)   He walked amongst the Trial Men
      In a suit of shabby gray:
      A cricket cap was on his head,
      And his step seemed light and gay;
      But I never saw a man who looked
      So wistfully at the day.

16. Which stanza did you   16. A B C D E
    put first?
17. Which stanza did you   17. A B C D E
    put after (A)?
18. Which stanza did you   18. A B C D E
    put after (B)?
19. Which stanza did you   19. A B C D E
    put after (C)?
20. Which stanza did you   20. A B C D E
    put after (D)?

(A)   She's creeping slowly up past Quarantine,
      A shameless, shaggy rover of the sea;
      A commercial vagrant, dirty and serene,
      A salty chevalier of beggary.

(B)   No silken gowns sweep o'er her painted
      boards,
      She comes or goes and no one seems to
      care;
      A little fuel and grub are her rewards,
      She'll leave at any time for anywhere.

(C)   The stuff her better sisters couldn't take,
      Unsavory bits that lost the regular run;
      She fetched 'em 'cross the world for she
      must make
      A little profit when the year is done.

(D)   She'll bluster till her anchor clatters out—
      She'll fidget, yank and grumble with the
      tide;
      Yet she grins a little 'neath her battered
      snout,
      Proud because there's cargo in her hide.

21. Which stanza did you   21. A B C D E
    put first?
22. Which stanza did you   22. A B C D E
    put after (A)?
23. Which stanza did you   23. A B C D E
    put after (B)?
24. Which stanza did you   24. A B C D E
    put after (C)?
25. Which stanza did you   25. A B C D E
    put after (D)?

(A)   How much more praise deserved thy
      beauty's use.
      If thou couldst answer "This fair child of
      mine

Shall sum my count and make my old excuse,''
Proving his beauty by succession thine!
(B) When forty winters shall besiege thy brow
And dig deep trenches in thy beauty's field,
Thy youth's proud livery, so gazed on now,
Will be tattered weed, of small worth held:
(C) This were to be new made when thou art old,
And see thy blood warm when thou feel'st it cold.
(D) Then being asked where all thy beauty lies,
Where all the treasure of thy lusty days,
To say, within thine own deep-sunken eyes,
Were an ill-eating shame and thriftless praise.

26. Which stanza did you put first?   26. A B C D E
27. Which stanza did you put after (A)?   27. A B C D E
28. Which stanza did you put after (B)?   28. A B C D E
29. Which stanza did you put after (C)?   29. A B C D E
30. Which stanza did you put after (D)?   30. A B C D E

TEST 3 *Suggested Time: 20 Minutes*
Each of the following selections contains a missing line. Beneath each are four lines that could complete the passage. Only one of the four is entirely satisfactory. The others all have a definite deficiency. By circling the letters provided to the right, for each of the four lines, mark

(A) if the line is acceptable
(B) if the line is not satisfactory because of a defect in rhythm or meter
(C) if the line is not acceptable because of style or tone
(D) if the line is inappropriate in meaning

Life has loveliness to sell,
  Music like a curve of gold,
Scent of pine trees in the rain,
  Eyes that love you, arms that hold,
And for your spirit's still delight,

_____

1. Ships of the air with the speed of light.   1. A B C D

2. Holy thoughts that star the night.   2. A B C D
3. Great thoughts the minds of yore endite.   3. A B C D
4. The best wishes of all your friends in sight.   4. A B C D

Since brass, nor stone, nor earth, nor boundless sea,
But sad mortality o'er sways their power,
How with this rage shall beauty hold a plea,

_____

5. When it is so fragile, like a flower?   5. A B C D
6. When o'er its head the face of hope doth glower?   6. A B C D
7. Whose action is no stronger than a flower?   7. A B C D
8. Who cannot make the game go any slower!   8. A B C D

I walked a mile with Sorrow
  And ne'er a word said she;
But, oh, the things I learned from her

_____

9. When Sorrow walked with me.   9. A B C D
10. As Error rained on me.   10. A B C D
11. Which circumstance should have uncovered for me.   11. A B C D
12. When Sorrow gave to me my misery.   12. A B C D

Because I could not stop for death,
He kindly stopped for me:
The carriage held but just ourselves

_____

13. And none whom I could see.   13. A B C D
14. Proud and private, for all to see.   14. A B C D
15. The cabbie and little old me.   15. A B C D
16. And immortality.   16. A B C D

Not enjoyment, and not sorrow,
  Is our destined end or way;
But to act, that each tomorrow

_____

17. Finds us with enough energy for the day.   17. A B C D
18. Revives to live another day.   18. A B C D
19. Finds us farther than today.   19. A B C D
20. Leadeth thee on thy true way.   20. A B C D

My mind to me a kingdom is,
Such present joys therein I find,

_____

That world affords or grows by kind.
Though much I want which most would
have,
Yet still my mind forbids to crave.

21. You too cannot afford to miss.
                        21. A B C D

22. Content and fed by no bliss.   22. A B C D
23. That it excels all other bliss.   23. A B C D
24. Ah Joys! Beyond all other bliss.
                        24. A B C D

See, the day begins to break,
And the light shoots like a streak
Of subtle fire; the wind blows cold,

_____

25. Whilst the morning doth unfold;
                        25. A B C D

26. And the rising sun doth unfold;
                        26. A B C D

27. It's time to get up and be bold;
                        27. A B C D

28. Rise and shine, ye beggars bold;
                        28. A B C D

There are a number of us creep
Into this world to eat and sleep,
And know no reasons why they're born
But merely to consume the corn,
Devour the cattle, fowl, and fish,

_____

29. And waste away with every wish.
                        29. A B C D

30. Without even having an ambitious wish.
                        30. A B C D

31. No love! No hate! No joy! No wish!
                        31. A B C D

32. And leave behind an empty dish.
                        32. A B C D

TEST 4   *Suggested Time: 20 Minutes*

Each of the following selections contains a missing
line. Beneath each are four lines which could complete the passage. Only one of the four is entirely
satisfactory. The others all have a definite deficiency. By circling the letters provided to the right,
for each of the four lines, mark

  (A) if the line is acceptable
  (B) if the line is not satisfactory because of a de-
fect in rhythm or meter
  (C) if the line is not acceptable because of style
or tone
  (D) if the line is inappropriate in meaning

He clasps the crag with crooked hands;
Close to the sun in lonely lands,
Ringed with the azure world, he stands.
The wrinkled sea beneath him crawls;
He watches from his mountain walls,

_____

1. Swiftly down he swoops; in vain the victim
calls.   1. A B C D
2. And like a thunderbolt he falls.   2. A B C D
3. As night within his shadow falls.
                        3. A B C D
4. O Eagle! Mightiest bird of all! 4. A B C D

   Yes; quaint and curious war is!
   You shoot a fellow down
   You'd treat if met where any bar is,

_____

5. Or help to half a crown.   5. A B C D
6. O Mighty War, with cruelty ever strown!
                        6. A B C D
7. And at him you would never frown.
                        7. A B C D
8. And never throw him out of town.
                        8. A B C D

   The written word
   Should be clean as bone,
   Clear as light,

_____

   Two words are not
   As good as one

9. Sheer in tone.   9. A B C D
10. Like unto brass that shone. 10. A B C D
11. Firm as stone.   11. A B C D
12. Containing sweetness of tone. 12. A B C D

These I have loved:
  White plates and cups, clean-gleaming,
Ringed with blue lines; and feathery, faery dust;
Wet roofs, beneath the lamp-light; the strong crust
Of friendly bread; and many-tasting food;

_____

13. Courage, justice and the kindly work of the
good;   13. A B C D
14. I must not forget to mention old wood;
                      14. A B C D
15. Rainbows; and the blue bitter smoke of wood;
                      15. A B C D
16. Finally, I also enjoy the smell of burning wood;
                      16. A B C D

Death stands above me, whispering low
I know not what into my ear;
Of his strange language all I know

_____

17. I argue vehemently my time is near.
                      17. A B C D
18. 'Tis love alone I've learned to fear.
                      18. A B C D
19. The fee he asks is much too dear.
                      19. A B C D
20. Is, there is not a word of fear.   **20.** A B C D

    I was angry with my friend:
    I told my wrath, my wrath did end.
    I was angry with my foe:

_____

21. I told it not, my wrath did grow.
                      21. A B C D
22. He was nothing but a so and so.
                      22. A B C D
23. In his heart I let it grow.   **23.** A B C D
24. Silent, fearful, I let it grow.   **24.** A B C D

    I made you many and many a song
      Yet never once told all you are—
    It was as though a net of words

_____

25. Tried real hard to catch a star.
                      25. A B C D
26. Flexed up to catch a star.   **26.** A B C D
27. Were flung to catch a star.   **27.** A B C D
28. Far flung tried in vain to catch a star.
                      28. A B C D

    No longer mourn for me when I am dead
    Then you shall hear the surly sullen bell

_____

    From this vile world, with vilest worms to dwell.

29. The church bell shrill to all that I am fled.
                      29. A B C D
30. Give warning to the world that I am fled.
                      30. A B C D
31. With glee so gay announce that I am fled.
                      31. A B C D
32. In the light of the day that I am fled.
                      32. A B C D

TEST 5 *Suggested Time: 20 Minutes*
Each of the following selections contains a missing line. Beneath each are four lines which could complete the passage. Only one of the four is entirely satisfactory. The others all have a definite deficiency.

By circling the letters provided to the right, for each of the four lines, mark

(A) if the line is acceptable
(B) if the line is not satisfactory because of a defect in rhythm or meter
(C) if the line is not acceptable because of style or tone
(D) if the line is inappropriate in meaning

    Mock on, mock on, Voltaire, Rousseau:
    Mock on, mock on: 'tis all in vain!
    You throw the sand against the wind,

_____

1. And back it flies to you with power amain.
                      1. A B C D
2. And the wind wafts it back again.
                      2. A B C D
3. And the wind blows it back again.
                      3. A B C D
4. Once more its full force to regain.
                      4. A B C D

    I traveled among unknown men,
      In lands beyond the sea;
    Nor, England! did I know till then

_____

5. The affinity you had for me.   **5.** A B C D
6. The depths of every lea.   **6.** A B C D
7. Fully your significant worth to me.
                      7. A B C D
8. What love I bore to thee.   **8.** A B C D

    I strove with none, for none was worth my strife.
    Nature I loved and next to Nature, Art:

_____

    It sinks, and I am ready to depart.

9. I warmed both hands before the fire of life;
                      9. A B C D
10. Fired with struggle and woe, the beacon of my life;   **10.** A B C D
11. Unto each and every one comes the fire of life;
                    11. A B C D
12. Cursed ones! Now see the fire of my life;
                    12. A B C D

    I could think in the withered grass
    Spring's budding wreaths we might discern;
    The violet's eye might shyly flash

_____

13. And wintry ice to come be seen.

              13. A B C D

14. And young leaves shoot among the fern.

              14. A B C D

15. And green chlorophyl among the fern.

              15. A B C D

16. Renewal and a rebirth in this Spring's return.

              16. A B C D

       I dare not ask a kiss,
        I dare not beg a smile,
      Lest having that or this,

_____

17. I could then be developing a new style.

              17. A B C D

18. The worms with death could then revile.

              18. A B C D

19. I might grow proud the while.   19. A B C D

20. Thou couldst me then revile.   20. A B C D

  Sound, sound the clarion, fill the fife!
    To all the sensual world proclaim,

_____

    Is worth an age without a name.

21. A day or an hour devoted to glorious life.

              21. A B C D

22. One glorious hour without my wife.

              22. A B C D

23. Years devoid of unwonted strife.

              23. A B C D

24. One crowded hour of glorious life.

              24. A B C D

    Come, read to me some poem
      Some simple and heartfelt lay,
    That shall soothe this restless feeling,

_____

25. And toss right out the fears of day.

              25. A B C D

26. And banish the thoughts of day.

              26. A B C D

27. And leave me with nothing to say.

              27. A B C D

28. And turn my labor into light play.

              28. A B C D

  O world, thou choosest not the better part!
  It is not wisdom to be only wise,
  And on the inward vision close the eyes,

_____

29. But it is wisdom to believe the heart.

              29. A B C D

30. And never let that inner motor start.

              30. A B C D

31. But it is best to settle in the heart.

              31. A B C D

32. To your ideals and humanity's cries.

              32. A B C D

ANSWER KEY: ADDITIONAL MASTERY TESTS

TEST 1

1. (D)	9. (D)	17. (D)	25. (B)
2. (B)	10. (A)	18. (C)	26. (D)
3. (A)	11. (B)	19. (A)	27. (A)
4. (C)	12. (C)	20. (B)	28. (C)
5. (D)	13. (B)	21. (A)	29. (A)
6. (A)	14. (D)	22. (D)	30. (D)
7. (B)	15. (C)	23. (B)	31. (C)
8. (C)	16. (A)	24. (C)	32. (B)

TEST 3

1. (D)	9. (A)	17. (B)	25. (A)
2. (A)	10. (D)	18. (D)	26. (D)
3. (C)	11. (B)	19. (A)	27. (B)
4. (B)	12. (C)	20. (C)	28. (C)
5. (B)	13. (D)	21. (D)	29. (D)
6. (D)	14. (B)	22. (B)	30. (B)
7. (A)	15. (C)	23. (A)	31. (C)
8. (C)	16. (A)	24. (C)	32. (A)

TEST 2

1. (D)	9. (E)	17. (C)	25. (C)
2. (C)	10. (A)	18. (D)	26. (B)
3. (A)	11. (D)	19. (E)	27. (C)
4. (E)	12. (C)	20. (A)	28. (D)
5. (B)	13. (E)	21. (A)	29. (E)
6. (B)	14. (B)	22. (D)	30. (A)
7. (C)	15. (A)	23. (E)	
8. (D)	16. (B)	24. (B)	

TEST 4

1. (B)	9. (D)	17. (B)	25. (C)
2. (A)	10. (C)	18. (D)	26. (D)
3. (D)	11. (A)	19. (C)	27. (A)
4. (C)	12. (B)	20. (A)	28. (B)
5. (A)	13. (D)	21. (A)	29. (C)
6. (C)	14. (C)	22. (C)	30. (A)
7. (B)	15. (A)	23. (D)	31. (D)
8. (D)	16. (B)	24. (B)	32. (B)

TEST 5

1. (B)	9. (A)	17. (B)	25. (C)
2. (C)	10. (D)	18. (D)	26. (A)
3. (A)	11. (B)	19. (A)	27. (D)
4. (D)	12. (C)	20. (C)	28. (B)
5. (C)	13. (D)	21. (B)	29. (A)
6. (D)	14. (A)	22. (D)	30. (C)
7. (B)	15. (C)	23. (C)	31. (D)
8. (A)	16. (B)	24. (A)	32. (B)

4. Terms of Literary Analysis

An understanding of the concepts of the literary terms in the following glossary will enable you to better interpret the prose passages in the Literature test. Use the glossary for both study and reference.

GLOSSARY

abstract idea A general statement about a quality or state, about a class of persons, objects, ideas. It is opposed to a specific fact or concrete statement.

> abstract: Wealth corrupts the soul.
> concrete: I read *Tom Jones*.

abstract noun Refers to a quality or state. It is opposed to a concrete noun that refers to a specific object or person.

> abstract nouns: *love, honor, courtesy*
> concrete nouns: *house, dog, person*

adage A proverb, or familiar wise saying.

> Early to bed, early to rise
> Makes a man healthy, wealthy
> And wise.

allegory A literary form in which some or all of the characters are embodiments of abstract ideas. It is a story which carries a second meaning along with its surface story. Bunyan's *Pilgrim's Progress*.

alliteration Repetition of the initial sound in words. This device, while effective in poetry and polyphonic prose can be obtrusive in ordinary writing.
> To sit in solemn silence

allusion A casual reference to some character, person, fact, idea, or event. The reader is expected to see the application of the allusion to the thought being expressed.

> He sees himself as another confident Hercules assigned to clean out the rubbish of the centuries.

ambiguity When used as a derogatory term, refers to the lack of clarity that beclouds meaning when more than one interpretation is highly possible.

> He didn't know, she said, he was to go.
> (Who commanded him to go?)

Ambiguity may also be used to describe the richness in poetry that "gives room for alternative reactions to the same piece of poetry." William Epsom referred with praise to the seven types of this kind of ambiguity.

anachronism A device describing something placed in an inappropriate period of time. It may be an unintentional error, or it may be used deliberately for effect.

> Daniel Boone leveled his tommy gun at the mass of attacking renegades.

analogy A comparison of two things alike in certain aspects.

Analogies are always dangerous because we tend to assume that since two people or things are similar in one or more respects, they should necessarily be similar in others.

> Since we both come from the same hometown, we should have similar ambitions.

anecdote A brief, pointed, or humorous story sometimes included in a larger whole. It lacks the complicated plot of a short story. It is an effective device for beginning a speech or driving home a realization.

antagonist   The main character opposed to the author's principal character.

The antagonist need not be a villain. In a story dealing with Satan, the protecting angel could be the antagonist.

anthology   A collection of prose or poetry selections. Many of the textbooks used in English courses in literature are anthologies.

anticlimax   The arrangement of details in such an order that the unimportant suddenly appears at the point where the critical or serious detail should be found. Anticlimax is a flaw in a story in which the hero has an unpredicted allergy attack just when he is to lead his troops into battle. It can be an effective device in humorous material.

We talked boldly of daring raids to come on the enemy supply lines. We boasted of bloody deeds we would accomplish; and fell asleep over the emptied glasses of beer.

antithesis   A rhetorical device in which contrasted words, clauses, or ideas are balanced.

Love and hate, desire and fulfillment gave his life purpose and robbed him of peace of mind.

Antithesis must be used sparingly; too many sentences containing this dramatic approach gives the material a heavy, artificial tone.

antonomasia   The use of a proper noun as a common name. It is a type of allusion in which the reader must see the relationship between the person referred to and the present subject.

Beware of him! He is another Hitler!

aphorism   A short, pithy statement of a principle or precept.

Life is short; art is long.

apostrophe   A rhetorical device in which the author addresses a personified abstraction or a person not present.

Poverty, touch not his hopes!

This device is restricted in its use in prose because of the intensity it generates.

archaism   A word or phrase no longer used in actual speech.

quoth   eftsoon   methinks

This is a facile, often too facile, device for dating a speech or work.

argument   Refers, as a literary term, to the summary of the plot placed at the beginning of a section or chapter. *Paradise Lost* contains an argument summarizing the main lines of action at the beginning of each Book.

assonance   The similarity in sound of vowels following different consonants, usually in stressed syllables.

Like a diamond in the sky

With rhymes, the consonants following the vowel must be the same: *fat, bat*.

In assonance the consonants are different: *fact, bad*. Assonance is a device that can effectively lead to euphony (pleasant-sounding word combinations) if used sparingly in prose.

atmosphere   The tone and mood established by the totality of a literary work. The atmosphere of a comedy is light while that of a tragedy tends to be somber.

autobiography   A literary work in which the author describes major events in his past. A *diary* emphasizes inner rather than outward manifestations. *Memoirs* stress reactions, impressions, people met. A *journal* is more private and more episodic.

balanced sentence   A sentence in which words, phrases, or clauses are set off against each other in position so as to emphasize contrast or similarity in meaning.

You may eat to live, but he lives to eat.

The balanced sentence is not favored in present-day writing because the cleverness of the writing tends to obscure the meaning behind the words.

bathos   Another term for anticlimax, a sudden descent from the ladder leading to greater significance, a going from the sublime to the ridiculous, from the heights of the important to the level of trivia. Bathos can be evidenced in action or words.

Advance the fringed curtains of thy eyes
And tell me what comes yonder.

bibliography   A list of books, articles, publications on a particular subject. Scholarly works follow formalized procedures in handling bibliographies.

biography   The account of the life of a person.

blurb   A description of the contents of a book, included on its cover or dust jacket to entice prospective purchasers.

bombast   Grandiloquent, ranting, insincere, extravagant language.

From the depths of sincerity and honesty, we decry, with all the emphatic force at our command, the scurrilous, unfounded accusations brought forth as so obvious an attempt to obfuscate the truth in our just and modest claims.

Bombast is a derogatory term, describing an emotionalized letting go of all controls in writing.

brevity   A complimentary term implying the use of only those words needed to express an idea—and no more. Brevity is essential to forceful expression. In the telegraphic style found in some headlines and in the dialogue of popular television detective tales, brevity has been carried too far: "Saw the oncoming car. Tried to swerve. Went into skid. Three occupants of other car died. Horribly." Such stylizing is not acceptable in general writing.

burlesque   The type of humorous writing which satirizes and imitates a literary convention, style, or attitude. *Don Quixote* was written as a burlesque of the medieval romance so popular in Cervantes' Spain.

cacophony   Harsh combinations of sound.

blue spurt of a lighted match

The experienced writer may use cacophony as a device to emphasize action related to his dialogue, but in expository writing, he will avoid having the sound of his words interfere with the flow of meaning. Cacophony is the opposite of *euphony*.

caricature   A character or action exaggerated for satiric or humorous effect. A limited number of personal qualities is usually selected for such an exaggeration.

circumlocution   A roundabout expression, one that avoids a direct label.

"He is a man who avoids telling or revealing in direct terms any item that may put him in a bad light, despite the needs of the listener!"

"Simply then, he's a liar!"

clarity   "Absolute accordance of expression to idea." To achieve clarity, the accurate word should be specific and concrete.

classic   (1) A literary work which has achieved a recognized position for its superior qualities: Shakespeare's *Hamlet*.
(2) A literary work that helped set the pattern in a previous period and therefore has historical importance: Eliot's *Silas Marner*.

cliché   An expression which the author or reader feels has been so overused that it has lost its forcefulness.

as smart as a whip   as quiet as mice

Note that the cliché label may be in the mind of the reader or the writer. What may be a cliché to one may be new and exciting to the other!

climax   (1) An arrangement in which the chief point of interest is reached at the end.
(2) The moment in the plot at which a crisis reaches its highest intensity and is resolved. Narrative and expository material benefit from being planned toward reaching a climax.

coherence   A work has coherence when the relationship of one part to another is clear and intelligible. Words, phrases, clauses, sentences, paragraphs, and chapters are the units which show coherence through progressive and logical arrangement. Illogical arrangement results in lack of coherence.

colloquial   The level of speech in everyday conversation. Words and expressions must be appropriate to the level of the material. Expressions labeled as belonging to the colloquial level are avoided in Standard and Formal Levels of writing. Since the level of usage planned for the Achievement Tests is the Standard, the colloquial level can be marked wrong even though it is acceptable in everyday conversation.

comedy   *a.* An amusing presentation usually with a happy ending   *b.* any literary work with a happy ending   *c.* any literary work dealing with satire or humor. Note that humor is not essential under definition (*b*).

comic relief   A humorous scene inserted in a serious or tragic work to relieve tension and so heighten the tragic emotion by contrast. The porter scene in *Macbeth*, following the slaying of the king, is the classic example of comic relief at its most effective level.

conceit   A complex or far-fetched comparison.

> Her eyes are suns that blind

Because of the time such comparisons take for analysis, they had long fallen into disrepute. However, many modern writers attempting to reach the complexities of present-day living have revived the conceit. When the comparison is startling and appropriate, the effect is commendable; when the comparison confuses the reader or leads to too great an overrefinement, then it is worthy of condemnation.

concrete noun   Stresses the tangible, that which can be seen, heard, felt. It is close to the specific, the particular. The concrete has actual existence and can be experienced: The stone before me is *concrete*. Concrete terms are the converse of abstract nouns: *Honesty* is an abstract term. Effective writing tends to be concrete. Vague, unclear writing tends toward the abstract.

confidant   A character to whom another reveals his most intimate feelings and intentions. *Confidante* is the feminine form. Hamlet's trusted friend, Horatio, was his *confidant*.

conflict   The struggle which grows out of the interplay of opposing forces in a plot.

connotation   The implications or suggestions evoked by a word. *Connotation* is distinguished from *denotation*, which refers to the objective values only. Scientific writing stresses denotative values. The scientist avoids using terms that have differing connotations for his readers. The literary artist uses connotation to add emotionality.

convention   Any generally accepted literary device or form. The soliloquy in which a character ex-

presses his innermost thoughts and feelings to the audience was an Elizabethan convention.

denotation   A word's most literal and limited meaning, the person, thing, or idea to which a word refers exclusive of attitudes or feelings which the writer or speaker may have. The denotation of *cow* is its dictionary definition of the mature female of cattle. When *cow* is used to describe a human being, then the connotative values of the word are being used. The propagandist specializes in milking a word of its full connotation: *coward, national pride, one hundred percent patriot!*

denouement   The events following the final climax of a story, the final unraveling and setting straight, the solution of the mystery, the explanation of all misunderstandings.

deus ex machina   Coming from the Latin, means literally *god from the machine*. In Greek drama, one of the conventions allowed a god to be lowered onto the stage to rescue one of the characters. The term today is a derogatory one, referring to any artificial device for resolving difficulties. Serious writers avoid such a device since the resolution of difficulties should grow from the action itself. The story line is weakened and the reader's credulity is strained when an unexpected and improbable happening is employed to make things turn out "right."

diction   The choice and arrangement of words. The kind of diction used must be appropriate to the literary form, the subject, and the style of the period. Formal diction is inappropriate in a play set in a crude farm or in a city slum. . . . Slang and regional expressions are inappropriate when interspersed in writing that calls for standard or formal usage.

didactic   A label applied to a literary work when its principal aim is to give guidance in moral, ethical, or religious matters. Didactic is a neutral term when applied by those who accept teaching as the purpose of the material. Didactic becomes a derogatory term when the reader feels that the writer overemphasizes moral values and distorts events to achieve these aims.

digression   Unrelated material inserted in a discussion. It is a violation of unity in formal essays. It is a standard device in the personal essay. It is that which puts an audience to sleep in college lectures and lowers grades on themes.

dramatic irony   When the words or acts of a character carry a meaning unperceived by him but understood by the audience or reader. The irony lies in the contrast between the speaker's intended meaning and the realization of the others: the character who unknown to himself is dying makes elaborate plans for his future with his bride-to-have-been.

dynamic character   One who changes as the result of the plot action. Usually the protagonist is dynamic, and his growth and development as a reaction to circumstance create the central interest in the story line. Macbeth and Lady Macbeth are dynamic in that they change. Dynamic characters are contrasted with static, stereotyped characters who remain dominated by a single quality throughout the story. The television detective who remains unchanged in his approach to the challenges of his job is static.

economy of expression   A term of praise, implying the use of the minimum number of words necessary for clarity and emphasis.

empathy   The feeling of identity that a reader has when he becomes so involved with a character in a play or novel that he experiences the emotionality that he thinks the character is going through. With *sympathy* we feel for the other; with *empathy* we feel as we think the other feels.

emphasis   The planning of elements so that the important items, ideas, facts, personalities are stressed.

epigram   A witty, pointed, terse saying

"Life consists of sobs, sniffles, and smiles, with sniffles predominating."

epilogue   (1) A concluding statement at the end of a speech or play.
(2) An appendix added after the conclusion of a play or story. An epilogue may be the conclusion of a speech, the final remarks of an actor addressed to the audience, or a scene added after the main action of a drama has ended. An epilogue is the opposite of a prologue.

epithet   A word or group of words used to characterize a person.

Jude *the Obscure*   Harold *the Brave*   *wily* Ulysses

essay   A short prose work stressing the author's opinion on one topic. The personal essay stresses revelation of personal reactions. The formal essay develops an idea or expresses a point of view.

euphemism   A rhetorical device for conveying a harsh or unpleasant concept pleasantly or gently.

pass away in place of *die*

euphony   The juxtaposition of words and sounds that blend together pleasantly. Writers use assonance, phrase rhythms, and alliteration as the principal rhetorical devices to achieve euphony. When used to excess, such devices can result in bombast or a tone of insincerity.

exposition   The type of writing in which explanations are stressed. Narrative writing tells a story; descriptive writing has as its purpose description of a scene, person, or process; in argumentation, the writer either attacks or defends a point of view. Expository writing tells how something is done or how something works.

fable   (1) A short moral tale usually having animals as its characters: the stories of Aesop, La Fontaine.
(2) A story or anecdote that is labeled as untrue.

farce   A humorous play depending on exaggerated, improbable situations. The humor is based on horseplay, coarse wit, gross incongruities: the typical Three Stooges' television movie.

fiction   A narrative writing based on the author's free use of experience and imagination rather than on history or fact. Novels and short stories are examples of fiction.

figurative language   Writing that includes one or more of the various figures of speech: simile, metaphor, apostrophe. The literal meaning of the words is avoided in favor of the connotative values. Figurative language is the basis of poetry; overuse of this type of writing makes prose vague and difficult to understand.

figures of speech Those forms of expression that are different from the ordinary modes in order to emphasize or make the meaning more effective. (See Devices of Poetry on page 221.) These devices are most effective when used sparingly in prose; otherwise the reader's attention is caught by the device rather than the meaning.

flashback A device whereby the reader or audience views scenes or incidents that occurred prior to the opening scene: A man is walking toward the gallows. The next scene is a flashback to his childhood and the action that led to his present plight.

foreshadowing A device in which the author drops hints or prepares the reader for an event that will come later.

formal essay An essay written to explain an idea or to persuade the reader to adapt a point of view. It is serious, dignified, logically organized.

fustian Bombastic or pompously ornate language.

The heavens will cease holding a protective canopy over our earthly endeavors ere I consent to being associated in such unspeakable knavery!

genre A literary type classified by form and technique: domestic novel, formal essay, etc.

generalization A statement that applies to a group or a series. It is opposed to a fact which deals with one instance. Writers must beware of the emptiness that results from the overuse of generalizations. The more a generalization is restricted by qualifications, the more effective it becomes: *All generalizations are false, including this one* is the generalization that I accept as valid.

hero (heroine) One capable of brave, courageous deeds. Because *hero* has connotations that confuse, the preferred term for the main character in a story is protagonist. In a tale in which the main character is villainous, *protagonist* is more appropriate than *hero* as the labeling term.

historic present The present tense used to describe past events. In some narratives, the writer will switch from the past tense to the present when attempting to dramatize a scene. This device is not in favor among modern writers.

homily A literary term used to describe a work which lectures its readers and urges them to adhere to high moral standards: a typical Sunday sermon.

hyperbole A rhetorical term for conscious exaggeration.

There were millions of people packed into that subway train!

interior monologue A recording of the thoughts and emotional experiencings of a character on one or more levels of consciousness. It is the technique employed by James Joyce in *Ulysses*. In a *soliloquy,* the revelations are limited to one level of consciousness, to one thought process.

inversion A rhetorical device used for emphasis, consisting of the transposing of words out of their usual order.

A man filled with fears and doubts I saw.

irony The expression of the opposite of what is intended.

You are truly kind to me!

Irony is more strained and less bitter than sarcasm, its close relative.

irrelevant The label attached to material that does not continue the development of a thread of thought or action, something added which begins another idea. Irrelevant material or irrelevant details cause a significant lowering of grades in college themes.

journalese The term used to characterize the style patterns of the headlines and sports columnists of the daily press—clipped sentences, neologisms, slang, euphemisms. Most of the news items of today, copied from the releases of the press agencies, are written in Standard English.

King's English The term used for an expression that is fully accepted on the Standard Written English level of usage.

levels of usage The speech, pronunciation, diction, and structure of the language as a means of communication with differing groups and differing purposes. The levels of usage are similar to the levels of diction:

(1) *Formal* The level employed in doctoral theses, presidential messages, state documents, international communications, textbooks.

(2) *Standard* The level expected in newspaper editorials, student writing, television discussions, lectures. It is the level tested for in the College Board Achievement Tests.

(3) *Colloquial* The level of informal conversations, telephone discussions.

(4) *Nonstandard* The level of usage limited to regional groups and slang. Such usage is correct—in its appropriate place, but not on college and college entrance themes.

literal Accurate to the letter. A *literal* translation is one that follows the exact meaning of the original. A *literal* interpretation avoids figurative connotations. *Rosy* cheeks taken literally creates a frightening image!

litotes The denial of the opposite to achieve intensity and emphasis. Litotes is a form of understatement: She is *not stupid*. This answer is *not wrong*.

loose sentence A sentence in which the ideas follow their logical order, subject followed by predicate, main clause followed by adverbial clauses. It is the basic pattern in conversation and informal writing.

He reconstructed the fallen building block by block with infinite patience and with a complete disregard of time and cost.

malapropism An error in diction caused by the substitution of one word for another similar in sound but different in meaning.

I would by no means wish that a daughter of mine be a *progeny* of learning. (Should be *prodigy*)

Malaproprisms result from the misuse of big words intended to impress.

maxim A short, concise statement based on experience and giving some practical advice.

If you cannot beat them, join them!

Maxims are often used as the topic sentence or summary sentence in expository writing.

melodrama A play based on a sensational, romantic plot with emphasis on emotional jolts for the audience. The typical melodrama has a happy ending achieved over a course of improbable events in which the good are rewarded and the wicked ones punished. Soap operas and typical television drama are prime examples of this genre.

mise-en-scène The stage setting of a play: scenery, costumes, properties of a theatrical production.

mood The tone of a literary work: *thoughtful, light, somber*.

negative criticism Fault-finding without the presentation of steps for correction.

nonfiction Literature based on actual occurrences, on facts. It is the term associated with histories, biographies, textbooks.

nonstandard The level of slang, dialectal variations, regionalisms. College students are supposed to be able to recognize this level and avoid mingling it with the standard use and diction required for work in required and elective courses.

novel A long story, extended fictional prose narrative. It is a representation of life in fictional narrative.

omniscient author An author who shifts from the objective exterior world into the subjective interior world of a number of characters. He feels free to comment at any time on the significance of events or reactions.

oxymoron The figure of speech describing seemingly contradictory terms used to create a paradox: *sad optimist, hardworking idler, conspicuous by his absence*.

parable A short, simple story containing a moral lesson. The parable of the Prodigal Son is one of the best known examples of this genre.

paradox A seemingly contradictory or absurd statement which may actually contain a basic truth. It is a rhetorical device used for emphasis.

"We need a man who can climb to the top and remain on the level."

parallelism The balancing of similar items: word against word, clause against clause, sentence against sentence. It is the device that leads to balanced sentences.

It is not what he has, or even what he does which expresses the worth of a man, but what he is.

Parallelism is another effective device for achieving sentence variety and for increasing the intensity of audience reaction. However, this one too must be used sparingly; its overuse leads to cluttering and rhetoric, airy thoughts without substance.

paraphrase A restatement in different words. The paraphrase, unlike a précis or summary, may be as long as the original.

parody A satirical imitation of a poem or other writing. The devices employed by Poe in his poems are so theatrical that his style has led to the many parodies that have been published in imitation of his most famous works.

pathetic fallacy A projection in which human characteristics are attributed to inanimate objects.

The heavens weep with you in your sorrow.

pedantry A derogatory term used to label a display of learning for its own sake. It is applied to a style in which the author uses an excess of sequipedalianisms, quotations, foreign phrases, allusions, name-dropping.

periodic sentence A sentence in which the meaning is suspended until the end of the sentence, in which the main clause appears last.

By not arriving on time and by deliberately misinterpreting the directive, thus revealing his rejection of our suggestion, Harold brought our plan to a halt.

The periodic sentence when used exclusively gives a heavy tone to writing. It is best employed when interspersed among loose sentences to gain variety.

personal essay A prose work in which the author expresses an intimate reaction or indulges in self-revelation. The theme in which you reminisce about the advantages that have accrued to you from being the only child is a *personal essay*; when you seriously and objectively write about the main advantages and disadvantages in being an only child, then it becomes a *formal essay*.

personification The device in which inanimate objects and abstraction are referred to as having life or personality.

Good Fortune, come and be my companion, if only for a brief interlude!

Personification has fallen into disfavor in modern prose writing.

platitude An overused generalization uttered as though it were fresh and original. Polonius' advice to Laertes is the classic example: *Neither a borrower nor lender be*.

pleonasm The label applied when more words than necessary are used to convey an idea: *write* it *down, spell* the word *out, walk on foot, hear* it *with my own ears.*

poetic justice The good are rewarded and the evil punished. Poetic justice becomes a derogatory term when the author applies its principles with a heavy brush to the action in a plot.

poetic license The privilege claimed by authors to depart from the expected—normal order, diction, rhyme, pronunciation, grammar.

positive criticism Fault-finding, but with remedies being suggested. In the rational world of colleges, student themes must contain positive criticism to achieve maximum grades in most instances.

précis A summary or abstract. A précis usually contains less than half the number of words found in the original.

prologue A preface or introduction, usually to a play.

prose All forms of written and oral communication that lacks the regular rhythmic pattern of verse. It consists of connected ideas, not listings.

prose rhythms A constant flow of accent that is not recurrent in a regular pattern as in verse. Prose rhythm is an element of style.

protagonist The main character around whom the plot evolves. The protagonist is not necessarily a *hero* or *villain*. He may be the thief or the protecting officer of the law, depending upon the emphasis of the author.

provincial   Narrow in point of view or approach. A derogatory term when applied to a writer who sees universal problems only in terms of himself and his immediate surroundings.

pseudonym   A fictitious name assumed by a writer: *Mark Twain* (Samuel Clemens).

purple patch (passage)   A selection in which the author seems to overstrain for effect, relying heavily on rhetorical devices and emotional tones. A purple patch is usually more rhythmic than most prose. It contains a strongly emotional tone marked by figures of speech and poetic diction. *Purple patch* is a derogatory term when used in modern criticism.

redundancy   Needless repetition: repeat it *again*; descend *down*.

relevant   Appropriate; on the topic; fitting. Relevant material and relevant arguments are effective additions to a theme.

rhetorical figure   A specific arrangement of words for emphasis: *inversions, rhetorical question, apostrophes*. Rhetorical figures do not alter the meaning of the words employed as do figures of speech (similes, metaphors).

rhetorical question   A question that is asked, not to elicit information, but to achieve a stylistic effect. It is often used by a speaker to add dramatic emphasis at the beginning of a thought unit.

Why don't our opponents accept our challenge? Let me tell you why! . . .

sarcasm   A statement of the opposite of what is meant, a bitter, derisive statement of disapproval.

I am so glad to see that you are well enough to interfere with my plans!

Sarcasm is caustic, intended to hurt.

satire   A type of writing which ridicules or denounces human vices and frailties. Horatian satire stresses a sophisticated, amused comment on vice or folly. Juvenalian satire is bitter, vehement, unamused in its denunciation.

setting   The time and place in which the action of the plot occurs.

slang   A nonstandard level of diction and usage. Slang consists of newly coined words and phrases and familiar words and phrases with meanings that have not been accepted on the colloquial or standard levels.

Cool it!   It's *a gas!*   He's *hip*.

slapstick   Comedy characterized by physical action such as throwing pies or falling into the swimming pool in formal clothing.

stereotype   The expected, the customary, a generalized pattern applied in a specific instance. A *stereotyped character* or *stereotype* is a stock character—the hard-boiled detective, the sweet, self-sacrificing, and graying pre-Freudian mother. A *stereotyped solution* is one that is found in most stories in a specific pattern. A *stereotyped plot* is one that contains no surprises for the audience. A *stereotyped idea* is a facile generalization. *Stereotype* and *stereotyped* are usually terms of derogation.

static character   A character centering about a single quality; one that does not grow or change during the action of the plot. Such characters usually surround the more complex, dynamic characters around whom the plot evolves. Hamlet is dynamic; Polonius is static.

stock character   Stereotype that appears regularly in certain literary forms: the drunkard, the villain, the hero, and the heroine of the "cowboy stories," the private eye of most detective tales.

stock situation   A frequently recurring incident or series of incidents found in the plot in a specific genre. Pick any incident or series of incidents in the typical "western" as your example.

style   (1) The verbal pattern that characterizes a writer or writings.

Carl Sandburg's style is easily imitated.

(2) Excellence

He has style!

subjective   Personal, limited to one person's standards, reactions, feelings, impressions, evaluations. *Subjective* is opposed to *objective*, which stresses external, verifiable by others, followed accepted standards. The personal essay is subjective; the formal essay tends to be objective.

One's impressions of an experience are subjective; an evaluation of the advantages and disadvantages of city living in statistical terms would be objective. The best college themes give the objective evidence followed by subjective reactions.

suspension The basic device in the periodic sentence in which the meaning is suspended until the end of the sentence.

Block by block, with infinite patience and with complete disregard of time and cost, he reconstructed the fallen building.

synopsis A summary, a condensation of a work. The synopsis should contain fewer words than the original.

tall tale A story of extravagant occurrences told for humorous effects. The element of belief or plausibility is in evidence in only some of the details of the story. The exploits of Paul Bunyan are typical tall tales.

theme (1) Student themes are papers written on one topic. They may center around personal reactions or evaluations of readings.
(2) The theme of a literary work is its central idea.

thesis (1) A formal essay, longer than a theme and resulting from research.
(2) A proposition to be defended or proved formally: The thesis of the author is that intelligence is mainly the result of environmental factors.

tirade A long uninterrupted speech usually condemnatory.

I am so tired of his long *tirades* on how much more responsible youth was in his day.

tone The quality of a work that reflects the mood and the attitude of the writer as expressed in the passage. Some typical adjectives used to describe tone are *formal, ironic, cynical, humble, irreverent, melodramatic, objective*. Some typical nouns: *acceptance, anger, despair, joy, optimism, relief, resignation, reverence, self-pity, sorrow, urgency*.

tragedy (1) An unfortunate occurrence.
(2) A plot that follows the classic or Aristotelian definition: disaster in the life of a ruler brought about inevitably as a result of a flaw in his character.
(3) A plot that follows the contemporary definition: an important series of related events in the life of a person significant to the audience, such events leading to an unhappy ending. The protagonist may be the victim of a flaw in his own character, forces in society, or forces in nature. The tone is one of great dignity and seriousness.

tragic flaw The defect in the protagonist which leads to his downfall.

unity Oneness. Each element and each larger part of a work should be about one thing or tend to produce one effect. All the parts should be so related that the work is an organic whole. The introduction of an irrelevant detail destroys unity.

universality The ability of a work to appeal to a wide segment of the reading public, generation after generation.

variety Evasion of monotony in choice of words, structure of sentences, repetition of rhetorical devices, approaches to climaxes. The need for variety can be carried to extreme through the use of doubtful synonyms and inappropriate rhetorical devices.

verisimilitude The quality of reality possessed by plot, episode, setting or character. The reader is willing to accept as representation of truth those elements that possess verisimilitude.

villain An evil character opposing the forces of good found in the hero. The villain, however may be the protagonist, the main character in a story. In *Don Juan*, the main character is the villain of the action.

TEST OF MASTERY

I.   Read each of the following sentences carefully. Then circle the appropriate letter in the answer column. Select

(A) if the sentence contains irony
(B) if the sentence contains a hyperbole
(C) if the sentence contains litotes
(D) if the sentence contains parallelism
(E) if the sentence contains none of these devices

1. Such faith can move mountains.
1. A B C D E

2. To see and hear but not to judge and evaluate are our present goals.
2. A B C D E

3. This decision was not a foolish one.
3. A B C D E

4. So you think you made a wise choice!
4. A B C D E

5. It was a night that I shall long remember.
5. A B C D E

6. Rhetoric is the art of ruling the minds of men.
6. A B C D E

7. Hitch your wagon to a star.
7. A B C D E

8. The spirit is willing, but the flesh is weak.
8. A B C D E

9. The enemy is not stupid!
9. A B C D E

10. The eyes of the tortured were pools filled with the darkness of the Hell fires.
10. A B C D E

II.   Read each of the following passages carefully. Then circle the appropriate letter in the answer column. Select

(A) if what is described is a parody
(B) if what is described is a fable
(C) if what is described is a novel
(D) if what is described is a tall tale
(E) if what is described is none of the above

11. Hamlet meets a more sophisticated Ophelia, who breaks down his guard by accusing him of lacking a sense of humor. She convinces him to visit her psychiatrist, who gives him a tranquilizer that cures him of his anxieties.
11. A B C D E

12. The bees decide that the moon is responsible for the lowered production in their hives. Upon consultation with the learned Queen Ant, they learn that if they avoid contact with red clover, they will destroy the moon. The Inner Party, headed by the drones, rejects the suggestion because it is unscientific. The Outer Party then declares war on the others, and an incendiary destroys the hive and all in it.
12. A B C D E

13. In a long rambling story, the author contrasts the growing years of three girls who had attended the same grade school.
13. A B C D E

14. The author reveals how he had felt during the years he had been a member of the President's Cabinet.
14. A B C D E

15. Henry felt that he would like to test some of the basic beliefs in our present society. He thought that he could prove that intelligence was a product of environment only and that it could be improved indefinitely. He decided to experiment with beagles. In order to reach significant results he decided to speed up the rate of learning of his subjects by tripling the speed of life around them. Humans spoke, walked, reacted three times faster than usual when in the laboratory. The beagles were forced to eat and react three times faster than the nonexperimental group.

The results were astounding. The beagles were soon doing problems in elementary algebra and studying the principles of physical anthropology. The experiment came to an unexpected ending when the beagles died of old age at the chronological age of two; the speed-up had caused them to age nine times faster!
15. A B C D E

16. The water droplets and dust particles in the air revolt against the inexorable forces of law that force them into cloud formations.
16. A B C D E

17. A fictitious character recalls the main events that changed him from being a self-centered adolescent into a responsible adult.
17. A B C D E

18. Tired of back-alley shenanigans, a handsome tomcat learns to type and persuades an agent to have his memoirs published. The moral that it pays to reform is stressed in this success story.
18. A B C D E

19. The owner of a racehorse discovers that the racer loves fast music. The faster the music, the greater the speed. A subminiature tape recorder is placed in the horse's ear, and he wins race after race with incredible speed. The scheme comes to an abrupt end when the horse

learns that he can listen to the music—and not run; in fact he seems to derive greater enjoyment by standing still.

                                        19. A B C D E

20. After reading the sonnet "How Do I Love Thee?" a teenage activist is inspired to write a poem addressed to the world, "How Do I Hate Thee? / Let Me Count the Ways."

                                        20. A B C D E

III.   Read each of the following sentences. Then circle the appropriate letter in the answer column. Select

   (A) if the sentence contains alliteration
   (B) if the sentence contains an allusion
   (C) if the sentence contains an analogy
   (D) if the sentence contains an epithet
   (E) if the sentence contains an oxymoron

21. The philanthropist was merciless in his kindness.   **21.** A B C D E

22. The daily drudgery drowned his ambition in its sameness.   **22.** A B C D E

23. The wily politician allowed us to speak at length without committing himself.
                                        23. A B C D E

24. This could so easily be his Waterloo!
                                        24. A B C D E

25. I don't see how you can disagree since I like the plan!   **25.** A B C D E

26. Who can have kind words for a gentle executioner!   **26.** A B C D E

27. I read the report on Alexander the Great.
                                        27. A B C D E

28. His other plan was successful; this one too should succed.   **28.** A B C D E

29. The common man has need for a Roosevelt in this time of crisis!   **29.** A B C D E

30. What swimmer could survive in such wild waters!   **30.** A B C D E

IV.   Read each of the following carefully. Then circle the letter of the pair of words that would best complete each statement.

31. An abstract statement is a general statement. It is opposed to a _____ fact or _____statement.

   (A) vague . . . . specific
   (B) general . . . . indefinite
   (C) specific . . . . concrete
   (D) definite . . . . false

32. A loose sentence is the basic pattern in _____ and _____writing.
   (A) arguments . . . . letter

   (B) debates . . . . informal
   (C) books . . . . informal
   (D) conversation . . . . informal

33. Satire _____human frailties; _____satire stresses sophisticated, amused comment.
   (A) praises . . . . American
   (B) exposes . . . . modern
   (C) ridicules . . . . Horatian
   (D) ridicules . . . . Juvenalian

34. Tragic flaws are _____in the _____which inevitably lead to disaster.
   (A) plants . . . . plot
   (B) devices . . . . action
   (C) defects . . . . protagonist
   (D) characters . . . . story

35. The reader is willing to accept as a representation of _____those elements that possess   _____.
   (A) truth . . . . verisimilitude
   (B) life . . . . vitality
   (C) evil . . . . tragedy
   (D) action . . . . plot

36. A literary form in which all or some of the characters are the embodiment of _____ideas is called a(n) _____.
   (A) novel . . . . novel
   (B) abstract . . . . allegory
   (C) modern . . . . journal
   (D) imaginative . . . . allegory

37. A(n) _____lacks the _____plot of a short story although they resemble each other in other respects.
   (A) anecdote . . . . complicated
   (B) adage . . . . novel
   (C) maxim . . . . involved
   (D) paradox . . . . simple

38. Dramatic irony occurs when the words or acts of a character carry a meaning _____him but _____ the audience.
   (A) clear to . . . . not understood by
   (B) developed by . . . . perceived by
   (C) avoided by . . . . known to
   (D) unperceived by . . . . understood by

39. Economy of expression results from the use of _____number of words necessary for _____.
   (A) necessary . . . . expression
   (B) minimum . . . . clarity
   (C) realistic . . . . emphasis
   (D) given . . . . delivery

40. _____and _____are examples of fiction.
   (A) Biographies . . . . memoirs
   (B) Essays . . . . lyrics
   (C) Short stories . . . . novels
   (D) Novels . . . . essays

41. A sentence in which the ideas follow their _____order is called a _____sentence.
- (A) inverted . . . . loose
- (B) logical . . . . loose
- (C) psychological . . . . periodic
- (D) inverted . . . . dramatic

42. The device in which _____is referred to as having personality is called _____.
- (A) contraction . . . . metonomy
- (B) a person . . . . drama
- (C) an animal . . . . irony
- (D) an abstraction . . . . personification

43. A(n) _____generalization uttered as though it were original is a(n)_____.
- (A) logical . . . . principle
- (B) overused . . . . realization
- (C) trite . . . . cliché
- (D) novel . . . . ideal

44. Criticism becomes _____when _____are suggested.
- (A) negative . . . . remedies
- (B) positive . . . . remedies
- (C) valid . . . . results
- (D) carping . . . . faults

45. The _____character around whom the plot evolves is called the _____.
- (A) static . . . . hero
- (B) dynamic . . . . villain
- (C) minor . . . . prologue
- (D) main . . . . protagonist

46. _____repetition is called _____.
- (A) Unintentional . . . . humor
- (B) Intentional . . . . style
- (C) Needless . . . . redundancy
- (D) Humorous . . . . needless

47. A question for which a(n) _____is not anticipated is a _____question.
- (A) answer . . . . rhetorical
- (B) reaction . . . . double-barreled
- (C) discussion . . . . legal
- (D) reply . . . . dramatic

48. A(n) _____of a work is called a(n) _____.
- (A) interpretation . . . . thesis
- (B) condensation . . . . synopsis
- (C) criticism . . . . précis
- (D) reproduction . . . . essay

49. A _____of prose selections is called a(n) _____.
- (A) criticism . . . . critique
- (B) summary . . . . aphorism
- (C) reproduction . . . . classic
- (D) collection . . . . anthology

50. A(n) _____is a _____description of a book.
- (A) blurb . . . . complimentary
- (B) circumlocution . . . . vague

- (C) confidant . . . . secret
- (D) inversion . . . . critical

V. In the space provided, write T if the statement is true; F if the statement is not true.

_____ **51.** A familiar wise saying is called an allegory.

_____ **52.** A word that is no longer in use is called an archaism.

_____ **53.** The account of a person's life as told by his brother is an autobiography.

_____ **54.** Harsh combinations of sounds are examples of cacophony.

_____ **55.** A caricature is a well-rounded, realistic presentation of a character.

_____ **56.** A cliché is a type of rhetorical question.

_____ **57.** A clown may be used to supply comic relief.

_____ **58.** A conceit is an exaggerated impression of one's own importance.

_____ **59.** Conflict and climax are synonyms.

_____ **60.** Homily and sermon are synonymous terms.

_____ **61.** Similes cannot be taken literally.

_____ **62.** Oxymoron is the denial of the opposite.

_____ **63.** An aphorism is similar to a maxim.

_____ **64.** Scenery is basic to mise-en-scène.

_____ **65.** A paradox contains antithesis.

_____ **66.** Pathetic fallacies are based on parables.

_____ **67.** A paraphrase is closer to a synopsis than to a précis.

_____ **68.** Pleonasm is a type of personification.

_____ **69.** A platitude is closer to a cliché than to an aphorism.

_____ **70.** Both prose and poetry contain rhythms.

_____ **71.** Stock characters are usually dynamic.

_____ **72.** Suspension is the basic device of the loose sentence.

_____ **73.** The protagonist cannot be villainous.

_____ **74.** A tirade is a work of praise.

_____ **75.** Abstractions play important roles in allegories.

VI. Circle the letter of the word or phrase that best completes each of the following statements.

76. When more than one interpretation is possible, the result is _____.
- (A) analogy
- (B) circumlocution
- (C) ambiguity
- (D) conflict

77. The _____is the main character opposed to the author's principal character.
- (A) protagonist

(B) antagonist
(C) villain
(D) setting

78. The author who has Delilah awaken Samson to the ringing of an alarm clock has used the device of _____.
(A) anachronism
(B) oxymoron
(C) digression
(D) epigram

79. Calling another a Solomon is using the device called _____.
(A) aphorism
(B) assonance
(C) antonomasia
(D) confidant

80. An author's choice and arrangement of words reveals his level of _____.
(A) diction
(B) digression
(C) mood
(D) prose

81. A literary work whose principal aim is teach moral values is _____.
(A) figurative
(B) ironic
(C) relevant
(D) didactic

82. The author who interrupts the action of the play to insert a scene of a previous time is employing a(n) _____.
(A) anachronism
(B) flashback
(C) prologue
(D) epilogue

83. The writer who has traveled little and concentrates on describing only what he has actually experienced tends to be _____.
(A) précis
(B) irrelevant
(C) provincial
(D) universal

84. George Eliot is an example of a(n) _____.
(A) pseudonym
(B) inversion
(C) antonomasia
(D) apostrophe

85. *What was good for your father should be good for you* is an example of _____.
(A) an anecdote
(B) an analogy
(C) anticlimax
(D) universality

86. The phrase *to see, to feel, to know, but not to judge, to favor or condemn* is an example of _____.
(A) anticlimax
(B) atmosphere
(C) assonance
(D) antithesis

87. An emotionalized letting go of all controls in writing is called _____.
(A) bombast
(B) bathos
(C) brevity
(D) burlesque

88. *Love* and *patriotism* are examples of _____.
(A) concrete terms
(B) parallelism
(C) abstract terms
(D) comic relief

89. A confidant could not be the _____.
(A) heroine
(B) villain
(C) protagonist
(D) antagonist

90. *Mother, helping hand, understanding attitude* have a pleasant _____ for most people.
(A) denotation
(B) connotation
(C) verisimilitude
(D) analogy

91. The white hat and white horse of the hero in a western tale are accepted _____ of that genre.
(A) digressions
(B) epigrams
(C) epithets
(D) conventions

92. How the hero and heroine will live happily ever after is usually developed in the _____.
(A) prologue
(B) climax
(C) denouement
(D) setting

93. The reader who exclaims, "I know exactly how the main character felt at that moment," has experienced _____.
(A) empathy
(B) exposition
(C) interior monologue
(D) inversion

94. Narrative writing based on imagination rather than fact could *not* be _____.
(A) a novel
(B) a short story
(C) a poem
(D) a biography

95. Fustian is similar to _____.
    (A) exposition
    (B) bombast
    (C) interior monologue
    (D) subjectivity
96. When an author digresses, the material is usu-
    ally labeled as _____.
    (A) irrelevant
    (B) relevant
    (C) journalese
    (D) litotes
97. A malapropism is similar to a(n) _____.
    (A) maxim
    (B) slang expression
    (C) pun
    (D) homily
98. The author who tells a story strictly from the
    point of view of the protagonist's younger
    brother is not _____.
    (A) subjective
    (B) paradoxical

    (C) sarcastic
    (D) omniscient
99. The author who reveals his insecurity by mak-
    ing excessive use of quotations from authori-
    ties is in danger of being labeled _____.
    (A) objective
    (B) provincial
    (C) pedantic
    (D) universal
100. *Pleonasm* is to *redundancy* as *maxim*
    is to _____.
    (A) *precept*
    (B) *short story*
    (C) *essay*
    (D) *homily*
101. Slapstick would not be found during the climax
    of a _____.
    (A) farce
    (B) comedy
    (C) novel
    (D) tragedy

ANSWER KEY: TEST OF MASTERY

I.	II.	III.	IV.	
1. (B)	11. (A)	21. (E)	31. (C)	41. (B)
2. (D)	12. (B)	22. (A)	32. (D)	42. (D)
3. (C)	13. (C)	23. (D)	33. (C)	43. (C)
4. (A)	14. (E)	24. (B)	34. (C)	44. (B)
5. (E)	15. (D)	25. (C)	35. (A)	45. (D)
6. (E)	16. (B)	26. (E)	36. (B)	46. (C)
7. (B)	17. (C)	27. (D)	37. (A)	47. (A)
8. (D)	18. (B)	28. (C)	38. (D)	48. (B)
9. (C)	19. (D)	29. (B)	39. (B)	49. (D)
10. (B)	20. (A)	30. (A)	40. (C)	50. (A)

V.		VI.		
51. (F)	64. (T)	76. (C)	89. (B)	
52. (T)	65. (T)	77. (B)	90. (B)	
53. (F)	66. (F)	78. (A)	91. (D)	
54. (T)	67. (F)	79. (C)	92. (C)	
55. (F)	68. (F)	80. (A)	93. (A)	
56. (F)	69. (T)	81. (D)	94. (D)	
57. (T)	70. (T)	82. (B)	95. (B)	
58. (F)	71. (F)	83. (C)	96. (A)	
59. (F)	72. (F)	84. (A)	97. (C)	
60. (T)	73. (F)	85. (B)	98. (D)	
61. (T)	74. (F)	86. (D)	99. (C)	
62. (F)	75. (T)	87. (A)	100. (A)	
63. (T)		88. (C)	101. (D)	

The Literature Test

Section S I X : Practice Tests in Literature

1. *Four Practice Tests*

2. *Answers to Practice Tests*

To Do Your Best

1. This is a test of your ability to read literary passages. Therefore you should read the passage first; do not endanger your understanding by looking at the questions first.

2. The first reading should be a rapid one. From it you should be able to gather what the general topic is.

3. Your second reading should be sentence by sentence. The test of comprehension at this point is your being able to follow the thought sequence from sentence to sentence. Try to pick out the topic sentence in this process.

4. Remember, you are *not* being marked on how many times you read the selection. Credit is given for the accuracy of your answers. Therefore, reread the passage sentence by sentence again if necessary. And then again!

5. If you still find the passage unyielding, then you can consider going on to the next and then coming back to this one. The time lapse will help; you will be pleased at the way the selection suddenly comes into focus during this second visit.

6. Follow the questions in order. This procedure helps since the answer to one question is often dependent on what had gone before.

7. Do not forget that you are being tested on your ability to do critical reading. Before answering a question on a portion of the passage, reread the section; do not depend on your memory!

8. In questions of content, find your answers in the selection. Do not rely on your previous knowledge. This is a test of reading, not memory.

9. Use the process of elimination to select the answer. Even if you identify the "correct" answer at first glance, eliminate the others, and thus eliminate the possibility of careless acceptance of the second best.

10. You *can* guess. In fact, it is generally to your advantage to guess if you can eliminate one or more of the choices for a question. However, because of the way the tests are scored, guessing randomly is not likely to increase your score.

11. Do not dawdle or worry yourself into tension over a question or selection. If you find it very difficult, then go on to the next. If you have time, then you can return later. The passages and questions are varied; some you will find more difficult than others. The next one may be one that you can answer quickly, and then when you have finished, you can go back.

12. Pace yourself to answer as many questions as possible. However do not feel discouraged if you do not finish before the time is up, or if you have not had time to return to the questions you skipped. The form of the test that you are taking may be one that very few if any students are expected to finish.

13. Read in order!

FIRST THE DIRECTIONS: you have to know what is expected before you can give correct answers!

THEN THE SELECTION: this is a test of reading.

FINALLY, THE QUESTIONS IN ORDER: there is no shortcut!

Time Limit

The test that you will take consists of approximately 60 multiple-choice questions and will be an hour long, with fifteen additional minutes for preparation. The practice tests that follow will enable you to assess the speed with which you can work under examination conditions. However, do not strive for speed at first. Be as thorough and as accurate as you can be without dawdling when you take the initial practice tests; speed will come. It little profits to finish first—with errors of omission and careless haste!

PRACTICE TEST ONE

ANSWER SHEET

1	Ⓐ Ⓑ Ⓒ Ⓓ Ⓔ	21 Ⓐ Ⓑ Ⓒ Ⓓ Ⓔ	41 Ⓐ Ⓑ Ⓒ Ⓓ Ⓔ
2	Ⓐ Ⓑ Ⓒ Ⓓ Ⓔ	22 Ⓐ Ⓑ Ⓒ Ⓓ Ⓔ	42 Ⓐ Ⓑ Ⓒ Ⓓ Ⓔ
3	Ⓐ Ⓑ Ⓒ Ⓓ Ⓔ	23 Ⓐ Ⓑ Ⓒ Ⓓ Ⓔ	43 Ⓐ Ⓑ Ⓒ Ⓓ Ⓔ
4	Ⓐ Ⓑ Ⓒ Ⓓ Ⓔ	24 Ⓐ Ⓑ Ⓒ Ⓓ Ⓔ	44 Ⓐ Ⓑ Ⓒ Ⓓ Ⓔ
5	Ⓐ Ⓑ Ⓒ Ⓓ Ⓔ	25 Ⓐ Ⓑ Ⓒ Ⓓ Ⓔ	45 Ⓐ Ⓑ Ⓒ Ⓓ Ⓔ
6	Ⓐ Ⓑ Ⓒ Ⓓ Ⓔ	26 Ⓐ Ⓑ Ⓒ Ⓓ Ⓔ	46 Ⓐ Ⓑ Ⓒ Ⓓ Ⓔ
7	Ⓐ Ⓑ Ⓒ Ⓓ Ⓔ	27 Ⓐ Ⓑ Ⓒ Ⓓ Ⓔ	47 Ⓐ Ⓑ Ⓒ Ⓓ Ⓔ
8	Ⓐ Ⓑ Ⓒ Ⓓ Ⓔ	28 Ⓐ Ⓑ Ⓒ Ⓓ Ⓔ	48 Ⓐ Ⓑ Ⓒ Ⓓ Ⓔ
9	Ⓐ Ⓑ Ⓒ Ⓓ Ⓔ	29 Ⓐ Ⓑ Ⓒ Ⓓ Ⓔ	49 Ⓐ Ⓑ Ⓒ Ⓓ Ⓔ
10	Ⓐ Ⓑ Ⓒ Ⓓ Ⓔ	30 Ⓐ Ⓑ Ⓒ Ⓓ Ⓔ	50 Ⓐ Ⓑ Ⓒ Ⓓ Ⓔ
11	Ⓐ Ⓑ Ⓒ Ⓓ Ⓔ	31 Ⓐ Ⓑ Ⓒ Ⓓ Ⓔ	51 Ⓐ Ⓑ Ⓒ Ⓓ Ⓔ
12	Ⓐ Ⓑ Ⓒ Ⓓ Ⓔ	32 Ⓐ Ⓑ Ⓒ Ⓓ Ⓔ	52 Ⓐ Ⓑ Ⓒ Ⓓ Ⓔ
13	Ⓐ Ⓑ Ⓒ Ⓓ Ⓔ	33 Ⓐ Ⓑ Ⓒ Ⓓ Ⓔ	53 Ⓐ Ⓑ Ⓒ Ⓓ Ⓔ
14	Ⓐ Ⓑ Ⓒ Ⓓ Ⓔ	34 Ⓐ Ⓑ Ⓒ Ⓓ Ⓔ	54 Ⓐ Ⓑ Ⓒ Ⓓ Ⓔ
15	Ⓐ Ⓑ Ⓒ Ⓓ Ⓔ	35 Ⓐ Ⓑ Ⓒ Ⓓ Ⓔ	55 Ⓐ Ⓑ Ⓒ Ⓓ Ⓔ
16	Ⓐ Ⓑ Ⓒ Ⓓ Ⓔ	36 Ⓐ Ⓑ Ⓒ Ⓓ Ⓔ	56 Ⓐ Ⓑ Ⓒ Ⓓ Ⓔ
17	Ⓐ Ⓑ Ⓒ Ⓓ Ⓔ	37 Ⓐ Ⓑ Ⓒ Ⓓ Ⓔ	57 Ⓐ Ⓑ Ⓒ Ⓓ Ⓔ
18	Ⓐ Ⓑ Ⓒ Ⓓ Ⓔ	38 Ⓐ Ⓑ Ⓒ Ⓓ Ⓔ	58 Ⓐ Ⓑ Ⓒ Ⓓ Ⓔ
19	Ⓐ Ⓑ Ⓒ Ⓓ Ⓔ	39 Ⓐ Ⓑ Ⓒ Ⓓ Ⓔ	59 Ⓐ Ⓑ Ⓒ Ⓓ Ⓔ
20	Ⓐ Ⓑ Ⓒ Ⓓ Ⓔ	40 Ⓐ Ⓑ Ⓒ Ⓓ Ⓔ	60 Ⓐ Ⓑ Ⓒ Ⓓ Ⓔ

PRACTICE TEST ONE

Total Time: One Hour
Time begun .... Time ended .... Time used ....

DIRECTIONS: This test consists of selections from literary works and questions on their content, form, and style. After reading each passage or poem, choose the best answer to each question and blacken the corresponding space on the answer sheet.

NOTE: Pay particular attention to the requirement of questions that contain the words NOT, LEAST, or EXCEPT.

Questions 1–8:   Read the following passage carefully before you choose your answers.

Our eyes can see nothing behind us. A hundred times a day we laugh at ourselves when we laugh at our neighbors; and we detest in others the faults which are much more glaring in
(5) ourselves, and with marvelous impudence and thoughtlessness we express our astonishment at them. Only yesterday I had the opportunity to hear a man, an intelligent and well-mannered person, ridiculing with as much humor as apt-
(10) ness, the fatuity of another who pesters everybody with his pedigrees and his alliances, which are more than half imaginary (for they are most ready to pounce upon this silly subject whose quality is most doubtful and least certain). And
(15) this man, if he had retired within himself, would have seen that he was hardly less extravagant and tedious in publishing and extolling his wife's family prerogatives. Oh, the meddlesome presumption with which the wife sees herself
(20) armed by the hands of her own husband!

As if she were not mad enough already,
You now provoke her to greater madness.
(Terence)

I do not mean that no man should judge unless
(25) he himself be spotless, for then no man could judge; not even if he were free from the same kind of blemish. But I do mean that our judgment, when laying blame on another who is in question, should not save us from self-judg-
(30) ment. It is a charitable office in one who cannot rid himself of a fault to endeavor nonetheless to rid another of it, in whom it may have taken less deep and stubborn root.

1. The first sentence sets the tone of the selection by containing an example of

(A) a clever simile
(B) an intended ambiguity
(C) a dated expression
(D) an unintentional hyperbole
(E) none of the above

2. The examples given in the selection are of

(A) perceptive conversationalists
(B) introverted gossipers
(C) intellectually gifted listeners
(D) politically sensitive socialites
(E) concerned parents

3. The author's thesis is that

(A) husbands are no different from all other men
(B) man is very simple to understand
(C) the faults we find in others are usually our own
(D) man can, when he wants to, be very objective
(E) we are such poor judges of ourselves

4. The "meddlesome presumption" made by the wife results in all of the following EXCEPT

(A) both spouses talking on the same topic
(B) revelation of family trivia
(C) justification of choice of conversational topics
(D) a similarity in point of view
(E) the wife's questioning the husband's conclusions

5. Which of the following best describes the purpose of the quotation in the selection?

(A) It serves to prove the preceding sentence by showing how thoughtless wives can be in their criticizing their husbands.
(B) It serves to prove the second sentence by showing that wives can be provoked into misjudgments by their husbands' laughter.
(C) It serves to prove the truth in the sentence that follows the quotation by proving that only those without fault can judge others.
(D) It is a serious indictment of marriage.
(E) It serves to prove the truth in the preceding sentence that husbands are responsible for the distorted views expressed by their wives.

6. Which of the following best expresses the thought development in the selection?

   (A) The author presented his thesis early in the selection and then proceeded to prove it through logic and example, ending with a final summary that brings the reader back to the major premise.
   (B) Through the use of initial definition of terms and examples, the author leads us to a logical acceptance of his thesis in the final sentences.
   (C) He quickly presented an insight that he wanted to impart to the reader, followed it by examples, and then explored kindred aspects through statements and example.
   (D) He took the general topic of laughter and tried to explain it through example and quotation.
   (E) He took the general topic of self-criticism and then wrote in random fashion on whatever thoughts came to him, in a psychological rather than logical fashion.

7. In the selection, the author does NOT

   (A) present alternative actions for objectionable ones
   (B) include himself as a guilty one
   (C) think that genial laughter is a curative
   (D) expose the self-centered
   (E) pass judgment on others

8. The author's attitude toward the reader is best expressed in which of the following statements?

   (A) In his superior wisdom the author attempts to correct the weaknesses of the reader.
   (B) He accepts the reader as an equal who will stand beside him on the sidelines and laugh at his fellowmen.
   (C) He is a master teacher helping his reader find wisdom before he makes mistakes.
   (D) The social evils of the world will be corrected by the reader if the author can make him aware of these evils.
   (E) He sets high standards for the reader and expects him to reach them for the betterment of society.

Questions 9–18: Read the following selection carefully before you choose your answers.

   Skimming lightly, wheeling still,
       The swallows fly low
   Over the field in clouded days,
       The forest-field of Shiloh—

(5) Over the field where April rain
    Solaced the parched one stretched in pain
        Through the pause of night
        That followed the Sunday fight
        Around the church of Shiloh—
(10) The church so lone, the log-built one,
    That echoed to many a parting groan
            And natural prayer
            Of dying foemen mingled there—
    Foemen at morn, but friends at eve—
(15)   Fame or country least their care:
    (What like a bullet can undeceive!)
        But now they lie low,
    While over them the swallows skim,
        And all is hushed at Shiloh.

9. Which of the following best explains the function of the images in the poem?

   (A) All of the images are generalized except for the church so that becomes the central image of the poem.
   (B) The images pile up one after the other to emphasize the vastness of the silence that covers the countryside.
   (C) Detail after detail is added to each image so that the image carries the thought content of the poem.
   (D) The images are all presented vaguely and simply so that they will not interfere with the message of the poem.
   (E) The images logically connect one with the other, one building on the other to bring into focus the last new image presented in the lines 16–20.

10. The image of the swallow is used to
    (A) show the horrors of war
    (B) emphasize the difference between then and now
    (C) introduce the reader gradually to the poem's message
    (D) give peaceful motion to the horrible scene
    (E) show that nature is always in harmony

11. The line "what like a bullet can undeceive" reveals the author's
    (A) love of humanity
    (B) need for consolation
    (C) attitude toward religion
    (D) attitude toward the issues fought over
    (E) need for recognition

12. Which of the following best expresses the author's purpose?

(A) He used expansion of images to clarify the reader's thinking about man and nature.
(B) He contrasted a series of objective images to show how insignificant man is.
(C) He contrasted image and style in order to intensify the reader's sense of horror.
(D) He blended sights and sounds to intensify the idyllic landscape.
(E) He used peaceful images to lull the reader into an acceptance of his message.

13. The spring rain "solaced" the wounded because it

I. brought them back to consciousness
II. eased their pain
III. satisfied their thirst
(A) I only
(B) II only
(C) III only
(D) II and III
(E) I, II, and III

14. All of the following are mentioned to emphasize contrast or irony EXCEPT

(A) April rain
(B) church of Shiloh
(C) friends at eve
(D) parting groan
(E) hushed at Shiloh

15. Which of the following expresses the theme of this selection?

(A) the beauties of the natural scene
(B) the indestructibility of nature
(C) man's insignificance
(D) the vastness of nature
(E) war is wrong

16. The fact that the fighting took place on Sunday is taken advantage of by the poet

(A) to develop dramatic irony
(B) to enhance the image of the forest-fields
(C) to develop the primitiveness of the church
(D) to set the scene for the battle
(E) to give the men a chance to pray

17. In the first line the poet attempts to

(A) picture war's destructive turmoil
(B) show the mercilessness of war

(C) arouse the sympathy of the reader
(D) horrify the reader
(E) imitate the swallows' flight pattern

18. The author emphasizes the personal tragedy for each of the casualties by

(A) describing the battlefield today
(B) describing the field on a cloudy day
(C) omitting which side won
(D) making the field rain-soaked
(E) omitting the preparation for battle

Questions 19–26: Read the following paragraph carefully before you choose your answers.

If nature be regarded as the teacher and we poor human beings as her pupils, the human race presents a very curious picture. We all sit together at a lecture and possess the necessary
(5) principle for understanding it, yet we always pay more attention to the chatter of our fellow students than to the lecturer's discourse. Or, if our neighbor copies something, we sneak it from him, stealing what he may himself have
(10) heard imperfectly, and add to it our own errors of spelling and opinion.

19. Which of the following best explains the structure of this selection?

(A) Through expansion and example, the author developed his thoughts, leading to his final topic sentence.
(B) He began with a topic sentence and through examples explained it.
(C) He began with his topic sentence and through contrast expanded it.
(D) He presented his thesis and then used logical development to convince the reader.
(E) He began with his thesis and then used the weight of authority and insight to prove it.

20. Which of the following best expresses the author's contention?

(A) We are all poor imitators.
(B) Nature is the best teacher.
(C) Man is a slow learner.
(D) Man is a curious animal.
(E) We should see things for ourselves.

21. The author pictures nature as

(A) the principal of a teaching institution
(B) antagonistic to the needs of humanity

(C) an unappreciated guide
(D) an unwilling teacher
(E) a law-giver

22. The lecturer referred to is

   (A) humanity
   (B) the expert
   (C) our neighbor
   (D) time
   (E) nature

23. This selection can be classified as

   (A) an anecdote
   (B) a moralizing sermon
   (C) a fiction
   (D) an allegory
   (E) an incident

24. We human beings are "poor" because

   (A) we are economically deprived
   (B) we have so little in comparison to what na-
       ture has
   (C) we have such little understanding
   (D) we have so little strength to cope with the
       forces of nature
   (E) we are always so envious of others in our
       fight for survival

25. The tone of this selection can best be described
    as

   (A) cynical
   (B) joyful
   (C) indignant
   (D) philosophical
   (E) solemn

26. The approach of the author is

   (A) destructive
   (B) positive
   (C) negative
   (D) neutral
   (E) nonjudgmental

Questions 27–40: Read the following poem carefully before you choose your answers.

    I had been hungry all the years;
    My noon had come, to dine;
    I, trembling, drew the table near,
(4) And touched the curious wine.

    'Twas this on tables I had seen,
    When turning, hungry, lone,

    I looked in windows, for the wealth
(8) I could not hope to own.

    I did not know the ample bread,
    'Twas so unlike the crumb
    The birds and I had often shared
(12) In Nature's dining-room.

    The plenty hurt me, 'twas so new,—
    Myself felt ill and odd,
    As berry of a mountain bush
(16) Transplanted to the road.

    Nor was I hungry; so I found
    That hunger was a way
    Of persons outside windows,
(20) The entering takes away.

27. The poet's main idea may best be expressed as:

   (A) Ambition can drive us along many strange
       paths.
   (B) Often we desire most that which we really
       do not want.
   (C) We soon learn that our ideals have feet of
       clay.
   (D) The striving for is more rewarding than ac-
       complishment.
   (E) The striving for is more satisfying than the
       reward itself.

28. The bread and wine mentioned in this poem
    were

   (A) the symbols of a religious service
   (B) things she needed for survival
   (C) the beauties of nature
   (D) the goals she had sought
   (E) the material aspects of life

29. The poem is organized primarily according to
    the principle of

   (A) chronology in that it presents each of the
       events in the order in which it occurred
   (B) cause and effect in that it shows what the
       poet did to bring about each of the results
   (C) derivation in that she presents a concrete
       situation and then evolves a principle to ex-
       plain it
   (D) exemplification in that the poet presented
       a statement and then proceeded to prove
       it through example
   (E) classification in that she attempted to sort
       out the different attitudes man and nature would
       have under these circumstances

30. The mood in lines 8–11 is one of

(A) hope
(B) envy
(C) joy
(D) despair
(E) love

31. "Curious" in the phrase "the curious wine" describes the

(A) appearance of the wine
(B) taste of the wine
(C) reaction of the owner
(D) attitude of the guests
(E) attitude of the poet

32. The first line must be taken

(A) figuratively
(B) literally
(C) joyfully
(D) ironically
(E) philosophically

33. The "ample bread" in line 9 symbolizes

I. worldly awards
II. security that comes with success
III. the applause of the critics
(A) I only
(B) II only
(C) III only
(D) I and III
(E) I, II, and III

34. During the struggle for recognition, the poet had all of the following EXCEPT

(A) ambition
(B) ability
(C) human friendship
(D) privations
(E) consoling nature

35. Line 2 implies that
(A) success had come to her slowly
(B) she had despaired of ever being successful
(C) success had come to her too late in life
(D) success had come to her suddenly
(E) success had come to her after striving for it

36. The comparison between the poet and birds in lines 11–12

(A) is apt because it makes the reader sense the poet's closeness to nature
(B) is awkward since the reader is given a ludicrous image
(C) is striking because of the implied comparison between nature's vastness and man's unlimited potential
(D) is effective because it shows how puny the poet and birds are
(E) is ineffective because it does not help to develop the ideas of the poem

37. The comparison between the poet and the berry of a mountain bush in the fourth stanza

(A) emphasizes the difficulties she had gone through
(B) de-emphasizes the role she has been playing
(C) stresses the duration of the apprenticeship period
(D) emphasizes the insignificance of success and her feeling of inadequacy
(E) emphasizes the change in circumstances

38. The diction of the selection is best defined as mainly

(A) formal and emotional
(B) symbolic and dialectal
(C) colloquial and florid
(D) nonstandard and abstract
(E) colloquial and philosophical

39. In lines 16–20, key words that must be supplied are

(A) for more food
(B) once and for all
(C) of life
(D) of the room
(E) curious

40. The poet's purpose was to

(A) present a social problem and convince the reader to take sides
(B) show the beauty of nature so that all can enjoy
(C) express a deep-felt emotional reaction to be shared with the reader
(D) share an insight with the reader
(E) delight the reader through the presentation of a pleasing realization

Questions 41–48: Read the following selection carefully before you choose your answers.

Among all the famous sayings of antiquity, there is none that does greater honor to the author, or affords greater pleasure to the reader (at least if he be a person of a generous and
(5) benevolent heart), than that of the philosopher, who, being asked what "countryman he was," replied, that he was, "a citizen of the world."— How few are there to be found in modern times who can say the same, or whose conduct is con-
(10) sistent with such a profession!—We are now become so much Englishmen, Frenchmen, Dutchmen, Spaniards, or Germans, that we are no longer citizens of the world; so much the natives of one particular spot, or members of
(15) one petty society, that we no longer consider ourselves as the general inhabitants of the globe, or members of that grand society which comprehends the whole human kind.

Did these prejudices prevail only among the
(20) meanest and lowest of the people, perhaps they might be excused, as they have few, if any, opportunities of correcting them by reading, traveling, or conversing with foreigners; but the misfortune, is, that they infect the minds, and
(25) influence the conduct, even of our gentlemen; of those, I mean, who have every title to this appellation but an exemption from prejudice, which however, in my opinion, ought to be regarded as the characteristical mark of a gentle-
(30) man; for let a man's birth be ever so high, his station ever so exalted, or his fortune ever so large, yet if he is not free from national and other prejudices, I should make bold to tell him, that he had a low and vulgar mind, and had no just
(35) claim to the character of a gentleman. And in fact, you will always find that those are most apt to boast of national merit, who have little or no merit of their own to depend on; than which, to be sure, nothing is more natural: the
(40) slender vine twists around the sturdy oak, for no other reason in the world but because it has not strength sufficient to support itself.

41. All of the following are evidence that the selection was not written recently EXCEPT

(A) belief in the commonality of all human beings
(B) length of sentences
(C) meaning of "gentleman"
(D) use of "characteristical"
(E) use of "meanest and lowest of the people"

42. The tone of the passage is best termed

(A) smug
(B) joyful
(C) scornful
(D) elegiac
(E) exhortative

43. The author would approve of the concepts behind all of the following EXCEPT

(A) the European Common Market
(B) theories of racial equality
(C) exploration of Antarctica
(D) apartheid
(E) the UN

44. The word "comprehends" in line 18 is used to mean

(A) understands
(B) takes in
(C) misinterprets
(D) denies
(E) classifies

45. In the analogy in lines 40–42, the sturdy oak represents

(A) nationalities
(B) gentlemen
(C) foreigners
(D) lower classes
(E) mankind

46. The author developed the first paragraph through

(A) the use of specific examples
(B) logical presentation of counter arguments
(C) balancing of ideas
(D) application of the topic sentence to the present
(E) use of contrast in the effects of the topic sentence

47. The second paragraph supports the main thesis through

(A) mustering of relevant facts
(B) disproving basic arguments of the opposition
(C) statement of specific examples
(D) citing authority
(E) relying on name-calling

48. The author does NOT explain

(A) what he means by a citizen of the world
(B) what is wrong with nationalism
(C) what he means by being a gentleman
(D) what he means as a basic characteristic of a low and vulgar mind
(E) how people can develop into being citizens of the world

Questions 49–55:   Read the following poem carefully before you choose your answers.

Do not weep, maiden, for war is kind.
Because your lover threw wild hands
   toward the sky
And the affrighted steed ran on alone,
Do not weep.
(5) War is kind.

Hoarse, booming drums of the regiment,
Little souls who thirst for fight,
These men were born to drill and die.
The unexplained glory flies above them,
(10) Great is the battle-god, great, and his
   kingdom—
A field where a thousand corpses lie.

Do not weep, babe, for war is kind.
Because your father tumbled in the yellow
   trenches,
Raged at his breast, gulped and died,
(15) Do not weep.
War is kind.

Swift blazing flag of the regiment,
Eagle with crest of red and gold,
These men were born to drill and die.
(20) Point for them the virtue of slaughter,
Make plain to them the excellence of
   killing
And a field where a thousand corpses lie.

Mother whose heart hung humble as a
   button
On the bright splendid shroud of your son,
(25) Do not weep.
War is kind.

49. Which of the following best expresses the effect of the repetition of the last lines of the first stanza?

(A) It summarizes the action in the poem.
(B) It shows the speaker's moral shock.
(C) It helps place the blame where it should be.
(D) It lessens the tension brought about by the horrors described.
(E) It makes the poem seem unreal.

50. The reader rather than the author must supply the explanation for the line

(A) "A field where a thousand corpses lie"
(B) "Raged at his breast, gulped and died"
(C) "Because your love threw wild hands toward the sky"
(D) "War is kind"
(E) "The unexplained glory flies above them"

51. In the second stanza the poet does NOT state that

(A) insignificant men become soldiers
(B) soldiers are born to be trained and die on the battlefield
(C) the god of battle increases his kingdom with each battle
(D) the drums beat a desire to fight into the spirits of the soldiers
(E) what the men will gain by fighting

52. The flag of the regiment is "swift blazing" because

(A) it is being burned by the enemy
(B) it is carried swiftly at the head of the charge
(C) it has a red emblem and is carried by the flagbearer
(D) it has the eagle of Napoleon on it
(E) the cannon fire ignites it

53. Which of the following best explains the effect of the poet's use of clichés throughout the entire poem?

(A) The clichés weaken the poet's message and destroy its effectiveness.
(B) The clichés go unnoticed by the reader.
(C) Because so many of the clichés are deliberately repeated, there is an intensifying of the feeling of horror.
(D) The clichés allow the poet to express a complex thought simply.
(E) The reader laughs at the poet's ineptness, because the poem assumes the tone of a folk ballad.

54. The ironic theme of the poem is best stated as

(A) war must be considered inevitable
(B) war is really kind in that it provides such an exciting spectacle on the battlefield
(C) war is kind to the rulers and generals of the world
(D) children can grow up well in this atmosphere

(E) people should not weep for soldiers merely because they died

55. This poem was written before

(A) cavalry was used in battles
(B) cities were bombed and gutted
(C) trench warfare
(D) drums ordered the battle charge
(E) armies numbered in the thousands

Questions 56–60:   Read the following poem carefully before you choose your answers.

    Ninety and going strong,
Gray in dated neatness,
    Unweighted, timeless, drab,
She sat with clouded vision,
(5)   Faint smile and folded hands,
Entombed in transparent walls.
"Pleased to see you again," she said
    To each, untuned, she said,
    "Pleased to see you again."
(10) With pride, with fear,
    With scorn, with disbelief,
We sat by and
    Talked of things and things.

56. The word "things" in line 13 is used to

(A) condemn the visitors for their attitude
(B) arouse sympathy for the woman
(C) emphasize the impact of the woman's condition on her visitors
(D) show the callousness of the visitors
(E) reveal the unconcern of the visitors

57. The old woman described in the first 6 lines

(A) is unable to be reached
(B) is impatient with the visitors
(C) is one who died long ago and lives in the memories of the visitors
(D) joins in the conversation
(E) puts the visitors at ease

58. A reaction that would NOT have been expressed by at least one of the visitors is

(A) "I'm so glad that she's reached this ripe old age!"
(B) "I hope this never happens to me!"
(C) "Is she always this way?"
(D) "Why does it have to end this way for her!"
(E) "She was such a beautiful person!"

59. The theme of the poem is

(A) the serenity of old age
(B) our inability to accept senility
(C) the social graces of the aging
(D) the fate of all in their nineties
(E) the rewards of living

60. The word "sat" in line 4 is repeated in line 12 to

(A) show the inactivity of the group
(B) slow down the action in the poem
(C) intensify her reaction to the visitors
(D) show her control over the feelings of the visitors
(E) contrast her relaxed manner with their tense acceptance

ANSWER KEY: PRACTICE TEST ONE

1. (B)	10. (B)	19. (B)	28. (D)	37. (E)	46. (A)	55. (B)
2. (B)	11. (D)	20. (E)	29. (C)	38. (E)	47. (E)	56. (C)
3. (C)	12. (C)	21. (C)	30. (B)	39. (D)	48. (B)	57. (A)
4. (E)	13. (E)	22. (E)	31. (E)	40. (D)	49. (B)	58. (D)
5. (E)	14. (D)	23. (D)	32. (B)	41. (A)	50. (D)	59. (B)
6. (C)	15. (E)	24. (B)	33. (A)	42. (D)	51. (E)	60. (E)
7. (A)	16. (A)	25. (D)	34. (C)	43. (D)	52. (C)	
8. (B)	17. (E)	26. (C)	35. (E)	44. (B)	53. (C)	
9. (A)	18. (C)	27. (D)	36. (C)	45. (E)	54. (C)	

DETERMINING YOUR RAW SCORE

1. Tabulate Totals
   Number Right _____
   Number Wrong _____
   Number Omitted _____

2. Enter Number Right   A _____
   Divide Number Wrong by
   4 and put result here   B _____

3. Subtract B from A. This
   results in your RAW
   SCORE   _____

   The subtraction of ¼ point for each incorrect answer adjusts for the effect of random guessing.

EVALUATING YOUR PERFORMANCE

Excellent	56–60
Very Good	47–55
Good	35–46
Average	25–34
Below Average	16–24
Unsatisfactory	15 or Below

PRACTICE TEST TWO

ANSWER SHEET

1 Ⓐ Ⓑ Ⓒ Ⓓ Ⓔ	21 Ⓐ Ⓑ Ⓒ Ⓓ Ⓔ	41 Ⓐ Ⓑ Ⓒ Ⓓ Ⓔ
2 Ⓐ Ⓑ Ⓒ Ⓓ Ⓔ	22 Ⓐ Ⓑ Ⓒ Ⓓ Ⓔ	42 Ⓐ Ⓑ Ⓒ Ⓓ Ⓔ
3 Ⓐ Ⓑ Ⓒ Ⓓ Ⓔ	23 Ⓐ Ⓑ Ⓒ Ⓓ Ⓔ	43 Ⓐ Ⓑ Ⓒ Ⓓ Ⓔ
4 Ⓐ Ⓑ Ⓒ Ⓓ Ⓔ	24 Ⓐ Ⓑ Ⓒ Ⓓ Ⓔ	44 Ⓐ Ⓑ Ⓒ Ⓓ Ⓔ
5 Ⓐ Ⓑ Ⓒ Ⓓ Ⓔ	25 Ⓐ Ⓑ Ⓒ Ⓓ Ⓔ	45 Ⓐ Ⓑ Ⓒ Ⓓ Ⓔ
6 Ⓐ Ⓑ Ⓒ Ⓓ Ⓔ	26 Ⓐ Ⓑ Ⓒ Ⓓ Ⓔ	46 Ⓐ Ⓑ Ⓒ Ⓓ Ⓔ
7 Ⓐ Ⓑ Ⓒ Ⓓ Ⓔ	27 Ⓐ Ⓑ Ⓒ Ⓓ Ⓔ	47 Ⓐ Ⓑ Ⓒ Ⓓ Ⓔ
8 Ⓐ Ⓑ Ⓒ Ⓓ Ⓔ	28 Ⓐ Ⓑ Ⓒ Ⓓ Ⓔ	48 Ⓐ Ⓑ Ⓒ Ⓓ Ⓔ
9 Ⓐ Ⓑ Ⓒ Ⓓ Ⓔ	29 Ⓐ Ⓑ Ⓒ Ⓓ Ⓔ	49 Ⓐ Ⓑ Ⓒ Ⓓ Ⓔ
10 Ⓐ Ⓑ Ⓒ Ⓓ Ⓔ	30 Ⓐ Ⓑ Ⓒ Ⓓ Ⓔ	50 Ⓐ Ⓑ Ⓒ Ⓓ Ⓔ
11 Ⓐ Ⓑ Ⓒ Ⓓ Ⓔ	31 Ⓐ Ⓑ Ⓒ Ⓓ Ⓔ	51 Ⓐ Ⓑ Ⓒ Ⓓ Ⓔ
12 Ⓐ Ⓑ Ⓒ Ⓓ Ⓔ	32 Ⓐ Ⓑ Ⓒ Ⓓ Ⓔ	52 Ⓐ Ⓑ Ⓒ Ⓓ Ⓔ
13 Ⓐ Ⓑ Ⓒ Ⓓ Ⓔ	33 Ⓐ Ⓑ Ⓒ Ⓓ Ⓔ	53 Ⓐ Ⓑ Ⓒ Ⓓ Ⓔ
14 Ⓐ Ⓑ Ⓒ Ⓓ Ⓔ	34 Ⓐ Ⓑ Ⓒ Ⓓ Ⓔ	54 Ⓐ Ⓑ Ⓒ Ⓓ Ⓔ
15 Ⓐ Ⓑ Ⓒ Ⓓ Ⓔ	35 Ⓐ Ⓑ Ⓒ Ⓓ Ⓔ	55 Ⓐ Ⓑ Ⓒ Ⓓ Ⓔ
16 Ⓐ Ⓑ Ⓒ Ⓓ Ⓔ	36 Ⓐ Ⓑ Ⓒ Ⓓ Ⓔ	56 Ⓐ Ⓑ Ⓒ Ⓓ Ⓔ
17 Ⓐ Ⓑ Ⓒ Ⓓ Ⓔ	37 Ⓐ Ⓑ Ⓒ Ⓓ Ⓔ	57 Ⓐ Ⓑ Ⓒ Ⓓ Ⓔ
18 Ⓐ Ⓑ Ⓒ Ⓓ Ⓔ	38 Ⓐ Ⓑ Ⓒ Ⓓ Ⓔ	58 Ⓐ Ⓑ Ⓒ Ⓓ Ⓔ
19 Ⓐ Ⓑ Ⓒ Ⓓ Ⓔ	39 Ⓐ Ⓑ Ⓒ Ⓓ Ⓔ	59 Ⓐ Ⓑ Ⓒ Ⓓ Ⓔ
20 Ⓐ Ⓑ Ⓒ Ⓓ Ⓔ	40 Ⓐ Ⓑ Ⓒ Ⓓ Ⓔ	60 Ⓐ Ⓑ Ⓒ Ⓓ Ⓔ

PRACTICE TEST TWO

Total Time: One Hour
Time begun .... Time ended .... Time used ....

DIRECTIONS: This test consists of selections from literary works and questions on their content, form, and style. After reading each passage or poem, choose the best answer to each question and blacken the corresponding space on the answer sheet.

NOTE: Pay particular attention to the requirement of questions that contain the words NOT, LEAST, or EXCEPT.

Questions 1–6:   Read the following passage carefully before you choose your answers.

The division of Europe into a number of independent states, connected, however, with each other, by the general resemblance of religion, language, and manners, is productive of
(5) the most beneficial consequences to the liberty of mankind. A modern tyrant, who should find no resistance either in his own breast, or in his people, would soon experience a gentle restraint from the example of his equals, the dread
(10) of present censure, the advice of his allies, and the apprehension of his enemies. The object of his displeasure, escaping from the narrow limits of his dominions, would easily obtain, in a happier climate, a secure refuge, a new fortune
(15) adequate to his merit, the freedom of complaint, and perhaps the means of revenge. But the empire of the Romans filled the world, and when that empire fell into the hands of a single person, the world became a safe and dreary prison for
(20) his enemies. The slave of Imperial despotism, whether he was condemned to drag his gilded chain in Rome and the senate, or to wear out a life of exile on the barren rock of Seriphus, or the frozen banks of the Danube, expected his
(25) fate in silent despair. To resist was fatal, and it was impossible to fly. On every side he was encompassed with a vast extent of sea and land, which he could never hope to traverse without being discovered, seized, and restored to his ir-
(30) ritated master. Beyond the frontiers, his anxious view could discover nothing, except the ocean, inhospitable deserts, hostile tribes of barbarians, of fierce manners and unknown language, or dependent kings, who would gladly
(35) purchase the emperor's protection by the sac-

rifice of an obnoxious fugitive. "Wherever you are," said Cicero to the exiled Marcellus, "remember that you are equally within the power of the conqueror."

1. Which of the following contains the principal idea of this selection?

(A) Europe of today is better than the Europe of Rome because of the many different states.
(B) Liberty survives better in a world of many nations than in a world empire.
(C) Emperors can punish more relentlessly than kings.
(D) The slaves of Roman despotism could not escape punishment.
(E) The Romans were less humane than are the citizens of modern Europe.

2. Which of the following expresses the purpose of the final sentence?

(A) The author used authority to prove the cruelty of Roman rulers.
(B) The author brings in an irrelevance to show his scholarship.
(C) The author cites an authority to prove how all controlling Rome was.
(D) The author uses the quotation to summarize his thesis.
(E) The author uses contrast to prove his initial statement.

3. The independent states protect liberty better than could Rome because

(A) one country could declare war on another
(B) a refugee could be extradited
(C) one country could overcome another
(D) an escaped rebel could set up forces for liberation in the safety of another country
(E) the tyrant could have a treaty that would cause the other countries to drive out his enemies

4. There was no hope for rebellion against Rome because

(A) the rulers were ruthless
(B) there was no place to flee
(C) the people were too loyal
(D) the nations feared Rome too much
(E) the known world was too small

5. Which of the following expresses the thought pattern followed by the author of this selection?

   (A) He set up two premises, one dealing with modern Europe and the other with ancient Rome and then gave examples to prove his contentions.
   (B) He developed a chronological sequence to tie events together, leading to the climax in his final sentence.
   (C) He used amplification, stating a premise in his first sentence and then explaining the premise in other words in each of the following sentences.
   (D) He connected cause and effect, balancing one sentence with the next to build to his final premise.
   (E) He logically built on facts stated in his first sentence and, avoiding facts and examples, used logical proof to derive the thought presented in his final sentence

6. The diction and style of this passage are best defined as

   (A) allegorical and stately
   (B) emotional and judgmental
   (C) studied and scholarly
   (D) floridly oratorical
   (E) abstract and philosophical

Questions 7–15:   Read the following passage carefully before you choose your answers.

Miss Sally Appleby,
Madam,
        Understanding you have a parcel of heart, warranted sound, to be disposed of, shall be
(5) willing to treat for said commodity, on reasonable terms; doubt not, shall agree for same; shall wait of you for further information, when and where you shall appoint. This the needful from
                    Yours etc.
(10)   Gam. Pickle

        This laconic epistle, simple and unadorned as it was, met with as cordial a reception from the person to whom it was addressed, as if it had been couched in the most elegant terms that del-
(15) icacy of passion and cultivated genius could supply; nay, I believe, was the more welcome on account of its mercantile plainness; because when an advantageous match is in view, a sensible woman often considers the flowery profes-
(20) sions and rapturous exclamations of love as en-

snaring ambiguities, or at best impertinent preliminaries, that retard the treaty they are designed to promote; whereas Mr. Pickle removed all disagreeable uncertainty by descending at
(25) once to the most interesting particular.

7. It can be inferred from his letter that Pickle is

   (A) a cold-hearted exploiter
   (B) a lover too shy to say what he means
   (C) an arrogant snob
   (D) a man too rushed to enjoy life
   (E) a thoroughgoing pragmatist

8. All of the following are true of the letter EXCEPT that its

   (A) opening and closing courtesies suggest that the two people may not be well acquainted
   (B) avoidance of the pronoun "I" makes it seem impersonal
   (C) tone is insincere
   (D) clipped phrases sound hurried
   (E) purpose is practical

9. The narrator's comments (lines 12–25) about the letter are designed to

   (A) dispel any favorable impression the reader might have of Pickle
   (B) confirm the reader's expectation that Sally Appleby would be insulted by the letter
   (C) distract the reader from the letter's offensive tone
   (D) show the superiority of the narrator's taste to that of Pickle or Sally Appleby
   (E) indicate that the letter is more appropriate than it might seem

10. According to the narrator, Miss Appleby's reaction to the letter makes clear that she values

   (A) success over happiness
   (B) directness over decoration
   (C) humility over assertiveness
   (D) style over substance
   (E) her welfare over that of others

11. The phrase "delicacy of passion" (lines 14-15) means

   (A) refinement of feeling
   (B) concealment of emotion
   (C) shyness and coyness
   (D) feeble affection
   (E) witty expression

12. The statement made in lines 18–24 is presented in which of the following ways?

   (A) As a general truth that helps the reader understand the incident
   (B) As a controversial statement requiring closer examination
   (C) As an excuse made up by Pickle for his unconventional behavior
   (D) As a cynical observation made by the narrator
   (E) As a belief held by the rich, but not by the poor

13. As used by the narrator, the effect of such phrases as "elegant terms" (line 14), "delicacy of passion" (line 15), "flowery professions" (lines 19-20), and "rapturous exclamations" (line 20) is to

   (A) indicate the narrator's appreciation of true love letters
   (B) stress the narrator's contempt for emotion
   (C) satirize the language of conventional love
   (D) reveal the deeply sentimental nature of language
   (E) mock Pickle's futile attempt at fine language

14. Which of the following best describes the effect of the words "advantageous" (line 18), "match" (line 18), "treaty" (line 22), and "promote" (line 23)?

   (A) They imply that the commercialism of marriage is degrading.
   (B) They provide a contrast to the phrase "mercantile plainness" (line 18).
   (C) They suggest that marriage is like a sporting contest.
   (D) They echo the commercial and legal metaphors of Pickle's letter.
   (E) They elaborate on the analogy between marital and international strife.

15. The narrator's attitude toward a sensible woman's consideration in regard to marriage is best described as

   (A) heavily ironic
   (B) bitterly disapproving
   (C) strongly defensive
   (D) gently satirical
   (E) somewhat shocked

Questions 16–20: Read the following passage carefully before you choose your answers.

The men and women who make the best boon companions seem to have given up hope of doing something else. They have, perhaps, tried to be poets and painters; they have tried to be
(5) actors, scientists, and musicians. But some defect of talent or opportunity has cut them off from their pet ambitions and thus left them with leisure to take an interest in the lives of others. Your ambitious man is selfish. No matter how
(10) secret his ambition may be, it makes him keep his thoughts at home. But the heartbroken people—if I may use the word in a mild benevolent sense—the people whose wills are subdued to fate, give us consolation, recognition, and wel-
(15) come.

16. The best companions, according to this selection are

   (A) people who still have their pride and their ambitions
   (B) those who are benevolent
   (C) those who have succeeded in the arts
   (D) those who have secret ambitions
   (E) those who recognize their own failures

17. The tone of the passage is best termed

   (A) joyful
   (B) sincere
   (C) solemn
   (D) scornful
   (E) argumentative

18. For those who would question the meaning of *boon*, the author explains the words in terms of

   (A) poets and painters
   (B) pet ambitions
   (C) consolation, recognition, and welcome
   (D) ambitious man
   (E) defect of talent or opportunity

19. Which of the following is LEAST true of boon companions?

   (A) They look for rewards in the appreciation of others.
   (B) They are ships that are rudderless and without sails.
   (C) The basis of their interest in others is not jealousy or envy, but failure—their own failure.

(D) They no longer think of getting ahead.

(E) They are born and not made so by circumstances.

20. A boon companion must be

(A) trustworthy
(B) secretive
(C) interesting
(D) open
(E) lively

Questions 21–26:   Read the following poem carefully before you choose your answers.

> I have not told my garden yet,
> Lest that should conquer me;
> I have not quite the strength now
> (4) To break it to the bee.
> I will not name it in the street,
> For shops would stare, that I,
> So shy, so very ignorant,
> (8) Should have the face to die.
> The hillsides must not know it,
> Where I have rambled so,
> Nor tell the loving forests
> (12) The day that I shall go,
> Nor lisp it at the table,
> Nor heedless by the way
> Hint that within the riddle
> (16) One will walk to-day!

21. The poem deals with

(A) love
(B) eternity
(C) nature
(D) death
(E) joy

22. The thought of the poem is revealed

(A) in line 1
(B) in line 16
(C) in the first stanza
(D) not until the last stanza
(E) in lines 6–8

23. The attribution of human qualities to the non-human stresses

(A) the poet's interests in the world around her
(B) nature's love of all human beings
(C) the folly of man's efforts to control nature
(D) that man alone knows the inevitability of death
(E) that nature is not concerned about man

24. Line 2 is the key that unlocks the reason for her

I. not revealing her mortality
II. attributing human emotions to inanimate objects
III. feeling so bashful and unknowing
(A) I only
(B) II only
(C) III only
(D) I and III
(E) I, II, and III

25. The mood of the poet is one of

(A) acceptance
(B) rebellion
(C) expectancy
(D) desire
(E) anguish

26. The diction and tone of this selection are best characterized as

(A) simple and intimate
(B) studied and ornate
(C) didactic and philosophical
(D) purposive and moralistic
(E) indirect and studied

Questions 27–33:   Read the following selection carefully before you choose your answers.

Subjects are apt to be as arbitrary in their censure as the most assuming kings can be in their power. If there might be matter for objections, there is not less reason for excuses; the (5) defects laid to his charge are such as may claim indulgence from mankind.

Should nobody throw a stone at his faults but those who are free from them, there would be but a slender shower.

(10)   What private man will throw stones at him because he loved, or what prince because he dissembled?

If he either trusted, or forgave his enemies, or in some cases neglected his friends, more (15) than could be in strictness be allowed, let not those errors be so arraigned as to take away the privilege that seemeth to be due to princely frailties. If princes are under the misfortune of being accused to govern ill, their subjects have (20) the less right to fall hard upon them, since they generally do so little to be governed well.

The truth is, the calling of a king, with all its glittering, hath such an unreasonable weight upon it that they may rather expect to be la-

(25) mented than to be envied for being set upon a
pinnacle, where they are exposed to censure if
they do not do more to answer men's expectations than corrupted nature will allow.
　　　It is but justice therefore to this Prince to give
(30) all due softenings to the less shining part of his
life; to offer flowers and leaves to hide, instead
of using aggravations to expose them.
　　　Let his royal ashes then lie soft upon him,
and cover him from harsh and unkind censures;
(35) which though they should not be unjust, can
never clear themselves from being unfitting.

27. The selection was most likely part of a

(A) parliamentary debate defending a monarch
(B) culminating effort to dethrone a king
(C) campaign to restore a monarch's reputation
(D) series of speeches calling for support of the
king in a governmental crisis
(E) series of eulogies on the death of a king

28. This king did not

(A) place his trust in the wrong people
(B) show ingratitude to his friends
(C) rise above pettiness
(D) make errors that angered his subjects
(E) expose his weaknesses to his subjects

29. The writer asks that a king be excused because

(A) he is a human being
(B) he tried his best
(C) he was not worthy of the office
(D) he did not seek this high office
(E) his enemies were too numerous

30. When the king erred, he did so for any one of
the following reasons EXCEPT

(A) he trusted his friends too much
(B) he knew he was above criticism
(C) he did not have the fullest cooperation of
the people
(D) the burden of ruling led the people to expect
more from him than is humanly possible
(E) he was too willing to forgive his enemies

31. In lines 33-34, the author stands behind the belief that

I. kings can do no wrong
II. the errors of kings are to be forgiven and
forgotten
III. dead kings leave unblemished records
(A) I only

(B) II only
(C) III only
(D) I and III
(E) I, II, and III

32. In the first sentence the author

(A) asks the people to suspend judgment until
the facts are all in
(B) plays on the loyalty of the people to the
present government
(C) pleads with the people not to make the same
errors made by monarchs
(D) insists on unquestioning reverence for the
king
(E) expresses confidence in the sense of obligation of the people

33. The rhetorical question in lines 10-12 is based
on the assumption that

(A) the king loved his subjects
(B) all rulers tell untruths at times
(C) the king never disregarded the truth
(D) the king's faults made him capricious
(E) the king made no grave errors

Questions 34-40: Read the following selection
carefully before you choose your answers.

　　　To those puny objectors against cards, as nur-
turing the bad passions, she would retort, that
man is a gaming animal. He must be always
trying to get the better in something or other:—
that this passion can scarcely be more safely
(5) expended than upon a game at cards: that cards
are a temporary illusion; in truth, a mere drama;
for we do but *play* at being mightily concerned,
where a few idle shillings are at stake, yet, during the illusion, we *are* as mightily concerned
(10) as those whose stake is crowns and kingdoms.
They are a sort of dream-fighting; much ado;
great battling, and little blood shed; mighty
means for disproportioned ends; quite as di-
verting, and a great deal more innocuous, than
many of those more serious *games* of life, which
(15) men play, without esteeming them to be such.—
　　　With great deference to the old lady's judgment on these matters, I think I have experienced some moments in my life, when playing
at cards *for nothing* has even been very agree-
able. When I am in sickness, or not in the best
(20) spirits, I sometimes call for the cards, and play
a game at piquet *for love* with my cousin
Bridget—Bridget Elia.

34. Which of the following expresses the writer's attitude toward the old lady?

    (A) He was thoroughly convinced by her arguments.
    (B) He disagreed with her and told her so.
    (C) When she was in command, he followed her and obeyed, but he let her know that she was morally wrong.
    (D) He never argued with her, but he could also see reasons for disagreeing with her.
    (E) She was a quarrelsome old woman, and he did not want to argue with her.

35. The old woman favored playing cards for money because

    (A) other people did it
    (B) it imitated real life but without damaging penalties
    (C) it gave her a chance to be with people
    (D) the excitement was good for her
    (E) it gave her a chance to analyze people and their motives

36. The author fails to describe all of the following EXCEPT

    (A) the game piquet
    (B) how he felt about playing cards for stakes
    (C) whether he played cards with the old lady
    (D) his relationship to the old lady
    (E) the effect on him of playing cards without stakes

37. The mood of the writer is best interpreted as one of

    (A) anger
    (B) doubt
    (C) understanding
    (D) surprise
    (E) awe

38. Which of the following best describes the style of the passage?

    (A) It uses simple, direct statements to give clarity to the passage.
    (B) It builds up to a climax by placing subordinate clauses first.
    (C) It is telegraphic in that subjects and occasionally predicates are omitted.
    (D) It uses a piling up of clauses to give speed to the direction of the paragraphs.
    (E) It imitates conversation by using italics and parenthetical elements.

39. The effect of the style is best explained as one that

    (A) shows that the sophisticated reader can enjoy this material
    (B) makes the author seem to be an intimate friend of the reader
    (C) antagonizes the less sophisticated reader
    (D) shows the author as unable to make up his mind
    (E) shows that the succeeding generations cannot accept the values of their predecessors

40. A reason for playing cards, acceptable to the author but not mentioned by the old lady, is

    (A) it is a good way to spend time that is heavy and may become profitable
    (B) it can lead to the lessening of tension between relatives and friends
    (C) it is good mental exercise
    (D) it can help another
    (E) it can teach us to get along in polite society

Questions 41–47: Read the following selection carefully before you choose your answers.

> To him who in the love of nature holds
> Communion with her visible forms, she speaks
> A various language; for his gayer hours
> She has a voice of gladness, and a smile
> (5) And eloquence of beauty, and she glides
> Into his darker musings, with a mild
> And healing sympathy, that steals away
> Their sharpness, ere he is aware. When thoughts
> Of the last bitter hour come like a blight
> (10) Over thy spirit, and sad images
> Of the stern agony, and shroud, and pall,
> And breathless darkness, and the narrow house,
> Make thee to shudder and grow sick at heart;—
> Go forth, under the open sky, and list
> (15) To Nature's teachings, while from all around—
> Earth and her waters, and the depths of air—
> Comes a still voice:—

41. The "still voice" that is heard is that of

    (A) man speaking to man
    (B) conscience speaking to those who can listen
    (C) death that comes to all

(D) nature that surrounds us

(E) earth, the mother of us all

42. The underlying subject of the passage is

(A) man's ability to conquer all except personal death

(B) love's ability to help us to live better

(C) man's inhumanity to man

(D) the eternal struggle between the forces of good and of evil

(E) achieving oneness with nature

43. The mood of the selection is best interpreted as one of

(A) excitement

(B) doubt

(C) bravery

(D) agony

(E) sincerity

44. The selection is a paraphrase of

(A) nature's wonders

(B) wandering through nature

(C) let nature take its course

(D) Mother Nature

(E) curiosities of nature

45. This selection is marred for modern readers by

I. the use of dated poetic devices

II. the poet's attitude toward fear of death

III. the poet's separation of mankind from nature

(A) I only

(B) II only

(C) III only

(D) I and III

(E) I, II, and III

46. A word in this selection that is in danger of losing its traditional meaning is

(A) nature

(B) gayer

(C) blight

(D) communion

(E) musings

47. The voice is "still" because it is

(A) internalized

(B) everpresent

(C) so overwhelmingly clear

(D) universal

(E) the equivalent of Everyman

Questions 48–56: Read the following selection carefully before you choose your answers.

For while the tired waves, vainly breaking
    Seem here no painful inch to gain,
Far back, through creeks and inlets making,
(4)   Comes silent, flooding in, the main
And not by eastern windows only,
    When daylight comes, comes in the light,
In front the sun climbs slow, how slowly,
(8)   But westward, look, the land is bright.

48. The mood of this selection is one of

(A) doubt

(B) hesitation

(C) optimism

(D) awe

(E) surprise

49. In line 1, "tired waves" is an example of

(A) personification

(B) exaggeration

(C) irony

(D) simile

(E) contrast

50. Literally the *main* is

(A) the masses of humanity

(B) renewing flow

(C) the principles of life

(D) sunlight

(E) land mass

51. Which of the following best expresses the main idea of the selection?

(A) Man cannot live by fear and anxiety.

(B) We should not concern ourselves over details.

(C) Nature is our ally.

(D) Progress is a slow process.

(E) In our concern over what we see, we miss the greater significances.

52. A poetic device used sparingly by modern writers and found perhaps too frequently in this selection is

(A) rhyming

(B) simplification

(C) sarcasm

(D) metaphor

(E) inversion

53. Which of the following folk sayings best characterizes the thought content of the poem?

(A) Look before you leap.
(B) The worst hour is just before the dawn.
(C) Look for the silver lining.
(D) The best caution is precaution.
(E) Seeing is believing.

54. Which of the following best explains the versification of the poem?

(A) Its increasing regularity imitates the natural phenomena described.
(B) The metrical differences from line to line show the movement of masses of humanity from event to event.
(C) The alternation of line length suggests the alternation of events in life itself.
(D) Its variations in rhythm echo the flow of emotion of the people involved.
(E) The metrical differences from line to line interfere with the communication of thought from the poem to the reader.

55. Which of the following statements best characterizes an aspect of line 7?

(A) The sudden introduction of the sun changes the thought development.
(B) The majestic description of the rising sun illuminates the author's message.
(C) The use of alliteration causes the line to imitate the speed of the sun.
(D) The use of inversion adds awe and power to the sight of the rising sun.
(E) The sun is brought into sharp contrast to the tired waves.

56. Which of the following statements best characterizes line 8?

(A) Through contrast with the image in line 4, the author adds detail to his imagery.
(B) Through repetition of inversion, the poet defines his terms.
(C) Through imitation of natural movement, he clarifies his purpose.
(D) Through parallelism with the image in line 4, the poet widens the implications in the selection.
(E) Through alliteration the poet shows the narrowing spotlight of reality.

Questions 57–60: Read the following selection carefully before you choose your answers.

> All hail to thee, computer!
> Unworn by countless runs,
>   Pristine sounds and printed symbols
> Spew in awesome order
> (5)   Without variation
>   At each command.
> Unnatural offspring of a creature's frenzy
> You mock the sane chaos
>   The directionless selection
> (10)   Of all else.

57. The best paraphrase of "a creature's frenzy" in line 7 is

(A) an insane urge
(B) nature's plan
(C) a wild animal's whim
(D) humanity's imagination
(E) a creator's will

58. The "offspring" in line 7 is unnatural because

(A) of its high speed and potential accuracy
(B) of its absolute logic
(C) it lacks direction
(D) it is unselective
(E) it is revolutionary

59. In the last four lines, the poet

(A) uses the computer as an example of how nature can be tamed
(B) characterizes the universe as having no ultimate purpose
(C) belittles all that people invented before the computer
(D) shows how even the computer can fail
(E) discusses none of the above

60. The staccato effect of the first four lines

(A) imitates the sounds and movements of the storage disks in action
(B) catches the speed and tempo of modern America
(C) reveals the poet's condemnation of the computer as a creative tool
(D) expresses the poet's fear of being mastered by the computer's superiority
(E) concerns none of the above

ANSWER KEY: PRACTICE TEST TWO

1. (A)	10. (B)	19. (E)	28. (C)	37. (C)	46. (B)	55. (C)
2. (D)	11. (A)	20. (D)	29. (A)	38. (E)	47. (A)	56. (D)
3. (D)	12. (A)	21. (D)	30. (B)	39. (B)	48. (C)	57. (D)
4. (B)	13. (C)	22. (E)	31. (C)	40. (D)	49. (A)	58. (B)
5. (A)	14. (D)	23. (A)	32. (C)	41. (D)	50. (B)	59. (B)
6. (C)	15. (D)	24. (D)	33. (D)	42. (E)	51. (E)	60. (A)
7. (E)	16. (E)	25. (E)	34. (D)	43. (E)	52. (E)	
8. (C)	17. (B)	26. (A)	35. (B)	44. (D)	53. (C)	
9. (E)	18. (C)	27. (E)	36. (C)	45. (A)	54. (A)	

DETERMINING YOUR RAW SCORE

1. Tabulate Totals
   Number Right _____
   Number Wrong _____
   Number Omitted _____

2. Enter Number Right   A _____
   Divide Number Wrong by
   4 and put result here   B _____

3. Subtract B from A. This
   results in your RAW
   SCORE   _____

   The subtraction of ¼ point for each incorrect answer adjusts for the effect of random guessing.

EVALUATING YOUR PERFORMANCE

Excellent	55–60
Very Good	44–54
Good	35–43
Average	23–34
Below Average	15–22
Unsatisfactory	14 or below

PRACTICE TEST THREE

ANSWER SHEET

1	Ⓐ Ⓑ Ⓒ Ⓓ Ⓔ	21 Ⓐ Ⓑ Ⓒ Ⓓ Ⓔ	41 Ⓐ Ⓑ Ⓒ Ⓓ Ⓔ
2	Ⓐ Ⓑ Ⓒ Ⓓ Ⓔ	22 Ⓐ Ⓑ Ⓒ Ⓓ Ⓔ	42 Ⓐ Ⓑ Ⓒ Ⓓ Ⓔ
3	Ⓐ Ⓑ Ⓒ Ⓓ Ⓔ	23 Ⓐ Ⓑ Ⓒ Ⓓ Ⓔ	43 Ⓐ Ⓑ Ⓒ Ⓓ Ⓔ
4	Ⓐ Ⓑ Ⓒ Ⓓ Ⓔ	24 Ⓐ Ⓑ Ⓒ Ⓓ Ⓔ	44 Ⓐ Ⓑ Ⓒ Ⓓ Ⓔ
5	Ⓐ Ⓑ Ⓒ Ⓓ Ⓔ	25 Ⓐ Ⓑ Ⓒ Ⓓ Ⓔ	45 Ⓐ Ⓑ Ⓒ Ⓓ Ⓔ
6	Ⓐ Ⓑ Ⓒ Ⓓ Ⓔ	26 Ⓐ Ⓑ Ⓒ Ⓓ Ⓔ	46 Ⓐ Ⓑ Ⓒ Ⓓ Ⓔ
7	Ⓐ Ⓑ Ⓒ Ⓓ Ⓔ	27 Ⓐ Ⓑ Ⓒ Ⓓ Ⓔ	47 Ⓐ Ⓑ Ⓒ Ⓓ Ⓔ
8	Ⓐ Ⓑ Ⓒ Ⓓ Ⓔ	28 Ⓐ Ⓑ Ⓒ Ⓓ Ⓔ	48 Ⓐ Ⓑ Ⓒ Ⓓ Ⓔ
9	Ⓐ Ⓑ Ⓒ Ⓓ Ⓔ	29 Ⓐ Ⓑ Ⓒ Ⓓ Ⓔ	49 Ⓐ Ⓑ Ⓒ Ⓓ Ⓔ
10	Ⓐ Ⓑ Ⓒ Ⓓ Ⓔ	30 Ⓐ Ⓑ Ⓒ Ⓓ Ⓔ	50 Ⓐ Ⓑ Ⓒ Ⓓ Ⓔ
11	Ⓐ Ⓑ Ⓒ Ⓓ Ⓔ	31 Ⓐ Ⓑ Ⓒ Ⓓ Ⓔ	51 Ⓐ Ⓑ Ⓒ Ⓓ Ⓔ
12	Ⓐ Ⓑ Ⓒ Ⓓ Ⓔ	32 Ⓐ Ⓑ Ⓒ Ⓓ Ⓔ	52 Ⓐ Ⓑ Ⓒ Ⓓ Ⓔ
13	Ⓐ Ⓑ Ⓒ Ⓓ Ⓔ	33 Ⓐ Ⓑ Ⓒ Ⓓ Ⓔ	53 Ⓐ Ⓑ Ⓒ Ⓓ Ⓔ
14	Ⓐ Ⓑ Ⓒ Ⓓ Ⓔ	34 Ⓐ Ⓑ Ⓒ Ⓓ Ⓔ	54 Ⓐ Ⓑ Ⓒ Ⓓ Ⓔ
15	Ⓐ Ⓑ Ⓒ Ⓓ Ⓔ	35 Ⓐ Ⓑ Ⓒ Ⓓ Ⓔ	55 Ⓐ Ⓑ Ⓒ Ⓓ Ⓔ
16	Ⓐ Ⓑ Ⓒ Ⓓ Ⓔ	36 Ⓐ Ⓑ Ⓒ Ⓓ Ⓔ	56 Ⓐ Ⓑ Ⓒ Ⓓ Ⓔ
17	Ⓐ Ⓑ Ⓒ Ⓓ Ⓔ	37 Ⓐ Ⓑ Ⓒ Ⓓ Ⓔ	57 Ⓐ Ⓑ Ⓒ Ⓓ Ⓔ
18	Ⓐ Ⓑ Ⓒ Ⓓ Ⓔ	38 Ⓐ Ⓑ Ⓒ Ⓓ Ⓔ	58 Ⓐ Ⓑ Ⓒ Ⓓ Ⓔ
19	Ⓐ Ⓑ Ⓒ Ⓓ Ⓔ	39 Ⓐ Ⓑ Ⓒ Ⓓ Ⓔ	59 Ⓐ Ⓑ Ⓒ Ⓓ Ⓔ
20	Ⓐ Ⓑ Ⓒ Ⓓ Ⓔ	40 Ⓐ Ⓑ Ⓒ Ⓓ Ⓔ	60 Ⓐ Ⓑ Ⓒ Ⓓ Ⓔ

PRACTICE TEST THREE

Total Time: One Hour
Time begun .... Time ended .... Time used ....

DIRECTIONS: This test consists of selections from literary works and questions on their content, form, and style. After reading each passage or poem, choose the best answer to each question and blacken the corresponding space on the answer sheet.

NOTE: Pay particular attention to the requirement of questions that contain the words NOT, LEAST, or EXCEPT.

Questions 1–12: Read the following selections carefully before you choose your answers.

Let us spend one day as deliberately as Nature, and not be thrown off the track by every nutshell and mosquito's wing that falls on the rails. Let us rise early and fast, or break fast,
(5) gently and without perturbation; let company come and let company go, let the bells ring and the children cry,—determined to make a day of it. Why should we knock under and go with the stream? Let us not be upset and overwhelmed
(10) in that terrible rapid and whirlpool called a dinner, situated in the meridian shallows. Weather this danger and you are safe, for the rest of the way is down hill. With unrelaxed nerves, with morning vigor, sail by it, looking another way,
(15) tied to the mast like Ulysses. If the engine whistles, let it whistle till it is hoarse for its pains. If the bell rings, why should we run? We will consider what kind of music they are like. Let us settle ourselves, and work and wedge our feet
(20) downward through the mud and slush of opinion, and prejudice, and tradition, and delusion, and appearance, that alluvion which covers the globe, through Paris and London, through New York and Boston and Concord, through church
(25) and state, through poetry and philosophy and religion, till we come to a hard bottom and rocks in place, which we can call *reality,* and say, This is, and no mistake; and then begin, having a *point d'appui,* below freshet and frost and fire,
(30) a place where you might found a wall or a state, or set a lamp-post safely, or perhaps a gauge, not a Nilometer, but a Realometer, that future ages might know how deep a freshet of shams and appearances had gathered from time to
(35) time. If you stand right fronting and face to face

to a fact, you will see the sun glimmer on both its surfaces, as if it were a scimitar, and feel its sweet edge dividing you through the heart and marrow, and so you will happily conclude your
(40) mortal career. Be it life or death, we crave only reality. If we are really dying, let us hear the rattle in our throats and feel cold in the extremities; if we are alive, let us go about our business.
(45) Time is but the stream I go a-fishing in. I drink at it; but while I drink I see the sandy bottom and detect how shallow it is. Its thin current slides away, but eternity remains. I would drink deeper; fish in the sky, whose bottom is pebbly
(50) with stars. I cannot count one. I know not the first letter of the alphabet. I have always been regretting that I was not as wise as the day I was born. The intellect is a cleaver; it discerns and rifts its way into the secret of things. I do
(55) not wish to be any more busy with my hands than is necessary. My head is hands and feet. I feel all my best faculties concentrated in it. My instinct tells me that my head is an organ for burrowing, as some creatures use their snout
(60) and fore-paws, and with it I would mine and burrow my way through these hills. I think that the richest vein is somewhere hereabouts; so by the divining rod and thin rising vapors I judge; and here I will begin to mine.

1. According to this selection our major goal as human beings is to

(A) avoid the responsibilities placed on us
(B) fill our thoughts with nature
(C) find out from others what they think is best
(D) see things as they are
(E) be aware ever of the passing time

2. He feels that he was wiser the day he was born than he is today because

(A) he was fully protected from the evils of society then
(B) his mind had not been corrupted by society
(C) he was a feeling and not thinking creature
(D) he had people who loved him
(E) he had much time to his credit

3. An act that the author would not consider "going with the stream" would be

(A) reading the morning newspaper
(B) exploring through experimentation
(C) talking a long walk

(D) being introspective

(E) consulting with colleagues

4. According to the writer, we can find *reality* through

(A) reading and thinking

(B) relaxing and feeling

(C) experiencing

(D) thinking and feeling

(E) avoiding our fellow men

5. Dinner occurred in the author's household

(A) when most people ate breakfast

(B) at noon

(C) toward evening

(D) whenever he was hungry

(E) when the guests arrived

6. In line 63, the "thin rising vapors" are

(A) the lifting fog

(B) mists on the mountain tops

(C) research studies

(D) the promises of success

(E) beginnings of speculation

7. The rails mentioned in the first sentence contains the image of

(A) a subway train chugging into a station

(B) a locomotive pulling the freight trains

(C) one of the supports of a picket fence

(D) a path through the woods

(E) the road of living

8. The author believes all of the following EXCEPT

(A) most of us live guided by illusions, not reality

(B) the author is capable of uncovering truths

(C) his greatest joy comes from reveling in his perceptions

(D) his goal in life is to reveal reality to others

(E) the mind and not the heart or the senses is the key to successful living

9. The tone achieved by the author is deliberately developed through

(A) detached observations

(B) startling generalizations

(C) distorted values

(D) sophisticated judgments

(E) revelation of partial truths

10. To keep his reader alert, the writer used all of the following devices EXCEPT

(A) rhetorical questions that the author did not answer

(B) phrases to be taken figuratively rather than literally

(C) anecdotes

(D) seemingly contradictory statements

(E) an extensive vocabulary

11. The author fears most

(A) contact with his fellow men

(B) being filled with superstitions

(C) dying

(D) living routinely

(E) what others will think of him

12. The author does NOT

(A) tell us his formula for success

(B) tell us how to avoid wasting time

(C) where he can be most productive

(D) give us examples of what he found

(E) tell us the rewards for pursuing reality

Questions 13–20: Read the following paragraph carefully before you choose your answers.

You are not to consider that every new and personal beauty in art abrogates past achievement as an Act of Parliament does preceding ones, or that it is hostile to the past. You are to (5) consider these beauties, these innovations, as enrichments, as variations, as additions to an existing family. How barbarous you would seem if you were unable to bestow your admiration and affection on a fascinating child in (10) the nursery without at once finding yourselves compelled to rush downstairs and cut its mother's throat, and stifle its grandmother. These ladies may still have their uses.

13. Which of the following best explains the organization pattern of the selection?

(A) Selectivity—that is, the author stresses one detail in the first sentence and then develops and enhances that detail in the remaining sentences

(B) Application—that is, the author states a basic principle in the initial sentence and then applies it to prove its worth

(C) *Reductio ad absurdum*—that is, the author presents an idea and then proves it worthless by citing inapplicable extremes

(D) Universality—that is, the author presents a fact as a premise and then shows its lasting truth through examples

(E) Explication—that is, the author presents a statement in the first sentence and then proceeds to explain and illustrate that one idea

14. The tone of the selection is

(A) conciliatory
(B) argumentative
(C) persuasive
(D) didactic
(E) bitter

15. The author employed all of the following devices EXCEPT

(A) analogies
(B) innovative examples
(C) humor
(D) appropriate vocabulary
(E) extended comparison

16. Which of the following statements best states the thesis of this selection?

(A) Artists rebel against the traditions of the preceding generations.
(B) Beauty in art is a changeable concept.
(C) Art has values that transcend all movements.
(D) The artist consciously avoids imitation.
(E) The progress of art is a continuum.

17. In line 12, "stifle" is used to mean

(A) quiet
(B) subdue
(C) repress
(D) murder
(E) discourage

18. Which of the following best expresses the effect of the last sentence?

(A) It adds to the intense horror in the example.
(B) It assures the sophisticated reaction to the example by the reader.
(C) It adds humor to intensify the effect of the preceding sentence.
(D) It adds a final example to further prove the validity of the author's premise.
(E) It adds the necessary fact to prove what precautions are necessary.

19. The child in the nursery is compared to

(A) an Act of Parliament
(B) the artist
(C) the work of young artists
(D) personal beauty
(E) past achievement

20. Which of the following best describes the comparison in the third sentence?

(A) inappropriate and in bad taste
(B) accurate and harmonious
(C) startling but appropriate
(D) absurd and nauseating
(E) confused and vulgar

Questions 21–28: Read the following poem carefully before you choose your answers.

Whether on earth, in air or main,
Sure everything alive is vain!
   Does not the hawk all fowls survey
As destined only for his prey?
(5) And do not tyrants, prouder things,
Think men were born for slaves to kings?
   When the crab views the pearly strands,[1]
Or Tagus[2] bright with golden sands,
Or crawls beside the coral grove
(10) And hears the ocean roll above,
   "Nature is too profuse," says he,
"Who gave all these to pleasure me!"
   When bordering pinks and roses bloom
And every garden breathes perfume,
(15) When peaches glow with sunny dyes,
Like Laura's cheek when blushes rise,
When with huge figs the branches bend,
When clusters from the vine depend,
The snail looks round on flower and tree
(20) And cries, "All these were made for me!"

21. The meaning implied by the author's use of *vain* is

(A) foolish
(B) self-centered
(C) useless
(D) autocratic
(E) haughty

22. Which of the following best describes the development of the thought in this selection?

(A) Digression—that is, the author presents a

[1] Oyster beds.
[2] River in Spain and Portugal, renowned for gold dust in its waters.

thesis and then wanders off into various by-ways suggested by the thesis
(B) Analogy—that is, the author attempts to prove his thesis by showing comparable situations in which it works
(C) Classification—that is, the poet neatly puts many things into a group that proves his contention
(D) Chronology—that is, he presents each event in order of its occurrence
(E) Exemplification—that is, he presents a premise and then proceeds to prove it by piling up examples

23. The tone of the poem is

(A) humorous
(B) persuasive
(C) authoritative
(D) somber
(E) defensive

24. The author broke the strict logic of his plan when he

(A) wrote of crabs
(B) quoted the snail
(C) compared the color of Laura's cheek to that of a peach
(D) mentioned the Tagus
(E) put the hawk before the tyrants

25. The "prouder things" in line 5 identify

   I. hawks
  II. fowls
 III. rulers
(A) I only
(B) II only
(C) III only
(D) I and III
(E) I, II, and III

26. Which of the following rhyming pairs contains a synonym forced into use to complete the rhyme?

(A) survey-prey (lines 3–4)
(B) things-kings (lines 5–6)
(C) bloom-perfume (lines 13–14)
(D) dyes-rise (lines 15–16)
(E) tree-me (lines 19–20)

27. The word "depend" in line 17 means

(A) to trust
(B) to hang down

(C) to be undecided
(D) to be determined by
(E) to be pending

28. Which of the following did the author NOT do?

(A) Include apt illustrations
(B) Present an insight into the attitudes of living organisms
(C) Explain the value of his insight
(D) See human responses in nonhuman creatures
(E) Offer proof of the universality of the insight

Questions 29–34:   Read the following poem carefully before you choose your answers.

I saw a man pursuing the horizon;
Round and round they sped.
I was disturbed at this;
I accosted the man.
(5) "It is futile," I said,
"You can never—"
"You lie," he cried,
and ran on.

29. Which of the following best expresses the poet's thesis?

(A) Men spend their lives in trying to obtain the impossible.
(B) Some men try in vain to achieve the impossible.
(C) Some men try in vain to help their fellows.
(D) Only the foolish try to correct others.
(E) It is difficult to make men see the futility in dreams.

30. All of the following are characteristic of the style EXCEPT

(A) it speeds along—as rapidly as the man
(B) its message is vague
(C) it contains no poetic diction
(D) it is based on a dramatic confrontation
(E) the characters gain universality by not being described

31. Which of the following is LEAST clear to the reader?

(A) why the speaker is disturbed
(B) why the man's actions were futile
(C) why the man said, "You lie"
(D) why the speaker called the action futile
(E) how the incident ended

32. What is the function of the last line?

(A) to suggest the wisdom in the poet's suggestion
(B) to reemphasize the image in the first line
(C) to help the reader see the poem as an adage
(D) to emphasize the stubborn qualities in man
(E) to show that the central experience in the selection has universality

33. The one word that may be selected as the one to disturb the harmony of diction is

(A) horizon
(B) futile
(C) pursuing
(D) accosted
(E) cried

34. The tone of this passage is best defined as

(A) oratorical
(B) declamatory
(C) philosophical
(D) simplistic
(E) bombastic

Questions 35–44: Read the following selection carefully before you choose your answers.

Thoreau had no humor, and this implies that he was a sorry logician. Himself an artist in rhetoric, he confounds thought with style when he undertakes to speak of the latter. He was for-
(5) ever talking of getting away from the world, but he must be always near enough to it, nay, to the Concord corner of it, to feel the impressions he makes there. He verifies the shrewd remark of Sainte-Beuve, "*On touche encore à son temps*
(10) *et trèsfort, même quand on le repousse.*"[1] This egotism of his is a Stylites pillar after all, a seclusion which keeps him in the public eye. The dignity of man is an excellent thing, but therefore to hold one's self too sacred and precious
(15) is the reverse of excellent. There is something delightfully absurd in six volumes addressed to a world of such "vulgar fellows" as Thoreau affirmed his fellowmen to be. I once had a glimpse of a genuine solitary who spent his win-
(20) ters one hundred and fifty miles beyond all human communication, and there dwelt with his rifle as his only confidant. Compared with this, the shanty on Walden Pond has something of the air, it must be confessed, of the Hermitage
(25) of La Chevrette. I do not believe that the way

[1] We are still very much a part of our time, even when we reject it.

to a true cosmopolitanism carries one into the woods or the society of musquashes. Perhaps the narrowest provincialism is that of Self; that of Kleinwinkel is nothing to it. The natural man,
(30) like the singing birds, comes out of the forest as inevitably as the natural bear and the wildcat stick there. To seek to be natural implies a consciousness that forbids all naturalness forever. It is as easy—and no easier—to be natural in a
(35) *salon* as in a swamp, if one does not aim at it, for what we call unnaturalness always has its spring in a man's thinking too much about himself. "It is impossible," said Turgot, "for a vulgar man to be simple."

35. Which of the following best expresses the development of the thought content of the selection?

(A) Through causality, the author associates cause and effect to develop his thesis.
(B) Through concretization, he delivers generalization followed by example to prove his thesis.
(C) Through explication, he cites authority and example to explain his topic sentence.
(D) Through partition, he divides each aspect of the discussion into small aspects and then cites authority to prove his contention.
(E) Through assimilation, he begins with specific examples, quotations, and generalizations to reach his climactic conclusion.

36. The attitude of the writer toward Thoreau is best characterized by which of the following?

(A) admiring
(B) caustic
(C) genial
(D) confused
(E) objective

37. The writer characterizes Thoreau as

(A) a solitary genius
(B) a natural man
(C) a misunderstood mystic
(D) a sohisticated cosmopolite
(E) a confused thinker

38. The basic contradiction in Thoreau according to this critic lies in

(A) Thoreau's living one hundred and fifty miles away from all human communication
(B) Thoreau's having a rifle as his only companion

(C) Thoreau's coming out of the forest

(D) Thoreau's selection of Walden

(E) Thoreau's writing about his experiences

39. To support his contentions, the writer of this selection did NOT resort to

(A) authority

(B) allusions

(C) ridicule

(D) using Thoreau's writing to prove his point

(E) defining his terms

40. The writer is NOT critical of Thoreau's

(A) way of life

(B) expressed philosophy

(C) style of dress

(D) subject matter

(E) appeal to his readers

41. An ironic aspect of this selection is that

(A) Thoreau did not have a chance to answer the critic

(B) the critic goes out of his way to prove that he himself has a sense of humor

(C) Walden has survived this criticism

(D) the natural man can live in the city as well as the country

(E) logic is of little concern to a writer

42. According to this critic

(A) provincialism is unrelated to solitariness

(B) cosmopolitanism depends upon cities

(C) egotism develops in the public eye

(D) naturalism does not depend on provincialism or cosmopolitanism

(E) naturalism develops from self-consciousness

43. The critic implies that the Hermitage of La Chevrette was

(A) anything but popular

(B) anything but natural

(C) anything but provincial

(D) anything but cosmopolitan

(E) anything but solitary

44. The author deduces that Thoreau could not be a hermit because

(A) Thoreau really did not want to be one

(B) society admired Thoreau too much

(C) New Englanders of the time were dependent on each other

(D) Thoreau did not know what he wanted to be

(E) he had too many companions

Questions 45–49:   Read the following poem carefully before you choose your answers.

I met a seer.
He held a book in his hands,
The book of wisdom.
"Sir," I addressed him,
(5) "Let me read."
"Child—" he began.
"Sir," I said,
"Think not that I am a child,
For already I know much
(10) Of that which you hold;
Aye, much."
He smiled.
Then he opened the book
And held it before me.
(15) Strange that I should have grown so suddenly blind.

45. The author's purpose in this poem was to

(A) expose the cruelty of old age

(B) warn youth not to be adventurous

(C) explore man's inhumanity to man

(D) expose ignorance

(E) reveal a psychological truth

46. The shortness of the lines

(A) deprives the reader of values

(B) adds to the simpleness of tone

(C) develops a sense of awe

(D) gives the child a chance to act

(E) emphasizes the wisdom of the seer

47. Which of the following best states the effect of the last sentence?

(A) It is an anticlimax which repeats a realization already clear to the reader.

(B) It provides a philosophical conclusion that the narrator had much to atone for.

(C) It provides the ironic conclusion that we must pay for knowledge.

(D) It brings into focus the contrast between the narrative style and the variety of interpretations possible.

(E) It sharpens the reader's sense of horror at the impulsiveness of man.

48. All of the following are crucial words in interpreting the selection EXCEPT

(A) seer
(B) book of wisdom
(C) I know much
(D) child
(E) suddenly blind

49. The last sentence could mean

I. the truth in the book was more than he could absorb
II. the wisdom in the book made him realize how little he knew shorn of human error
III. he was punished for his presumption, and the gods blinded him

(A) I only
(B) II only
(C) III only
(D) II and III
(E) I, II, and III

Questions 50–54: Read the following paragraph carefully before you choose your answers.

A house without books is like a room without windows. No man has a right to bring up his children without surrounding them with books, if he has the means to buy them. It is wrong to (5) his family. Children learn to read by being in the presence of books. The love of knowledge comes with reading and grows upon it. And the love of knowledge, in a young mind, is almost a warrant against the inferior excitement of passions and vices.

50. The author reveals a fear of

(A) knowledge learned from books
(B) emotions
(C) authority
(D) people's ability to obey laws and regulations
(E) education

51. The tone of this selection is

(A) genial
(B) exhortatory
(C) pessimistic
(D) assuring
(E) adulatory

52. The author attempts to convince the reader through

(A) citing examples
(B) amassing statistics
(C) appealing to the reader's sentiment
(D) logical development of an idea
(E) generalization

53. Which of the following does the author stress as important in the learning process?

(A) the ability of the instructor
(B) the type of textbook being used
(C) the educational level of one's friends and relatives
(D) atmosphere
(E) the intelligence level of the children

54. According to the author the best that a parent can give his child must include

(A) sensitivity to the rights of others
(B) understanding of self
(C) willingness to follow worthwhile ideals
(D) fear of propaganda
(E) love of knowledge for its own sake

Questions 55–60: Read the following selection carefully before you choose your answers.

Yet notwithstanding this weight of authority, and the universal practice of former ages, a new species of dramatic composition has been introduced under the name of *sentimental* comedy, in which the virtues of private life are exhibited, rather than the vices exposed; and the distresses rather than the faults of mankind make our interest in the piece. These comedies have had of late great success, perhaps from their novelty, and also from their flattering every man in his favorite foible. In these plays almost all the characters are good, and exceedingly generous; they are lavish enough of their *tin* money on the stage, and, though they want humor, have abundance of sentiment and feeling. If they happen to have faults or foibles, the spectator is taught not only to pardon, but to applaud them, in consideration of the goodness of their hearts; so that folly, instead of being ridiculed, is commended, and the comedy aims at touching our passions without the power of being truly pathetic. In this manner we are likely to lose one great source of entertainment on the stage; for while the comic poet is invading the province of the tragic muse, he leaves her lovely sister quite neglected. Of this, however, he is no way solicitous, as he measures his fame by his profits.

55. The purpose of the writer is to

    (A) condemn sentimental comedy
    (B) praise sentimental comedy
    (C) turn the reader away from this type of play
    (D) evaluate sentimental comedy
    (E) interest the general public in this type of comedy

56. The purpose of the playwright who is responsible for these comedies is

    (A) to make money by giving the audience what it wants
    (B) to improve the moral standards of the audience
    (C) to expose human vices to the audience
    (D) to discuss the moral and political issues of the day
    (E) to entertain the audience and help them forget the evils of the day

57. The characters in these plays lack
    (A) a sense of right and wrong
    (B) ability to live lavishly
    (C) deep feelings
    (D) human weaknesses
    (E) a sense of the ridiculous

58. The author feels that sentimental comedy

    (A) will be just a passing style
    (B) is one of the great contributions of his age
    (C) deals with superficial aspects of life
    (D) enhances the audience's appreciation of suffering
    (E) sets beneficial examples for the audience to follow

59. The writers of previous generations would condemn sentimental comedy because

    (A) it distorts the audience's view of life
    (B) it stresses emotions rather than thought
    (C) it makes the audience smug and complacent
    (D) it confuses dramatic forms
    (E) it proves the worth of ordinary men

60. A trait not possessed by the characters in these plays is

    (A) generosity
    (B) ability to react emotionally
    (C) a deepened sense of virtue
    (D) self-centeredness
    (E) sensitivity to the social issues of the day

ANSWER KEY: PRACTICE TEST THREE

1. (D)	10. (C)	19. (C)	28. (C)	37. (E)	46. (B)	55. (D)
2. (B)	11. (D)	20. (C)	29. (E)	38. (D)	47. (D)	56. (A)
3. (D)	12. (D)	21. (B)	30. (B)	39. (E)	48. (A)	57. (E)
4. (D)	13. (E)	22. (E)	31. (D)	40. (C)	49. (B)	58. (C)
5. (B)	14. (D)	23. (C)	32. (B)	41. (B)	50. (B)	59. (D)
6. (E)	15. (B)	24. (E)	33. (D)	42. (D)	51. (B)	60. (E)
7. (C)	16. (E)	25. (D)	34. (D)	43. (E)	52. (E)	
8. (D)	17. (D)	26. (D)	35. (C)	44. (C)	53. (D)	
9. (B)	18. (B)	27. (B)	36. (B)	45. (E)	54. (E)	

DETERMINING YOUR RAW SCORE

1. Tabulate Totals
   Number Right _____
   Number Wrong _____
   Number Omitted _____

2. Enter Number Right   A _____
   Divide Number Wrong by
   4 and put result here   B _____

3. Subtract B from A. This
   results in your RAW
   SCORE   _____

   The subtraction of ¼ point for each incorrect answer adjusts for the effect of random guessing.

EVALUATING YOUR PERFORMANCE

Excellent	57–60
Very Good	47–56
Good	38–46
Average	26–37
Below Average	16–25
Unsatisfactory	15 or below

PRACTICE TEST FOUR

ANSWER SHEET

1 Ⓐ Ⓑ Ⓒ Ⓓ Ⓔ	21 Ⓐ Ⓑ Ⓒ Ⓓ Ⓔ	41 Ⓐ Ⓑ Ⓒ Ⓓ Ⓔ
2 Ⓐ Ⓑ Ⓒ Ⓓ Ⓔ	22 Ⓐ Ⓑ Ⓒ Ⓓ Ⓔ	42 Ⓐ Ⓑ Ⓒ Ⓓ Ⓔ
3 Ⓐ Ⓑ Ⓒ Ⓓ Ⓔ	23 Ⓐ Ⓑ Ⓒ Ⓓ Ⓔ	43 Ⓐ Ⓑ Ⓒ Ⓓ Ⓔ
4 Ⓐ Ⓑ Ⓒ Ⓓ Ⓔ	24 Ⓐ Ⓑ Ⓒ Ⓓ Ⓔ	44 Ⓐ Ⓑ Ⓒ Ⓓ Ⓔ
5 Ⓐ Ⓑ Ⓒ Ⓓ Ⓔ	25 Ⓐ Ⓑ Ⓒ Ⓓ Ⓔ	45 Ⓐ Ⓑ Ⓒ Ⓓ Ⓔ
6 Ⓐ Ⓑ Ⓒ Ⓓ Ⓔ	26 Ⓐ Ⓑ Ⓒ Ⓓ Ⓔ	46 Ⓐ Ⓑ Ⓒ Ⓓ Ⓔ
7 Ⓐ Ⓑ Ⓒ Ⓓ Ⓔ	27 Ⓐ Ⓑ Ⓒ Ⓓ Ⓔ	47 Ⓐ Ⓑ Ⓒ Ⓓ Ⓔ
8 Ⓐ Ⓑ Ⓒ Ⓓ Ⓔ	28 Ⓐ Ⓑ Ⓒ Ⓓ Ⓔ	48 Ⓐ Ⓑ Ⓒ Ⓓ Ⓔ
9 Ⓐ Ⓑ Ⓒ Ⓓ Ⓔ	29 Ⓐ Ⓑ Ⓒ Ⓓ Ⓔ	49 Ⓐ Ⓑ Ⓒ Ⓓ Ⓔ
10 Ⓐ Ⓑ Ⓒ Ⓓ Ⓔ	30 Ⓐ Ⓑ Ⓒ Ⓓ Ⓔ	50 Ⓐ Ⓑ Ⓒ Ⓓ Ⓔ
11 Ⓐ Ⓑ Ⓒ Ⓓ Ⓔ	31 Ⓐ Ⓑ Ⓒ Ⓓ Ⓔ	51 Ⓐ Ⓑ Ⓒ Ⓓ Ⓔ
12 Ⓐ Ⓑ Ⓒ Ⓓ Ⓔ	32 Ⓐ Ⓑ Ⓒ Ⓓ Ⓔ	52 Ⓐ Ⓑ Ⓒ Ⓓ Ⓔ
13 Ⓐ Ⓑ Ⓒ Ⓓ Ⓔ	33 Ⓐ Ⓑ Ⓒ Ⓓ Ⓔ	53 Ⓐ Ⓑ Ⓒ Ⓓ Ⓔ
14 Ⓐ Ⓑ Ⓒ Ⓓ Ⓔ	34 Ⓐ Ⓑ Ⓒ Ⓓ Ⓔ	54 Ⓐ Ⓑ Ⓒ Ⓓ Ⓔ
15 Ⓐ Ⓑ Ⓒ Ⓓ Ⓔ	35 Ⓐ Ⓑ Ⓒ Ⓓ Ⓔ	55 Ⓐ Ⓑ Ⓒ Ⓓ Ⓔ
16 Ⓐ Ⓑ Ⓒ Ⓓ Ⓔ	36 Ⓐ Ⓑ Ⓒ Ⓓ Ⓔ	56 Ⓐ Ⓑ Ⓒ Ⓓ Ⓔ
17 Ⓐ Ⓑ Ⓒ Ⓓ Ⓔ	37 Ⓐ Ⓑ Ⓒ Ⓓ Ⓔ	57 Ⓐ Ⓑ Ⓒ Ⓓ Ⓔ
18 Ⓐ Ⓑ Ⓒ Ⓓ Ⓔ	38 Ⓐ Ⓑ Ⓒ Ⓓ Ⓔ	58 Ⓐ Ⓑ Ⓒ Ⓓ Ⓔ
19 Ⓐ Ⓑ Ⓒ Ⓓ Ⓔ	39 Ⓐ Ⓑ Ⓒ Ⓓ Ⓔ	59 Ⓐ Ⓑ Ⓒ Ⓓ Ⓔ
20 Ⓐ Ⓑ Ⓒ Ⓓ Ⓔ	40 Ⓐ Ⓑ Ⓒ Ⓓ Ⓔ	60 Ⓐ Ⓑ Ⓒ Ⓓ Ⓔ

PRACTICE TEST FOUR

Total Time: One Hour
Time begun .... Time ended .... Time used ....

DIRECTIONS: This test consists of selections from literary works and questions on their content, form, and style. After reading each passage or poem, choose the best answer to each question and blacken the corresponding space on the answer sheet.

NOTE: Pay particular attention to the requirement of questions that contain the words NOT, LEAST, or EXCEPT.

Questions 1–8:   Read the following selection carefully before you choose your answers.

> There is a pleasure in the pathless woods,
> There is a rapture on the lonely shore,
> There is society, where none intrudes,
> (4) By the deep Sea, and music in its roar:
> I love not Man the less, but Nature more,
> From these our interviews, in which I steal
> From all I may be, or have been before,
> (8) To mingle with the Universe, and feel
> What I can ne'er express, yet cannot all
>   conceal.

1. The poet used the word "interviews" in line 6 to characterize his experiences because

   (A) nature communicated with him on a one-to-one basis
   (B) he learned so much from the experiences
   (C) nature lectured him
   (D) nature enjoyed his being there
   (E) his feelings exchanged vibrations with his surroundings

2. Which of the following expresses the poet's principal thought?

   (A) Contact with man corrupts the soul.
   (B) Joys of nature can be absorbed by man.
   (C) Contact with nature brings us close to a oneness with the Universe.
   (D) Only by expressing his feelings in words can the poet communicate with his fellow men.
   (E) Man can better his position in society through contacts with nature.

3. The poet advocates all of the following EXCEPT

   (A) seeking renewal away from big cities
   (B) taking mountain trips without companions
   (C) gaining a new identity through contemplation of the inanimate
   (D) studying the creatures of wild nature
   (E) striving to hear the music of the spheres

4. Which of the following best defines the function of the repetition in the first three lines?

   (A) It sets a note of sincerity for the reader.
   (B) It clarifies the author's purpose.
   (C) It slows down the flow of images in the poem.
   (D) It adds a note of cacophony to attract the attention of the reader.
   (E) It adds a note of simplicity to a complex idea.

5. The poet used all of the following devices EXCEPT

   (A) capitalization for emphasis
   (B) specific instances
   (C) generalizations
   (D) intentional ambiguity
   (E) statements that seem contradictory

6. In line 6, "steal" means

   (A) take wrongfully
   (B) take by force
   (C) appropriate entirely
   (D) come secretly
   (E) slip away

7. The tone of this selection is

   (A) mystical
   (B) ironic
   (C) humorous
   (D) skeptical
   (E) destructive

8. The poet avoided specific imagery in order to

   (A) arouse the reader's curiosity
   (B) have the reader agree with his thesis
   (C) goad the reader into an intellectual experience
   (D) have the reader sense the immensity he felt
   (E) keep his concept at an understandable level

Questions 9–15:   Read the following poem carefully before you choose your answers.

Yet let us ponder boldly—'tis a base
Abandonment of reason to resign
Our right of thought—our last and only place
(4) Of refuge; this, at least, shall still be mine:
Though from our birth the faculty divine
Is chain'd and tortured—cabin'd, cribb'd, confined,
And bred in darkness, lest the truth should shine
(8) Too brightly on the unprepared mind,
The beam pours in, for time and skill will couch the blind.

9. "Yet let us ponder boldly" in line one may be paraphrased in prose as

(A) let's give it a try
(B) think daringly and without fear
(C) come to think of it
(D) did you ever realize
(E) let me tell you how I feel

10. Which of the following best expresses the poet's main idea?

(A) Education leads us to intellectual freedom.
(B) Thinking without goals to aim at is a sterile accomplishment.
(C) Freedom of thought is mankind's most essential lever.
(D) Divine faculties are lost when we are imprisoned.
(E) We must seek refuge from base abandonment.

11. In line 5, "divine" could mean all of the following EXCEPT

(A) godlike
(B) god-given
(C) a quality of the gods
(D) a guessed-at quality
(E) marvelous

12. The poet makes use of repetition in line 6 to

(A) emphasize the power of the mind
(B) emphasize the powers of evil
(C) slow down the flow of his thoughts
(D) pile up image after image to clarify his concepts
(E) give as large a scope to the enumeration of the forces of ignorance

13. The poet contends that

(A) society should protect the young from mature thoughts
(B) there is no danger in planning boldly
(C) society cripples our ability to think during the educational process
(D) thinking cannot cause any permanent damage to the thinker
(E) thoughts can be dangerous

14. A synonym for the word *base* in the first line is

(A) *fundamental*
(B) *correct*
(C) *evil*
(D) *righteous*
(E) *erroneous*

15. A quality of the right of thought NOT mentioned by the poet is

(A) it causes no irreversible damage
(B) it is irrepressible
(C) it is often under attack
(D) without it we become unreasoning creatures
(E) it can lead to error

Questions 16–20:   Read the following selection carefully before you choose your answers.

It is natural for man to indulge in the illusions of hope. We are apt to shut our eyes against a painful truth, and listen to the song of the siren till she transforms us into beasts. Is this the part
(5) of wise men, engaged in a great and arduous struggle for liberty? Are we disposed to be of the number of those who having eyes see not, and having ears hear not the things which so nearly concern their temporal salvation?
(10) For my part, whatever anguish of spirit it may cost, I will to know the whole truth—to know the worst and to provide for it.

16. The writer equates the "illusions of hope" with

(A) the search for truth
(B) temporal salvation
(C) anguish of spirit
(D) painful truth
(E) false interpretations

17. If we are to have liberty, we must

(A) have anguish of spirit
(B) have illusions

(C) have hope

(D) know the facts

(E) have courage

18. By "temporal salvation," line 8, the author most likely meant

(A) spiritual deliverance

(B) nationalistic aspirations

(C) innermost security

(D) safety in their daily lives

(E) timely concerns

19. The advantage in knowing the truth is that

(A) we can then struggle for liberty

(B) we can disregard hope

(C) we can provide for all possibilities

(D) we can overcome the worst

(E) we will not be beasts

20. This selection was most likely written during

(A) a period of prosperity

(B) during the Depression

(C) a war of independence

(D) a time of political stress

(E) a national debate

Questions 21–28: Read the following passage carefully before you choose your answers.

Other faces there were, too, of men who (if the brevity of their remembrance, after death, can be augured from their little value in life) should have been represented in snow rather (5) than marble. Posteriorly will be puzzled what to do with busts like these, the concretions and petrifactions of a vain self-estimate; but will find, no doubt, that they serve to build into stone walls, or burn into quicklime, as well as (10) if the marble had never been blocked into the guise of human heads.

But it is an awful thing, indeed, this endless endurance, this almost indestructibility, of a marble bust! Whether in our own case, or that (15) of other men, it bids us sadly measure the little, little time during which our lineaments are likely to be of interest to any human being. It is especially singular that Americans should care about perpetuating themselves in this mode. (20) The brief duration of our families, as a hereditary household, renders it next to a certainty that the great-grandchildren will not know their father's grandfather, and that half a century hence, at furthest, the hammer of the auctioneer

(25) will thump its knockdown blow against his blockhead, sold at so much for the pound of stone! And it ought to make us shiver, the idea of leaving our features to be a dusty-white ghost among strangers of another generation, who will (30) take our nose between their thumb and fingers (as we have seen men do by Caesar's), and infallibly break it off if they can do so without detection!

21. In this passage, marble busts become symbolic of

(A) man's foolish attempts to transcend time

(B) the extravagant aspirations of the artist

(C) the loneliness of man in his own time

(D) the hardness of man's heart

(E) nature's triumph over civilization

22. The "other faces" mentioned in line 1 should have been represented in snow because they

(A) were cold-hearted and arrogant

(B) did not wish to be remembered

(C) failed to remember their friends

(D) did not merit a permanent memorial

(E) were not respected by their friends

23. The speaker's tone in lines 7–11 is best described as

(A) arrogant and patronizing

(B) shocked and indignant

(C) mildly disappointed

(D) reluctantly approving

(E) contemptuously ironic

24. As it is used in line 26, the word "blockhead" functions as a

(A) play on words

(B) literary allusion

(C) reference to the sculptor

(D) nonsense word

(E) paradoxical term

25. In the second paragraph, the speaker implies that American families are characterized by their

(A) contempt for foreigners

(B) lack of interest in their own past

(C) indifference to fine works of art

(D) overindulgence of their children and grandchildren

(E) eagerness to acquire and exhibit wealth

26. The "shiver" described in line 27 is occasioned by

(A) the coldness of our graves
(B) fear of the disrespect of those who come after us
(C) apprehension about what our ghosts will do
(D) horror at the corruption of our bodies
(E) the knowledge that we must come to dust

27. As it is used in line 28, the image of the ghost suggests something that is

(A) pitiful
(B) ominous
(C) vindictive
(D) restless
(E) ageless

28. According to the passage, which of the following properties of marble is most important to those who have busts of themselves made?

(A) Beauty
(B) Translucence
(C) Usefulness
(D) Coldness
(E) Durability

Questions 29–34: Read the following poem carefully before you choose your answers.

Never love unless you can
Bear with all the faults of man!
Men sometimes will jealous be,
Though but little cause they see,
And hang the head in discontent,
(6) And speak what straight they will repent.
Men that but one saint adore,
Make show of love to more;
Beauty must be scorned in none,
Though but truly served in one:
For what is courtship but disguise?
(12) True hearts may have dissembling eyes.
Men, when their affairs require,
Must awhile themselves retire;
Sometimes hunt, and sometimes hawk,
And not ever sit and talk:—
If these and such-like you can bear,
(18) Then like, and love, and never fear!

29. One fault of man not mentioned in the selection is

(A) men often tell untruths to their beloved
(B) men are sometimes jealous of their beloved

(C) men must sometimes pay attention to another while still thinking themselves loyal to their beloved
(D) men tend to be too truthful when asked a direct question
(E) men cannot long be idle in talk, but must have games and sports

30. The advice in the poem is intended for the

(A) widows
(B) lovelorn
(C) eligible females
(D) widowers
(E) wives

31. In line 12, "dissembling eyes" belong to those who

(A) are angry
(B) hide the truth
(C) are courting
(D) are impatient or annoyed
(E) are in love

32. The tone of the selection can best be interpreted as

(A) sophisticated
(B) scornful
(C) naive
(D) cynical
(E) optimistic

33. The poet in this poem assumes

(A) that not all men react in the same fashion
(B) that all men resemble courtiers in courting
(C) all courtship contains elements of cheating
(D) love is an irresistible force
(E) men are inconsistent

34. A premise upon which the poet based his advice is that

(A) the beloved is a saintly person
(B) no woman can love a man who is jealous
(C) women prefer men who hunt and fish
(D) women normally do not know the faults of their beloved
(E) love does not have its base in ordinary emotions and routines of life

Questions 35–46: Read the following passage carefully before you choose your answers.

"It's not the two thousand I regret," answered the lady, and a big tear rolled down her

cheek. "It's the fact itself that revolts me! I cannot put up with thieves in my house. I don't
(5) regret it—I regret nothing; but to steal from me
is such ingratitude! That's how they repay me
for my kindness. . . ."

They all looked into their plates, but Mashenka fancied after the lady's words that every
(10) one was looking at her. A lump rose in her
throat; she began crying and put her handkerchief to her lips.

"*Pardon*," she muttered. "I can't help it. My
head aches. I'll go away."

(15) And she got up from the table, scraping her
chair awkwardly, and went out quickly, still
more overcome with confusion.

"It's beyond everything!" said Nikolay Sergeitch, frowning, "What need was there to
(20) search her room? How out of place it was!"

"I don't say she took the brooch," said Fedosya Vassilyevna, "but can you answer for
her? To tell the truth, I haven't much confidence
in these learned paupers."

(25) "It really was unsuitable, Fenya. . . . Excuse
me, Fenya, but you've no kind of legal right to
make a search."

"I know nothing about your laws. All I know
is that I've lost my brooch. And I will find the
(30) brooch!" She brought her fork down on the
plate with a clatter, and her eyes flashed angrily.
"And you eat your dinner, and don't interfere
in what doesn't concern you!"

Nikolay Sergeitch dropped his eyes mildly
(35) and sighed. Meanwhile Mashenka, reaching her
room, flung herself on her bed. She felt now
neither alarm nor shame, but she felt an intense
longing to go slap the cheeks of this hard, arrogant, dull-witted, prosperous woman.

(40) Lying on her bed she breathed into her pillow
and dreamed of how nice it would be to go and
buy the most expensive brooch and fling it into
the face of this bullying woman. If only it were
God's will that Fedosya Vassilyevna should
(45) come to ruin and wander about begging, and
should taste all the horrors of poverty and dependence, and that Mashenka, whom she had
insulted, might give her alms! Oh, if only she
could come in for a big fortune, could buy a
carriage, and could drive noisily past the windows so as to be envied by that woman!

35. Which of the following describes an event that
had NOT taken place before the initial dialogue?

(A) A valuable brooch had disappeared mys-
teriously.

(B) The mistress of the house had searched the
rooms of her employees.
(C) One of the employees had been openly accused of taking the valuable piece of
jewelry.
(D) The mistress of the house was greatly dis-
tressed by the loss.
(E) The mistress of the house feels that the thief
had to be one of her employees.

36. The author characterizes the mistress of the
house by the following appellations:

(A) lady, Nikolay, Mashenka
(B) Fedosya Vassilyevna, Fenya, Nikolay Ser-
geitch
(C) Mashenka, Fenya, lady
(D) Fenya, lady, Fedosya Vassilyevna
(E) Nikolay, Fenya, Mashenka

37. Fenya is a

(A) first name
(B) familiar form, a shortened form
(C) formal class name like Miss
(D) last name
(E) middle name

38. The term *learned paupers* implies that Mashenka is

(A) the lady of the house
(B) a poor relative
(C) the husband's secretary
(D) the governess
(E) one of the servants

39. The character of the lady of the house is developed through

(A) inner thoughts of the guests
(B) author's description
(C) description of appearance and surround-
ings
(D) her gracious acceptance of the inevitable
(E) dialogue and action

40. Mashenka's daydream reveals her to be

(A) jealous of the riches of Fedosya Vassi-
lyevna
(B) envious of the wealth displayed by others
around her
(C) an old, disillusioned woman
(D) sensitive to the rights of others
(E) feeling rejected and degraded

41. Nikolay Sergeitch sees injustice in what had been done to Mashenka and

    (A) demands that such actions be apologized for
    (B) insists that such actions not be repeated
    (C) approves of the harsh measures
    (D) tells the authorities
    (E) sidesteps a confrontation

42. The author's basic means of characterization is

    (A) foreshadowing
    (B) action and dialogue
    (C) use of descriptive adjectives and evaluative statements
    (D) soliloquies
    (E) dramatic irony

43. At this point in the story, the reader's sympathies are with

    (A) the butler
    (B) Mashenka
    (C) Nikolay
    (D) Fedosya
    (E) the thief

44. The word that checks our sympathy from going completely to the lady in the first paragraph is

    (A) thousand
    (B) regret
    (C) thieves
    (D) revolts
    (E) ingratitude

45. The characters who will most likely receive further refinement are

    I. Nikolay and Mashenka
    II. Mashenka and Fedosya
    III. Nikolay and Fedosya
    (A) I only
    (B) II only
    (C) III only
    (D) I and II
    (E) I, II and III

46. Dramatic contrast is achieved by

    (A) juxtaposing Mashenka's agitation and politeness with the lady's aggressive insinuations
    (B) Nikolay's telling what was done and what should have been done

    (C) Mashenka's crying in bed when filled with agitation
    (D) the lady's remaining at the table while Mashenka leaves
    (E) juxtaposing the remarks of Fedosya Vassilyevna and those of Nikolay Sergeitch

Questions 47–55: Read the following poem carefully before you choose your answers.

No man's defects sought they to know;
So never made themselves a foe.
No man's good deeds did they commend;
So never raised themselves a friend.
(5) Nor cherished they relations poor,
That might decrease their present store;
Nor barn nor house did they repair,
That might oblige their future heir.
They neither added nor confounded;
(10) They neither wanted nor abounded.
Each Christmas they accounts did clear
And wound their skeins round the year.
Nor tear nor smile did they employ
At news of public grief or joy.
(15) When bells were rung, and bonfires made,
If asked, they ne'er denied their aid:
Their jug was to the ringers carried,
Whoever either died or married.
Their dry log at the fire was found,
(20) Whoever was deposed or crowned.
    Nor good, nor bad, or fools, nor wise;
They would not learn, nor could advise:
Without love, hatred, joy, or fear,
They led—a kind of—as it were:
(25) Nor wished, nor cared, nor laughed, nor cried;
And so they lived; and so they died.

47. The couple described in this selection can best be described as

    (A) autocratic
    (B) benevolent
    (C) despotic
    (D) self-centered
    (E) conceited

48. The couple lacked

    (A) a reason for living
    (B) money
    (C) sense of duty
    (D) relatives
    (E) neighbors

49. An expected reaction by readers to the last line would be

(A) "I was sorry to see them go"
(B) "They had led a good life"
(C) "They were good people"
(D) "The end is inevitable"
(E) "So what!"

50. Lines 11–12 point out that

(A) they did not celebrate Christmas
(B) they did not celebrate New Year's Day
(C) Christmas time only signified that it was time to clear debts.
(D) they did not make New Year's resolutions
(E) they disliked the festive atmosphere

51. In line 17, "Their jug was to the ringers carried" means

(A) their supplies were carried to the top
(B) they tipped the attendants at church ceremonies, as was expected
(C) the professionals always respected them for their cooperation
(D) their products were used in many places
(E) they lost money in unwise investments

52. Which of the following were missing from their lives?

I. Enemies
II. Deep emotions
III. A sense of duty
(A) I only
(B) II only
(C) III only
(D) I and II
(E) I, II, and III

53. According to the poet we become nonentities when we

(A) praise others for their deeds
(B) object to the conduct of others
(C) try to learn from others
(D) do only the expected
(E) help others to raise their sights in life

54. The tone of this selection is best termed

(A) joyful
(B) amused
(C) scornful
(D) solemn
(E) optimistic

55. Line 24 implies that

(A) they were proud of their accomplishments
(B) they had a feeling of satisfaction from doing what they did
(C) they understood life's values
(D) they regretted the path they took
(E) they never lived fully

Questions 56–60: Read the following poem carefully before you choose your answers.

"Had I the choice . . ."
"But I did try; I really tried!"
Neither tastes,
Nor tests,
(5) Nor proves:
Commas, not periods;
Partials, never fulfillment.

56. To the poet, the two quotations represent

(A) success
(B) willingness
(C) resignation
(D) perseverance
(E) condemnation

57. "Neither" in line 15 refers to

(A) commas
(B) the two who are quoted in lines 1 and 2.
(C) periods
(D) partials
(E) fulfillment

58. Line 3 emphasizes that those who spoke

(A) are not afraid to face difficulties
(B) refuse to be discouraged
(C) are prone to look for excuses
(D) practice what they preach
(E) do not become totally involved

59. The nouns in the last two lines contrast

(A) beginning and end
(B) aspirations and failure
(C) plateaus and completion
(D) satisfaction and hunger
(E) leaders and followers

60. Based on the ideas in this selection, the writer would agree

(A) that success will come next time if these people try harder

(B) that these people are born losers, and they should never have tried
(C) that the taste of victory is a heady wine available only to a very few
(D) that you must never stop before you achieve victory or defeat
(E) with none of the above

ANSWER KEY: PRACTICE EXAMINATION FOUR

1. (E)	10. (C)	19. (C)	28. (E)	37. (B)	46. (A)	55. (E)
2. (C)	11. (D)	20. (C)	29. (D)	38. (D)	47. (D)	56. (C)
3. (D)	12. (E)	21. (A)	30. (C)	39. (E)	48. (A)	57. (B)
4. (A)	13. (D)	22. (D)	31. (B)	40. (E)	49. (E)	58. (E)
5. (B)	14. (C)	23. (E)	32. (A)	41. (E)	50. (C)	59. (C)
6. (E)	15. (E)	24. (A)	33. (B)	42. (B)	51. (B)	60. (E)
7. (A)	16. (E)	25. (B)	34. (A)	43. (B)	52. (D)	
8. (D)	17. (D)	26. (B)	35. (C)	44. (E)	53. (D)	
9. (B)	18. (D)	27. (A)	36. (D)	45. (B)	54. (C)	

DETERMINING YOUR RAW SCORE

1. Tabulate Totals
   Number Right _____
   Number Wrong _____
   Number Omitted _____

2. Enter Number Right   A _____
   Divide Number Wrong by
   4 and put result here   B _____

3. Subtract B from A. This
   results in your RAW
   SCORE   _____

   The subtraction of ¼ point for each incorrect answer adjusts for the effect of random guessing.

EVALUATING YOUR PERFORMANCE

Excellent	55–60
Very Good	44–54
Good	35–43
Average	23–34
Below Average	15–22
Unsatisfactory	14 or below

CHOOSING A COLLEGE

For every question you have,
Barron's guides have the right answers.

BARRON'S COLLEGE GUIDES

AMERICA'S #1 RESOURCE FOR EDUCATION PLANNING.

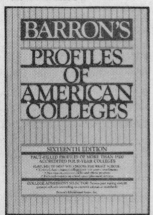
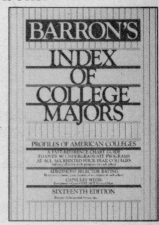

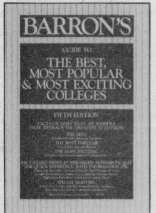